KU-629-858

Commando
FOR ACTION AND ADVENTURE

THE DIRTY DOZEN

Published in 2005 by Carlton Books Limited
An imprint of the Carlton Publishing Group
20 Mortimer Street
London W1T 3JW

A catalogue record for this book is available from the British Library.

ISBN 1 84442 307 7

Printed and bound in India
10 9 8 7 6 5 4 3 2

Commando
FOR ACTION AND ADVENTURE

THE DIRTY DOZEN

THE BEST 12 COMMANDO COMIC BOOKS EVER!

EDITED BY GEORGE LOW, EDITOR OF COMMANDO

CARLTON
BOOKS

Contents

Introduction

It has not been an easy task choosing the books for this collection. Since the first issue of Commando in 1961, there have been so many good stories and so much good artwork, both in black-and-white and colour, to appreciate. It was in 1963 that I joined the ranks of the Commando staff, and it has been very entertaining remembering a story here, an artist or writer there … all of them part of the team which has kept Commando going over the years.

FROM TWO SIDES THE BRITISH SOLDIERS WENT IN, WITH RIFLE, GRENADE AND SHINING BAYONET.
LEAVE IT TO THE POOR OLD INFANTRY, EVERY TIME.

The writers who dreamt up the ideas came from all walks of life, and many of the early ones had seen service during the Second World War at many levels. That gave them an edge when it came to the background and general knowledge of the subject. It has been harder for today's writers, but many have dug deep to research and develop their plots. The artists, armed with their own references and using the many we also supplied, tried to portray the equipment and uniforms as closely as possible. The British artists had a head start, but those from Spain, Italy and South America proved to be no slouches. Overall, they have done remarkably well.

THE MUSTANGS FLUNG THEMSELVES AT THE GUN EMPLACEMENTS, THEIR GUNS SPITTING HEAVY-CALIBRE BULLETS. ROGER GROOM TORE IN WITH A FEROCITY THAT FRIGHTENED ALAN.
STEADY ON, RED TWO. SAVE SOME AMMO FOR THE TRIP HOME.
NO! I'LL SHOW OWEN AND THE REST OF YOU THAT I'M NO COWARD!

Our readers have also played a big part, and almost everybody I talk to can remember the first Commando they read, or the one which became their favourite. Old copies turn up in attics or at car boot sales and the need to collect them is born again. Queries crop up regularly … who drew this, what story featured a timid private who lost his memory and turned into a battle-crazy hero? We can usually come up with an answer and that is only right … the interest these fans show is so encouraging and proof of the enjoyment so many readers get out of comics in general.

THE TWO DUNGEON GUARDS HAD BEEN HAVING A PEACEFUL GAME OF CARDS WHEN THE PARTISANS SWOOPED.
HA, YOUR GAMES ARE OVER FOR THE NIGHT!
GOTT IN HIMMEL... AAARGH!
PIETRO THEN GRABBED A BUNCH OF KEYS, AND THE LIBERATION OF THE CAPTURED PARTISANS MOVED ONE STAGE FURTHER.

But what exactly is Commando? It's a comic drawn for boys with enough text added to make it a good read. So only boys turn the pages? No, Dad and Granddad check it out too … not forgetting uncles and older cousins. So much so at times that our younger readers have asked for back copies to be addressed specifically to them ... or Mum ... to avoid the long wait when they get into older hands.

'Training Manuals' is also another description I have heard from serving members of Her Majesty's Forces. No names, no pack drill, but a few N.C.O.s have admitted to leaving copies lying around for officers to find. Improves tactics greatly, we have been informed.

THE INTRUDERS WERE MET BY A HAIL OF FIRE FROM THE SHADOWS.
AAGHH!
ACHTUNG, AN AMBUSH!

I hope then that you like what you find here. Perhaps there is an old favourite you had all but forgotten … a certain story or a certain artist's style. And if it is the first time you have come across Commando, remember that it is never too late to enjoy what you have just discovered. Like old soldiers, old comics never die....

George Low.

George Low,
EDITOR, COMMANDO

MOTOR TORPEDO BOAT
VOSPER 1940 CLASS

Equipment of the Second World War - No.15

P
O
M
L
K
H
G
F
A
I
C
E
B
D
J
N

"The little ships of the mosquito fleet" is what they were called—but what a mighty sting these mosquitoes carried! Roaring along at anything up to 45 miles an hour, they covered our coastal waters with a network of sudden danger to any Nazi vessel that ventured too close. They also specialised in cross-Channel beat-ups, working in close co-operation with their friends the motor gun-boats.

A LIFE RAFT
B FOC'S'LE & CREW QUARTERS (STARBOARD SIDE)
C GALLEY
D OFFICERS' QUARTERS & WARD-ROOM
E MAGAZINE
F SIREN
G BRIDGE
H WHEELHOUSE
I RADIO CABIN
J MIDSHIPS FUEL TANKS: 1605 GALLS.
K 21" TORPEDO TUBES
L POWER OPERATED TURRET WITH TWIN .5" MACHINE GUNS
M READY AMMUNITION LOCKER
N THREE PACKARD ENGINES
O DEPTH CHARGES

LENGTH – 72 ft.
BEAM – 19 ft.
DISPLACEMENT – 47 TONS
TOP SPEED – 40 KNOTS

INLAND NAVY

THE BATTLE HONOURS OF THE ROYAL NAVY IN THE SECOND WORLD WAR SPANNED THE WHOLE GLOBE. BRAVE MEN IN FINE SHIPS FOUGHT IN THE ATLANTIC, THE PACIFIC, THE NORTH SEA, THE ARCTIC OCEAN... THE PROUD LIST IS ALMOST ENDLESS.

BUT ONE SMALL BAND OF SAILORS WON THEIR GLORY FAR FROM THE HIGH SEAS, WITHOUT LOSING SIGHT OF LAND. THEIR BATTLEGROUND WAS THE QUIET, UNKNOWN CANALS AND RIVERS OF FRANCE WHERE THEY RAN THE GAUNTLET IN A FEROCIOUS DUEL THEY DARE NOT LOSE...

IN THE EARLY DAYS OF THE WAR, WHEN THE ALLIED ARMIES COULD DO NOTHING BUT WATCH THE GERMAN ADVANCE, THE BRITISH NAVY WERE INVOLVED IN ACTION IN ALL CORNERS OF THE WORLD.
THAT SHOULD TEACH THE HUNS TO STAY CLOSER TO HOME!

BUT NOT ALL THE NAVY SHARED IN THE FIGHTING. SOME HUNG AROUND AND WAITED IMPATIENTLY FOR THEIR TURN OF THE ACTION. ONE SUCH MAN WAS LIEUTENANT PETER POWELL. SWIMMING AND FISHING WERE FUN, BUT HE WANTED ACTION.
HERE I AM LOUNGING IN MALTA, AND THERE'S A WAR ON! YOU'D THINK WE WOULD BE DOING SOMETHING MORE USEFUL.
DON'T WORRY, OUR TURN WILL COME. WE'LL JUST HAVE TO WAIT UNTIL THE WAR REACHES THIS PART OF THE WORLD.

BUT PETER COULDN'T WAIT. EVERY DAY HE EXERCISED HIS MOTOR TORPEDO BOAT CREW IN THE HOPE THAT IF HIS CHANCE CAME, HE WOULD BE READY.
NOT BAD, LADS. I'LL SEE IF WE CAN GET A PLANE TO TOW A TARGET FOR US SOON.
NOT FLAMIN' BAD, 'E SAYS. AND I'M ONLY A COOK, NOT A GUNNER.
ON PETER'S BOAT ALL MEN WERE GUNNERS, AND THEY WERE KEPT IN PRACTICE.

PETER'S CREW SOMETIMES MOANED AMONG THEMSELVES ABOUT THE LACK OF ACTION AND THE EXTRA WORK THEY DID, BUT UNDERNEATH IT ALL THEY WERE PROUD OF BEING IN THE TOP MTB OF THE FLOTILLA.
YEAH, MATE, YOU SAY WHAT YOU WANT, BUT WE'RE THE BEST CREW AND YOU KNOW IT. WE SHOOT TEN TIMES BETTER THAN YOUR LOT DO!
HMS
YOU COULDN'T HIT A BARN DOOR FROM FIFTEEN YARDS! WAIT TILL WE GET INTO SOME ACTION.

IN THE RELATIVE SAFETY OF THE MEDITERRANEAN, THE MTB CREWS COULD LAUGH AND JOKE, BUT NEARER THE FIGHTING THE SITUATION WAS NOT SO FUNNY. IN DIJON –
PROFESSEUR DUVAL, FRANCE IS ILL. ONE SHARP BLOW FROM LES BOCHES AND SHE WILL COLLAPSE. YOU MUST GET OUT.
I KNOW. MY EXPERIMENTS MUST NOT FALL INTO THE HANDS OF THE NAZIS. I HAVE WRITTEN TO A FRIEND IN ENGLAND TO HELP ME GET MY INVENTION OUT OF THE COUNTRY.
PROFESSEUR HENRI DUVAL HAD STARTED WORK ON A COMPLETELY NEW FORM OF WEAPONRY. IN THE HANDS OF THE NAZIS THERE WAS NO KNOWING WHAT DAMAGE COULD BE DONE.

DUVAL'S DISTRESS SIGNAL QUICKLY REACHED THE HIGHEST AUTHORITIES BACK IN BRITAIN.
IS THIS IDEA ANY GOOD?
NOT RIGHT NOW, BUT IT HAS IMMENSE POSSIBILITIES. IF THE NAZIS GET HOLD OF IT, THE OUTCOME COULD BE DIS-ASTROUS.

RESCUE SUGGESTIONS OF ALL KINDS WERE PUT FORWARD, BUT IT WAS THE NAVY'S WHICH SEEMED THE MOST FEASIBLE.
WE'RE SENDING THE MALTA MTB FLOTILLA HOME. PERHAPS IT COULD MOTOR THROUGH FRANCE ON THE RIVERS AND CANALS, AND PICK UP DUVAL AT DIJON.
THE ADMIRAL'S PLAN WAS QUICKLY APPROVED AND SET IN MOTION.

BUT THE BRITISH AUTHORITIES WERE NOT THE ONLY ONES TO HEAR OF DUVAL'S FINDINGS. SIX HUNDRED MILES AWAY, IN ANOTHER CAPITAL CITY, TOP OFFICIALS WERE DISCUSSING THE SAME SITUATION.
SO,GUREN, YOU WILL HEAD STRAIGHT FOR DIJON AND CAPTURE THIS FRENCH INVENTOR AND HIS WORK. PICK YOUR MEN AND MAKE YOUR PLANS.
THE INVASION OF FRANCE IS CLOSE. I WILL HAVE TO WORK QUICKLY.
HAUPTSTURMFÜHRER LUDWIG GUREN OF THE S.S., ONE OF THE NAZIS' MOST RUTHLESS OFFICERS, WAS ALREADY WORKING IT OUT IN HIS HEAD.

BACK IN MALTA THE ORDERS FROM WHITEHALL CAME THROUGH, MUCH TO THE DISGUST OF THE MTB CREWS.
IT WASN'T EASY TO CONVINCE THEM THAT A TRIP THROUGH FRANCE MIGHT NOT BE A HOLIDAY.
ESPECIALLY YOUNG POWELL. HE WAS FUMING. IF THE EYETIES JOIN THE WAR, WE WILL NEED THEM BACK HERE QUICKLY, TOO.

THE MTB FLOTILLA WERE CERTAINLY NOT PLEASED AT GOING INLAND TO REACH HOME. THEY KNEW THAT THE BOATS WERE BUILT FOR SPEED AND NOT DESIGNED TO CRAWL SLOWLY UP RIVERS AND CANALS.
LOOKS LIKE BAD WEATHER BREWING UP. THIS MIGHT NOT BE NICE AT ALL.
HMS
NONSENSE. WE CAN STAND UP TO ANY-THING.

PETER KNEW ONLY TOO WELL THE POWERFUL HIGH OCTANE PETROL ENGINES WERE NOTORIOUSLY FICKLE.
KEEP HER INTO THE WIND, COX'N. AND PRAY THAT THERE ISN'T AN ENGINE FAILURE NOW.

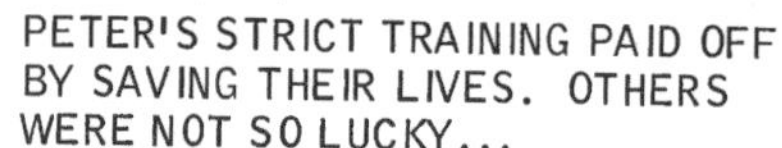
PETER'S STRICT TRAINING PAID OFF BY SAVING THEIR LIVES. OTHERS WERE NOT SO LUCKY...

SHE'S 'AD IT. NOT A FLAMING CHANCE.

THE SUDDEN STORM BLEW ITSELF OUT AS QUICKLY AS IT HAD ARISEN, BUT NOT BEFORE IT HAD CLAIMED ITS VICTIM. ONLY FIVE BOATS ENTERED THE RHÔNE ESTUARY.

LUCKY BLIGHTERS.
YEAH, I WOULDN'T MIND A BIT OF A FRENCH HOLIDAY MY-SELF.

THE VOYAGE UP THE RHÔNE WAS UNEVENTFUL. IT WAS A HOLIDAY TRIP...

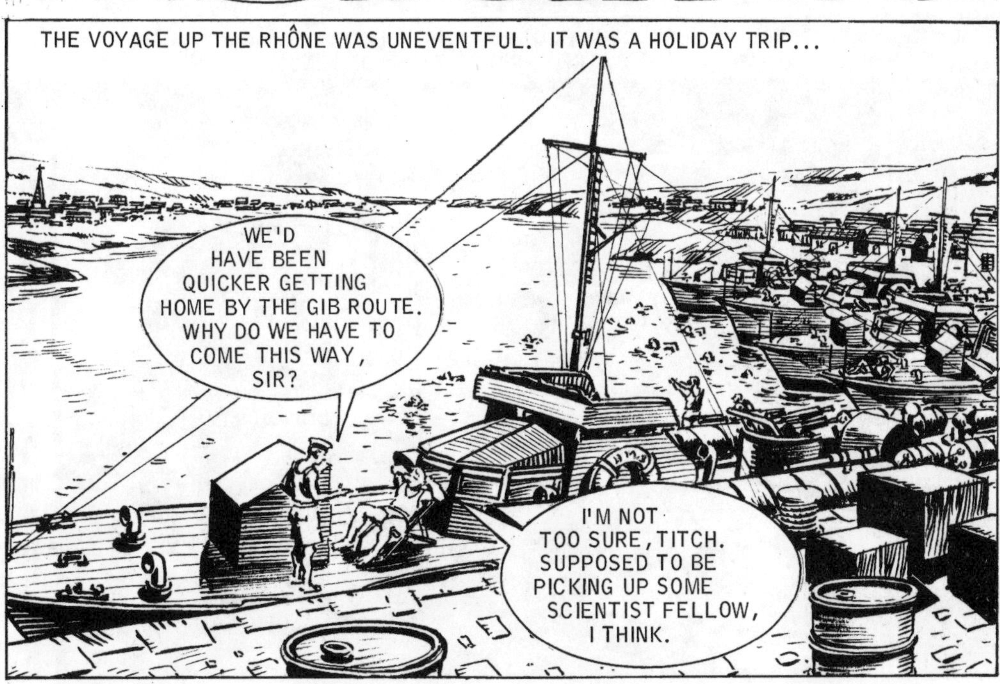
WE'D HAVE BEEN QUICKER GETTING HOME BY THE GIB ROUTE. WHY DO WE HAVE TO COME THIS WAY, SIR?
I'M NOT TOO SURE, TITCH. SUPPOSED TO BE PICKING UP SOME SCIENTIST FELLOW, I THINK.

BUT PETER'S CREW SOON FOUND OUT. ON REACHING DIJON, THE LITTLE SCIENTIST AND HIS EQUIPMENT WERE WAITING TO BE COLLECTED.
I HOPE YOU HAVE A PLEASANT TRIP, PROFESSOR DUVAL.
I WILL NOT BE HAPPY UNTIL WE ARE SAFE IN ENGLAND, LIEUTENANT.
PETER WAS COMPLETELY UNAWARE AS TO HOW VALUABLE HIS CARGO WAS.

BY MEANS OF CANAL AND RIVER THE FLOTILLA CONTINUED ON ITS WAY TO PARIS AND THE CHANNEL, BUT ON THE LAST STRETCHES OF THE WIDE, WINDING SEINE...
HOLY MACKEREL, ANDY. GO GET THE BOSS FAST.

THE NEWS WAS BAD. HITLER HAD THROWN HIS WELL-TRAINED AND ARMED COLUMNS INTO THE ATTACK, AND THE FRENCH WERE REELING. PETER CALLED THE OTHER MTB COMMANDERS TOGETHER.
I THOUGHT THIS WOULD HAPPEN. I SUGGEST FULL SPEED, LIEUTENANT. THE NAZIS WILL CUT THROUGH FRANCE LIKE A HOT KNIFE THROUGH BUTTER.
LET'S NOT PANIC. I'M SURE THEY WILL NEVER GET AS FAR AS THIS. WE ARE TOO FAR AHEAD, ANY-WAY.
BUT DUVAL WAS NOT SO SURE. HE KNEW THE EFFICIENCY OF HIS COUNTRY'S INVADERS.

DUVAL WAS SOON TO BE PROVED RIGHT. THE GERMANS ADVANCED QUICKLY, SMASHING ALL BEFORE THEM.
PAH, THEY FIGHT LIKE OLD WOMEN. ENGLAND WILL BE NEXT.
57

THE BRITISH AND FRENCH PUT UP A GALLANT RESISTANCE WHEREVER POSSIBLE.
JERRY DIDN'T LIKE THAT, HARRY. RECKON THEY HAVEN'T MET THE ROYAL WEST-SHIRES BEFORE.
AND THEY WON'T BE IN SUCH A RUSH TO MEET THEM AGAIN, MATE.

BUT EVEN THEIR DISCIPLINE AND COURAGE COULD NOT HOLD OUT AGAINST THE OVERWHELMING FORCES ARRAYED AGAINST THEM...
WE ARE BEING OUTFLANKED, AND MORE OF OUR FORCES ARE BEING DRIVEN BACK TOWARDS DUNKIRK. WE'LL JUST HAVE TO SPLIT INTO SMALL GROUPS AND MAKE OUR OWN WAY TO THE COAST.

THE GERMAN SPEARHEAD MOVED FAST AND MANY BRITISH UNITS WERE CUT OFF, INCLUDING THE COMPANY UNDER THE COMMAND OF CAPTAIN DAVE STANDISH, AN ABLE OFFICER.
MUST BE MORE THAN ONE PORT IN FRANCE, SIR. CAN'T WE TRY ANOTHER ROUTE?
RIGHT, MEN. WE'LL JUST HAVE TO FIGHT OUR WAY FORWARD, OR THERE'LL BE NO DUNKIRK FOR US.
DAVE WAS ALWAYS READY TO LISTEN TO ADVICE, AND HE REACHED FOR HIS MAP.

WE'LL HEAD FOR LE HAVRE. THE NAZIS DON'T SEEM TO BE HEADING THAT WAY YET.
GOOD IDEA, CAPTAIN. JERRY WILL HAVE TO RUN TO CATCH US, EH?
Le Havre
THE ROYAL WESTSHIRES WERE CERTAINLY NOT QUITTING. THEY WERE HEADING HOME AND IT WOULD TAKE A LOT TO STOP THEM.

MEANWHILE, TWO HUNDRED MILES FURTHER WEST, A PICKED UNIT OF GERMAN STORM TROOPERS WERE RACING TOWARDS DIJON, AND MEETING LITTLE OPPOSITION.
HURRY UP, DRIVER. WE MUST GET THIS IDIOT DUVAL BEFORE HE FLEES THIS ACCURSED COUNTRY.
GUREN WAS DESPERATE TO CARRY OUT HIS MISSION, FOR HE SAW GLORY AND MEDALS AHEAD IF HE BROUGHT IT OFF.

BUT WHEN THEY REACHED DIJON AN UNPLEASANT SURPRISE AWAITED THEM...
SPEAK, YOU DOG! WHERE IS DUVAL?
GONE. HE HAS BEEN GONE SINCE A LONG TIME.

GUREN, HOWEVER, WAS QUICK TO FIND OUT ABOUT THE FRENCHMAN AND THE MTBs. BUT BY THAT TIME THE FLOTILLA HAD PASSED PARIS. GUREN WOULD HAVE TO MOVE SHARPLY.
LOOKS QUIET ENOUGH, DON'T IT?
YEAH, BUT THE RADIO NEWS AIN'T SO GOOD, IS IT? LOOKS LIKE OUR ARMY'S ON THE RUN.

DUVAL WAS WORRIED TOO...
I FEEL SURE THE NAZIS WILL BE LOOKING FOR ME. THEY OFFERED ME A LOT OF MONEY TO GO TO GERMANY BUT I REFUSED.
DON'T PUSH THE PANIC BUTTON, PROFESSOR. ACCORDING TO THE RADIO THEY AREN'T ANYWHERE NEAR DIJON YET.

PETER DIDN'T KNOW, BUT BARELY A MILE AWAY CAPTAIN DAVE STANDISH AND THE REMAINS OF HIS COMPANY WERE TRYING TO ESCAPE BACK HOME.
WE AREN'T MOVING FAST ENOUGH. AT THIS RATE WE HAVEN'T A HOPE OF REACHING THE COAST.
AND THEY HADN'T MUCH HOPE OF HOLDING OFF THE NAZIS EITHER. CONSTANT ATTACKS HAD CUT THEIR STRENGTH TO A LITTLE OVER THIRTY MEN.

ON PETER'S BOAT, TITCH KEPT A CAREFUL LOOKOUT. THEY HADN'T SEEN A GERMAN YET, BUT THERE WAS NO POINT IN TAKING UNNECESSARY RISKS.
LOOK, SIR! GERMAN SOLDIERS.
ACTION STATIONS, MEN! LET'S HAVE A LOOK, TITCH.
THE SOLDIERS HAD SEEN THE BOATS TOO...BUT THEY WEREN'T GERMANS.
ARE YOU THINKING WHAT I AM, SERGEANT?
SURE AM. CAPTURE ONE OF THOSE THINGS, AND THEY COULD DO MY BLISTERS A LOT OF GOOD.

DAVE'S MEN WERE QUICKLY READY FOR BATTLE.
HOLD YOUR FIRE UNTIL I GIVE THE WORD. THEN BLAST THEM.

THE MTB CREWS WERE ALSO PREPARED.

WAIT TILL YOU CAN SEE WHAT YOU'RE AIMING AT BEFORE YOU FIRE, COOKIE.

SURE THING, SKIP.

IT LOOKED AS IF NOTHING WAS GOING TO STOP A TERRIBLE MISTAKE, BUT BY AN IRONIC TWIST A STUPID BLUNDER SAVED A DREADFUL MASSACRE.
LOOK WHERE YOU'RE GOING, NOBBY, FOR PETE'S SAKE!
ORDINARY SEAMAN TED BRANNAN TOPPLED MAJESTICALLY INTO THE CANAL.

ALERTED BY THE SUDDEN CRY, STANDISH STUDIED THE BOATS CAREFULLY THROUGH HIS BINOCULARS.
THEY'RE MTB s! BUT FOR ALL WE KNOW THEY COULD BE CAPTURED ONES...
THAT SHOUT DIDN'T SOUND LIKE GERMAN TO ME, SIR.

DAVE DECIDED TO TRY A WHITE FLAG AND FIND OUT IF THERE WAS A GERMAN TRICK OR NOT.
THAT AIN'T NO JERRY. WHO ELSE WOULD WEAR A KHAKI UNIFORM?
I THINK YOU'RE RIGHT. YOU'D BETTER BE, OR YOU'RE IN TROUBLE, ME LAD, FOR FALLING IN THE CANAL.

AS THE TWO SIDES GOT CLOSER IT WAS CLEAR THAT A NASTY INCIDENT HAD ONLY JUST BEEN AVERTED BY THE SEAMAN'S PLUNGE.
HMS
COULD WE CADGE A LIFT WITH YOU CHAPS? DON'T WANT TO SPEND THE REST OF THE WAR BEHIND BARBED WIRE!
YOU'RE WELCOME. IT'LL BE A BIT CRAMPED, BUT BRING YOUR MEN ABOARD.

DAVE'S COMPANY QUICKLY FILED ABOARD THE FIVE BOATS. THE SIGHT OF THE UNTIDY BOAT AND CREW WAS A QUICK SOURCE OF AMUSEMENT.

HMS

BLIMEY, THIS BOAT LOOKS LIKE A DISASTER AREA!

KEEP YOUR MUDDY FEET OFF THE DECK, SOLDIER. I ONLY SCRUBBED IT THIS MORNING.

WITH EVERYONE ON BOARD, DAVE ADVISED THE FLOTILLA TO SLOW DOWN, BUT PETER QUICKLY PUT HIM IN HIS PLACE.
I THINK A MORE CAUTIOUS APPROACH MIGHT BE MORE IN ORDER HERE.
I'M IN COMMAND OF THIS FLOTILLA, AND WE ARE GOING FULL BLAST FOR THE CHANNEL. I GET SEASICK IN THESE TIDDLY RIVERS.

TO THE NORTH THE WAR WENT ON AND THE MEN LISTENED ANXIOUSLY TO EVERY BROADCAST. NEWS CAME THROUGH OF THE DUNKIRK EVACUATION.
I WISH I'D BEEN THERE. I'D BE IN BLIGHTY INSTEAD OF BEING HERE STILL.
YOU AND ME BOTH, MATE. THE SQUAREHEADS WILL HAVE MORE TROOPS TO SEND DOWN THIS WAY NOW.

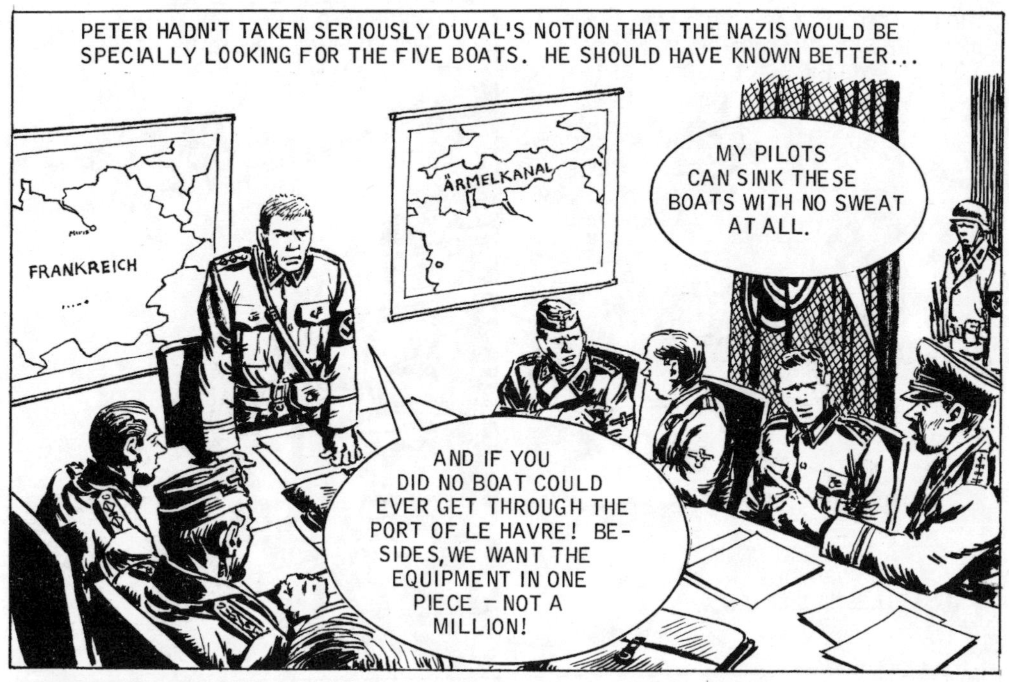
PETER HADN'T TAKEN SERIOUSLY DUVAL'S NOTION THAT THE NAZIS WOULD BE SPECIALLY LOOKING FOR THE FIVE BOATS. HE SHOULD HAVE KNOWN BETTER...
FRANKREICH
ÄRMELKANAL
MY PILOTS CAN SINK THESE BOATS WITH NO SWEAT AT ALL.
AND IF YOU DID NO BOAT COULD EVER GET THROUGH THE PORT OF LE HAVRE! BESIDES, WE WANT THE EQUIPMENT IN ONE PIECE – NOT A MILLION!

AS THE FLOTILLA MADE ITS WAY TOWARDS THE COAST, DAVE WAS QUICK TO MENTION THE POSSIBILITIES OF AN AIR ATTACK.
I THINK YOU UNDERESTIMATE THE NAZIS' AIR POWER. HAVE YOU EVER SEEN THEM IN ACTION?
NONE OF US HAS EVER SEEN A GERMAN – EITHER IN THE AIR OR AT SEA.
BUT PETER WAS SOON TO HAVE FIRST-HAND EXPERIENCE OF THE LUFTWAFFE.

THE LIEUTENANT WAS CONFIDENT, BUT UP IN THE SKY A PATROL OF Ju87 DIVE-BOMBERS WERE EQUALLY CONFIDENT.
A NICE EASY TARGET, REINHARDT, EH?
A PRACTICE RUN FOR REAL BATTLESHIPS LATER, SIR.
IF GUREN HAD SEEN THE STUKA CREWS HE WOULD HAVE GONE MAD. HE WANTED THE MTBs INTACT.
ATTACK FORMATION — GO!

THE MTBs WERE QUICK TO NOTICE THE STUKA ATTACK, BUT THEY WERE OVER-CONFIDENT AS THE SCREAMING AIRCRAFT CAME HURTLING OUT OF THE SUN.
GET READY, MEN! HERE COME SOME TROUBLE-MAKERS.
WHAT A NOISE! LIKE A MILLION BANSHEES WERE AFTER YOU.

AS PETER SAW THE STUKAS PEEL OFF, AND HEARD THE GHASTLY SCREECH OF THEIR APPROACH, HE WONDERED IF HE SHOULD HAVE LISTENED TO DAVE STANDISH...
I WAS WRONG. IF WE HAD BEEN MORE CAUTIOUS, WE WOULD HAVE BEEN READY FOR THIS. NOW MY MISTAKE IS GOING TO COST MEN'S LIVES.

AS THE FIRST STUKA SCREAMED OUT OF ITS DIVE THE COMBINED FORCE OF SOLDIERS AND SAILORS REPLIED THEIR ANGER WITH EVERY FORM OF GUN THEY HAD.
COME ON, COOKIE. LET'S SEE YOU USE THAT THING!
WHAT DO YOU THINK I'M DOING? THROWING DARTS?

THAT IS A SMALL BOAT, BUT IT CAN STILL SHOOT. STILL WANT A BATTLE-SHIP?

THE NAZI NEVER SAW HIS BATTLESHIP...

A LUCKY SHOT PIERCED THE FUEL TANK, ENGULFING THE STUKA IN A BALL OF FLAME.

AARGH!

BUT THE BATTLE WAS ONE-SIDED. THE MTBs COULD NOT HOPE TO MATCH THE DIVE-BOMBERS.

AARGH!
GUT! NOW WE SHOW THEM WHO THE MASTERS ARE.

A SECOND MTB WAS HIT, THE ONE CARRYING DUVAL'S CRATES, BUT NOT HIS NOTES WHICH WERE ON PETER'S BOAT.
LOUSY MURDERERS!
WHAT DO YOU EXPECT FROM THEM? THAT IS THE NAZI WAY.
URGH!

BUT THE SLAUGHTER HAD NOT GONE UN-NOTICED. FAR ABOVE, TWO COMMONWEALTH R.A.F. PILOTS WERE HAPPILY DIS-OBEYING ORDERS WHICH FOR-BADE THEM TO PATROL SO DEEP INTO FRANCE.
SHALL WE JOIN THE PARTY, BUTCH? IT DOESN'T LOOK PRIVATE.
SURE THING, BUDDY. BETTER BE QUICK THOUGH. WE'RE SUPPOSED TO BE BACK AT BASE!

THE TWO HURRICANES ROARED INTO THE BATTLE, EAGER TO DISPOSE OF THE LUMBERING STUKAS.
NOW THAT AIN'T FAIR PLAY, SPORT. LET'S SEE HOW YOU LIKE THE SAME.
ONE OF THE PILOTS, COBBER CANTWELL, HAD BEEN AN AUSSIE BUSH PILOT BEFORE THE WAR.

ARGH!
YOU ASKED FOR THIS, YELLA BELLY.
THE HATE-FILLED GUNNER OF THE STUKA PAID THE PRICE FOR HIS ACTIONS, AND THE DIVE-BOMBERS FOUND THAT IT WAS THEIR TURN TO BE SITTING DUCKS.

BUT THE TWO REMAINING STUKAS CONTINUED TO PRESS HOME THEIR ATTACK EVEN UNDER FIRE FROM THE FIGHTERS AND THE TORPEDO BOATS.
THAT GUNNER IS TOO GOOD. BUT HE'S HAD IT NOW...

BUT COBBER WAS IN TROUBLE TOO. WHEN GERMAN BULLETS SMASHED INTO HIS ENGINE, THE AUSTRALIAN KNEW IT WAS TIME TO BALE OUT.
I'M BALING OUT, BUTCH. THIS CRATE WON'T STAY UP LONG.
RIGHT, BUDDY. HOPE YOU GET BACK HOME OK...

AS THE AUSTRALIAN SLOWLY DESCENDED, THE REMAINING BOATS PREPARED TO PICK UP SURVIVORS.
WE'D BETTER RESCUE THAT PILOT.
IT'S A GOOD JOB THEY TURNED UP. WITHOUT THEM WE'D BE ALL AT THE BOTTOM OF THE RIVER.

COBBER CANTWELL WAS PICKED UP, WET AND ANGRY.
I'LL NEVER LIVE IT DOWN. IMAGINE BEING SHOT DOWN BY A STUKA!
NEVER MIND, AUSSIE! YOU GOT YOUR OWN BACK.

AS THE THREE REMAINING BOATS MOORED UNDER SOME WILLOWS, PETER AND DAVID TOOK STOCK.
MORE BAD NEWS. THE FRENCH HAVE SURRENDERED, AND THE GERMANS HAVE TAKEN LE HAVRE.
I FEARED AS MUCH.

PETER DECIDED THAT DIFFERENT TACTICS WOULD HAVE TO BE USED.
FROM HERE ON WE MOVE BY NIGHT AND HIDE DURING THE DAY.

IF PETER WAS ANNOYED IT WAS NOTHING COMPARED TO THE ANGER GENERATED BY A FURIOUS GUREN IN A NEARBY LUFTWAFFE MESS.
YOU IDIOTS! AGAINST ORDERS YOU ATTACKED THESE BOATS, AND NOW THAT VITAL INFORMATION IS AT THE BOTTOM OF THE RIVER!
WE ONLY SANK TWO BOATS TODAY. THE INFORMATION YOU NEED MAY WELL BE STILL INTACT.

FOR ALL HIS BLUSTER AND NASTINESS, GUREN WAS NO FOOL. HE KNEW THERE WAS STILL A GOOD CHANCE OF CAPTURING THE FRENCHMAN'S WORK, SO HE DROVE HURRIEDLY TO A NEARBY PANZER UNIT FOR ASSISTANCE.
OUR TANKS NEED SERVICING AND THE RIVER AREA IS TOO MARSHY AND NOT TANK COUNTRY. THE ONLY THING I CAN DO IS SEND MOTOR-CYCLE SCOUTS TO TRY TO LOCATE THE BOATS FOR YOU.
WELL, GET ON WITH IT! I WANT THEM FOUND IMMEDIATELY.

ON THE MTB s THE SEAMEN AND SOLDIERS COULD FEEL THE ENEMY CLOSING AROUND THEM AND TENSION QUICKLY LED TO BAD TEMPER. SMALL, UNIMPORTANT DETAILS BECAME BIG...
YOU BROWN BUFFOON. THAT THERE IS MY BUNK AND NO PONGO IS GOING TO 'AVE IT.
IT'S YOURS BETWEEN FOUR AND EIGHT. IT AIN'T FOUR YET, SO IT'S STILL MINE.

A BATTLE ROYAL WAS ABOUT TO BREAK OUT BUT PETER AND DAVID HEARD THE COMMOTION.

IF YOU'VE NOTHING BETTER TO DO THAN QUARREL, YOU CAN BOTH GO ON AN EXTRA GUARD DUTY, NOW!

IT'S MY BUNK, SIR. I DON'T SEE WHY I SHOULD HAVE TO GIVE IT UP FOR THAT CREEP!

MEANWHILE, AS THE TORPEDO BOATS HID UNDER THE SHELTER OF THE WILLOW TREES, TWO MOTOR-CYCLES AND SIDECARS ROARED NEARBY IN A FRANTIC EFFORT TO FIND GUREN'S PREY.
ALL WE HAVE TO DO IS FIND SOME TORPEDO BOATS, THE CAPTAIN SAYS.
AND THEN WHAT? A TORPEDO BOAT IS A BIT BIGGER THAN THIS USELESS MACHINE!

AS WELL AS BEING SMALLER THAN THE MTB s, THE MOTORBIKES WERE ALSO EVERY BIT AS NOISY, WHICH WAS JUST AS WELL...

LISTEN, I CAN HEAR MOTOR BIKES.
WE'D BETTER WARN THE OTHERS IN CASE IT'S JERRY ON A RECCE.

WITH EVERYONE ALERT TO THE DANGER THE THREE BOATS LAY SILENT, WITH EVERY MAN ABOARD ANXIOUSLY WAITING FOR THE BIKES TO ROAR OFF AGAIN.

NOTHING HERE. LET'S GO HOME.
WAIT A MINUTE. MY FEET ACHE. I'M GOING TO COOL THEM IN THE WATER.

MEANWHILE ON THE BOATS, THE WESTSHIRES WERE PREPARING THEMSELVES FOR BATTLE...

JUST IN CASE THEY DO SEE US. WE DON'T WANT TO MAKE A NOISE, DO WE?

THE GERMAN WITH THE SORE FEET HAD STROLLED DOWN TO THE RIVER BY NOW, AND HE SAW MORE THAN HE BARGAINED FOR.

MEIN GOTT, THE BOATS! I HAD BETTER PRE-TEND NOT TO HAVE SEEN ANYTHING YET.

BUT THE UNFORTUNATE GERMAN HAD ALREADY BEEN SPOTTED.
IT DIDN'T LOOK AS IF HE HAD NOTICED ANY-THING.
WE CAN'T AFFORD TO TAKE THE RISK. SERGEANT, TAKE TWO MEN AND MAKE SURE HE DOESN'T RE-PORT US.
FOLLOWING THEIR CAPTAIN'S ORDERS, THE SOLDIERS QUICKLY LEFT THE MTB.

ONE OF THEM SPRANG SILENTLY INTO ACTION. THERE COULD BE NO SHOOTING...
URGH!

WAITING ON THE HILL TOP, THE GERMANS BEGAN TO GET A LITTLE BIT ANXIOUS WHEN THEIR MATE DIDN'T RETURN.
HE MAY HAVE FOUND THOSE ACCURSED BRITISH BOATS.
MORE LIKELY HE IS PLAYING A STUPID JOKE ON US. WE'D BETTER LOOK ANYWAY.

WITH THE GERMAN BODY OUT OF SIGHT, THE WESTSHIRES WAITED FOR THEIR PREY. THEY HAD BEEN THROUGH PRACTICES LIKE THIS MANY TIMES BEFORE BUT NOW THEY WERE READY FOR THE REAL THING.
NO NOISE. GRAB THEIR GUNS AS THEY FALL, IN CASE ONE GOES OFF.

AS THE UNSUSPECTING GERMANS WALKED WEARILY PAST, DAVE'S MEN MOVED IN LIKE A TEAM OF VETERANS.
THIS'LL TEACH YOU TO COME NOSEYING, SQUAREHEAD!
ARGH!

WITH THE MOTOR-CYCLE PATROL WIPED OUT, THERE REMAINED THE JOB OF DISPOSING OF THE EVIDENCE.
THAT'S BETTER. THE BODIES ARE WELL HIDDEN IN THE BUSHES. MY CHAPS WERE DESPERATE FOR A BIT OF ACTION.
MINE STILL ARE. THEY'RE GETTING A BIT FED UP OF THIS CONTINUAL RUNNING FROM THE JERRIES.

THE WESTSHIRES HAD PROVED THEIR WORTH AGAIN – AND SAID SO.
WE CAN TAKE CARE OF THE GERMAN ARMY. YOU FISHHEADS JUST DRIVE THIS LITTLE TUB HOME.
YOU LOAFING LANDLUBBER. IF YOU CAN TAKE CARE OF THE JERRIES, WHY ARE YOU HITCHING A LIFT WITH US?

THE TENSION HAD BUILT UP TO BOILING POINT IN THE MTB CREWS, AND IT HAD TO ESCAPE.
ROTTEN PONGO!
CUT IT OUT, ALL OF YOU!

THE FRUSTRATED MEN CAME QUICKLY TO ATTENTION, AND LISTENED SHEEPISHLY AS DAVE AND PETER SPOKE TO THEM.
I WON'T SAY MUCH. IT ISN'T EASY TO DO SO MUCH WAITING AND HIDING, BUT YOU ARE TRAINED MEN, NOT A RABBLE.
THE GERMANS HOLD LE HAVRE. I DON'T THINK THEY WILL LIKE US CRUISING THROUGH, SO HOLD YOUR ENERGY FOR THE ENEMY. THAT'S ALL.

REALISING THEIR STUPID MISTAKE AND HOW MUCH THEY WERE GOING TO HAVE TO DEPEND ON EACH OTHER, THE ANGRY MEN SOON MADE UP.

SORRY, MATE. DON'T KNOW WHAT CAME OVER ME.
HMS
AW, FORGET IT. WE'RE ALL A BIT TENSED UP, LIKE.

BUT TROUBLE STRUCK BEFORE THE MTBs EVEN REACHED LE HAVRE.
BLIMEY, I'D BETTER TELL THE SKIPPER.
YEAH. IT DOESN'T LOOK TOO GOOD AT ALL.
PETER HAD THOUGH THE ONLY RE-MAINING HURDLE TO CROSS WAS TO GET THROUGH LE HAVRE. NOW HE HAD ANOTHER.
HMS
HMS
I DON'T KNOW HOW IT HAPPENED, SIR. MAY-BE A LEAK SOMEWHERE, BUT WE'RE GETTING LOW ON FUEL.
THAT'S ALL WE NEED!

REALISING SOMETHING HAD TO BE DONE, DAVID QUICKLY GOT TOGETHER A PARTY OF MEN TO SEARCH THE SURROUNDING AREA FOR ANY LIKELY SOURCE OF FUEL.
THANKS FOR TAKING SOME OF OUR LADS, DAVE. BEST OF LUCK, AND REMEMBER – PETROL, NOT DIESEL.
DON'T WORRY, WE'LL GET SOME IF IT TAKES US THE REST OF THE WAR!

AS THE RAIDING PARTY LEFT, PETER AND THE REMAINING SEAMEN PREPARED FOR THE WORST, MOVING WHAT PETROL THEY HAD LEFT INTO ONE MTB.

WHAT ARE YOU DOING?
WE'VE GOT TO FACE IT. THERE ISN'T MUCH CHANCE OF US GETTING FUEL, OR OF GETTING THE RAIDING PARTY BACK. WITH ONE BOAT AND THE REMAINING FUEL WE STILL HAVE A CHANCE.

THE PROFESSOR FOUND IT HARD TO BELIEVE THAT PETER WOULD LEAVE BEHIND HIS COMRADES.

LOOK, PROFESSOR, IT'S MY JOB TO GET YOU BACK TO BRITAIN NO MATTER THE COST. SO UNLESS THEY ARE BACK WITHIN TWENTY-FOUR HOURS, WE'RE MOVING ON.

THE RAIDING PARTY WERE NOT HAVING MUCH SUCCESS...

MIGHT AS WELL BE ON THE MOON. NOTHING BUT LOTS OF EMPTI-NESS HERE.
WE'D BETTER FIND SOME PETROL FAST, OTHERWISE IT'LL BE A SHORT WAR FOR US!

ONLY ONE MAN AMONG THE PARTY HAD A ROUGH IDEA OF THE COUNTRYSIDE THEY HAD FOUND THEMSELVES IN. COBBER CANTWELL POINTED AHEAD.

THERE'S AN AIRFIELD OVER THAT WAY, I RECKON. LOOKED LIKE THE LUFT-WAFFE HAD PLASTERED IT, LAST TIME I FLEW OVER IT.
OK. WE'LL HEAD FOR IT AND SCOUT AROUND.

BUT COBBER WAS FORGETTING THAT FLYING OVER AN AREA AT THREE HUNDRED MILES PER HOUR AND WALKING ON THE GROUND WERE TWO DIFFERENT THINGS.

MAKE FOR THE FARMHOUSE, MEN. WE'LL SEE IF WE CAN GET ANY HELP THERE.
LOOKS AS IF YOU WERE MISTAKEN, AUSSIE. NO AIRFIELD AROUND HERE.

AT THE FARMHOUSE, THE RAIDERS WERE PLEASED TO BE MET BY FRIENDLY FACES.
ANYONE WHO FIGHTS THE BOCHE IS A WELCOME VISITOR AT MY HOUSE.
WE HATE THE BOCHE. THEY HAVE TAKEN ONE SON AND THE OTHER WE THINK IS A PRISONER. IF THERE IS ANYTHING WE CAN DO...

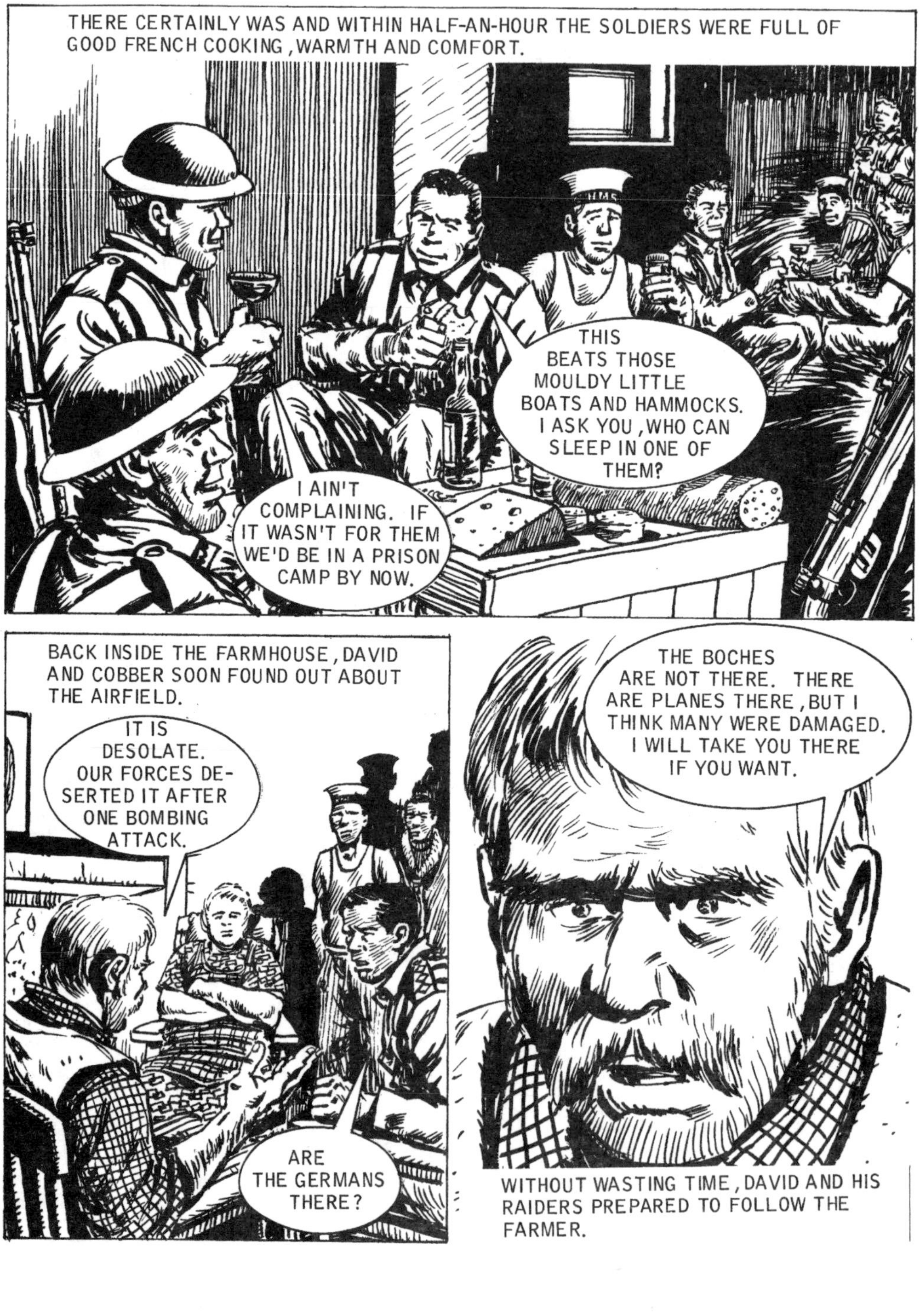

THERE CERTAINLY WAS AND WITHIN HALF-AN-HOUR THE SOLDIERS WERE FULL OF GOOD FRENCH COOKING, WARMTH AND COMFORT.

THIS BEATS THOSE MOULDY LITTLE BOATS AND HAMMOCKS. I ASK YOU, WHO CAN SLEEP IN ONE OF THEM?

I AIN'T COMPLAINING. IF IT WASN'T FOR THEM WE'D BE IN A PRISON CAMP BY NOW.

BACK INSIDE THE FARMHOUSE, DAVID AND COBBER SOON FOUND OUT ABOUT THE AIRFIELD.
ARE THE GERMANS THERE?
IT IS DESOLATE. OUR FORCES DESERTED IT AFTER ONE BOMBING ATTACK.

THE BOCHES ARE NOT THERE. THERE ARE PLANES THERE, BUT I THINK MANY WERE DAMAGED. I WILL TAKE YOU THERE IF YOU WANT.
WITHOUT WASTING TIME, DAVID AND HIS RAIDERS PREPARED TO FOLLOW THE FARMER.

THE COUNTRYSIDE CHANGED AS THE RAIDERS ARRIVED AT THE AIRFIELD. IT LOOKED DESERTED, BUT DAVE WASN'T TAKING ANY CHANCES.
LOOKS OK. MOVE IN QUIETLY AND HAVE A LOOK. MARSH AND WALKER, GO FIRST. IF IT'S OK, COME BACK AND GIVE US THE WORD.
I'LL GO TOO. I KNOW MY WAY AROUND AIRFIELDS, AND ONE IS MUCH LIKE ANOTHER.

THE THREE SCOUTS MOVED STEALTHILY THROUGH THE EMPTY BUILDINGS BUT FOUND NO SIGN OF LIFE.
SUFFERING SNAKES, LOOK AT THE WAY THE CLOWNS PARKED. SITTING DUCKS FOR ANY STUKA.
NO SIGN OF ANY FUEL IN HERE, ANYWAY. LET'S TRY ANOTHER HANGAR.

THE THREE RAIDERS COULDN'T BELIEVE WHAT THEY SAW IN THE NEXT HANGAR.
WELL, I'LL BE A KANGAROO'S AUNTIE! HALF THAT LOT WILL BE MORE THAN ENOUGH TO GET US HOME.
SOMETHIN' FISHY ABOUT THIS LOT, THOUGH. DOESN'T LOOK RIGHT...

THE YOUNG PRIVATE'S SUSPICIONS WERE CORRECT. SOMEONE HAD BEEN THERE BEFORE THEM.
HANDS UP. THAT FUEL WILL TAKE YOU NO-WHERE.
WE 'AVE BEEN FILLING THOSE CANS SINCE THE REST FLED. IT WILL BE USED ONE DAY.

THE FRENCHMEN WERE AIR FORCE MEN WHO HAD STAYED ON THE BASE TO SALVAGE WHAT THEY COULD TO CONTINUE THE FIGHT AGAINST THE GERMAN INVADERS, FROM THE WOODS AND HILLS.

LET'S MAKE A DEAL. I CAN SEE YOU ARE A PILOT, AND I RECKON YOUR MATES ARE GROUND CREW, RIGHT? HOW WOULD YOU LIKE TO KEEP FIGHTING IN THE AIR?

THAT UNFORTUNATELY IS NOT POSSIBLE. YOU HAVE SEEN THE WAY OUR GENERALS WERE UNABLE TO EVEN PARK OUR AIRCRAFT.

COBBER WAS QUICK TO SUGGEST THE POSSIBILITIES OF THE FRENCHMEN COMING BACK TO BRITAIN TO JOIN THE R.A.F. AND THEIR LEADER, JULES MAURIER, LISTENED WITH INTEREST.
IF YOU GIVE US THE FUEL, YOU COULD COME BACK WITH US AND JOIN THE R.A.F.
WHAT ABOUT IT, FROGGIE? YOU'D DO MORE DAMAGE WITH THE R.A.F. THAN YOU WOULD HERE.

THE FRENCH WERE ENTHUSIASTIC AND WERE PREPARED TO ACCEPT THE RISKS OF THE LAST STAGE OF THE VOYAGE.

ARE YOU CERTAIN THAT THE R.A.F. WILL TAKE A FRENCHMAN TO FLY FOR THEM?
MATE, WE ALREADY GOT YANKS, CZECHS, POLES – THE LOT. ANYONE WHO CAN HANDLE A PLANE IS NEEDED. THE BIG SHOW WILL COME WHEN THE NAZIS TRY TO INVADE US.

IT WAS HARD, LABORIOUS WORK CARRYING THE FUEL BACK TO THE BOATS, BUT MANY WILLING HANDS HELPED. AND BEST OF ALL, THE GERMANS HAD NO IDEA WHAT HAD HAPPENED.

LOOK, SKIP! THOSE ARMY BODS HAVE GOT US SOME PETROL.
JUST IN TIME TOO. ANOTHER TWO HOURS AND WE WOULD HAVE BEEN FORCED TO LEAVE WITHOUT THEM.

PETER SHUDDERED TO THINK OF THE BOATS BEING CRAMMED WITH HIGHLY INFLAMMABLE FUEL, BUT IT WAS NECESSARY IF THEY WANTED TO GET BACK HOME.

PETER PREPARED FOR THE FINAL BATTLE, BUT AS HE DID SO, A FAMILIAR FACE WAS ALSO PREPARING FOR ACTION...
THE LUFT-WAFFE HAVE LET ME DOWN. THE ARMY WERE JUST AS BAD. IT SEEMS THESE MTBs ARE GHOST BOATS. THEY MUST BE FOUND AND DESTROYED.
THEY HAVE NOT PASSED LE HAVRE, HERR GUREN. OF THAT I AM CERTAIN.
MAKE SURE THEY DO NOT. IT IS IMPERATIVE THEY ARE STOPPED. DO NOT MAKE MISTAKES, OR IT WILL BE THE WORSE FOR YOU.
JAWOHL! DO NOT WORRY. THEY WILL NOT ESCAPE US.

THE NAVAL OFFICER HAD PLANNED WELL. HE WAS A PROFESSIONAL SAILOR AND HE KNEW HOW TO TRAP THE TORPEDO BOATS.

YOU SEE THE BOOM. IT OPENS ONLY TO ALLOW OUR BOATS IN AND OUT. IT WILL BE IMPOSSIBLE FOR THE TORPEDO BOATS TO GET OUT.
IT HAD BETTER BE.

BACK AT THE BOATS, TENSION WAS ONCE AGAIN BUILDING UP. AFTER HIDING FOR SO LONG EVERYONE KNEW THAT THE FINAL STRUGGLE FOR ESCAPE WAS GETTING CLOSER.

IF WE ONLY KNEW WHAT WAS COMING.
YEAH. WE MIGHT BE SAILING INTO A TRAP.

MEANWHILE, UP ON BRIDGE, A LOCAL FRENCHMAN WAS PUTTING FORWARD HIS IDEAS TO THE FLOTILLA LEADER.
TELL THE LIEUTENANT YOUR PLANS, JACQUES.
I AM FROM LE HAVRE, SIR. I COULD GO INTO THE TOWN FOR A DAY AND PERHAPS I MAY LEARN SOMETHING OF THE RIVER DEFENCES.

THE PLAN WAS APPROVED IMMEDIATELY. THE GALLANT FRENCHMAN SET OFF AND THE BOATS ONCE AGAIN SETTLED DOWN TO WAIT.
THIS WAITING IS GETTING ME DOWN.
I FEEL A BIT LIKE A BIT OF CHEESE IN A MOUSETRAP.

AS THE DAY PROGRESSED, THE CREWS OF THE TORPEDO BOATS, ALONG WITH THEIR ARMY FRIENDS, PREPARED FOR BATTLE.
RIGHT, MEN. PREPARE TO GO, WE CAN'T WAIT ANY LONGER.
OH WELL, IN FOR A PENNY, IN FOR A POUND!

THE BOATS WERE ABOUT TO MOVE OUT IN A MAD DASH THROUGH THE HARBOUR WHEN THE LOYAL FRENCHMAN GOT BACK, EXHAUSTED AFTER HIS LONG JOURNEY.

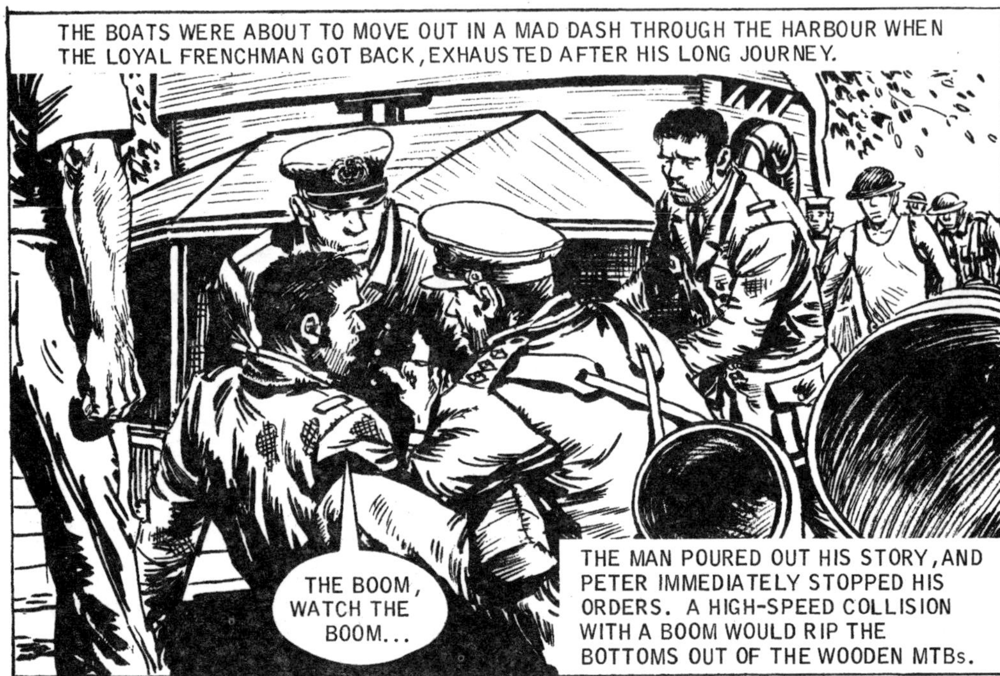
THE BOOM, WATCH THE BOOM...
THE MAN POURED OUT HIS STORY, AND PETER IMMEDIATELY STOPPED HIS ORDERS. A HIGH-SPEED COLLISION WITH A BOOM WOULD RIP THE BOTTOMS OUT OF THE WOODEN MTBs.

NOW THEY KNEW WHAT LAY AHEAD. UNLESS THE BOOM NET WAS DESTROYED IN SOME WAY, THE TORPEDO BOATS WOULD NEVER MAKE THE OPEN SEA.

WHAT DO WE DO NOW, THEN? WE'VE NO EXPLOSIVES AND IF WE USED TORPEDOES THEY WOULD GO STRAIGHT THROUGH THE NET.

PETER REALISED THE PROBLEM, BUT THERE WAS LITTLE HE COULD DO.

BUT TITCH WHO HAD BEEN LISTENING CLOSELY TO HIS SKIPPER'S CONVERSATION, CAME UP WITH A SOUND BUT DANGEROUS IDEA.
HMS
WHY DON'T WE DROP SOME DEPTH CHARGES NEXT TO THE NET, SKIP? WE COULD WAIT TILL DARK, THEN ONE OF THE BOATS COULD GO UP-RIVER AHEAD OF THE REST AND BLOW IT UP.

THE IDEA SEEMED A GOOD ONE, BUT PETER SOON FOUND PROBLEMS.
WHAT ABOUT SHORE-GUNS, TITCH? AS SOON AS WE BLOW UP THE NET, THE JERRIES WOULD REALISE WHAT WAS GOING ON AND BLAST US ALL OUT OF THE WATER.
HMS

DAVE STANDISH HOWEVER, HAD THE ANSWER TO THAT PROBLEM.
YOU FORGET YOU'RE CARRYING HALF A COMPANY OF HIS MAJESTY'S ROYAL WESTSHIRES. JUST DROP US OFF A MILE FROM THE GUNS AND WE'LL SORT THEM OUT.

PETER EVENTUALLY AGREED WITH THE PLAN – THERE WERE NO ALTERNATIVES LEFT NOW.

OK, THEN. WE'LL MOVE DOWN RIVER FOR ABOUT TEN MILES THEN YOU CAN TAKE YOUR MOB AND SILENCE ANY GUNS.

FINE. I'LL GET MY MEN READY AS QUICK AS I CAN.

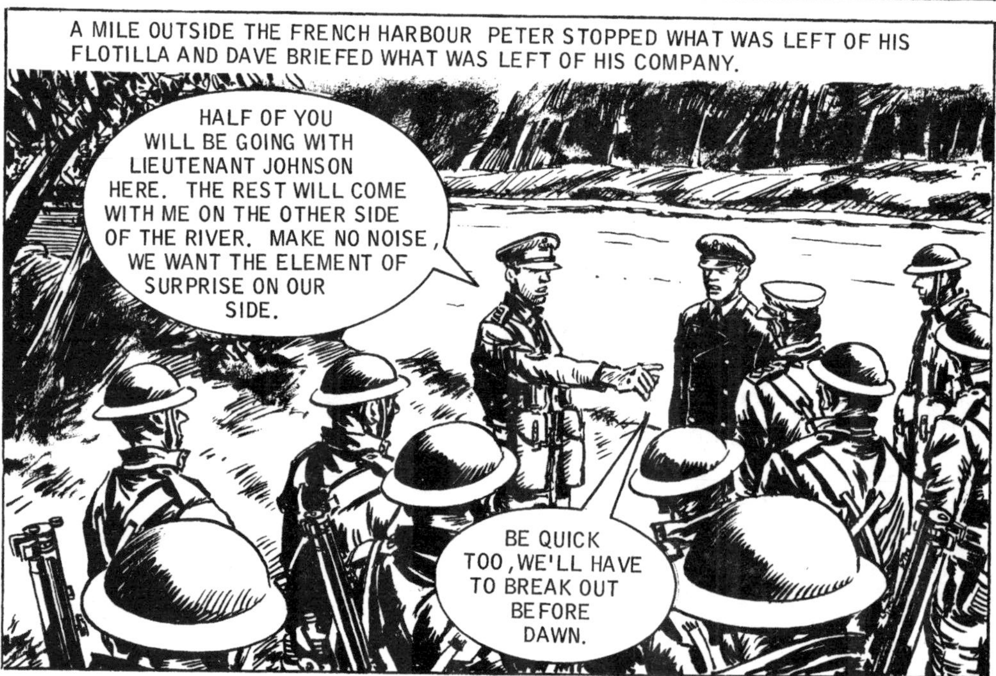
A MILE OUTSIDE THE FRENCH HARBOUR PETER STOPPED WHAT WAS LEFT OF HIS FLOTILLA AND DAVE BRIEFED WHAT WAS LEFT OF HIS COMPANY.
HALF OF YOU WILL BE GOING WITH LIEUTENANT JOHNSON HERE. THE REST WILL COME WITH ME ON THE OTHER SIDE OF THE RIVER. MAKE NO NOISE, WE WANT THE ELEMENT OF SURPRISE ON OUR SIDE.
BE QUICK TOO, WE'LL HAVE TO BREAK OUT BEFORE DAWN.

WITHIN HALF AN HOUR DAVE AND HIS SECTION OF THE COMPANY HAD FOUND THEIR PREY.
REMEMBER, BE QUICK AND SILENT. IF WE BUNGLE THIS, THERE'LL BE NO CHRISTMAS CAKE FOR US.

THE RAIDERS MOVED IN AS IF THEY HAD PRACTISED IT FOR YEARS. WITHIN SECONDS IT WAS ALL OVER.
URGH!
GOOD WORK, MEN.
THEIR JOB DONE, THE ATTACKERS MOVED QUICKLY BACK TO THE BOATS.

BACK AT THE BOATS, PETER WAS BEGINNING TO LOSE HIS PATIENCE.

GET A MOVE ON, YOU LOT. WE'LL NEVER GET HOME AT THIS RATE.
HOLD YOUR HORSES. WE'RE GOING AS FAST AS WE CAN.

WITH EVERYONE ON BOARD THE MTB s ROARED OFF, PETER'S BOAT WELL IN FRONT FOR THE ATTACK ON THE NET.

AS THEY RACED CLOSER AND CLOSER TO THE NET, PETER AND HIS CREW PREPARED FOR THE SHARPEST U-TURN THEY HAD EVER ATTEMPTED.

WE MUST BE COMING UP TO THE NET, I CAN SEE THE FLOATS. GET READY, COOKIE, WE'RE GOING TO DO A SHARP TURN.
SURE THING, SKIP.

WITH ONLY FEET TO SPARE, THE TORPEDO BOAT TURNED AND THE TWO SAILORS WERE QUICK TO DISPOSE OF THE DEPTH-CHARGES.

RIGHT, SKIPPER. LET'S GET OUT OF HERE BEFORE WE GO UP WITH 'EM!
DON'T WORRY ABOUT GETTING AWAY, COOKIE. THIS BOAT 'ERE HAS GOT THE FASTEST ACCELERATION IN THE NAVY.

LUCKILY TITCH WAS RIGHT. PETER'S MTB HAD MANAGED TO REJOIN THE REMAINDER OF THE FLOTILLA BEFORE THE CHARGES WENT OFF.

UP SHE GOES!

WITH THE HARBOUR ENTRANCE NOW OPEN THE THREE TORPEDO BOATS MADE A QUICK DASH FOR THE CHANNEL.

AS THEY RACED THROUGH THE HARBOUR, EVERYONE EXPECTED TO BE MET BY A HAIL OF FIRE. BUT THE INFANTRY HAD SEEN TO THAT.

FOR ONCE YOU DID A JOB WELL, SOLDIER. THAT MAKES A CHANGE!

FIRE AT WILL, MEN. LET'S CONFUSE THEM AS MUCH AS POSSIBLE.

THE FLOTILLA HAD CERTAINLY CAUSED CONFUSION. THE SENIOR GERMAN NAVAL OFFICER SAT IN HIS OFFICE AND TRIED TO RE-ORGANISE HIS DEFENCES, DESPITE BEING DISTRACTED BY A FUMING GUREN.

YOU DOLT, WHAT IS GOING ON?
I SEE. HAVE THE E-BOAT FLOTILLA READY. THEY CAN CAST OFF AS SOON AS POSSIBLE.

GUREN COULD NO LONGER KEEP HIS TEMPER...
THE FÜHRER WILL HAVE YOUR HEAD FOR THIS, FOOL. WHY DON'T YOU BLAST THEM OUT OF THE WATER WITH YOUR COASTAL GUNS?
THE NAZI OBVIOUSLY HAD NOT BEEN CHECKING HIS DEFENCES.
HE FOUND IT IMPOSSIBLE TO BELIEVE THAT A FEW LITTLE BOATS COULD ESCAPE HIM AFTER ALL HIS PLANNING.
CALM YOURSELF, GUREN. ALL IS UNDER CONTROL. THEY HAVE ESCAPED THROUGH THE BOOM NET, BUT OUR E-BOATS WILL CATCH THEM.
I WILL GO WITH YOUR BOATS AND PERSONALLY FINISH THOSE VERDAMMT ENGLANDERS.
THE PENT UP TENSION WAS RELEASED ON THE TWO BOATS IN THE FORM OF RED-HOT LEAD.
EXHILARATING STUFF. WOULDN'T HAVE MISSED IT FOR THE WORLD.
WAIT TILL WE'RE HOME BEFORE YOU SAY THAT. THERE'S A LOT OF CHANNEL STILL TO CROSS.

THE MTBs DISHED OUT AS MUCH PUNISHMENT TO THE SHORE INSTALLATIONS AS THEY COULD.
AARGH!

IT WOULD HAVE BEEN A MIRACLE IF ALL THE BOATS HAD ESCAPED SCOT-FREE.
URGH!
BUT THE INJURED WERE RUSHED BELOW DECKS AND THE BOATS CONTINUED ON THEIR RACE TO FREEDOM.

THE MTBs SPED OUT INTO THE RIVER ESTUARY, BUT AS PETER HAD SAID, THEY WERE NOT YET HOME. GUREN WAS NOT GOING TO GIVE UP.

GET GOING! MOVE!

PETER KNEW THAT THE SLIM RAKED ENEMY E-BOATS WOULD BE FOLLOWING HIM. HE KNEW NOW THAT THEY WERE BIGGER, FASTER AND BETTER ARMED THAN HIS BOATS.
MADE IT. HOME FOR BACON AND EGGS.
DON'T BE TOO SURE, CHUM. LOOK BEHIND YOU!

ONCE OUT INTO THE OPEN SEA HOWEVER, THE MTBs HAD NO PROBLEM IN LOSING THEIR PREDATORS.
PUT THAT CIGARETTE OUT! WE DAREN'T LET THOSE E-BOATS SEE EVEN THE SMALLEST LIGHT.
THE LIEUTENANT'S RIGHT – WATCH YOUR STEP, LADS.

LESS THAN A QUARTER OF A MILE AWAY THE E-BOATS WERE LOOKING, BUT NOT WITH MUCH LUCK.
SO YOU CANNOT FIND THEM. WHAT SORT OF A NAVY DO WE HAVE?
I DO NOT THINK THEY ARE FAR AWAY. THE ENGLISH-MAN IS NOT STUPID. IF HE WAS RUNNING FULL OUT WE WOULD HEAR HIM.

BUT SUDDENLY A STROKE OF BAD LUCK HIT THE MTB FLOTILLA. THE HEAVY CLOUDS BROKE, REVEALING ALL THE BOATS.
CRIKEY, THAT'S DONE IT NOW.
ACHTUNG! OVER THERE.

IT WAS A BITTER BLOW, BUT PETER'S MIND WAS WORKING FURIOUSLY AS HE PLOTTED THEIR NEXT MOVE.
FULL AHEAD. GET THOSE PETROL CANS READY TO TOSS OVER WHEN I GIVE THE WORD.
WE WON'T GET MUCH EXTRA SPEED BY TOSSING A FEW DRUMS OVER-BOARD.

BUT PETER'S AIM WAS NOT TO LIGHTEN THE BOAT – HE HAD ANOTHER PLAN.
GET SOME SMOKE UP, LADS. AND QUICK!

AS THE E-BOATS SPED INTO THE SMOKE SCREEN AFTER THEIR PREY, PETER GAVE THE ORDER TO FIRE... BUT NOT AT THE GERMAN VESSELS.
FIRE AT THE PETROL CANS. AND HIT THEM, LADS. OUR LIVES DEPEND ON IT.

AND THE GUNNERS DID NOT MISS THE CANS. THE PLAN WORKED PERFECTLY AND THE HUNGRY FLAMES LICKED AT THE SPEEDING GERMAN CRAFT.
MEIN GOTT, WE ARE ON FIRE!
ABANDON SHIP!
20
ONE BOAT WAS SOON A BLAZING WRECK.

AND WHEN THE REMAINING TWO E-BOATS EMERGED FROM THE BURNING INFERNO, ANOTHER SURPRISE AWAITED THEM.
HOW DO YOU LIKE THE NAVY IN ACTION, MATE? NOT SO DUSTY, EH?
FIRE ONE, FIRE TWO.
OK, YOU'VE MADE YOUR POINT. JUST SINK THOSE TWO CONTRAPTIONS AND GET US HOME.

THE TORPEDOES RAN TRUE...
ARGH!
THAT SORTED THAT LITTLE LOT OUT, EH!

AND GUREN DID CATCH UP WITH PROFESSOR DUVAL – BUT NOT IN THE WAY HE EXPECTED...

YOU WILL ALL PAY FOR THIS. SOON OUR ARMY WILL BE IN LONDON AND YOU WILL PAY DEARLY.

BELT UP, JERRY, OR I'LL DUMP YOU BACK IN!

AS DAWN BROKE THAT MORNING, THE COASTAL STATION AT AN ENGLISH PORT SAW AN UNUSUAL SIGHT.
BLIMEY, BERT. WE DIDN'T HAVE ANY TORPEDO BOATS OUT LAST NIGHT, DID WE?
NOPE. WE'D BETTER GET ONTO THE TOP BRASS.

THE MTB FLOTILLA ENTERED HARBOUR AS HEROES. AGAINST ALL THE ODDS THEY HAD SAILED RIGHT THROUGH FRANCE, OUTWITTING THE GERMAN FORCES ALL THE WAY. WHAT HAD STARTED OUT AS A HOLIDAY TRIP, ENDED UP AS ONE OF THE WAR'S MOST DARING ADVENTURES.

WELL, WE EVENTUALLY MADE IT, BUT I'LL NEVER WANT A HOLIDAY LIKE THAT AGAIN!
ME, NEITHER. MIND YOU, IT WAS FUN WHILE IT LASTED. I CAN'T WAIT TO HAVE ANOTHER CRACK AT THE LIKES OF GUREN!
Commando
THE END

Your next four exciting Commando books are out in three weeks!
Make sure you get:—

"JUNGLE CRAZY" ***"THE HIDDEN ROCKETS"***

"CARRIER SQUADRON" ***"AFTER D-DAY"***

INTO ACTION

WEAPONS THAT MADE HISTORY

LEE-ENFIELD RIFLE

THIS is the famous Lee-Enfield rifle, the British infantryman's best friend in two World Wars. Probably the best-known rifle in the world, it started its career in 1907, and has been around ever since. It's even in military use today in some places, and it's a great favourite as a sporting rifle in the U.S.A.

So accurate is it that the sights can be set to 2,000 yards range. That's a fantastic distance to fire a rifle and still hit the target.

It also had the fastest rate of fire of any bolt-action rifle in the world – in fact, the Germans thought they were up against machine guns when they faced Lee-Enfield fire in 1914.

RILEY'S RIFLE

DEATH AND DESTRUCTION WERE PART OF EVERYDAY LIFE IN THE GRIM MONTHS AT THE BEGINNING OF THE SECOND WORLD WAR. BUT A GIPSY'S CURSE...THAT WAS SOMETHING FROM CENTURIES LONG GONE BY AND FORGOTTEN.

AT LEAST THAT WAS THE REACTION OF PRIVATE BILL RILEY – JUST ANOTHER BRITISH SOLDIER, CLUMSIER THAN MOST, BUT WELL ARMED WITH THE FAMOUS LEE-ENFIELD RIFLE. HE JUST WASN'T THE TYPE TO BELIEVE IN WEIRD TALES – BUT HE'D SOON HAVE PLENTY TO THINK ABOUT AS THE FANTASTIC EVENTS BEGAN TO OCCUR...

THE CORNSHIRE REGIMENT CAME TO FRANCE IN EARLY 1940. WITH THEM CAME PRIVATE JEM "GIPSY" SMITH – A STRANGE, BROODING BLOKE WHO MADE NO EFFORT TO MAKE FRIENDS WITH THE OTHERS.

GIVES ME THE CREEPS, THAT SMITH! WHAT WITH HIS WAY WITH ANIMALS, AND HIS FUNNY EYES.

ME TOO! COULD SEE HIM PUTTING A CURSE ON SOMEONE. SPOOKY SORT OF COVE.

NOBODY KNEW IF SMITH WAS A REAL GIPSY, BUT THE NICK-NAME STUCK. THEY KNEW HE HAD WANDERED ALL OVER BRITAIN BEFORE THE WAR, AND THAT ALL ANIMALS TRUSTINGLY CAME TO HIM.

OF ALL HIS SECTION, SMITH HAD TIME FOR ONLY ONE MAN – PRIVATE BILL RILEY. THOUGH NOT EXACTLY BRIGHT, THE LITTLE PRIVATE HAD A HEART AS BIG AS HIS ARMY BOOTS.
WOTCHER, SMITHY. TALKING TO THE BIRDS AGAIN?
SOMETIMES THEY ANSWER, RILEY. THEY ARE NATURE'S CHILDREN, AS WE ALL ARE.

RILEY DIDN'T UNDERSTAND HALF THE THINGS HIS ODD FRIEND SAID, BUT THIS DIDN'T REALLY WORRY HIM. IT WAS ENOUGH TO HAVE THE MAN AS HIS MATE.
DON'T KNOW ABOUT THAT. ALL I KNOW IS I'M BORED. THOUGHT WE'D COME OVER HERE TO FIGHT JERRY... AIN'T EVEN SEEN ONE YET!
GIPSY QUIETLY SMILED. HE WASN'T SURPRISED THAT VERY NIGHT WHEN A MASSIVE GERMAN ASSAULT FLUNG BACK THE FRENCH FORCES WITH SHATTERING EASE.

BUT WHEN THEY CAME UP AGAINST THE CORNSHIRES, THE NAZIS WERE HALTED "DEAD" IN THEIR TRACKS.
THEY HAVE COURAGE, BUT WE HAVE COVER.
AN' THESE RIFLES, CHUM.
YES, THEY HAD THEIR RIFLES. THE BEST INFANTRY WEAPON IN THE WORLD – THE .303 LEE-ENFIELD.

IN THE MAIN THE REGIMENT FOUGHT HARD — BUT THERE WERE THOSE WHO DIDN'T. PRIVATES DAVE CADMAN, "OX" OXLEY AND "JACKO" JACKSON WERE THREE SKIVERS INTERESTED ONLY IN SAVING THEIR OWN SKINS.

KEEP LOW! I'M NOT STICKING MY HEAD OVER THAT WALL TO HAVE IT BLOWN OFF.

GOT TO HAND IT TO YOU, DAVE. YOU KNOW HOW TO FIX IT SO WE GET A SAFE SPOT.

LET THE MUGS HAVE THE GLORY!.

THE BULLYING CADMAN WAS THE NATURAL LEADER OF THE WEAK-WILLED PAIR.

YET ALL THE OTHERS FOUGHT BRAVELY. BUT STUBBORN AS THEY WERE IN DEFENCE, THANKS TO TOUGH, EXPERIENCED SERGEANTS LIKE COLIN COBB, THE CORNSHIRES WERE PUSHED OUT OF THEIR DEFENCES BY VASTLY SUPERIOR FORCES.
THAT'S IT, LADS, OUT WITH YOU. WE'RE FALLING BACK TO ANOTHER LINE OF DEFENCE.
CAN'T SAY I'M SORRY, SARGE. IT'S GETTIN' A BIT NOISY AROUND HERE.

WHEN THEY WITHDREW, COBB CONSULTED WITH HIS OFFICER, LIEUTENANT NEIL HARVEY.

WELL, WE'RE DUG IN WELL ENOUGH, BUT NOW THERE ARE REPORTS OF PARATROOPERS IN THIS WOOD. PROBABLY RUBBISH, BUT WE HAVE TO CHECK.

I'LL GET A DETAIL ON IT, SIR.

HARVEY WAS GREEN. YET, IF HE SURVIVED LONG ENOUGH, WOULD MAKE A GOOD OFFICER, AND THAT WAS THE OPINION OF COBB WHO WAS A GOOD JUDGE OF MEN.

GIPSY SMITH AND RILEY WERE AMONG THOSE CHOSEN BY THE CORPORAL WHO HAD BEEN ORDERED TO LEAD THE SMALL PATROL. THEY ENTERED THE WOOD, NOT REALLY EXPECTING TROUBLE, BUT READY SHOULD IT COME.

PARACHUTISTS! WONDER H.Q. DIDN'T REPORT GNOMES IN THE WOOD. JUST AS LIKELY!
DO NOT SCOFF, CORPORAL. THE WOODS HIDE FAR MORE THAN MOST PEOPLE EVER IMAGINE.

AT SMITH'S WORDS, RILEY GRINNED BROADLY. HE CERTAINLY HAD AN ODD CHUM. SOUNDED AS IF GIPSY WAS SAYING HE BELIEVED IN GNOMES...

OLD SMITHY IS CERTAINLY A CAUTION. BET HE SEES SPOOKS, TOO!

BUT THAT THOUGHT SOMEHOW CHILLED RILEY INTO GREATER ALERTNESS.

THE WOOD DID NOT HIDE PARATROOPERS BUT IT DID HOLD A TOUGH NAZI ADVANCE SQUAD.

KEEP ALERT! THIS FAR FORWARD WE SHOULD HAVE SURPRISE ON OUR SIDE, BUT THESE BRITISH ARE GOOD.

THE WOOD WAS QUIET. ONLY BEES DRONED, BIRDS MUTTERED SLEEPILY. BUT, WITH INSTINCTS SHARPER THAN MOST, GIPSY SMITH SUDDENLY SMELT DANGER.

WAIT – I FEEL SOMETHING, CORPORAL. THERE IS DANGER!
YOU WHAT, SMITH? I CAN'T SEE ANYTHING.

SMITH'S WARNING WAS TIMELY. HAD IT NOT COME, THE PARTY WOULD HAVE RUN SLAP INTO THE GERMANS, WHO OUTNUMBERED THEM.
COVER, QUICK! YOU WERE RIGHT, SMITH, BUT HOW YOU KNEW BEATS ME.
HE'S A QUEER ONE IS GIPSY.

SECONDS LATER A BROADSIDE OF BRITISH BULLETS OPENED THE BATTLE. A HOARSE BELLOW FROM THE NAZI CORPORAL SENT HIS MEN TO COVER.

COVER – SCHNELL!

AAGH!

IT WAS NO GREEN SECTION THE BRITISH PARTY HAD ENCOUNTERED, BUT VETERANS OF THE POLISH INVASION. SURPRISE HAD COST THEM TWO MEN, BUT THE SURVIVORS MELTED INTO THE UNDERGROWTH — DANGEROUS ADVERSARIES.

'ERE, WHERE THE 'ECK ARE THEY?

A WELL FLUNG STICK GRENADE SUPPLIED THE ANSWER — AND KILLED TWO OF THE BRITISH.

THE SAVAGE CRACK OF THE GERMAN GRENADE WAS FOLLOWED AT ONCE BY THE HEAVIER DETONATION OF A BRITISH GRENADE FLUNG BY GIPSY, WHICH ALSO CLAIMED VICTIMS.

AAGH!
NOW, WHERE ARE THE OTHER GERMANS?

THE FIGHT WAS SHORT BUT VICIOUS. GERMAN AND BRITISH WEAPONS MINGLED IN A SAVAGE SYMPHONY. THEN ABRUPTLY — SILENCE.
PHEW! I THINK I GOT ONE. HARD TO TELL IN THESE BUSHES. BETTER RELOAD QUICK. WHERE ARE THE REST OF THE LADS?

THERE WERE BUT THREE SURVIVORS OF THAT ENCOUNTER — GIPSY SMITH, PRIVATE RILEY . . . AND THE GERMAN CORPORAL.
A GERMAN STILL LIVES . . . OF THAT I'M SURE.

BUT AS SMITH HUNTED THE NAZI, HIS PREY HAD FOUND RILEY WHO WAS HAVING TROUBLE RELOADING, AND NEVER SAW THE DANGER.
BLASTED THING WON'T GO IN!
ACH, THIS IS TOO EASY. A GENTLE LOB . . .

BUT THE NAZI GRENADE GOT TANGLED IN SOME BRANCHES, ALTHOUGH IT SEEMED TO RILEY THE EARTH HAD EXPLODED AS THE MISSILE DETONATED.

AARGH — MY EARS!

THE NOISE AND THE BLAST KNOCKED THE WIND FROM HIM. HIS RIFLE WAS FLUNG TO ONE SIDE.

DAZED AND CONFUSED, RILEY STAGGERED AWAY, LEAVING HIS RIFLE WHERE IT LAY, BUT FORTUNATELY THE NAZI HAD RUN OUT OF AMMO.

HE'S GETTING CLEAR, THE SCHWEIN! I — I WHAT WAS THAT? SOMEONE TO MY LEFT...

IT WAS GIPSY SMITH, ALSO OUT OF AMMO BUT STILL WITH THE WILL TO FIGHT.

SO TWO MEN RESORTED TO COLD STEEL, HUNTING EACH OTHER LIKE ANIMALS.
ONE MAN, BY THE SOUND OF IT. ONE WHO MOVES QUIETLY, YET NOT QUIETLY ENOUGH.

THEN CAME THE CONFRONTATION BOTH KNEW WOULD MEAN DEATH FOR ONE –
LET'S SEE WHO MOVES THE FASTER.
YOU WILL DIE, SCHWEIN!

A FIERCE DUEL ENDED WITH THE NAZI KILLED, AND SMITH ALONE WAS STILL IN THAT WOOD, NEAR TO WHERE THE STUNNED RILEY HAD LET HIS RIFLE LIE.
THIS IS AN EVIL PLACE. I CAN SENSE EVEN MORE DEATH.
GIPSY SMITH LOOKED AROUND COLDLY, THE VISIONS BUILDING UP IN HIS BRAIN THAT OFTEN TOLD HIM OF THE FUTURE.

RILEY WAS MEANWHILE CLEAR OF THE WOOD AND FACING A ROCKET FROM SERGEANT COBB FOR HAVING LOST HIS RIFLE. THE LITTLE PRIVATE'S MUTTERED PROTEST THAT HE HAD BEEN LUCKY NOT TO LOSE HIS LIFE WAS SWEPT ASIDE.

LOSING YOUR RIFLE IS A CRIME, RILEY. WE NEED EVERY ONE, BUT YOURS WILL LIE THERE RUSTING!

BUT — BUT SARGE, I NEARLY GOT BLASTED!

THE APPEARANCE OF GIPSY CHEERED RILEY, AND COBB WAS NOT SHORT WITH GRUFF PRAISE.

GOOD LAD, SMITH. EVEN KEPT HOLD OF YOUR RIFLE — MORE THAN THIS APOLOGY HERE!

COBB STRODE OFF, UNAWARE OF JUST WHAT PART RILEY'S RIFLE WAS TO PLAY IN THE EVENTS AHEAD.

THAT NIGHT, IN THE VILLAGE THE CORNSHIRES HELD, GIPSY SMITH SUDDENLY STIFFENED AND STARED TOWARDS THE BLACK, GLOOMY WOOD IN THE BACKGROUND. CATCHING THE EXPRESSION GLEAMING IN THOSE DARK EYES, RILEY FELT FEAR CLUTCH HIM.

'ERE, WHAT IS IT, SMITHY?
THINGS THAT WILL BE... THAT MUST BE...

THE WORDS WERE EERIE AND GHOSTLY, ALMOST AS IF THEY HAD COME FROM THIN AIR.

STILL GRIPPED BY THE UNEASE SMITH'S WORDS HAD BROUGHT, RILEY MISSED THE STRANGE GLITTERING LOOK THE GIPSY SHOT ACROSS AT PRIVATES CADMAN, OXLEY AND JACKSON.

SO, THAT IS THE WAY OF IT. SO BE IT THEN.

FROM THE THREE HARD-CASES, SMITH'S EYES SLID TO THE PLATOON OFFICER. AS USUAL, LIEUTENANT HARVEY HAD A CHEERY WORD FOR ALL, AS WELL AS THE DOG AT HIS HEELS WHICH SERVED AS THE MEN'S MASCOT.

SO YOUNG. IT IS SAD – BUT INEVITABLE!

AND SILENTLY THIS STRANGE MAN TURNED OVER, AND SOON SLEPT SOUNDLY AND DEEPLY – ALTHOUGH HE HAD JUST FORESEEN HIS OWN DEATH AND THE BIZARRE EVENTS THAT WOULD UNFOLD FROM IT.

NEXT DAY, NEWS OF THE FURTHER ADVANCE BY THE GERMAN HORDES REACHED THE REGIMENT.

THAT'S IT THEN, SERGEANT. WE PROVIDE A REARGUARD WHILE THE MAIN BODY PULL BACK TO PREPARED POSITIONS. AND I'M STAYING HERE WITH THE FIRST SECTION, NO MORE ARGUMENT.

IF YOU SAY SO, SIR. THOUGH I STILL SAY I SHOULD TAKE THE FIRST GROUP.

THE INTENTION WAS TO PULL BACK ALL THE MEN IN A SERIES OF LEAP-FROG REARGUARDS.

AS HARVEY ASSEMBLED THE MEN WHO WERE TO FACE THE FIRST ATTACK WITH HIM, COBB EYED THREE MEN STONILY AND VOICED HIS OPINION.

WATCH CADMAN AND HIS TWO CRONIES, SIR. BAD TYPES – WOULDN'T TRUST 'EM.

GIVE THEM A CHANCE, SERGEANT. THEY'LL BE OK IF THE CHIPS ARE DOWN. WELL, SEE YOU AT MAIN BASE IN FOUR HOURS.

COBB'S WARNING WAS A WISE ONE. NONE OF THE THREE SKIVERS LIKED THE WAY THINGS WERE GOING AT ALL.
WE ACT AS HEROES, TO COVER THE REST AS THEY SCUTTLE OFF. WHAT DO THEY THINK WE ARE?
'S RIGHT! GOT US DOWN FOR MUGS, EH?

LIEUTENANT HARVEY DID NOT PULL ANY PUNCHES AS HE EXPLAINED THE CURRENT POSITION THEY FACED.
THINGS ARE NOT GOOD, CHAPS. WE ARE IN DANGER OF ENCIRCLEMENT. BUT IF WE MAINTAIN OUR TRADITION, WE SHOULD PULL OUT OF IT. RIGHT, TAKE UP YOUR POSITIONS IN THE WOOD.

GIPSY SMITH WAS THE FIRST MAN WHO MOVED TO OBEY, ALONE NOW THAT RILEY HAD BEEN EAR-MARKED BY SERGEANT COBB FOR EXTRA ATTENTION AND HAD ALREADY LEFT WITH THE OTHER SECTION.

IT WAS CADMAN WHO DECIDED TO TURN SULLEN RESENTMENT INTO POSITIVE ACTION.
LISTEN, ARE YOU TO GOING TO DIE HERE LIKE SHEEP, OR ARE YOU COMING WITH ME?
ER – WELL, I DUNNO! IT'S A SERIOUS THING, DOIN' A RUNNER.
THEY SHOOT BLOKES FOR IT! DESERTION IN THE FACE OF THE ENEMY.

CADMAN EYED HIS TWO CRONIES, THEN GAVE A SCORNFUL LAUGH. WHEN HE SPOKE AGAIN, IT WAS WITH A CONTEMPT THAT MADE THE WAVERING PAIR WINCE.
SCARED TO STAY, SCARED TO RUN. SURE, THEY SHOOT YOU FOR RUNNING — IF THEY CAN PROVE IT. WHAT'S JERRY GOING TO DO — HAND YOU BOTH A CIGAR?
HE'S RIGHT, OK. COUNT ME IN, CADMAN.
ALL RIGHT THEN, ME TOO. TO STAY WITH THIS LOT IS ASKING FOR IT!

MEANWHILE THE LIEUTENANT WENT ROUND HIS MEN, CHATTING CHEERFULLY TO THEM. SOON THEY WOULD BE FIGHTING FOR THEIR LIVES, YET THE YOUNG OFFICER HID HIS OWN TENSION AS HE ATTEMPTED TO EASE THEIRS.
SETTLING IN, SMITH? BE HAVING COMPANY SOON, I EXPECT.
AYE, I'M READY, SIR. SHOULD HIT THEM HARD, AS THEY WON'T EXPECT US TO BE WAITING HERE.

HARVEY RETAINED HIS CHEERFUL EXPRESSION AS HE LEFT SMITH. THEN, DESPITE CADMAN'S BANTER, HE CAUGHT SOMETHING IN THE SOLDIER'S EYES THAT MADE THE WORDS SOUND FALSE.
ALL OK, HERE, SIR. READY FOR OLD FRITZ TO SHOW HIS UGLY MUG!
GOOD SHOW, THEY WON'T KEEP US LONG. WE'LL GIVE THEM A BLOODY NOSE, THEN FALL BACK TO SERGEANT COBB'S LINE.
SOMETHING WRONG HERE! THESE THREE ARE UP TO SOMETHING.

BUT BIGGER TROUBLE WAS HEADING THEIR WAY –
PREPARE TO FIRE – FIRE!

A SIGHING MOAN – THEN THE FIRST SHELL EXPLODED, TO BE FOLLOWED BY ONE AFTER ANOTHER.
A NEAR ONE! YET IT IS NOT MY TIME YET...
AND CALMLY THE GIPSY AWAITED HIS FATE.

IT WAS NOW, WITH A CURTAIN OF SMOKE AND DUST BLOTTING OUT THE AREA, THAT CADMAN DECIDED TO MAKE HIS BREAK.
COME ON, THEN, NOW OR NEVER. THEY WON'T SEE US WITH ALL THIS GOING ON.
I'M WITH YOU, CADMAN. COME ON, JACKO.
ANYTHING'S BETTER THAN WAITING TO BE KILLED!

THE MORTAR STONK SLACKENED – THEN CEASED ALTOGETHER. IT WAS HARVEY WHO SPOTTED THE GAP NOW ON HIS POSITION'S FLANK.
THEY'VE RUN! COBB WAS RIGHT!

SATISFIED THAT THE DEFENDERS WERE SUITABLY SOFTENED BY THE BARRAGE, THE GERMANS STORMED FORWARD — INTO A HAIL OF BRITISH LEAD.
ACH, SO TOMMY DOES WANT TO FIGHT!
FORWARD FOR THE FATHERLAND!

BULLETS WHINED, WEAPONS HAMMERED AS MEN SCREAMED THEIR RAGE. SOME REMAINED CALM, SELECTING TARGETS COOLLY, LIKE LIEUTENANT HARVEY AND PRIVATE SMITH.
WELL DONE, SMITH. GOOD SHOOTING.
YOU DO WELL TOO, SIR, BUT THEY'RE SLIPPING THROUGH ON OUR FLANK.

BOTH HARVEY AND SMITH SAW THE ENEMY TRY TO SET UP A MACHINE GUN IN THE DESERTERS' POSITIONS.
SCHNELL, CARL. WE CAN CATCH THE SCHWEIN IN A CROSS-FIRE!

BOTH MEN LEAPT TO FORESTALL THE GERMANS.
GO BACK, SMITH! I CAN HANDLE THIS.
NOT ALONE, SIR. I'M COMING TOO.

THEY DEALT WITH THE NAZIS, THEN THE PAIR SWUNG THE MACHINE GUN AROUND AND OPENED UP ON THE ADVANCING ATTACKERS –
BET THE JERRY FACTORY WORKERS WOULD NEVER BELIEVE THIS WOULD HAPPEN TO THEIR GUN.
KEEP IT UP, SMITH. THEY DON'T LIKE THIS AT ALL.

BUT THE ODDS WERE TOO HEAVY. ONE BY ONE THE BRITISH RIFLES FELL SILENT AS SMITH AND HARVEY DID DEADLY WORK UNTIL THE AMMO WAS GONE.
THAT'S IT, SMITH. TIME TO GO, I THINK.
IT IS NOW! THOSE OF THE LADS WHO CAN'T HAVE GIVEN THE REGIMENT A NEW BATTLE HONOUR.

GIPSY SMITH WAS RIGHT. HE AND THE LIEUTENANT STOLE FROM THE SCENE WHERE ANOTHER LEGEND OF THE CORNSHIRES HAD BEEN BORN...
...AND THEY CARRIED WITH THEM THE THREE NAMES OF THE DESERTERS WHO HAD SOILED THE REGIMENT'S GOOD NAME. THEY WOULD SEE THEY WERE PUNISHED.

SO ON THEY WENT, SHAKING OFF HALF-HEARTED GERMAN PURSUIT.
I WONDER WHERE THE DOG GOT TO? HE BUZZED OFF QUICK WHEN THE SHOOTING STARTED. WENT EVEN QUICKER THAN CADMAN AND HIS PRECIOUS PAIR.
CAN'T BLAME THE DOG, SIR, BUT THOSE THREE HAVE NO EXCUSE.

CADMAN AND HIS CRONIES WERE AT THAT MOMENT NOT VERY FAR AHEAD — AND HOPELESSLY LOST.
OOOH, ME FEET! WE'VE BEEN GOIN' ROUND IN CIRCLES, IF YOU ASK ME.
STOP MOANING. WE'VE JUST TO KEEP OUR HEADS, THAT'S ALL.
WHAT DO WE DO, CADMAN? WE CAN'T KEEP FLOUNDERING ABOUT IN THIS BLASTED WOOD. IT'LL BE NIGHT SOON.

FURTHER BICKERING WAS CUT SHORT AS, WITH A RUSTLE OF BUSHES, HARVEY AND SMITH STEPPED INTO VIEW.

WELL, WELL. LOOK WHO WE HAVE HERE!

YOU! HOW DID YOU...

ANGRILY HARVEY STEPPED FORWARD, HIS WORDS SO HOT AND FIERCE THAT CADMAN ALONE COULD FACE HIM. YET EVEN HE WAS WHITE-FACED AND TREMBLING, BUT WHETHER FROM FEAR, SHAME, OR ANGER...
YOU THREE APOLOGIES FOR MEN MAKE ME SICK TO MY STOMACH!
IT – IT WAS HIS IDEA! WE JUST WENT ALONG.
SHUT UP, OXLEY! ALL RIGHT, SIR, JUST WHAT ARE YOU GOING TO DO ABOUT IT?

HARVEY SPOKE AGAIN, HIS TONE COLD AND BITTER. IT MADE THE THREE MORE UNEASY THAN HIS ANGER HAD DONE.
I'LL TELL YOU WHAT I'M GOING TO DO! FIVE MEN SURVIVED...BUT THREE WON'T DARE SHOW THEIR FACES WHEN I'VE TOLD MY STORY. SMITH HERE IS A WITNESS!

CADMAN FLINCHED. THEN HIS EYES GLEAMED AS HE THOUGHT SWIFTLY ABOUT WHAT HARVEY HAD SAID.
FIVE MEN SURVIVED? THAT MEANS JUST US HERE! AND THEM...

TURNING ON HIS HEEL, HARVEY MADE TO WALK AWAY, UNAWARE THAT CADMAN'S RIFLE HAD SWUNG UPWARDS. SMITH SAW IT THOUGH, BUT AN EXPRESSION OF CALM ACCEPTANCE SHOWED IN HIS FACE AS HE REALISED WHAT WAS ABOUT TO HAPPEN.
COME ON, SMITH, LET'S GO. THESE THREE CAN DO AS THEY WANT.
YES, WE CAN! WITH YOU PAIR OUT OF THE WAY!

LIEUTENANT HARVEY DIED BEFORE HE'D TAKEN TWO PACES FORWARD, WITH CADMAN'S BULLET IN HIS BACK.

AAGH!

YOU WON'T BE TELLING ANYONE ANYTHING, HARVEY. NOT NOW — OR EVER!

WITH A SNARL, CADMAN SWUNG TO FACE SMITH. THE GIPSY'S EYES WERE NOT MERELY UNAFRAID — BUT CALM AND MOCKING AS THEY BORED INTO HIS OWN.
RUN, BLAST YOU, SMITH! RUN!

FOR THE FIRST TIME SINCE STEPPING INTO THE CLEARING, SMITH SPOKE. HIS WORDS CHILLED THE THREE MEN TO THE SOUL.

SHOOT HIM, CADMAN!
I KNOW MY DEATH IS NEAR... BUT IT IS MURDER, AND WILL BE AVENGED. AS WILL THE LIEUTENANT'S MURDER.
WHAT'S THE MATTER? SHUT HIM UP FOR PETE'S SAKE!

OXLEY AND JACKSON, SNATCHING UP THEIR RIFLES, FIRED TOGETHER. THE TWO SHOTS MERGED INTO THE THIRD AS CADMAN AT LAST PULLED THE TRIGGER.

GOT HIM! THAT'S SHUT HIM UP FOR GOOD!
CURSE US, WILL HE? THAT'S SHOWN HIM!

SMITH STAGGERED BACK UNDER THE SHOCKING IMPACT – BUT INCREDIBLY DID NOT FALL. WHAT KEPT HIM UPRIGHT, WHERE DID HE FIND THE WILL TO SPEAK?
SOME THINGS CANNOT BE SILENCED. FROM THE GRAVE THEY CRY OUT FOR VENGEANCE. SO SHALL MY DEATH!
HE – HE WON'T DIE! CADMAN, WHAT'S HAPPENING?
I – I DON'T UNDERSTAND IT!

PANIC TOOK THE MEN – AND THEY FLED BLINDLY AWAY FROM THE FIGURE THAT STILL STOOD BEFORE THEM. THE HARSH, UNEARTHLY VOICE THAT HAD ISSUED FROM SMITH WAS UNNERVING.
I'M – I'M GETTING OUT OF HERE!
ME, TOO! HE – HE STARES RIGHT THROUGH ME.

THE THREE TERRIFIED MEN ALMOST RAN INTO THE ARMS OF A GERMAN PATROL IN THEIR HEADLONG FLIGHT. THERE WAS ONLY ONE THING TO DO — SEPARATE.
JERRIES — SCATTER! EVERY MAN FOR HIMSELF!
HIMMEL, WHAT'S GOING ON?

THE FIGURE OF SMITH SEEMED TO WATCH THE THREE MEN'S FLIGHT. THEN, AS IF GUIDED BY A STRANGE FORCE, IT LURCHED TO A SPOT TEN FEET AWAY.

THERE IT CRUMPLED, AND AN ARM MOVED TOWARDS A RIFLE DROPPED EARLIER BY SMITH'S ONLY FRIEND, PRIVATE BILL RILEY.

SO LIEUTENANT HARVEY WAS DEAD...AND SMITH PERISHED AS HE HAD FORESEEN THAT NIGHT BEFORE.

AND NOW A BRITISH RIFLE, JUST LIKE A THOUSAND OTHER LEE-ENFIELDS, WAS TO BE CAUGHT UP IN ONE OF THE ODDEST MYSTERIES OF THE WAR.

MEANWHILE OX OXLEY, NEVER CONSIDERED BRIGHT, WAS STILL RUNNING. HE WAS MORE INCLINED TO PANIC THAN HIS TWO COMPANIONS, AND HAD CERTAINLY TRAVELLED FASTER THAN THEM – BUT IN WHICH DIRECTION?

GOT TO REST... I'M DONE. CAN'T GO ON... LOST...

OXLEY HADN'T REALISED AT FIRST, BUT HIS HEADLONG FLIGHT HAD TAKEN HIM IN A CIRCLE. HE STAGGERED, SPENT, TO THE EXACT SPOT HE HAD STARTED FROM.
SHOULD BE WELL CLEAR NOW. MUST REST! THEN I'LL TRY AND GET BACK TO OUR LINES.

HAVING REGAINED HIS BREATH, OXLEY TOOK INTEREST IN HIS WHEREABOUTS, AND FOUND HIS EYES RESTING UPON THE BODY OF HARVEY.
EH? OH, NO – IT CAN'T BE! I MUST HAVE GONE IN A CIRCLE?

THERE WAS HARVEY, BUT WHERE WAS SMITH? THE GIPSY COULD NOT HAVE SURVIVED THREE BULLETS, SO OXLEY BEGAN A DESPERATE SEARCH.
I'VE GOT TO FIND HIM. I'VE GOT TO MAKE SURE HE'S DEAD!

AT LAST THE FRANTIC SEARCHER FOUND THE BODY OF GIPSY SMITH.

SO, HE IS DEAD. AND I CAN USE THAT RIFLE... UNLESS SMITH WANTS IT!

LAUGHING GRIMLY AT HIS OWN JOKE, OXLEY WALKED OVER AND PICKED UP RILEY'S RIFLE. HE WALKED AWAY WITHOUT A BACKWARD GLANCE.

A FEW HUNDRED YARDS FURTHER ON, OXLEY FELT THE FIRST STIRRINGS OF UNEASE.
IT – IT MUST BE IMAGINATION! BUT IT'S LIKE I'M BEING FOLLOWED...

THE FEELING GREW STRONGER – THEN SUDDENLY CAME THE DEFINITE SOUND OF A BODY PUSHING THROUGH THE UNDERGROWTH.
THERE IS SOMEONE! COME OUT, OR I'LL BLAST YOU!

THEN INTO THE OPEN CREPT LIEUTENANT HARVEY'S DOG. LOST AND BEWILDERED, IT HAD SOUGHT OUT THE COMPANY OF MAN.
PHEW, MY NERVES! FOR ONE MOMENT, I THOUGHT...

WITH A HOARSE SHOUT, OXLEY ATTEMPTED TO SHOO THE DOG AWAY – BUT IT SEEMED RELUCTANT TO GO.
HOP IT, MUTT! BEAT IT, DO Y'HEAR?

THE BIG MAN DECIDED HE MUST HAVE REST, AND SETTLED DOWN... AFTER COCKING THE RIFLE AND LEAVING IT WHERE HE COULD GRAB IT. HE WAS TOO TIRED TO CHASE THE DOG AWAY.
I'D SHOOT THE CUR, BUT I CAN'T RISK THE SHOT BEING HEARD BY THE JERRIES.

IT WAS AS WELL FOR OXLEY HE DID NOT SEE THE DOG SUDDENLY STIFFEN AND RISE TO HIS FEET. THEN, WITH A CURIOUS JERK OF ITS HEAD, GROWL WITH PLEASURE.

IT WAS ALMOST AS IF A FRIENDLY HAND WAS SCRATCHING THE ANIMAL BEHIND THE EARS.

SEEMING TO LOSE FEAR, THE DOG TROTTED TO WHERE OXLEY NOW LAY ASLEEP, SILENT SAVE FOR AN OCCASIONAL TWITCH AND MUTTERED WORD.
SHOOT! GO ON, SHOOT, CADMAN... THOSE EYES!
THE DOG WHINED QUIETLY, CREEPING CLOSER TO THE MAN.

THEN A WAGGING TAIL CAUGHT THE RIFLE, SENDING IT THUDDING TO THE GROUND. IT WAS COCKED, THE SAFETY CATCH WAS OFF – AND IT FIRED.

THE DOG FLED AND OXLEY MADE NO MOVE. ONE MURDERER OF GIPSY SMITH WAS STONE DEAD WITH A BULLET FROM RILEY'S RIFLE IN HIS BRAIN.

AND RILEY HIMSELF WAS PLEADING WITH SERGEANT COBB AT THAT VERY MOMENT IN THE POSITION NOW OCCUPIED BY THE CORNSHIRES. HE'D JUST LEARNED THAT COBB WAS TAKING TWO SOLDIERS TO TRY AND FIND OUT WHAT HAD HAPPENED TO HARVEY AND HIS MEN.

LET ME COME, TOO, SARGE. I WANT TO FIND OUT IF SMITH IS OK.
FORGET IT, RILEY. YOU STAY HERE OUT OF TROUBLE – AND THAT'S AN ORDER!

IT DIDN'T TAKE THE THREE MEN LONG TO FIND EVIDENCE OF THE UNIT'S LAST STAND.

THE LADS PUT UP ONE HECK OF A SCRAP.

MUST HAVE, TO SEND JERRY BACK ON HIS HEELS. BET THEY DIDN'T EXPECT SUCH A HARD FIGHT.

A SWIFT SEARCH BROUGHT PUZZLED FROWNS. HARVEY'S BODY WAS NOT THERE.
COULD HAVE BEEN TAKEN PRISONER, SARGE.
CAN'T FIND SMITH, EITHER – OR CADMAN, OXLEY AND JACKSON. YET THE MOB THAT HIT 'EM, ACCORDING TO INTELLIGENCE, AREN'T THE SORT TO TAKE PRISONERS. SOMETHING ODD HERE. DOESN'T FEEL RIGHT...

ABOUT TO TURN AWAY, THE FAMILIAR BARK OF A DOG BROUGHT THEM WHIRLING AROUND.
MISTER HARVEY'S DOG! IT'S ALMOST AS IF IT'S TRYING TO GET US TO FOLLOW IT.

THE THREE SET OFF AFTER THE DOG WHICH KEPT JUST AHEAD OF THEM, PAUSING NOW AND THEN TO MAKE CERTAIN THEY WERE FOLLOWING.

IT IS LEADING US TO SOMETHING. NOT UP THE GARDEN PATH, I HOPE.

THE DOG LED THEM DIRECTLY TO THE SPOT WHERE ITS DEAD MASTER LAY.
OH, NO – HARVEY! MUST HAVE BEEN HIT BAD, AND MADE IT THIS FAR BEFORE DROPPING.
TOUGH LUCK – HE WAS A GOOD TYPE.

THEN COBB'S EYES NARROWED. AFTER THE SHOCK HAD LEFT HIM, HIS SHARP EYES AND VAST EXPERIENCE TOOK IN THE POSITION OF THE WOUND – THEN THE WOUND ITSELF.
JUST A MINUTE... THAT WOUND! IT COULD HAVE BEEN ONE OF OUR RIFLES MADE THAT. AND IN THE BACK?

COBB'S MIND RACED. HARVEY SHOT IN THE BACK, AND THREE OF THE MEN MISSING WERE THE ONES HE HAD WARNED THE DEAD OFFICER ABOUT. DID IT ADD UP?

I MAY BE A SUSPICIOUS DEVIL, BUT IT COULD BE MURDER.

SOME BLOOD ON THE LEAVES THROUGH HERE!

THE SOLDIER'S CRY JERKED COBB FROM HIS GRIM MUSING. AS WELL AS THE BLOOD, THERE WERE SIGNS OF SOMEONE HAVING PASSED THROUGH THE FOLIAGE.

COULD HAVE BEEN THE LIEUTENANT OR ANOTHER OF THE LADS. HAVE A GOOD LOOK IN THERE. COULD BE ONE OF OUR WOUNDED.

THEY FOUND GIPSY SMITH'S BODY A LITTLE FURTHER ON. IT SEEMED TO CONFIRM THE SERGEANT'S WORST SUSPICIONS WHEN HE SAW SMITH HAD BEEN SHOT THREE TIMES.

FIRST HARVEY, NOW SMITH! BOTH WITH WOUNDS THAT LOOK LIKE MURDER!
ANYTHING UP, SARGE? YOU LOOK A BIT...
COBB ONLY SHOOK HIS HEAD. HE HAD NOTHING TO SAY YET.

THEY BURIED THE TWO MEN AS BEST THEY COULD, BUT COBB'S THOUGHTS WERE DARK AS THEY MADE THE JOURNEY BACK TO THEIR OWN LINES.

THESE THREE WILL HAVE SOME EX-PLAINING TO DO WHEN I FIND 'EM. I MAY BE WRONG, BUT ON THE OTHER HAND I WOULDN'T PUT ANYTHING PAST THEM.

A LITTLE FURTHER ON THEY CAME ACROSS THE DEAD OXLEY, SEEMINGLY ASLEEP AGAINST A TREE. COBB GAVE A GRUNT. THERE WERE CERTAIN QUESTIONS HE INTENDED TO ASK OXLEY.

IT'S OX OXLEY! ASLEEP, AS USUAL, BY THE LOOK OF IT.
WELL, WE'LL WAKE HIM UP!
AND I'LL GET A FEW ANSWERS FROM HIM AS TO JUST WHERE HIS PALS ARE.

BUT NOBODY COULD WAKE UP OXLEY NOW. HIS SLEEP WAS A DEEP AND LONG ONE.
COME ON, OXLEY! YOU, EH – THIS MAN'S DEAD!
LOOK, GOT IT IN THE HEAD.

COBB PICKED UP THE FALLEN RIFLE, AND ALMOST CAME UP WITH AN ACCURATE RECONSTRUCTION OF WHAT HAD HAPPENED.

MUST HAVE DROPPED OFF WITH THE RIFLE PROPPED UP, SAFETY CATCH OFF. IT SLIPPED AND BLAM – EXIT OXLEY. WHAT A STUPID WAY TO GO.

DIDN'T LIKE THE BLOKE, BUT IT'S ROTTEN LUCK ALL THE SAME!

THEN COBB, PURELY BY CHANCE, GLANCED AT THE DOG — AND GASPED, AS DID THE OTHER TWO.

BLIMEY, THAT DOG LOOKS AS IF . . .
. . . AS IF HE WERE HAVING HIS EARS SCRATCHED! STRUCK ME TOO.

IT COULD HAVE BEEN IMAGINATION, BUT THE WOOD SEEMED SUDDENLY COLDER . . .

. . . AND THE GLOOM AROUND THEM SEEMED THAT LITTLE BIT DARKER.

NEVER NOTICED JUST WHAT A CREEPY HOLE THIS WOOD IS. MUST BE A REACTION TO FINDING THE LADS AND HARVEY.

BACK AT THEIR LINES, SOME OF COBB'S UNEASE FADED, YET ENOUGH LINGERED TO CAUSE HIM TO BROOD.

I DON'T KNOW WHAT WENT ON IN THAT WOOD — DON'T SUPPOSE I'LL EVER KNOW. BUT THERE IS SOMETHING WRONG ABOUT IT ALL!

ONE GOOD THING HAD COME OUT OF IT. THE SERGEANT WAS ABLE TO GIVE RILEY BACK HIS RIFLE, THANKS TO THE SERIAL NUMBER ON IT.

HERE! AND IF YOU LOSE IT AGAIN...
THANKS, SARGE. I WON'T, BELIEVE ME!

THEN COBB'S GRIM FACE RELAXED. HE HAD, DESPITE ALL OUTER SHOW, A SOFT SPOT FOR THE CHEERFUL, CLUMSY PRIVATE.

I KNOW YOU MISS SMITH, RILEY. JUST WATCH OUT FOR YOURSELF, EH?
EH? ER – YES, SARGE! AND I'LL KEEP GOOD CARE OF MY RIFLE FROM NOW ON, DON'T YOU WORRY.

SO THE RIFLE WAS GIVEN THE MOST THOROUGH CLEANING IT HAD EVER HAD... AND IT STILL HAD A VITAL ROLE TO PLAY.

THEN CAME ORDERS TO PULL BACK, TO BE RELIEVED BY ANOTHER UNIT. ALSO, PRIVATE JACKO JACKSON APPEARED, HAVING MANAGED TO REACH SAFETY AFTER FLEEING FROM THE MURDER SCENE.

HELLO, SARGE. BOY, AM I GLAD TO BE BACK?

WELL, WELL! I THINK YOU MIGHT HAVE QUITE A TALE TO TELL, JACKSON!

JACKSON GRINNED, SECURE IN THE KNOWLEDGE THAT LIEUTENANT HARVEY AND GIPSY SMITH WERE DEAD.

HE SEEMED EAGER TO TELL HIS STORY.
WE GOT CUT OFF FROM THE MAIN GROUP, SARGE. WHEN WE RAN OUT OF AMMO, ALL WE COULD DO WAS PULL OUT.
SO THAT'S HOW IT HAPPENED, JACKSON — JUST LIKE THAT?

COBB'S EYES PROBED THE OTHER'S RELENTLESSLY, AND SOME OF JACKSON'S COMPOSURE BEGAN TO EBB.

HE — HE CAN'T BREAK DOWN MY STORY. I'M SAFE!

COBB WAS ABOUT TO PUSH FURTHER, SENSING THE UNEASE, WHEN THE REPLACEMENT OFFICER STRODE UP, THWARTING THE SERGEANT.

AH, SERGEANT COBB, I'M ANDERSON. TAKING THE PLACE OF POOR OLD HARVEY. DON'T SUPPOSE I'LL DO AS WELL, BUT WE'LL RUB ALONG, I DARE SAY.

THANK GOODNESS! COBB SMELLS A RAT, BUT I'LL KEEP OUT OF HIS WAY AS MUCH AS POSSIBLE. HE CAN'T PROVE A THING.

ER – YES, SIR! I – ER – DARE SAY.

ANDERSON CHATTED ON AS JACKSON SAUNTERED AWAY.
QUITE A SHOW THE LADS PUT UP IN THE WOOD, SERGEANT. PITY OLD HARVEY WENT WEST. DECENT FELLOW!
HE WAS, SIR. THE BEST OFFICER I'VE EVER SERVED UNDER.
AND I WON'T REST TILL I FIND OUT EXACTLY WHAT DID HAPPEN!

IT WAS JUST AFTER THE MEN HAD SETTLED IN THEIR BILLETS THAT JACKSON HEARD OF OXLEY'S DEATH. HE HAD BEEN TOO WORRIED ABOUT HIS OWN SAFETY TO GIVE HIS TWO MATES A SECOND THOUGHT.

YOU'RE LUCKY, JACKO. SEEMS ONLY YOU AND CADMAN SURVIVED THAT LOT IN THE WOOD. FANCY OLD OX SHOOTIN' HIMSELF.

OXLEY SHOOTING HIMSELF – WHAT THE HECK ARE YOU ON ABOUT?

JACKSON'S REACTION WAS STARTLING TO THE CASUALLY MENTIONED NEWS OF OXLEY'S DEATH. HE GRABBED AT THE SOLDIER –
OXLEY DEAD? IT'S LIES... I CAN'T BELIEVE IT!
'ERE, YOU GONE POTTY? OLD OXLEY'S RIFLE FELL AN' SHOT HIM. IT WASN'T MY FAULT!
CONTROLLING HIMSELF, JACKSON MUTTERED AN APOLOGY AND STOLE AWAY.

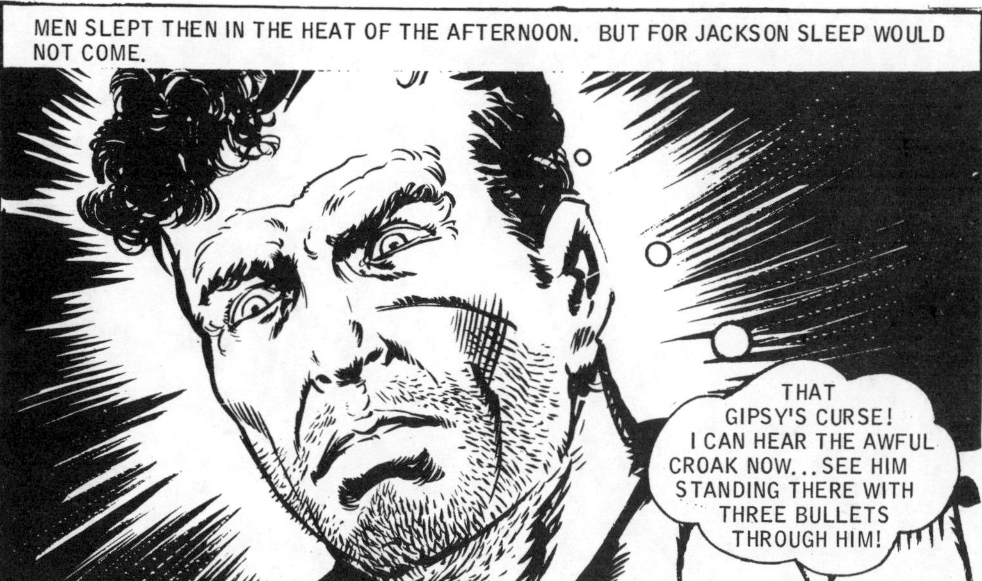
MEN SLEPT THEN IN THE HEAT OF THE AFTERNOON. BUT FOR JACKSON SLEEP WOULD NOT COME.
THAT GIPSY'S CURSE! I CAN HEAR THE AWFUL CROAK NOW... SEE HIM STANDING THERE WITH THREE BULLETS THROUGH HIM!
IT WAS A VERY ANXIOUS MAN WHO LAY THERE, JUMPING AT EVERY LITTLE UNEXPECTED NOISE.

AS THE WAR BLAZED FIERCELY AROUND THEM AGAIN, COBB DECIDED IT WAS TIME HE ENLISTED THE AID OF SOMEBODY ELSE. RILEY WAS THE NATURAL CHOICE.
LISTEN GOOD NOW, RILEY. BECAUSE YOU WERE SMITH'S MATE I WANT TO HEAR WHAT YOU THINK OF THIS...
RIGHT, SARGE.
RILEY LISTENED PATIENTLY AS COBB EXPLAINED HIS MISGIVINGS. THE YOUNG PRIVATE WILLINGLY AGREED TO HELP KEEP AN EYE ON JACKSON.

THIS TIME THE REGIMENT WAS LUCKY. THEIR JOB WAS TO GUARD A BRIDGE OVER THE RIVER BETWEEN THE WOOD AND THE VILLAGE, AND SERGEANT COBB PICKED JACKSON AS ONE OF THIS DETAIL.

JUST KEEP YOUR EYES OPEN, JACKSON. JERRY MIGHT BE CLOSER THAN WE THINK.

JUST PICKING ON ME, I BET! WELL, HE WON'T BREAK ME!

SO JACKSON BEGAN HIS LONELY VIGIL, AND UNPLEASANT THOUGHTS CAME TO MIND. THE FACE OF GIPSY SMITH SEEMED TO HAUNT HIS BRAIN.

HIS NERVES BEGAN TO STRETCH WITH THE MINUTES. THE SOUND OF WAR FADED AND THE COLD DARK WATER BELOW THE BRIDGE SEEMED TO GROW LOUDER, WHISPERING TO HIM ALONE. HE GLANCED DOWN –

AHH, WHAT'S THAT?

THERE, SHIMMERING IN THE WATER, WAS THE GHOSTLY, EERIE FACE OF GIPSY SMITH.

IT WAS AT THAT MOMENT THAT TWO FIGURES AND A DOG CREPT STEALTHILY ON TO THE BRIDGE, AND JACKSON DIDN'T SEE ANY OF THEM.
SOME SENTRY! WELL, I'LL LEARN HIM!
HE SEEMS INTERESTED IN THE FISH. GOOD JOB WE AIN'T A PAIR OF JERRIES.

AS THEY APPROACHED, HIS MUTTERING ROSE IN PITCH UNTIL THEY COULD HEAR EVERY WORD.
YOU'RE DEAD, SMITH — DEAD! YOU AND HARVEY!
THE MAN'S GONE MAD!

COBB GRASPED JACKSON'S SHOULDER AND THE MAN GAVE A DEMONIC SHRIEK.
AHHH, NO!
WHAT THE HECK?

WORDS POURED FROM JACKSON THEN, A TORRENT OF FEAR, HATE AND GUILT THAT MADE IT PLAIN JUST WHAT HAD HAPPENED IN THE WOOD.
SO YOU KNOW, EH? WE SHOT SMITH AND HARVEY... OXLEY, CADMAN AND ME. BUT SMITH WON'T DIE... HE'S BEHIND YOU, RILEY!
HE'S OFF HIS NUT!
COME ON, GIVE ME THAT RIFLE.

STILL YELLING, JACKSON BEGAN TO EDGE AWAY. AROUSED FROM SLEEP, THE OTHER SOLDIERS BECAME SILENT WITNESSES TO WHAT FOLLOWED.

GET AWAY, COBB! GIPSY SMITH SENT YOU, DIDN'T HE?

GIVE ME THAT RIFLE, LAD. I'M COMING TO GET IT!

THEN JACKSON, WITH A SPEED THAT WAS UNEXPECTED, RAISED HIS RIFLE AND FIRED. COBB FELT A HAMMER-BLOW STRIKE HIS SHOULDER.

THAT'S IT — THAT'S HOW I GOT RID OF SMITH!

SARGE, HE'S HIT YOU!

WITH A SNARL, JACKSON SWUNG TO FACE RILEY, BUT ALREADY THE YOUNG PRIVATE'S FINGER WAS TIGHTENING ON THE TRIGGER.
YE GODS!
AAGH!
A BULLET KILLED JACKSON IN MID-STRIDE — A BULLET FROM THE SAME RIFLE THAT HAD CUT DOWN OXLEY.

THE DOG CAME OVER TO NUZZLE RILEY AS HE LOOKED AT THE RIFLE IN HIS HANDS, FACE INCREDULOUS. IT HAD JUST SAVED HIS LIFE, BUT HE COULD HARDLY BELIEVE IT.

NEVER KNEW YOU COULD MOVE SO QUICK, RILEY.

IT WAS AS IF THE RIFLE HAD A LIFE OF ITS OWN, SARGE. JUST SEEMED TO LEAP UP AN' FIRE.

ENOUGH WITNESSES WERE ON THE BRIDGE TO TELL WHAT HAD HAPPENED THAT NIGHT AND TO CLEAR RILEY OF ANY BLAME. YET HE WAS STILL BEMUSED.
DON'T LOOK SO PUZZLED, RILEY. THERE'S NOTHING LIKE DANGER TO MAKE A MAN MOVE FAST.
MAYBE. BUT I'M SURE I FELT IT MOVE IN MY HANDS, SARGE. TALK ABOUT CREEPY!
A GRIM LOOK PASSED BETWEEN THE TWO MEN. THEY KNEW WHAT WAS GOING ON WAS MORE THAN THEY COULD FATHOM.

RILEY WAS THERE AS COBB WAS SEEN TO BEFORE BEING SENT BACK TO ENGLAND.

SO LONG, CHUM. BE BACK WITH YOU IN NO TIME.

SO LONG, SARGE. SEE YOU IN BLIGHTY – I HOPE.

THE SERGEANT'S WAR IN FRANCE WAS OVER, BUT THE REGIMENT STILL HAD A LOT OF FIGHTING TO DO.

BLIMEY, AIN'T YOU GOT NO NERVES, RILEY?
NOT WHILE I'VE GOT MY RIFLE, MATE. AIN'T GOING TO LOSE IT AGAIN.

YET RILEY NOW FELT A CALM CONFIDENCE, AND HIS RIFLE SAW PLENTY ACTION AS THE FULL WEIGHT OF THE GERMAN ONSLAUGHT HIT THEM AGAIN. HE SEEMED A NEW MAN, DIFFERENT FROM THE CLUMSY LITTLE FELLOW OF BEFORE.

AFTER ONE PARTICULAR ACT OF BRAVERY, LIEUTENANT ANDERSON, NOW A RESPECTED PART OF THE TEAM, APPROACHED THE CHEERY LITTLE PRIVATE WITH STARTLING NEWS.
WELL, RILEY, YOU'RE UP FOR A GONG. KEEP ON LIKE THIS AND YOU'LL BE A ONE-MAN ARMY.
HECK, A MEDAL? WAIT TILL OLD COBB GETS TO KNOW. HE'LL BUST!
AND HE BENT TO PAT HARVEY'S DOG WHICH NOW FOLLOWED HIM EVERYWHERE.

IN AN ENGLISH HOSPITAL AND IMPATIENT TO BE BACK IN THE ACTION, SERGEANT COBB DID HEAR OF RILEY'S MEDAL – AND WAS DELIGHTED.
WELL, GOOD OLD RILEY! PROPER LITTLE TERRIER HE TURNED OUT TO BE!
BUT HIS GRIN FADED AS HE READ THAT OF CADMAN THERE WAS STILL NO SIGN. JUST WHAT COULD HAVE HAPPENED TO THE LAST OF THE THREE KILLERS?

ACTUALLY, WHEN THE THREE MURDERERS HAD SEPARATED, CADMAN HAD PLUNGED AWAY FROM HIS TWO COMPANIONS, AS PANIC-STRICKEN AS THEM.
MUST GET CLEAR. MUST GET AWAY FROM THAT SPOT!

THEN HE HAD TAKEN A GRIP OF HIMSELF AND, AS EVER, THOUGHT OUT WHAT COURSE OF ACTION WOULD BE BEST FOR HIM.
PRISONERS, NOT OUR LOT. THE WAR'S OVER FOR THEM. NO MORE DODGING BULLETS.

SO HE GOT THE IDEA THAT HE THOUGHT WOULD ENSURE HE WOULDN'T HAVE TO RISK HIS NECK AGAIN.
WHY NOT SURRENDER? BETTER BE BEHIND WIRE THAN DEAD.

HE SIMPLY STEPPED INTO THE ROAD WITH HIS HANDS IN THE AIR.
KAMERAD . . . KAMERAD!
HIMMEL!

THE GERMANS' OBVIOUS SCORN WAS NOT PLEASANT, BUT CADMAN DIDN'T LET THIS THROW HIM.
ACH, THERE ARE SUCH IN EVERY ARMY. GO WITH YOUR COMRADES — IF THEY CAN STOMACH YOU!
ALL RIGHT, SNEER IF YOU WANT, BUT I'M SAFE NOW.

THE OTHER BRITISH DID NOT WELCOME HIM WITH OPEN ARMS. THEY THEMSELVES HAD FOUGHT HARD TO THE LAST BULLET.
HEROES, EH? GONG-HUNTING, DEATH-OR-GLORY BOYS!
SHUT UP! IT'S BAD ENOUGH WEARING THE SAME UNIFORM AS YOU, WITHOUT HEARING YOU SHOOT YOUR MOUTH OFF.

THEN A HURRICANE ON THE PROWL SPOILT THE MURDERER'S PLANS AS IT DIVED TO SHOOT UP THE EASILY-SEEN GERMAN GUARDS.
MAYBE SOME OF OUR LADS WILL BE ABLE TO MAKE A BREAK FOR IT.

IN PITCHED THE PRISONERS TO SEIZE THE GUARDS' GUNS, BUT CADMAN MADE NO MOVE.
NO, DON'T – THEY'LL SHOOT US ALL!
NOT TILL WE'VE GOT SOME OF THEM, CHUM!

CADMAN NEVER STAYED TO SEE HOW THE PRISONERS FARED. HE STAGGERED AWAY. FINALLY, ABOUT EXHAUSTED, HE FELL IN WITH A GROUP OF BATTLE-WEARY BRITISHERS HEADING FOR THE DUNKIRK BEACHES.

COME ON, LADS, JOIN THE MERRY THRONG.

I'D BETTER STICK WITH THIS MOB. I'VE JUST ABOUT HAD IT.

SO THE KILLER FINALLY REACHED THE EVACUATION AREA.

AND, AT THE SAME TIME, SO DID RILEY AND LIEUTENANT ANDERSON, WHOSE PATH TO THE BEACH HAD BEEN A FAR MORE HONOURABLE ONE.

I WOULDN'T HAVE MADE IT IF YOU HADN'T HELPED ME, RILEY. YOU JUST WOULDN'T LEAVE ME, THE DOG – OR THAT PRECIOUS RIFLE OF YOURS!

CAN'T LOSE THAT, SIR. SERGEANT COBB WOULDN'T BE PLEASED!

IT WAS A FISHING BOAT THAT PICKED UP RILEY, HIS OFFICER AND THE DOG, MANNED BY MEN WHO RESPECTED COURAGE.

WATCH ME RIFLE, CHUM! BE COMING BACK HERE WITH IT ONE DAY.

ALL RIGHT, MATE! HURRY UP BEFORE WE GET COMPANY FROM JERRY UPSTAIRS!

THE FISHING BOAT SPOTTED A LONE FIGURE STRUGGLING IN THE WATER JUST OFF-SHORE AND MADE FOR IT. DAVE CADMAN GRINNED – HIS DECISION TO SWIM OUT TOWARDS THE BOATS HAD PAID OFF.
HANG ON, MATE, WE'LL HAVE YOU OUT OF THERE.
AND NOT TOO SOON, EITHER!

THE VOICE BETRAYED CADMAN'S PRESENCE TO RILEY WHO WENT FORWARD TO INVESTIGATE –

IT'S CADMAN! WAIT TILL SERGEANT COBB GETS HOLD OF HIM...

RILEY!

BUT ABRUPTLY SHOCK TURNED TO UTTER HORROR AS CADMAN SAW THE GHOSTLY FACE OF GIPSY SMITH MATERIALISE FROM THIN AIR.

NO, NO – GO AWAY, BLAST YOU!

'ERE, WHAT'S HE ON ABOUT?

RILEY WASN'T QUITE AS PUZZLED AS THE OTHERS, BUT THEN THE DOG LEAPT UP, BARKING FURIOUSLY...
CALM DOWN, BOY... STEADY ON!
... DISLODGING RILEY'S RIFLE WHERE HE'D LEFT IT ON THE WHEELHOUSE ROOF.

CADMAN SAW THE RIFLE COMING, SAW THE GHOSTLY, SMILING FACE... AND FELL BACK GIBBERING INTO THE WATER.

AAGH!

THE HEAVY RIFLE BUTT HIT HIM FULL IN THE FACE – AND WITH FAR MORE FORCE THAN JUST A FALLING OBJECT.

THEN THERE WAS JUST THE EMPTY SURFACE OF THE COLD GREY SEA. CADMAN HAD VANISHED, THE THIRD AND LAST VICTIM OF THE GIPSY CURSE.
BLIMEY, WHAT WAS ALL THAT ABOUT?
MY RIFLE IS GONE... BUT IT'S DONE ITS WORK NOW!
AND, JUST FOR AN INSTANT, RILEY COULD HAVE SWORN HE SAW THE GHOSTLY, SMILING FACE HIMSELF.

THEY MADE IT SAFELY BACK TO ENGLAND AND RILEY GOT A BRAND NEW RIFLE. HE WAS A SERGEANT WHEN HE RETURNED TO FRANCE WITH THE INVADING ALLIES, THE DOG AT HIS HEELS AND VICTORY IN SIGHT.
KEEP AT IT, RILEY – BUT DON'T LOSE THAT RIFLE!
PIECE O' CAKE – NO PROBLEMS!
IT WAS COMPANY-SERGEANT MAJOR COBB'S STANDARD JOKE NOW, BUT HE AND RILEY OFTEN TALKED OVER THE BIZARRE EVENTS CENTRED ROUND THAT FIRST RIFLE. AND HOW NOTHING ELSE STRANGE HAD OCCURRED AFTER CADMAN HAD PERISHED...
Commando
THE END

Only two weeks to wait before you can get the next four great Commando books. Look out for:—

"SMITH VERSUS SCHMIDT" **"FRONT-LINE FEUD"**

"WEST TO FREEDOM" **"DEADLY CHOICE . . ."**

SUPERMARINE SPITFIRE MKXII

Aircraft of the Second World War — No. 1

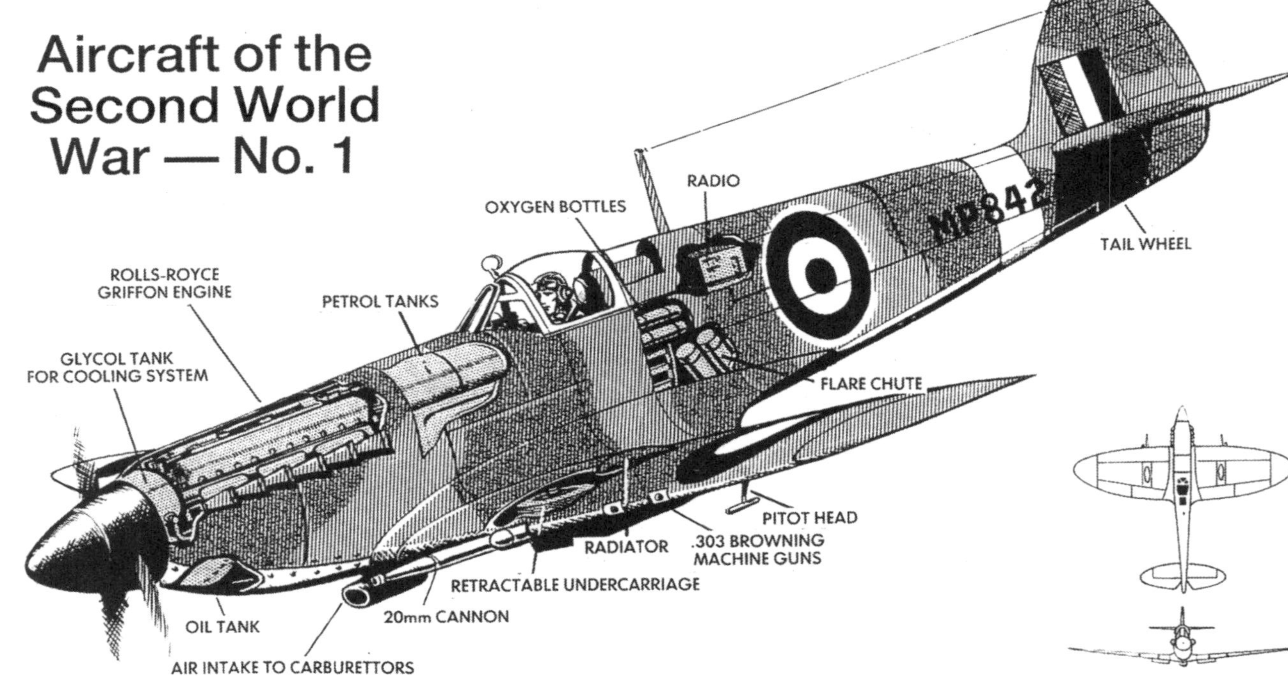
RADIO
OXYGEN BOTTLES
MP842
TAIL WHEEL
ROLLS-ROYCE GRIFFON ENGINE
PETROL TANKS
GLYCOL TANK FOR COOLING SYSTEM
FLARE CHUTE
PITOT HEAD
RADIATOR
.303 BROWNING MACHINE GUNS
RETRACTABLE UNDERCARRIAGE
20mm CANNON
OIL TANK
AIR INTAKE TO CARBURETTORS

RECKONED by many people to be the most beautiful aircraft ever to take to the air, the famous Supermarine Spitfire will always be remembered as the perfect fighting machine. This plane, along with the Hurricane, was the one that saved this country from invasion by winning the Battle Of Britain.

Designed before the war and first test-flown in 1936, the Spit was steadily improved and up-dated as the years went by. At the beginning of its service it had a Rolls Royce Merlin engine, eight machine guns and a top speed of 357 mph (574 km/h), while the latest models had Griffon engines, four 20 mm cannon plus bombs, and could zip along at 450 mph (725 km/h). A folding-wing version was built for the Fleet Air Arm too, and called the Seafire, while a very fast clipped-wing type was used to catch the German V-1 flying bombs over southern England in 1944.

During World War Two huge numbers of aircraft were built, compared to present-day air forces. The total production of Spitfires was 20,334 and there were 2954 Seafires!

ACES WILD
THERE HAD BEEN SOMETHING MYSTERIOUS ABOUT THE DEATH OF SPITFIRE PILOT MIKE SHAW. NOW HIS YOUNG BROTHER CLIVE WAS JOINING THE SAME SQUADRON, DETERMINED TO FIND OUT THE TRUTH. BUT THERE WERE A FEW SHOCKS IN STORE FOR CLIVE...

ABOVE THE SOUTH COAST OF ENGLAND IN 1940, A FEW SPITFIRES AND HURRICANES FLUNG THEMSELVES AGAINST THE MIGHT OF THE LUFTWAFFE. CLIVE, FRESH FROM TRAINING AND WITH THE RANK OF PILOT OFFICER, WAS CERTAINLY KEEN TO SEE SOME ACTION.

I'LL BE FLYING WITH THEM SOON. AND MAYBE I'LL FIND SOME ANSWERS TO A FEW QUESTIONS TOO.
JF650
JF655

FOR CLIVE IT WAS AN UNCANNY FEELING TO BE ON THIS AIRFIELD.
MIKE WAS PART OF ALL THIS BEFORE HE DIED.

CLIVE HAD HERO-WORSHIPPED MIKE. IT WAS HARD TO BELIEVE THAT MIKE HAD BEEN SHOT DOWN BY A LONE Me109 OVER FRANCE, BUT HIS PLANE HAD BEEN SEEN TO CRASH BY THE PILOT OF THE ACCOMPANYING SPITFIRE AND THE NAZIS HAD RECOVERED A BODY FROM THE WRECK.

ONCE IN HIS ROOM, CLIVE UNPACKED HIS LUGGAGE IN WHICH THERE WAS A BUNDLE OF LETTERS FROM MIKE — LETTERS THAT MADE CLIVE THINK THERE MIGHT BE MORE TO MIKE'S DEATH THAN MET THE EYE.
MIKE COULD DO ALMOST ANYTHING WITH A PLANE. HE'D HAD BATTLE EXPERIENCE IN THE SPANISH CIVIL WAR. HOW COULD HE HAVE BEEN SHOT DOWN BY A LONE MESSERSCHMITT WHEN THERE WAS ANOTHER SPITFIRE WITH HIM ON THAT PATROL?

MIKE HAD MORE THAN HINTED THAT SQUADRON LEADER PETER WILLIAMS WAS JEALOUS OF HIM AND WOULD LIKE TO SEE HIM POSTED.
THE OTHER MEN ADMIRED HIM AND KNEW HE'D MAKE A MARVELLOUS C.O. I CAN QUITE BELIEVE THE SQUADRON LEADER WAS JEALOUS OF MIKE.

BUT CLIVE WAS FAIR-MINDED. HE'D NEVER CONDEMN ANYONE ON A FEW LETTERS ALONE.
I'LL KEEP THESE LETTERS HIDDEN UNTIL I'VE GOT SOME-THING TO GO ON. AND I'LL SPEAK TO THE PILOT WHO FLEW WITH MIKE ON THAT LAST PATROL.

CLIVE SOON HAD A CHANCE TO MEET THE REST OF THE SQUADRON AND HE DISCOVERED THAT MIKE HAD NOT EXAGGERATED HIS POPULARITY.

ANOTHER DRINK, CLIVE?

YOUR BROTHER WAS A GRAND FELLOW AND A NATURAL PILOT.

CLIVE WAS OVERWHELMED BY THE PILOTS' PRAISE OF MIKE. EVERYONE SAID HOW MUCH THEY LIKED HIM, AND HOW WELL HE FLEW — EVERYONE EXCEPT SQUADRON LEADER PETER WILLIAMS.

WILLIAMS CERTAINLY ISN'T FRIENDLY. HE CHANGED THE SUBJECT PRETTY QUICKLY WHEN I STARTED TO TALK ABOUT MIKE. I WONDER WHY? GUILTY CONSCIENCE?

RESERVED AND QUIET, PETER WILLIAMS KEPT ON THE EDGE OF THE NOISY GROUP. HE DID NOT KNOW THAT HIS ACTIONS CAUSED CLIVE'S SUSPICIONS TO GROW.

LATER PILOT OFFICER NICKY THOMPSON TOOK CLIVE ROUND THE AIRFIELD. AND CLIVE WAS ABLE TO ASK HIS FIRST QUESTION.

I CAN'T SEE JF-SIX-FIVE-TWO ANYWHERE. WHO FLIES IT ANYWAY?
JF657

IMMEDIATELY CLIVE SENSED NICKY WAS UNEASY AT THE MENTION OF THE AIRCRAFT THAT FLEW WITH MIKE ON HIS LAST MISSION.

AND NICKY TRIED TO BRUSH THE QUESTION ASIDE.

DID YOUR BROTHER MENTION THAT PARTICULAR PLANE?
NO. THE OFFICIAL REPORT OF HIS DEATH MENTIONED IT. I'D LIKE TO TALK TO THE PILOT.

FOR SOME REASON CLIVE SENSED THAT NICKY WAS RELIEVED AT HIS ANSWER.

THAT'S NOT POSSIBLE. JF-SIX-FIVE-TWO WAS RALPH CLARK'S PLANE. HE WAS SHOT DOWN TWO WEEKS AGO.
OH, I'M SORRY.

CLIVE KNEW THAT NICKY MUST BE SPEAKING THE TRUTH FOR HE COULD EASILY CHECK. BUT HE ALSO FELT CERTAIN NICKY WAS KEEPING SOMETHING FROM HIM. THAT NIGHT –
THERE'S SOMETHING ODD ABOUT THAT SPITFIRE THAT FLEW WITH MIKE. IF I COULD FIND OUT WHAT, I'D BE CLOSER TO FINDING OUT MORE ABOUT MIKE'S DEATH. BUT WHERE DO I START?
IT SEEMED AN IMPOSSIBLE PROBLEM. BUT CLIVE DIDN'T GIVE UP EASILY. HE FELT SURE THE FUTURE WOULD PROVIDE HIM SOME CLUES.

IN THE FOLLOWING DAYS HE FLEW ON SEVERAL UNEVENTFUL PATROLS. AND THEN, ONE AFTERNOON –
JERRIES AT TEN O'CLOCK. BREAK FORMATION!
JF 660
GOOD GRIEF, I DIDN'T EVEN NOTICE THEM.

SUDDENLY THE SKY BECAME A BATTLEFIELD.
JF656
MIKE SCORED A KILL DURING HIS FIRST DOG-FIGHT. HE WROTE ME A LONG LETTER ABOUT IT.

CLIVE THREW HIS SPITFIRE INTO A WILD DIVE.
I CAN NEVER BE AS GOOD AS MIKE WAS BUT AT LEAST I'LL SHOW THE SQUADRON I'M GAME TO TRY.

INTENT ON HIS CHOSEN VICTIM, CLIVE HURTLED DOWN. HE DID NOT EVEN NOTICE THE SPITFIRE THAT HAD BANKED WILDLY TO AVOID HIM.
GOOD GRIEF, THAT'S CLIVE! HE'LL HAVE TO LEARN TO LOOK WHERE HE'S GOING.

CLIVE CONTINUED HIS RECKLESS DIVE.
HE'S A SITTING DUCK. HE HASN'T EVEN SEEN ME. I'LL GET THIS ONE — FOR MIKE.

BUT IF THE MESSERSCHMITT BELOW CLIVE HADN'T SEEN HIM, ONE ABOVE HIM HAD.
THAT STUPID ENGLANDER IS ASKING FOR TROUBLE, AND I SHALL OBLIGE.

CONCENTRATING ON HIS OWN QUARRY, CLIVE DIDN'T SEE THE TAILING Me109.
IT'S TOO EASY! I CAN'T MISS!

BUT HE HAD UNDER-
ESTIMATED HIS OPPONENT.
THE NAZI LOOPED ROUND
TO ATTACK FROM ABOVE.
GOOD GRIEF!
THE GERMAN WAS AN EXPERIENCED PILOT, AND HIS REACTIONS WERE RAZOR SHARP. HE HAD DELIBERATELY LET CLIVE THINK HE HAD AN EASY KILL.

AND A MOMENT LATER CLIVE'S PLANE SHUDDERED AS ENEMY BULLETS RAKED ITS WING.
HOW DID HE
GET BEHIND ME?
CLIVE WAS LEARNING THE ART OF DOG-FIGHTING THE HARD WAY.

HIS FIRST OPPONENT TOOK ALL CLIVE'S ATTENTION, BUT HIGH ABOVE HIM PETER WILLIAMS NOTICED THE SECOND MESSERSCHMITT CLOSE IN.
I'M NOT SURE CLIVE CAN MANAGE ONE JERRY YET, LET ALONE TWO. AND I DON'T THINK HE'S EVEN SEEN THAT OTHER ONE.

PETER DECIDED TO TAKE AN INTEREST IN THIS BATTLE.
PERHAPS I CAN EVEN OUT THE ODDS.

BUT THE LUFTWAFFE PILOT SAW HIS ATTACKER AND SHEERED ASIDE.
HIMMEL!

THE GERMAN SOON REALISED THAT HE HAD MET HIS MATCH. HE WENT INTO A VERTICAL CLIMB, BUT PETER WASN'T EASILY SHAKEN OFF.
I'M NOT GOING TO LOSE YOU NOW!

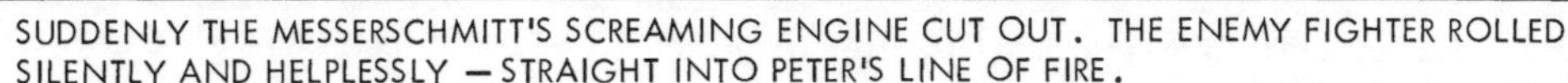
SUDDENLY THE MESSERSCHMITT'S SCREAMING ENGINE CUT OUT. THE ENEMY FIGHTER ROLLED SILENTLY AND HELPLESSLY — STRAIGHT INTO PETER'S LINE OF FIRE.

BULL'S-EYE!

THE STRICKEN MESSERSCHMITT PLUMMETED DOWN, GUSHING BLACK SMOKE.
YOU SHOULD HAVE PULLED OUT OF THAT CLIMB SOONER, JERRY.

BUT AS PETER LOOKED DOWN HE REALISED THAT THE BURNING MESSERSCHMITT WAS STILL CAPABLE OF CAUSING TROUBLE.

THAT JERRY'S HEADING STRAIGHT FOR CLIVE! IF HE DOESN'T WATCH OUT THERE'LL BE A COLLISION!

CLIVE WAS STILL BATTLING DESPERATELY. HE DID NOT NOTICE THE NEW DANGER UNTIL PETER'S VOICE SOUNDED URGENTLY.

SHAW, LOOK OUT ABOVE YOU!

HE DODGED AWAY JUST IN TIME.

THAT WAS TOO CLOSE FOR COMFORT!

BUT THE MESSERSCHMITT WAS SPIRALLING WILDLY, AND CLIVE'S OPPONENT WAS NOT SO LUCKY AS THE BLAZING WRECK CLIPPED HIS WING.

TEUFEL!

BLINDED BY THE SMOKE THE LUFTWAFFE PILOT BANKED WILDLY, AND GAVE CLIVE JUST THE OPENING HE WANTED.

GOT HIM – I'VE GOT HIM! IF MIKE COULD ONLY SEE ME NOW.
THE Me109 BURST INTO FLAMES ALMOST IMMEDIATELY.

AS HE WATCHED HIS FIRST KILL FLAMING DOWN, CLIVE SUDDENLY REALISED THAT THERE WERE NO MORE GERMAN PLANES NEAR HIM. THEN PETER'S VOICE SOUNDED IN HIS EARS.

JERRY SEEMS TO HAVE HAD ENOUGH. THEY'RE GOING HOME, SO I SUPPOSE WE'D BETTER DO THE SAME.

CLIVE REJOINED THE SQUADRON AND THEY FLEW BACK TOWARDS THE ENGLISH COAST.

I DIDN'T EVEN NOTICE THOSE JERRIES PULLING OUT... OR THAT BURNING MESSERSCHMITT UNTIL IT NEARLY HIT ME! YOU CERTAINLY NEED EYES IN THE BACK OF YOUR HEAD IN A DOG-FIGHT!
JF660

THE SQUADRON HAD SUFFERED NO CASUALTIES. IT HAD BEEN A SUCCESSFUL PATROL.

CLIVE WAS NATURALLY PROUD OF HIS FIRST KILL, BUT HE SOON FOUND THAT PETER DID NOT SHARE HIS ENTHUSIASM.

SHAW, I WANT TO TALK TO YOU. WHAT DO YOU MEAN BY THROWING YOUR PLANE ALL OVER THE PLACE LIKE AN IRRESPONSIBLE STUNT-PILOT?
BUT, SIR, I GOT A GERMAN. DIDN'T YOU SEE ME?

IT WAS QUITE THE WRONG THING TO SAY.
I SAW YOU NEARLY RAM A SPITFIRE! AND DIDN'T YOU SEE THAT BURNING MESSERSCHMITT BEFORE I WARNED YOU? A GOOD FIGHTER PILOT HAS TO WATCH THE WHOLE SKY, NOT JUST HIS OWN OPPONENT!

CHARACTERISTICALLY PETER DID NOT ADD THAT HE HAD SHOT DOWN THE MESSERSCHMITT HIMSELF AND PROBABLY SAVED CLIVE'S LIFE.

CLIVE WAS BEWILDERED. HE TURNED TO HIS FRIEND, NICKY, AS PETER WALKED AWAY.

WHAT'S THE MATTER WITH HIM? I SHOT DOWN A GERMAN. I THOUGHT HE'D BE PLEASED.
I'M AFRAID IT WAS YOUR FLYING, OLD BOY. NO OFFENCE, BUT I SAW YOU. YOU NEARLY COLLIDED WITH ONE OF OUR CHAPS. YOU REALLY MUST WATCH OUT IN FUTURE.

PETER'S ALWAYS ANXIOUS ABOUT PILOTS ENDANGERING THEIR LIVES BY WILD FLYING. HE EVEN HAD ONE CHAP TRANSFERRED BECAUSE HE LACKED DISCIPLINE. IT'S COMMON SENSE REALLY. THERE'S ENOUGH DANGER UP THERE AS IT IS.

CLIVE REALISED HE HAD MADE MISTAKES, BUT HE FELT THAT HIS KILL WAS AT LEAST WORTH A WORD OF PRAISE FROM HIS C.O. THE OTHER PILOTS CONGRATULATED HIM, BUT PETER NEVER MENTIONED THE INCIDENT AGAIN.

THE FOLLOWING MORNING CLIVE WAS STILL THINKING ABOUT PETER'S REACTIONS WHEN HE SUDDENLY REMEMBERED SOMETHING HIS C.O. HAD SUGGESTED TO HIM...

GOOD HEAVENS, I ALMOST FORGOT. I SAID I'D GIVE PETER SOME PERSONAL LETTERS TO FORWARD TO MY FAMILY IF ANYTHING HAPPENS TO ME. I'D BETTER TAKE THEM TO HIM NOW.

JF662

CLIVE HAD ALREADY WRITTEN THE LETTERS. HE COLLECTED THEM FROM HIS ROOM AND WENT TO PETER'S OFFICE.

NO ONE ANSWERED HIS KNOCK, SO HE PUSHED OPEN THE DOOR AND WENT IN.

I WONDER WHERE PETER IS? THERE'S A DRAWER WITH 'S' ON IT. I'LL PUT THEM IN THERE AND TELL PETER LATER ON.
Q
R
S
T
U
V

HE LOOKED THROUGH THE FILES, HOPING TO FIND ONE WITH HIS NAME ON IT. HE WASN'T PRYING. HE MERELY WANTED TO LEAVE HIS LETTERS IN A SAFE PLACE.

THEN HE FOUND A LOOSE SHEET OF PAPER WITH HIS NAME ON IT AND HIS CURIOSITY PROVED TOO STRONG TO RESIST.

IT'S A COPY OF A REQUEST FROM PETER WILLIAMS TO FIGHTER COMMAND, ASKING THEM NOT TO SEND ME TO THIS SQUADRON.

CLIVE DID NOT NOTICE THE DOOR OPEN UNTIL PETER SPOKE.

JUST WHAT THE BLAZES DO YOU THINK YOU'RE DOING, SHAW?

CLIVE QUICKLY EXPLAINED ABOUT HIS LETTERS, BUT HE STILL KEPT HOLD OF THE DUPLICATE REQUEST SHEET.

SO YOU SEE, SIR, I WAS LOOKING FOR A PLACE TO PUT MY LETTERS AND I COULDN'T HELP SEEING THIS. JUST WHY DIDN'T YOU WANT ME TO BE POSTED HERE?
I HAD NOTHING AGAINST YOU PERSONALLY, BUT I FELT THAT AN EXPERIENCED PILOT WOULD BE MORE USE TO US THAN A MAN FRESH FROM TRAINING.

BUT THAT ANSWER WASN'T GOOD ENOUGH FOR CLIVE. HE FORGOT HE WAS TALKING TO A SUPERIOR OFFICER AS MEMORIES OF MIKE'S LETTERS CAME FLOODING BACK.

DON'T YOU MEAN IT WAS BECAUSE I'M MIKE'S BROTHER? THIS WAS HIS FIRST SQUADRON TOO BUT HE SOON SHOWED HIS WORTH.

BUT BEFORE PETER COULD ANSWER THEY HEARD THE ALARM BELL AND A SHOUT OF "SCRAMBLE" FROM OUTSIDE. THE NEXT MOMENT BOTH WERE RACING FOR THEIR PLANES.

WITHIN MINUTES THE SQUADRON WAS AIRBORNE. CLIVE GLANCED ACROSS AT PETER'S PLANE.

THINGS ARE FITTING INTO PLACE NOW. HE DOESN'T WANT ME HERE AND HE'S GOING TO USE THE EXCUSE OF MY BAD FLYING TO GET ME TRANSFERRED. WELL, WE'LL SEE ABOUT THAT. FROM NOW ON I'LL FLY BY THE BOOK.

CLIVE STUCK TO THIS DECISION. HE LEARNED A GREAT DEAL IN THE DOG-FIGHTS THAT FOLLOWED. THEN ONE DAY HE CLAIMED HIS SECOND KILL.
I'VE GOT YOU THIS TIME, FRITZ!

BACK AT THE SQUADRON AIRFIELD HE HAD HIS VICTORY PAINTED UP.
THAT LOOKS VERY NICE.
BUT I'LL NEVER BE AS GOOD AS MIKE. IT'S TAKEN ME MONTHS TO GET MY SECOND JERRY. HE WROTE AND TOLD ME HE'D SHOT DOWN THREE IN HALF THIS TIME.

AS USUAL THE OTHER MEN QUICKLY AGREED WITH CLIVE.
HE WAS GOOD, OLD MIKE WAS. ONE OF THE BEST.
THE BEST. I'LL BUY YOU A DRINK ON IT, CLIVE.
OK, BE WITH YOU IN FIVE MINUTES.

CLIVE STARED AFTER THE MEN.
I BET THE MEN WANTED MIKE AS C.O. HE WAS AN ACE! BUT I'M NOT EVEN IN THE RUNNING...PROBABLY NEVER WILL BE. SO WHY DOESN'T PETER WANT ME HERE? WHAT'S HE AFRAID OF?
BUT ALTHOUGH CLIVE COULD NOT FORESEE IT, HIS VERY DECISION TO FLY BY THE BOOK WAS GOING TO LEAD TO SOME STARTLING DISCOVERIES.

IN THE FOLLOWING DAYS THE LUFTWAFFE REDOUBLED ITS EFFORTS, DETERMINED TO CRUSH THE R.A.F. ONCE AND FOR ALL. AND DAY BY DAY THE R.A.F. FIGHTER SQUADRONS FLUNG THEMSELVES INTO THE UNEQUAL BATTLE.
ENEMY AHEAD! BREAK FORMATION!
JF656
JF659

THE SQUADRON HAD ALREADY FLOWN ON A LONG ROUTINE PATROL. NEVERTHELESS THEY MET THE CHALLENGE OF THE MESSERSCHMITTS.
THEY OUTNUMBER US BY AT LEAST THREE TO ONE.

WITH SOME CLEVER MANOEUVERING, CLIVE GOT ON AN Me109's TAIL.
WITH A BIT OF LUCK I'LL MAKE THIS JERRY MY THIRD KILL.

THE MESSERSCHMITT STUNTED WILDLY, BUT CLIVE SOON REALISED HE WAS A MATCH FOR HIS OPPONENT.
ONLY A MATTER OF TIME NOW.

SUDDENLY CLIVE HEARD PETER'S VOICE IN HIS EARPHONES...
PULL OUT AND REFORM. WE'RE GOING HOME.
OH NO! THIS JERRY'S AS GOOD AS MINE.
BUT CLIVE WAS FLYING BY THE BOOK. OBEDIENTLY HE BANKED AWAY TO REJOIN THE SQUADRON. THE AMAZED MESSERSCHMITT PILOT CLIMBED THANKFULLY TOWARDS THE SUN.

ONE BY ONE THE SPITFIRES TRIED TO REFORM, BUT AS CLIVE GAINED HEIGHT HE HAPPENED TO GLANCE DOWN.

THAT FELLOW NEEDS HELP, AND I'M THE ONLY ONE NEAR ENOUGH TO GIVE IT.
JF 660

BUT PETER HAD GIVEN ORDERS TO PULL OUT. CLIVE HESITATED, STILL LOOKING DOWN. AND IN A DOG-FIGHT A MOMENT'S LOSS OF CONCENTRATION COULD PROVE FATAL.

IT NEARLY PROVED FATAL FOR CLIVE AS A PROWLING NAZI POUNCED.

YE GODS!

INSTINCTIVELY HE FLUNG HIS PLANE INTO A TIGHT TURN. ANOTHER LINE OF BULLETS RAKED HIS WING.
MY RADIO'S GONE DEAD. THE JERRY BULLETS MUST HAVE WRECKED IT.

THE WIND WHISTLED THROUGH THE SHATTERED COCKPIT CANOPY AS THE MESSERSCHMITT CLUNG TO CLIVE'S TAIL.
THIS FELLOW'S AN ACE. IT'S A MIRACLE HE DIDN'T SHOOT ME DOWN TO START WITH!

BUT THE LUFTWAFFE PILOT OBVIOUSLY HAD EVERY INTENTION OF MAKING GOOD HIS MISTAKE.
IT'S NO USE, HE'S TOO GOOD FOR ME. SOME OF MIKE'S SKILL WOULD COME IN HANDY NOW.

SUDDENLY A SHADOW PASSED OVER CLIVE'S SPITFIRE. GLANCING UP CLIVE RECOGNISED THE REGISTRATION NUMBER.

NICKY!

NICKY WAS A NATURAL PILOT WITH PLENTY OF BATTLE EXPERIENCE. HE WAS MORE THAN A MATCH FOR THE GERMAN.

KNOWING THAT NICKY HAD THINGS UNDER CONTROL, CLIVE LOOKED DOWNWARDS. THE SPITFIRE BELOW HIM WAS IN EVEN MORE TROUBLE NOW.
I'M OUT OF CONTACT WITH THE SQUADRON NOW, SO I'LL ACT ON MY OWN INITIATIVE. I CAN'T FLY AWAY WITHOUT TRYING TO HELP THAT PLANE.
JF 660

BUT AS SOON AS HE LEVELLED OUT HE RECEIVED A NASTY SHOCK.
MY CONTROLS AREN'T RESPONDING PROPERLY. THERE'S SOMETHING WRONG!
JF660

TOO LATE HE REALISED THAT HIS SPITFIRE HAD SUFFERED MORE THAN JUST A DAMAGED RADIO. THE MESSERSCHMITT, SENSING AN EASY VICTIM, WAS ON HIS TAIL SECONDS AFTER THE OTHER SPITFIRE DITCHED.

I'VE REALLY GOT MYSELF IN A MESS THIS TIME!

CLIVE WAS NO LONGER FLYING IN PARTNERSHIP WITH HIS PLANE. IT WAS A BATTLE TO KEEP THE SPITFIRE AIRBORNE AT ALL.

IT'S JUST LIKE FLYING IN SLOW MOTION! BUT I'LL JUST HAVE TO KEEP DODGING AND FIRING AND HOPE FOR THE BEST.

CLIVE KNEW THAT HOPING FOR THE BEST WAS NOT THE WAY TO WIN DOG-FIGHTS BUT HE KEPT ON FIGHTING AGAINST THE ODDS.

ANOTHER BURST LIKE THAT AND I'LL BE JOINING THAT SPITFIRE IN THE SEA.

BUT HE KNEW THAT WITH THE PERSISTENT NAZI ON HIS TAIL, HIS OWN LANDING MIGHT NOT BE SO SUCCESSFUL.

BUT CLIVE HAD FORGOTTEN NICKY. NICKY'S OWN DUEL HAD COME TO A SUDDEN, LETHAL END AND HE WAS ABLE TO TURN HIS ATTENTION TO HIS FRIEND AGAIN.

CLIVE'S PLANE LOOKS A BIT KNOCKED ABOUT.
NICKY'S SPITFIRE SCREAMED INTO A DIVE.

HIS SUDDEN ARRIVAL STARTLED THE LUFTWAFFE PILOT.

HIMMEL!

CLIVE HEAVED A SIGH OF RELIEF AS HE WRESTLED WITH HIS SLUGGISH PLANE WHILE NICKY CHASED THE NAZI.

GOOD OLD NICKY. I DON'T THINK THAT JERRY'S TOO HAPPY NOW!

CLIVE WAS RIGHT. THE GERMAN SOON DECIDED HE'D HAD ENOUGH AND CLIMBED SWIFTLY AWAY.

CLIVE GUESSED NICKY WOULD RADIO THE POSITION OF THE DITCHED SPITFIRE TO THE AIR-SEA RESCUE PATROL. BUT THEN HE SAW NICKY MAKING DESPERATE HAND SIGNALS TO HIM.

WHAT'S HE TRYING TO TELL ME? THERE AREN'T ANY MORE JERRIES AROUND. I WONDER WHAT'S BOTHERING HIM?

CLIVE CONCENTRATED ON KEEPING HIS DAMAGED SPITFIRE FLYING LEVEL. BUT AS THE ENGLISH COAST CAME NEARER, HIS ENGINE BEGAN TO COUGH AND PROTEST. IT WAS THEN HE REALISED WHAT NICKY HAD BEEN TRYING TO TELL HIM.

GOOD GRIEF! I'M NEARLY OUT OF FUEL.

NOW HE REALISED THAT PETER HAD KNOWN THE SQUADRON'S FUEL POSITION. THAT'S WHY HE HAD ORDERED THEM TO PULL OUT.

I SHOULD HAVE CHECKED MY FUEL GAUGE BEFORE, BUT THE DOG-FIGHT MADE ME FORGET EVERY-THING ELSE. I MAY HAVE TWO KILLS MARKED UP, BUT I'M STILL A BEGINNER.

THE TWO SPITFIRES FLEW LOW OVER THE SEA, THEIR ENGINES GRINDING ANGRILY.
NICKY'S FUEL TANK MUST BE AS EMPTY AS MINE. IF WE CAN ONLY MAKE LAND, WE MIGHT BE ABLE TO GET OUR KITES DOWN IN ONE PIECE.
CLIVE KNEW HOW VALUABLE EACH FIGHTER PLANE WAS TO THE UNDERMANNED BRITISH SQUADRONS.

ON THEIR LAST DROP OF FUEL THEY MANAGED TO REACH THE CLIFFS.
NICKY'S GOING TO MAKE IT. HOPE I CAN.

BUT NICKY'S SPITFIRE WAS IN GOOD ORDER AND RESPONDING WELL. CLIVE'S WAS NOW BEHAVING MORE ERRATICALLY THAN EVER.

NICKY'S OK. NOW DOWN WITH MY UNDERCART.

CLIVE SAW THE GROUND RUSHING UP TO MEET HIM. HE WRONGLY THOUGHT HIS UNDERCARRIAGE WAS DOWN AND HE TRIED TO LEVEL OUT.

EASY DOES IT – EASY!

HE MIGHT HAVE MADE IT IF HIS UNDERCARRIAGE HAD NOT JAMMED. HIS FIGHTER PLOUGHED INTO THE GROUND.
AAAAH!

MIRACULOUSLY UNHURT, CLIVE PUSHED BACK THE COCKPIT CANOPY AND STRUGGLED OUT. HE HAD HARDLY GONE A FEW STEPS BEFORE THE SPITFIRE EXPLODED.

GREAT SCOTT!

HE SOON CONTACTED NICKY WHO WAS ALSO UNHURT. THEY FOUND A TELEPHONE AND BEFORE LONG A LORRY ARRIVED TO PICK THEM UP AND RETURN THEM BACK TO THE AIRFIELD.

BACK AT THE BASE THEY FOUND THAT PETER WILLIAMS KNEW EXACTLY WHAT HAD HAPPENED IN THE AIR. AND HE WASN'T TOO PLEASED ABOUT IT.
IF YOU'D BEEN WATCHING YOUR REAR-VIEW MIRROR YOU'D HAVE SEEN THE MESSERSCHMITT THAT BOUNCED YOU. YOU'RE LUCKY TO BE ALIVE. SQUADRON FLYING ISN'T THE SAME AS JOY-RIDING, YOU KNOW!
I ONLY LOOKED DOWN FOR A SECOND, SIR. I SAW ANOTHER SPITFIRE IN TROUBLE...

IT WAS OBVIOUS THAT SPITFIRE WAS FINISHED. THERE'S A TIME FOR HEROICS, AND A TIME FOR COMMON SENSE. BEING OUT OF RADIO CONTACT'S NO EXCUSE.

BECAUSE YOU DIDN'T STOP TO THINK, YOU'VE WRITTEN OFF A VALUABLE SPITFIRE. IT'S ONLY SHEER LUCK THAT PILOT OFFICER THOMPSON DIDN'T DO THE SAME. I HOPE YOU'RE SATISFIED!

CLIVE WAS TEMPORARILY GROUNDED UNTIL A NEW PLANE COULD BE FOUND FOR HIM.
PETER'S RIGHT TO BE ANGRY THIS TIME. I BET THE OTHERS ALL WISH MIKE WAS HERE INSTEAD OF ME. HE'D NEVER HAVE GOT INTO A MESS LIKE THIS!
SCRAMBLE — SCRAMBLE!

ONE THING SURPRISED CLIVE — PETER DID NOT TRY TO USE THE INCIDENT TO GET HIM TRANSFERRED. BUT CLIVE STILL SUSPECTED PETER'S MOTIVES.
MAYBE PETER THINKS IT'S TOO OBVIOUS...GETTING ME TRANSFERRED FOR SOMETHING THAT COULD BE BAD LUCK. PERHAPS HE'S HOPING THAT WHEN I GET MY NEW SPITFIRE I'LL MAKE A REALLY STUPID MISTAKE. THEN HE'LL GET HIS CHANCE!

THE FOLLOWING WEEK CLIVE WAS DRIVEN TO A NEARBY AIRFIELD WHERE BATTLE-SCARRED FIGHTERS WERE REFITTED.
SO THIS IS MY NEW SPITFIRE. IT LOOKS A BIT SHAKY TO ME!
IT'S GOT A NICE ENGINE. WE'RE RATHER PROUD OF THE WAY WE MAKE NEW PLANES OUT OF OLD. EVEN YOUR SQUADRON LEADER FLEW ONE OF OUR RECONDITIONED SPITS FOR A WHILE.
THIS WAS NEWS TO CLIVE.
YOU'RE JUST SAYING THAT TO CHEER ME UP.
I'M NOT—LOOK IT UP IN OUR RECORDS IF YOU DON'T BELIEVE ME. YOU'VE GOT THE TIME WHILE THE MECHANICS GET YOUR PLANE OUTSIDE.

OUT OF CASUAL INTEREST CLIVE DID LOOK UP THE RECORDS. AND HE COULD HARDLY BELIEVE WHAT HE SAW.

JF – SIX-FIVE-TWO! THE SPITFIRE THAT WAS WITH MIKE WHEN HE WAS KILLED. PETER WILLIAMS MUST HAVE BEEN FLYING IT!

CLIVE QUESTIONED THE TECHNICAL OFFICER AND LEARNED THAT PETER HAD BEEN GIVEN A NEW SPITFIRE AFTER THE DATE OF MIKE'S DEATH. JF-652 HAD ONLY BEEN GIVEN THEN TO ANOTHER PILOT, A MAN WHO HAD ALSO LATER BEEN SHOT DOWN.

CLIVE FLEW BACK TO HIS BASE, HIS MIND A TURMOIL.

HOW DO I REALLY KNOW MIKE WAS SHOT DOWN BY A NAZI? THE OFFICIAL REPORT IS BASED ON PETER'S STORY, AND PETER WAS JEALOUS OF MIKE! HE'D HAVE BEEN GLAD TO GET RID OF HIM.

CLIVE REALISED THAT THE REST OF THE SQUADRON MUST HAVE KNOWN THAT PETER WAS WITH MIKE WHEN HE DIED.

THE OTHERS MUST HAVE KEPT QUIET OUT OF LOYALTY. BUT NOT ME! I DON'T OWE ANY LOYALTY TO THE MAN WHO KILLED MY BROTHER.

CLIVE FOUND PETER IN HIS OFFICE AND, WITH BARELY SUPPRESSED ANGER, TOLD HIM HE HAD DISCOVERED.
YOU'RE RIGHT. I WAS WITH YOUR BROTHER WHEN HE WAS SHOT DOWN. I HAD A SPECIAL REASON FOR NOT TELLING YOU. IF YOU'RE WISE YOU'LL DROP THE SUBJECT. IT WON'T DO ANY GOOD TO RAKE IT UP AGAIN.
IT WON'T DO YOU ANY GOOD, YOU MEAN. YOUR VERSION OF WHAT HAPPENED WAS LIES FROM START TO FINISH!

CLIVE CONTINUED ANGRILY.
MIKE WAS AN ACE! EVERYONE IN THE SQUADRON AGREES. HOW COULD ONE GERMAN OUTWIT BOTH OF YOU? I DON'T BELIEVE YOU MET A JERRY AT ALL.

CLIVE WAS NOT GOING TO LET THE MATTER DROP. SO THERE WAS ONLY ONE THING FOR THE SQUADRON LEADER TO DO...
THE TRUTH WAS WE WERE RETURNING FROM A RECCE PATROL WITH VALUABLE FILM AND WERE JUMPED BY A GERMAN. MIKE DIDN'T OBEY MY ORDER TO BREAK FOR HOME.
YOU MUST HAVE HAD THE FILM AND MIKE WAS PROTECTING YOU. HE WASN'T A COWARD!

PETER AT LAST REVEALED THE AWFUL TRUTH.
ENGLISH CHANNEL
YOU...
HE CERTAINLY WASN'T A COWARD, BUT HE WAS A USELESS PILOT. I DON'T KNOW WHAT HE TOLD YOU, BUT HE NEVER MADE A SINGLE KILL WHILE HE WAS WITH US. HE HATED TAKING ORDERS.

CLIVE STARED IN SHOCKED AMAZEMENT AS PETER CONTINUED.
MIKE WAS THE MOST UNPOPULAR MAN IN THE SQUADRON. HE WAS SELF-CENTRED AND BOASTFUL. WE WERE AFRAID YOU'D BE THE SAME.
BUT THE OTHER PILOTS HAVE ALWAYS PRAISED HIM!

OUT OF KINDNESS TO YOU. THEY REALISED HOW MUCH YOU HERO-WORSHIPPED MIKE. IT'S TRUE, CLIVE.

BUT WHY DID YOU NOT WANT ME HERE, THEN?
I DIDN'T WANT SOMEONE WHO MAY HAVE TURNED OUT LIKE YOUR BROTHER.

BUT CLIVE REFUSED TO BELIEVE PETER, EVEN WHEN THE OTHER MEN RATHER RELUCTANTLY BACKED PETER UP.
WE DIDN'T REALLY WANT TO LIE TO YOU, OLD BOY. WE JUST THOUGHT IT WAS THE KINDEST THING. WE HOPED YOU'D NEVER FIND OUT THE TRUTH.
I KNOW THE TRUTH. HE WAS AN ACE PILOT – THE BEST!

CONVINCED THAT THE SQUADRON WERE SIDING WITH PETER, CLIVE BECAME MORE AND MORE WITHDRAWN. HE ONLY SEEMED TO LIVE TO FIGHT.
ANOTHER KILL FOR CLIVE. HE'S PUSHING HIMSELF TOO HARD. IF HE DOESN'T RELAX, HE'LL CRACK UP.

PETER HAD ALSO NOTICED CLIVE'S BEHAVIOUR. HE SPOKE ABOUT IT TO NICKY.
CLIVE DOESN'T RECORD HIS KILLS ANY MORE BUT HE TAKES ENOUGH RISKS GETTING THEM.
I KNOW. HE WORRIES ME. HE'S DETERMINED NOT TO BELIEVE THE TRUTH ABOUT MIKE. HE JUST LIVES TO SHOOT DOWN GERMAN PLANES.

PETER HAD SEEN IT HAPPEN BEFORE. PILOTS WHO LIVED ONLY FOR THE NEXT DOG-FIGHT. PETER ALSO KNEW HOW THIS COULD END...

CLIVE'S AFRAID OF THE TRUTH, AND THAT'S DANGEROUS.

WE'LL HAVE TO KEEP AN EYE ON HIM IN THE AIR. IF HE GETS INTO REAL TROUBLE ONE OF US MIGHT BE ABLE TO HELP HIM OUT.

PETER KNEW THAT HE SHOULD REALLY ORDER CLIVE TO TAKE SOME LEAVE. BUT THE BATTLE OF BRITAIN WAS AT ITS HEIGHT, AND HE COULD NOT SPARE A SINGLE PILOT.

DURING THE MANY DOG-FIGHTS AND PATROLS THAT FOLLOWED, CLIVE REALISED THAT PETER WAS STICKING CLOSE TO HIM, AND HE FOUND HIS OWN EXPLANATION.

SQUADRON LEADER WILLIAMS SEEMS VERY FOND OF ME THESE DAYS. PERHAPS HE'S HOPING HE'LL GET ME ON MY OWN SOMETIME, AND THEN CLAIM THAT A MESSERSCHMITT SHOT ME DOWN TOO!
JF656

BECAUSE OF HIS SENSELESS HATE CLIVE ONLY NOTICED PETER FLYING NEAR HIM. HE DID NOT KNOW THAT NICKY ALSO STAYED CLOSE.

WAVE AFTER WAVE OF BLACK-CROSSED PLANES FLUNG THEMSELVES AT THE R.A.F. AND STILL THE SPITFIRES AND HURRICANES MET THE CHALLENGE. THEN ONE DAY, OVER FRANCE, PETER'S SQUADRON CLASHED WITH A GROUP OF Me109's WITH MANY KILLS MARKED UP ON THEIR TAIL-FINS.
WE HAVEN'T TANGLED WITH THIS BUNCH BEFORE. BUT IF THEIR TAILS ARE TELLING THE TRUTH THEY'RE A SQUADRON OF ACES!

CLIVE SOON DISCOVERED THEY WERE.
THIS JERRY'S GOOD, BUT I'LL DEAL WITH HIM LIKE MIKE WOULD.

THE TWO PLANES WHEELED IN A DEADLY DUEL.
I'VE GOT HIM NOW.

BUT WHENEVER CLIVE THOUGHT HE WAS THE VICTOR, HE SOON FOUND HE WAS MISTAKEN. THE MESSERSCHMITT FLICKED AWAY AT EXACTLY THE RIGHT MOMENT.
GOOD GRIEF!

THE GERMAN TURNED HIS EVASIVE ACTION INTO AN ATTACK.
THAT WAS TOO CLOSE!

CLIVE REALISED THE GERMAN WAS TOO GOOD FOR HIM. BUT INSTEAD OF TRYING TO BREAK AWAY, HE CIRCLED CLOSER.
I'M NOT GIVING UP NOW! ONE OF US IS GOING TO END UP IN FLAMES.
JF656
BUT CLIVE'S DUEL HAD NOT GONE UNNOTICED. SOME WAY ABOVE, PETER WAS WATCHING.
CLIVE SEEMS TO HAVE PICKED HIMSELF THE GERMAN SQUADRON LEADER. I THINK HE'LL NEED SOME HELP.
JF656

PETER'S SPITFIRE SCREAMED INTO A DIVE.
LET'S SEE IF I CAN SORT THIS OUT.
BUT BEFORE PETER REACHED CLIVE A SIXTH SENSE MADE HIM LOOK UP. HE SAW THE FLAMING BULK OF A STRICKEN MESSERSCHMITT HURTLING DOWN AT HIM.
BY THUNDER!

HE HAD LESS THAN A SECOND TO FLING HIS SPITFIRE TO SAFETY.
MADE IT — JUST!

PETER WAS BLINDED BY THE BLACK SMOKE.
WHERE'S CLIVE GOT TO?

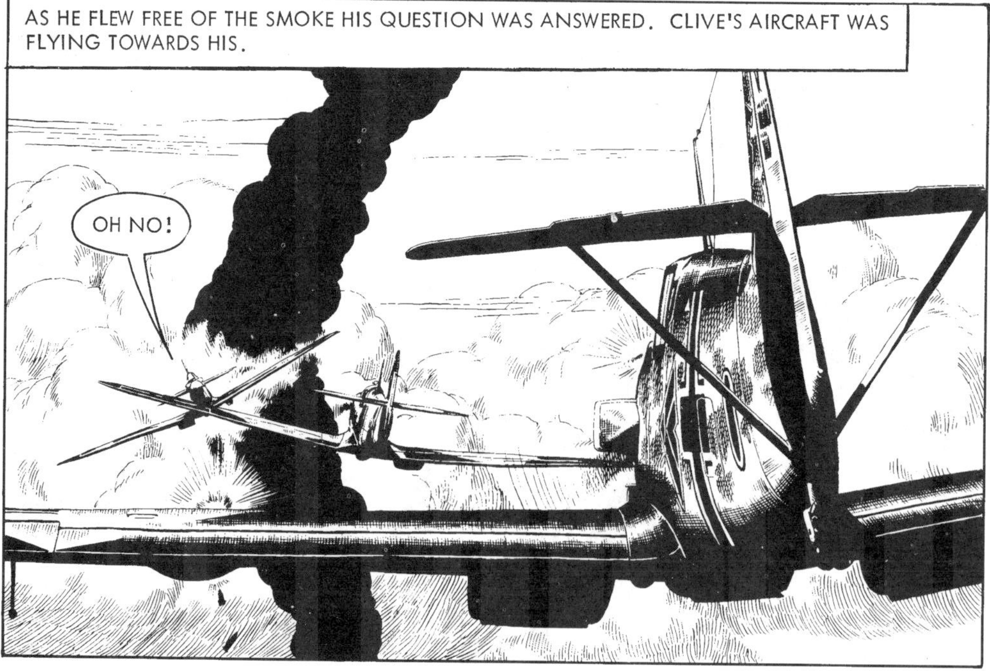
AS HE FLEW FREE OF THE SMOKE HIS QUESTION WAS ANSWERED. CLIVE'S AIRCRAFT WAS FLYING TOWARDS HIS.
OH NO!

THE TWO R.A.F. PILOTS WERE SAVED BY THEIR RAZOR-SHARP REACTIONS. CLIVE FLUNG HIS SPITFIRE OUT OF PETER'S WAY.
THE CLOT IS TRYING TO KILL ME — LIKE HE DID MIKE!

THE GERMAN ACE WAS NOT GOING TO MISS SUCH AN OPPORTUNITY.
HE'S GOT ME!
IT WAS TOO EASY!

AFTER HE HAD RECOVERED FROM HIS NEAR MISS, PETER CLASHED WITH THE NAZI. BUT HE WAS TOO LATE TO HELP CLIVE.

CAN'T JUMP, I'M TOO LOW. CAN'T PULL OUT — STICK'S JAMMED.
JF660

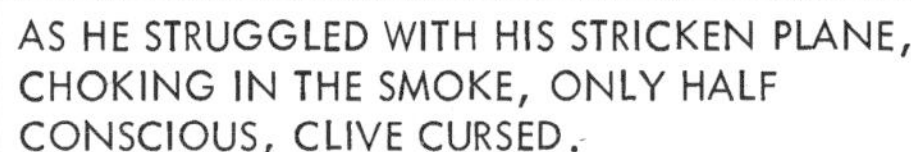
AS HE STRUGGLED WITH HIS STRICKEN PLANE, CHOKING IN THE SMOKE, ONLY HALF CONSCIOUS, CLIVE CURSED.

PETER FORCED ME INTO THE JERRY'S GUNS TO GET ME DONE AWAY WITH — JUST LIKE MIKE.

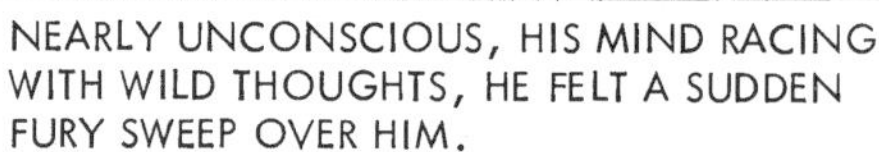
NEARLY UNCONSCIOUS, HIS MIND RACING WITH WILD THOUGHTS, HE FELT A SUDDEN FURY SWEEP OVER HIM.

I MUST LEVEL THIS PLANE OUT. I'M GOING TO STAY ALIVE!

HIS SPITFIRE HURTLED DOWN WITH AN EERIE SCREAM. BUT STILL CLIVE WAS DETERMINED TO STAY CONSCIOUS, HIS FURY GIVING HIM ALMOST SUPERHUMAN STRENGTH.
COME ON. COME UP!

CLIVE MANAGED TO STAY CONSCIOUS, FIGHTING ALL THE TIME. AND THEN, AT THE LAST MINUTE –
JUST MADE IT!

THE SPITFIRE HOWLED OVER THE TREE TOPS.

I'LL HAVE TO PUT HER DOWN SOON. SHE'S SHAKING TO PIECES.

JF660

TREES RUSHED AWAY BENEATH HIM, THEN GAVE WAY TO OPEN COUNTRY.

FIELDS! I'VE GOT TO GET DOWN THERE.

STILL FURIOUSLY ANGRY AT THE WAY HE THOUGHT PETER HAD TRIED TO KILL HIM, CLIVE FOUGHT TO STAY CONSCIOUS AS HE LANDED.

WHEELS DOWN...I'M GOING TOO FAST...NOT LEVEL. I'M GOING TO HIT THOSE TREES.

HE DIDN'T HIT THE TREES, BUT HIS WING PLOUGHED INTO THE GROUND.

OH NO, IT'S GOING TO TURN OVER!

BUT THE SPITFIRE SLEWED SUDDENLY TO A SHATTERING HALT, FLINGING CLIVE AGAINST THE INSTRUMENT PANEL.

AARGH!

ONLY WILL POWER ENABLED HIM TO STAGGER FROM THE WRECK.

I'M ALIVE. PETER'S FAILED!

AS HE REACHED THE TREES HIS SPITFIRE EXPLODED INTO FLAMES. BUT HE DID NOT EVEN NOTICE THE BLAZE. EXHAUSTION CLAIMED HIM, AND HE PITCHED FORWARD.

UUUGH!

WHEN CLIVE REGAINED CONSCIOUSNESS HE WAS IN A SHUTTERED ROOM. A MAN SAT NEXT TO HIM.
WHAT HAPPENED?
DON'T BE AFRAID, MONSIEUR. YOU ARE SAFE. I SAW YOUR PLANE CRASH AND SEARCHED FOR YOU. LUCKILY I FOUND YOU BEFORE THE GERMANS.

CLIVE BEGAN TO FEEL THE EFFECTS OF HIS DESPERATE BATTLE FOR LIFE. HIS HANDS HAD BEEN BURNED, AND NOW HE REALISED QUITE CLEARLY WHAT HAD ACTUALLY HAPPENED.
WHAT A FOOL I'VE BEEN. PETER DIDN'T TRY TO KILL ME. HE WAS TRYING TO HELP ME. IT WASN'T HIS FAULT HE NEARLY RAMMED ME. IT WAS JUST AN ACCIDENT.

AND CLIVE REALISED SOMETHING ELSE...
BY RIGHTS I SHOULD BE DEAD! I ONLY PULLED THROUGH BECAUSE I WAS SO DETERMINED TO OUTWIT PETER. THAT GAVE ME STRENGTH. SO IN A STRANGE KIND OF WAY, PETER'S REALLY SAVED MY LIFE!
THE GERMANS WERE STILL SEARCHING FOR CLIVE SO HE LAY HIDDEN FOR A WEEK. THE LONG HOURS ALONE IN THE ROOM GAVE HIM PLENTY OF TIME FOR THOUGHT. AND HE FOUND MUCH OF HIS PREVIOUS ANGER AND BITTERNESS DISAPPEARING.

THE FRENCHMAN, A POOR FARMER CALLED MARCEL, TOLD HIM THAT UNFORTUNATELY THE RESISTANCE COULD NOT WORK A SECOND 'MIRACLE' FOR HIM.
WE CALL IT OUR 'MIRACLE'. WE RESCUED A SPITFIRE PILOT BEFORE,DRESSED A DEAD GERMAN IN HIS UNIFORM AND PUT THE BODY IN THE PLANE. WE SET IT ON FIRE AND THE NAZIS THOUGHT THEY'D FOUND THE PILOT'S BODY. THE ENGLISH PILOT IS ALIVE TODAY.

A WILD IDEA OCCURED TO CLIVE. HE ASKED HIS COMPANION EXACTLY WHERE IN FRANCE THEY WERE. AND THEN HE KNEW THAT HIS IDEA COULD BE TRUE.
THIS IS WHERE MIKE'S PLANE CRASHED. HE WAS REPORTED BURNED. BUT SUPPOSING HE REALLY ESCAPED, SUPPOSING HE'S THE MAN THE RESISTANCE RESCUED?

CLIVE TRIED TO QUESTION THE FRENCHMAN FURTHER, BUT HE MET WITH A BLANK WALL.
I CAN'T TELL YOU ANYTHING MORE. THIS ENGLISHMAN NOW LEADS OUR RESISTANCE GROUP. IT WAS HIS OWN IDEA TO STAY HERE IN FRANCE AND HELP US.
CAN'T YOU EVEN TELL ME HIS NAME? IT'S VERY IM- PORTANT. I MUST KNOW!
BUT THE FRENCHMAN WOULD ONLY SHAKE HIS HEAD. AND NOTHING CLIVE COULD SAY MADE ANY DIFFERENCE.

WHEN HE HEARD A MONTH LATER THAT HIS ESCAPE ROUTE HAD BEEN ARRANGED, CLIVE MADE ONE LAST ATTEMPT TO CONTACT THE MYSTERIOUS ENGLISHMAN.

GIVE THIS NOTE TO YOUR ENGLISH FRIEND. IF HE REFUSES TO SEE ME AFTER READING IT I'LL NEVER MENTION THE SUBJECT AGAIN.
I SUPPOSE THERE'S NO HARM IN THAT.

IN THE NOTE CLIVE HAD PROVED HIS IDENTITY BY WRITING ABOUT THINGS ONLY HE COULD KNOW ABOUT HIS BROTHER.

THE NOTE WAS SUCCESSFUL. THAT EVENING A MAN CAME TO THE FARM. AND, DESPITE HIS BEARD, CLIVE RECOGNISED HIS BROTHER.

MIKE!
I COULDN'T REALLY LET YOU GO BACK TO ENGLAND WITHOUT SAYING HELLO!

THE FRENCHMAN LEFT QUIETLY AND THE TWO BROTHERS HAD A HUNDRED THINGS TO TALK ABOUT, BUT SOON THE CONVERSATION TURNED TO MIKE'S SERVICE WITH PETER. AND THERE WAS SOMETHING MIKE WANTED TO GET OFF HIS CHEST.
I FEEL REALLY ASHAMED ABOUT THOSE LETTERS I SENT YOU. THEY WERE A PACK OF LIES. I WAS A ROTTEN PILOT! NOT LIKE PETER WILLIAMS AND SOME OF THE OTHERS. THEY WERE NATURALS. I ENVIED THEM...

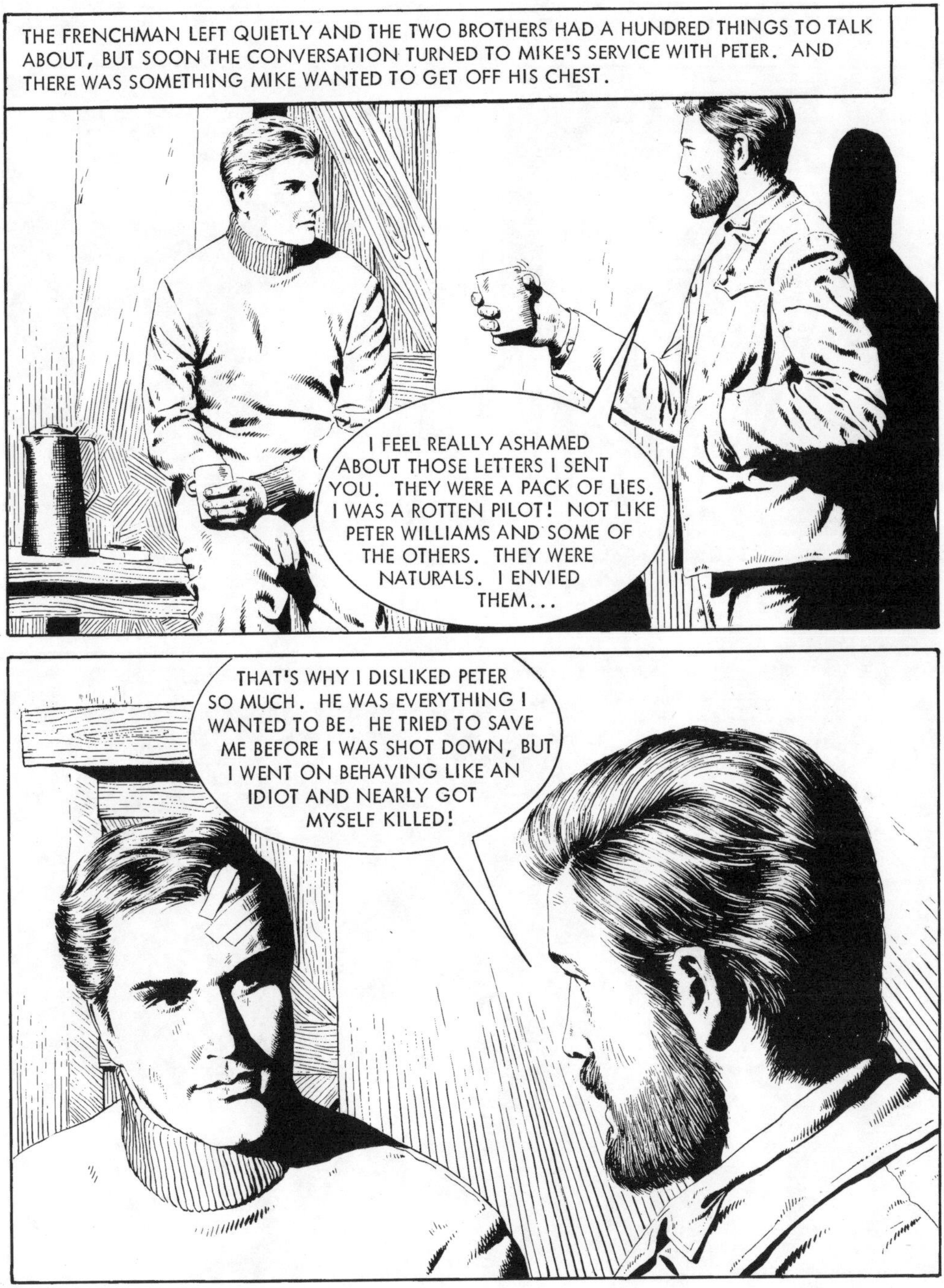

THAT'S WHY I DISLIKED PETER SO MUCH. HE WAS EVERYTHING I WANTED TO BE. HE TRIED TO SAVE ME BEFORE I WAS SHOT DOWN, BUT I WENT ON BEHAVING LIKE AN IDIOT AND NEARLY GOT MYSELF KILLED!

CLIVE REALISED THAT EVERYTHING PETER HAD TOLD HIM ABOUT MIKE WAS TRUE. BUT MIKE HAD CHANGED.
I'VE LEARNED A LOT SINCE I'VE BEEN IN FRANCE. I'M AN UNDER-COVER FIGHTER, LIKE I WAS IN SPAIN. THIS IS WHERE I WANT TO STAY!
MIKE ADDED THAT LONDON HAD NOW GIVEN HIM PERMISSION TO FIGHT ON IN FRANCE. THEY WERE EVEN SENDING ANOTHER TRAINED AGENT OUT TO HELP HIM. CLIVE WAS TO GO BACK TO ENGLAND ON THE SUBMARINE THAT BROUGHT THE AGENT OUT.

LATER THAT NIGHT CLIVE AND MIKE SAID GOOD-BYE ON A DESERTED STRETCH OF BEACH.
I DIDN'T GIVE THE SQUADRON MUCH CAUSE TO LIKE ME OR BE PROUD OF ME, BUT PERHAPS I'LL BE ABLE TO APOLOGISE TO THEM AFTER THE WAR.
I'VE GOT A FEW APOLOGIES OF MY OWN TO MAKE — ESPECIALLY TO PETER.

BACK AT HIS BASE CLIVE WAS WELCOMED WARMLY. HE TOLD ALL TO PETER AND NEVER PUT A FOOT OUT OF LINE AGAIN. THEN CAME THE DAY WHEN THEY LENT SUPPORT TO THE ALLIED ARMIES INVADING NAZI EUROPE.
THE WAR'S NEARLY OVER. SOON I'LL SEE MIKE AGAIN...
Commando
THE END

The next four all-action Commando books are out in two weeks!
Look out for:—

" WITCH-DOCTOR "
" FIRE IN THE FOREST "

" THE FORTUNES OF WAR "
" INTO THE JUNGLE "

DAIMLER ARMOURED CAR

Equipment of the Second World War — No. 5

CREW – 3

WEIGHT — 7112kg

LENGTH — 3962mm

WIDTH — 2438mm

HEIGHT — 2234mm

SPEED — 45mph (72km/h)

ENGINE — 95hp Daimler

ARMAMENT — 40mm cannon. Quick-firing 7.9mm machine gun, Bren gun can be mounted on turret rim.

ARMOUR — 16 millimetres thick

High mobility was the main feature of the Daimler Armoured Car. It could go backwards or forwards through all the gears at high speeds.

Used mainly for reconnaissance duties, this A/C could get out of trouble fast if it met any tanks — but it could also dish out plenty trouble when it had to.

TROUBLE SPOT
10

BRITISH, ITALIAN AND GERMAN CARS DUELLED FOR SUPREMACY ON THE RACING TRACKS OF PRE-WAR EUROPE, THEIR DRIVERS' NAMES HOUSEHOLD WORDS. BILL 'JUMBO' ROGAN OF BRITAIN, GINO GASTONI OF ITALY, AND THE NAZI HANS MULLER DICED REGULARLY FOR THE COVETED GRAND PRIX AWARDS. SOON THEY WOULD BE FACING EACH OTHER, NOT ON THE TRACK, BUT ON THE SHELL-TORN DESERT OF LIBYA. AND THE ONLY AWARD WOULD BE DEATH TO THE LOSER.

BERLIN, 1939 . THIS TIME, ON HIS HOME GROUND, MULLER HAD TO WIN. SCORNFULLY, HE LISTENED TO THE CHAFF BETWEEN HIS TWO ARCH-RIVALS.
HEY, JUMBO, THIS TIME I WIN, I THINK. ME FIRST, YOU SECOND, AND OUR GERMAN FRIEND THIRD. WHAT YOU SAY?
AH, GO ON, YOU OLD MACARONI MUNCHER. YOU'LL BE STARING UP MY EXHAUST THIS TIME.
BAH, THEY ARE LIKE CHILDREN.
THE NAZIS EXPECTED A VICTORY. AS A GLOOMY ANNOUNCER WAS PREDICTING TO LISTENERS IN AMERICA, IT LOOKED VERY MUCH LIKE THEY WOULD GET IT.
WELL, FOLKS, OUR BOY IS RIGHT OUT OF IT. THE ITALIAN AND THE BRITISHER ARE GIVING IT ALL THEY HAVE, BUT IT LOOKS LIKE THIS GUY MULLER HAS THE EDGE ON THEM BOTH.

BUT MULLER WAS NOT YET HOME AND DRY. ON THE LAST LAP, JUMBO FLOGGED HIS ENGINE AS IT HAD NEVER BEEN FLOGGED BEFORE, AND SCREAMED PAST GINO.
10
14
ONE DOWN AND ONE TO GO. IF THIS ENGINE HOLDS TOGETHER, I RECKON I CAN TAKE MULLER.

MULLER WAS AWARE OF THE DANGER. WITH A COLD SMILE, HE GUNNED THAT LITTLE BIT EXTRA OUT OF HIS ALREADY STRAINING ENGINE AS JUMBO CLOSED RELENTLESSLY.
I MUST NOT LOSE NOW. I MUST NOT!
12
I'LL TAKE YOU ON THE NEXT BEND, CHUM.

THE BEND RUSHED UP, THE TWO DRIVERS DETERMINED NOT TO BE FIRST TO LOSE SPEED. THEN, AS IT SEEMED CERTAIN BOTH CARS MUST LOCK TOGETHER ON THE TIGHT BEND, MULLER LOST CONTROL.
IF I CAN JUST... AHHHHH, NO!
14

JUMBO HAD SNATCHED VICTORY FROM THE HANDS OF THE NAZIS.
IT'S YOU LADS WHO OUGHT TO TAKE A BOW. YOU WERE UP ALL NIGHT ON THE CAR.
SO WERE YOU, JUMBO. AND YOU DROVE THE PERISHIN' THING.

GINO GASTONI HURRIED TO ADD HIS CONGRATULATIONS, BUT THERE WAS AN INTERRUPTION...
ROGAN! I DEMAND YOU WITHDRAW FROM THE PRIZE-GIVING. YOU FORCED ME OFF THE ROAD.

THERE WAS NO TRUTH IN THE ACCUSATION, BUT MULLER WAS INCENSED WITH RAGE AND THE SHAME OF HIS LAST-SECOND DEFEAT.
'ERE, WATCH IT, MATE.
I THINK JUMBO, HE CAN HANDLE THIS, NO?
MULLER'S HAYMAKER HIT NOTHING BUT SPACE. THEN HE WAS SENT ON THE WAY TO THE FLOOR.
SIT DOWN AND LISTEN TO REASON, WILL YOU?
I THINK, JUMBO, OUR FRIEND IS A BAD LOSER.

FOR THE SECOND TIME IN ONE DAY, MULLER HAD BEEN BESTED BY THIS UPSTART ENGLISHMAN. HE COMPLETELY LOST CONTROL AND SNATCHED UP A SPANNER.
NOBODY, NOBODY KNOCKS HANS MULLER DOWN.
AH, NAUGHTY, NAUGHTY.
IT JUST WASN'T MULLER'S DAY.
HAVE A NICE TRIP MY HOMICIDAL FRIEND.
AAAH!

THERE WAS BANTER IN GINO'S VOICE, BUT A QUIET MENACE IN HIS EYES.
WHAT THE —?
NOT TO WORRY, JUMBO. HERR MULLER HERE TRIPPED. I AM SURE HE WILL, IN FUTURE, BE MORE CAREFUL.
ALL RIGHT. TODAY, YOU BOTH WIN. BUT TO-MORROW? WE SHALL SEE.

THE TWO CHUMS PARTED THE NEXT DAY. BOTH WERE ONLY TOO AWARE OF THE SAVAGE VOICES RAISED IN MILITARY SONGS, AND THE TRAMP OF MARCHING FEET. WAR WAS COMING.
WELL, OLD FRUIT, SEE YOU IN ROME AT THE END OF THE YEAR. WHO KNOWS, YOU MAY EVEN WIN THIS TIME.
CERTAINLY I SHALL WIN, JUMBO. THAT IS, IF CERTAIN GENTLEMEN IN BERLIN AND ROME DON'T PREVENT US RACING AGAIN.

ONLY MONTHS LATER, JUMBO REMEMBERED GINO'S GLOOMY PREDICTION. BRITAIN AND GERMANY WERE AT WAR. IT WOULD ONLY BE A MATTER OF TIME BEFORE ITALY JOINED IN.

JUMBO WAS COMMISSIONED TO THE RANK OF LIEUTENANT IN AN ARMOURED CAR REGIMENT, AND BY THE TIME HIS REGIMENT REACHED LIBYA, ITALY HAD JOINED FORCES WITH HITLER.
WON'T BE LONG NOW, JUMBO OLD MAN. ONLY HOPE THE LADS AND I CAN SHOW 'EM.

JUMBO NEED NOT HAVE WORRIED ABOUT HIS REGIMENT'S PERFORMANCE IN COMBAT. LIKE OTHER BRITISH UNITS, THEY PROVED MORE THAN A MATCH FOR THE OPPOSING ITALIAN FORCES.
RIGHT ON THE NOSE. GOOD OLD "TUBBY". NOW FOR THE OTHERS.
MAMA MIA. RUN!

SAM SPOONER, JUMBO'S DRIVER, MADE IT PLAIN WHAT HE THOUGHT OF THE ITALIAN AS A FIGHTING MAN.
LOOK AT 'EM. NOT EVEN GOT THE SPIRIT TO MAKE A RUN FOR IT. WHAT A PERISHIN' ARMY.
MANY OF THEM DON'T AGREE WITH WHAT THEY FIGHT FOR, SAM. THEIR HEART JUST ISN'T IN IT.

'TUBBY' TRUBSHAW, JUMBO'S GUNNER, DIDN'T AGREE WITH SAM'S OPINION OF THE ITALIANS.

'ERE, YOU'RE NOT GIVING HIM THAT SPARE PAIR OF BOOTS, ARE YER?

AH, LEAVE OFF, SAM. LOOK AT THE POOR BLIGHTER. HIS FEET WOULD BE CUT TO BITS IN THE MARCH TO THE WIRE.

FOUR DAYS MARCH TO THE EAST, HANS MULLER WAS GIVING HIS OPINION OF THE ITALIANS.
AS ALLIES, THESE SCUM ARE USELESS.
YOU'RE A LITTLE HARD ON THEM, HANS. AMONG THEM CAN BE FOUND GOOD SOLDIERS.

MULLER, FRESH FROM THE WEHR-MACHT'S SWEEPING SUCCESSES IN FRANCE, WAS SUPREMELY CONFI-DENT.
IT WILL BE US, THE AFRIKA KORPS, WHO WILL SEND THE BRITISH SCUTTLING BACK ACROSS THE DESERT LIKE THE RATS THEY ARE.

THE NEXT DAY, JUMBO AND ANOTHER ARMOURED CAR RAN SLAP BANG INTO AN ITALIAN REARGUARD THAT PROVED BOTH SAM SPOONER AND MULLER TO BE VERY MISTAKEN ABOUT HOW AN ITALIAN COULD FIGHT.

AMBUSH! PUT YOUR FOOT DOWN, SAM. THAT LADDIE CAN SHOOT. WE'LL NEED THE WHOLE GROUP TO FLUSH THEM OUT.

JUMBO REPORTED BACK TO HIS TROOP THAT SOME ITALIANS, AT ANY RATE, WERE TIRED OF RUNNING. HIS C.O. GATHERED THE CAR COMMANDERS TOGETHER AT ONCE.

WELL, CHAPS, IT LOOKS AS IF THE ITALIANS DON'T WANT TO GIVE UP HALAFA VILLAGE WITHOUT PUTTING UP SOME SORT OF SHOW. JUMBO HERE CAN VOUCH FOR THE FACT THESE BLOKES CAN SHOOT, SO DON'T UNDERESTIMATE ANYTHING YOU MEET. IT MIGHT BITE.
RIGHT, SIR.

WHATEVER ELSE JUMBO'S CREW MIGHT LACK, IT WAS NOT CONFIDENCE.

WELL, SAM. IT LOOKS AS IF THEY WANT TO COME AND PLAY TODAY.

HUMPH! YOU CAN OUT-THINK 'EM, TUBBY CAN OUT-SHOOT 'EM, AND I CAN OUT-DRIVE 'EM.

MODEST OLD DEVIL, OUR SAM.

THE BRITISH FORCE NUMBERED EIGHT ARMOURED CARS. THE ITALIANS, CONFIDENT OF VICTORY, SALLIED OUT WITH TEN.

AMONG THE ITALIAN FORCE, THERE WAS A CERTAIN LIEUTENANT GINO GASTONI.

HEY, KEEP YOUR HEAD DOWN, CARLO, EH? OTHERWISE, THESE BRITISH, THEY SHOOT IT OFF.
DON'T YOU TAKE ANYTHING SERIOUS, GINO?

THEY DIDN'T KNOW IT, BUT JUMBO AND GINO, TWO COMRADES OF THE RACE TRACK, WOULD SOON BE TRYING ALL THEY KNEW TO KILL EACH OTHER.
GOOD OLD TUBBY — RIGHT ON THE NOSE! KEEP DODGING, SAM. THEY MEAN BUSINESS.
THEY HAVE HIT CARLO! LET US SEE IF WE CAN AVENGE HIM.
IN THE MELEE OF THE BATTLE ALL ORDER WAS LOST. STILL UNKNOWING, GINO AND JUMBO FOUND THEMSELVES HURTLING STRAIGHT TOWARDS EACH OTHER. THERE WAS ONLY ONE THING TO DO. FIRE, AND HOPE YOU'D GET YOUR MAN BEFORE HE GOT YOU!

IT SEEMED CERTAIN THAT BOTH JUMBO AND GINO WOULD DESTROY EACH OTHER, BUT FATE INTERVENED. AN ITALIAN CAR, PURSUED BY AN OPPONENT, SWEPT BETWEEN THE TWO BATTLE-LOCKED FRIENDS, AND TOOK BOTH SHELLS.

THEN, WITH A SUDDENESS THAT WAS STARTLING, IT WAS ALL OVER. THE ITALIANS BROKE OFF THE ENGAGEMENT, HEADING BACK FOR THE VILLAGE OF HALAFA.

PHEW, WHAT A FIGHT THAT WAS.

IT HAD BEEN A FIERCE BATTLE, WITH HEAVY LOSSES. BEFORE THEY WENT IN AGAIN, THE R.A.F. WOULD 'SOFTEN UP' THE ITALIANS.

WHEN THAT ONE CAME AT US HEAD ON, I THOUGHT WE'D HAD OUR LOT.
IF THAT OTHER CAR HADN'T CUT ACROSS AND COPPED IT, WE WOULD HAVE!

AFTER A HASTY MEAL, THE THREE CARS THAT HAD SURVIVED THAT SAVAGE ENCOUNTER WERE OFF INTO ACTION AGAIN, SUPPORTING THE INFANTRY THAT WERE TO TAKE THE VILLAGE OF HALAFA.

AHEAD OF THE BRITISH ATTACK, AN AIR STRIKE HOWLED DOWN ON THE ITALIAN POSITIONS IN THE VILLAGE.
THE R.A.F. MIGHT AT LEAST HAVE GIVEN ME TIME TO GET SOME PETROL IN MY CAR. ANOTHER FIVE MINUTES, AND I COULD HAVE BEEN AWAY.
IT LOOKS AS IF WE ARE THE LAST CREW OPERATIONAL HERE NOW.

BRITISH BOMBS KILLED ALL THE ITALIAN OFFICERS APART FROM GINO, AND SEVERELY WOUNDED THE C.O. DURING A LULL, GINO WAS SENT FOR.

WE MUST HOLD THIS VILLAGE AS LONG AS WE CAN. OUR FORCES MUST BE GIVEN TIME TO RE-GROUP ALONG OUR FRONT. YOU, AS THE ONLY OFFICER, MUST TAKE CHARGE.
I'LL DO MY BEST, SIR.

GINO DID HIS BEST. WHEN THE BRITISH ATTACK CAME, HE WAS MORE THAN READY FOR IT.

FIRE!

JUMBO'S CAR, IN THE LEAD, HAD CAUGHT THE FIRST ITALIAN SALVO SQUARE-ON. THE TRIO HAD GRABBED THEIR RIFLES AND BALED OUT.

TALK ABOUT OUT OF THE FRYING PAN INTO THE FIRE.
TOLD YOU THEY COULD SHOOT. THE INFANTRY WILL HAVE TO WORK ROUND THEIR FLANK.

FROM TWO SIDES THE BRITISH SOLDIERS WENT IN, WITH RIFLE, GRENADE AND SHINING BAYONET.

LEAVE IT TO THE POOR OLD INFANTRY, EVERY TIME.

THEY WERE CLOSELY FOLLOWED BY JUMBO AND HIS MATES, HANDLING THEIR RIFLES LIKE VETERANS.
I DIDN'T KNOW YOU LOT COULD HANDLE A RIFLE LIKE THAT!
WE DON'T SPEND ALL OUR TIME TOURING AROUND THE COUNTRY-SIDE, SOLDIER.
ONLY ONE PART OF THE VILLAGE DEFENCES HELD, AND THEN ONLY DUE TO THE BRAVERY OF GINO.
HOLD HARD, COMRADES. HOLD LONGER, AND THEY WILL RUN.

BUT THE BRITISH ATTACK WAS STRONG AND DETERMINED.
PILE IT ON, LADS.
AS LONG AS GINO WAS ON HIS FEET, THE ITALIANS WOULD NOT RUN. BUT THEN A GRENADE BLAST KNOCKED HIM TO THE GROUND.
THE DEFENCES CRACKED WIDE OPEN AND YELLING BRITISH INFANTRY CHASED THE NOW COMPLETELY SHATTERED ITALIANS BEFORE THEM LIKE STARTLED SHEEP.
ALL IS LOST. RUN FOR YOUR LIVES.

WHEN GINO, STUNNED BY THE BLAST OF THE GRENADE, REGAINED HIS SENSES, HE FOUND THAT THE VILLAGE WAS IN BRITISH HANDS.
SO WE HAVE LOST, THEN?
TOO TRUE, MATE. WELL, YOU SEEM OK. THE WAR'S OVER FOR YOU, ANYWAY.

AS THE ONLY ITALIAN OFFICER PRESENT, GINO, FOR ONCE SERIOUS, FORMALLY SURRENDERED THE VILLAGE TO THE BRITISH.

NO NEED TO BE SO SOLEMN, OLD CHAP.

MY COMRADES FOUGHT HARD FOR THIS VILLAGE. I SEE NO CAUSE FOR CELEBRATION OR AMUSEMENT WHEN I HAVE TO DELIVER OUR SURRENDER.

THERE WAS GREAT DIGNITY IN THE QUIETLY SPOKEN WORDS. BOTH BRITISH OFFICERS AT ONCE HONOURED GINO'S SURRENDER.

THANK YOU. YOU FOUGHT WELL. PERHAPS YOU WILL DO US THE HONOUR OF EATING WITH US.

FORMALITY OVER, GINO ACCEPTED THE BRITISH OFFICER'S INVITATION – AND GOT THE SURPRISE OF HIS LIFE.

JUMBO ... JUMBO ROGAN!
IT CAN'T BE ... GINO!

IF EITHER DOUBTED THE OTHER'S FRIENDSHIP, THEIR DOUBTS MELTED IN THE WARMTH OF EACH OTHER'S GREETING.
IT'S GOOD TO SEE YOU, JUMBO. AT LEAST YOU ARE NOT INJURED IN THIS MESS.
SAME HERE. WELL, AT LEAST YOU'RE OUT OF IT NOW.
WELL, WHAT DO YOU KNOW? HE WALKS INTO AN ENEMY BASE AND FINDS A FRIEND.

AT JUMBO'S WORDS, A STRANGE GLEAM CAME INTO GINO'S EYES. WAS THE WAR OVER FOR HIM? NOT IF HE COULD GET BEHIND THE WHEEL OF A TRUCK.

I CERTAINLY DON'T FANCY SPENDING TIME BEHIND WIRE. I WONDER?

THE NEXT DAY, STRONG BRITISH FORCES CAME UP, POISED FOR AN ATTACK THAT WAS TO SHATTER THE ITALIANS. WITH THEM CAME AN INTELLIGENCE MAJOR, BRUSQUE AND TO THE POINT.
THERE ARE CERTAIN QUESTIONS CONCERNING YOUR UNIT I WISH TO ASK.
ASK, BY ALL MEANS, BUT I CANNOT ANSWER THEM.
ENOUGH OF THAT, MATE. GET IN.

AN HOUR PASSED, AND THE SENTRY POSTED OUTSIDE THE TENT BEGAN TO BE UNEASY. IF INTERRUPTED, THE MAJOR WOULD HIT THE ROOF. BUT STILL...
NOT A CHEEP FOR TEN MINUTES NOW. MAYBE I OUGHT TO GO IN.

THE SENTRY DID, AND FOUND THE MAJOR BOUND AND GAGGED. THIS WAS ONE INCIDENT HE'D NEVER LIVE DOWN.
BLIMEY!
MMMMMMUMPH!

LATER THAT DAY, WHEN JUMBO TRIED TO SEE GINO, HE FOUND HE WAS TOO LATE.
YOUR EYTIE MATE BORROWED TRANSPORT AND DISAPPEARED. HALF HOPE HE MAKES IT.
NEVER DID GIVE UP EASY.

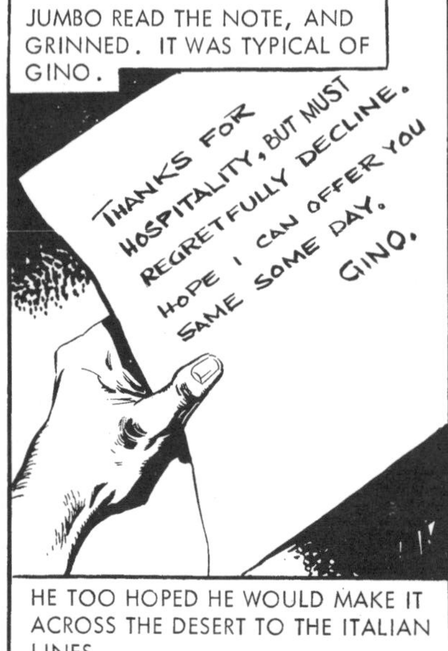
JUMBO READ THE NOTE, AND GRINNED. IT WAS TYPICAL OF GINO.
THANKS FOR HOSPITALITY, BUT MUST REGRETFULLY DECLINE. HOPE I CAN OFFER YOU SAME SOME DAY. GINO.
HE TOO HOPED HE WOULD MAKE IT ACROSS THE DESERT TO THE ITALIAN LINES.

GINO DID MAKE IT. AND, THREE WEEKS LATER, WAS ONCE MORE IN ACTION.

HELLO, WE HAVE COMPANY.

A PROWLING HURRICANE PILOT HAD SEEN, TO HIS DELIGHT, THE THREE PATROLLING CARS.
YIPPEE, THEY'RE SITTING DUCKS.

GUNS HAMMERING, HE CAME IN AT FULL THROTTLE, TO BE GREETED BY A CALM GINO COOLLY ANSWERING HIS FIRE.
YOU'LL HAVE TO DO BETTER THAN THAT TO FINISH GINO GASTONI!

THE HURRICANE MADE TWO PASSES, AND ON THE THIRD RAN INTO TROUBLE. RAKED WITH FIRE, AND FLYING TOO LOW TO RECOVER, IT HIT THE SAND WITH A SAVAGE RENDING NOISE.

WITHOUT HESITATION GINO LEAPT FROM HIS CAR, ORDERING HIS GUNNER TO HELP HIM DRAG THE BRITISH PILOT CLEAR OF THE SMOKING WRECK.
THE PLANE, SHE WILL GO UP ANYTIME.
WE CANNOT LEAVE HIM TO FRY. SAVE YOUR BREATH FOR LIFTING.

WITH SECONDS TO SPARE, THE SWEATING PAIR DRAGGED THE PILOT CLEAR.
THE HEAT IS TERRIBLE.
IT IS A LOT HOTTER IN THAT COCKPIT, THOUGH.
MINUTES LATER, THE EYES OF THE YOUNG PILOT FLICKERED OPEN.
I THINK PERHAPS YOU WILL BE A LITTLE DRY, NO? YOU ARE SAFE NOW.
I — I REMEMBER PRANGING. YOU MUST HAVE GOT ME OUT. THANKS.

AS THEY HEADED BACK TO BASE, GINO SPOTTED A MOUTH ORGAN IN THE BREAST POCKET OF HIS PRISONER.

THAT IS A HARMONICA, NO? DO YOU PLAY WELL? WHAT DO YOU KNOW?

I PLAY A BIT. WANT TO HEAR SOMETHING?

BACK AT GINO'S BASE, HIS C.O. WAS BRIEFING NEWLY-ARRIVED GERMAN REINFORCEMENTS. IN COMMAND OF THE REINFORCEMENTS WAS CAPTAIN HANS MULLER.

IT IS TIME THE BRITISH IN THIS SECTOR MET REAL SOLDIERS. I AND MY MEN HAVE BEEN SENT TO SUPPORT YOUR CRUMBLING FRONT. SHOW ME YOUR LINES OF DEFENCE.
ARROGANT PIG!

AT THAT MOMENT GINO SWEPT INTO CAMP, SINGING LOUDLY.
THAT YOUNG FELLOW IS LIEUTENANT GASTONI. A BIT WILD, BUT HIS BRAVERY IS WITHOUT QUESTION.
YOU DO NOT HAVE TO TELL ME ABOUT HIM. WE HAVE MET BEFORE.

AS GINO BADE A CHEERY FAREWELL TO HIS PRISONER, MULLER STRODE UP, OBVIOUSLY DISAPPROVING OF THE WHOLE THING.

WELL, GOOD LUCK. THE FOOD MAY BE TERRIBLE IN THE BIRD CAGE, BUT IT IS BETTER THAN GETTING KILLED OUT HERE.

IT'S THANKS TO YOU I'M AROUND AT ALL.

MULLER'S HARSH VOICE MADE GINO TURN. ALTHOUGH SURPRISED, HE LOST NONE OF HIS COMPOSURE.
SO, GASTONI, WE MEET AGAIN. STILL FOND OF THE BRITISH?
WELL, WELL — MULLER. STILL STRUTTING AROUND LIKE A MECHANICAL MAN.

MULLER FLUSHED ANGRILY, HIS HAND STRAYING TO HIS HOLSTER. THEN HE RELAXED.
AS I HAVE TO CO-OPERATE WITH YOU, I WILL OVERLOOK THIS. BUT TREAD CAREFULLY IN FUTURE.
THE GERMAN TURNED ON HIS HEEL AND STAMPED AWAY.

BEFORE THE OPPOSING FORCES LAUNCHED THEMSELVES AT EACH OTHER AGAIN, THERE WAS AN UNEASY LULL. THE TROOPS TRIED TO RELAX, AND, ON THE BRITISH FRONT, A SHOOTING COMPETITION WAS ORGANISED.

OK, MATE, ADMITTED YOUR BOY CAN SHOOT. BUT YOU HAVEN'T SEEN MY COMMANDER YET. I'VE GOT A PAIR OF ITALIAN BINOCULARS THAT SAYS HE'LL WIN FOR OUR UNIT.

DONE. I'LL MATCH YOUR BET WITH TWO TINS OF FAGS.

SAM SPOONER KNEW HIS CHIEF. JUMBO PUT EVERY BULLET IN THE MAGAZINE RIGHT THROUGH THE BULL.
3

IT WAS SHOOTING THAT BROUGHT GASPS OF WONDER AND ADMIRATION.

YOU WEREN'T JUST KIDDING, CHUM. HERE, YOUR BLOKE MADE OUR LAD LOOK SICK.

THEN ROMMEL'S EXPECTED ATTACK CAME. ALL ALONG THE BRITISH LINES, ARMOURED UNITS SWEPT FORWARD, DETERMINED TO CRASH THROUGH.
STEADY, LADS. KEEP YOUR HEADS, AND MAKE EVERY SHOT COUNT.

ON THEY CAME. MANY HOWEVER, WERE STOPPED IN THEIR TRACKS, DESTINED TO LITTER THE DESERT WITH THEIR STEEL HULKS.

OUT, QUICK! SHE IS ABOUT TO BLOW UP!

BUT FOR EVERY ONE DESTROYED, THERE WERE TEN MORE BEHIND. SLOWLY THE BRITISH BEGAN TO GIVE GROUND.

ON THE FLANKS, ROVING ARMOURED CAR UNITS SUPPORTED SMALL POCKETS OF INFANTRY DEFENDING KEY POINTS. JUMBO'S UNIT WAS TO HELP DEFEND HALAFA VILLAGE.
GLAD TO HAVE YOU. HOPE WE CAN HOLD THIS PLACE BETTER THAN OUR ITALIAN FRIENDS DID, EH?
SURE WE CAN. WE OUGHT TO PUT UP QUITE A DEFENCE, WHAT WITH YOUR LADS AND OUR FIVE CARS.

PLOTTING THE CAPTURE OF THE SMALL VILLAGE WAS HANS MULLER HIMSELF, SUPREMELY CONFIDENT WHAT THE OUTCOME OF THE FIGHT WOULD BE.

TOMORROW NIGHT AT THIS TIME, HALAFA VILLAGE WILL AGAIN BE IN AXIS HANDS. WITH GERMAN CARS AND INFANTRY TO SUPPORT YOU, IT SHOULD BE EASY. OF COURSE, THE VILLAGE SHOULD NOT HAVE FALLEN IN THE FIRST PLACE.

AT FIRST LIGHT NEXT MORNING, THE GERMAN AND ITALIAN FORCES SWUNG FORWARD.
UP VERY EARLY, AREN'T THEY?
I THINK WE COULD WORK A FLANKER WHICH COULD TAKE SOME OF THE WEIGHT OFF YOUR BOYS.

JUMBO'S UNIT PULLED OUT, BUT THEIR DUST BETRAYED THEM TO MULLER.
BRITISH. THEY ARE TRYING TO OUTFLANK US.

MULLER HAD PRECIOUS INFANTRY TRUCKS TO PROTECT. HE HEADED TOWARDS THE DUST CLOUD.

MUCH AS GINO DISLIKED THE GERMAN, HE COULD FIND NO FAULT WITH MULLER'S COURAGE.
BUT I THINK YOU WILL FIND THOSE BRITISH NOT SUCH EASY MEAT, MY PROUD HERR MULLER.
GINO AND HIS FELLOW ITALIANS HAD BEEN LEFT WITH THE JOB OF ESCORTING THE INFANTRY WHO WERE TO MAKE THE FINAL ATTACK ON THE VILLAGE.

GINO'S BINOCULARS SWUNG TO THE BRITISH FORCE, WHICH HAD JUST COME INTO VIEW. THEN THEY JERKED IN SURPRISE. FOR FRAMED IN THEM WAS JUMBO ROGAN, LOOKING CALM AND RESOLUTE.

THEY'RE COMING INTO RANGE, TUBBY. SAM, GET READY TO BREAK RIGHT, SOON AS I GIVE THE WORD.

ONE THING TRAINING COULD NEVER GIVE AN ARMOURED CAR COMMANDER WAS THE INSTINCT TO KNOW WHAT THE OTHER FELLOW WAS GOING TO DO.
NOW!
AND A SHELL BURST SIX YARDS AWAY, WHERE THE VEHICLE OUGHT TO HAVE BEEN.

ONE BRITISH COMMANDER HADN'T THIS ESSENTIAL QUALITY. A TURN MADE TOO SLOW, AND A SHELL SLAMMED INTO HIS CAR.

MULLER SHOWED NO MERCY, EVEN TO MEN OUT OF THE BATTLE.
GUN THEM DOWN. WE MUST HOLD THIS FORCE HERE WHILE OUR INFANTRY ATTACK THE VILLAGE.

COMRADE AVENGED COMRADE IN THE MAN-MADE HELL OF BARKING GUNS AND BURNING CORDITE.
BUT MULLER WAS ACHIEVING HIS PURPOSE. THE BRITISH ARMOUR WAS KEPT AWAY FROM THE VILLAGE IT WAS SUPPOSED TO DEFEND.

GINO, APPROACHING HALAFA, WAS PREPARING TO ATTACK IT. YET HE COULD STILL SPARE A THOUGHT FOR A FRIEND.

GOOD LUCK, JUMBO. GOOD LUCK TO US BOTH!

THE BRITISH HAD NO SUPPORTING ARMOUR, BUT THEY HAD ANOTHER EQUALISER – MINES.
AAARGH!
FOR A MOMENT THE ATTACK WAS THROWN INTO CONFUSION.
GOOD. NOW THEY'LL BE SCARED EVERY TIME THEY PLONK DOWN THEIR BIG FEET, BERT.
RIGHT, JIM. BUT THEY'LL BE ON US SOON.

THE MINES COULD NOT COVER EVERY SQUARE YARD OF GROUND, AND THE ITALIAN CARS BORED ON TO MEET THE BRITISH ANTI-TANK FIRE.
GOT YOU NOW, MY LAD.

THE BRITISH INFANTRY KNEW THE ODDS. THEY WOULDN'T LAST LONG, BUT EACH PRAYED THEY WOULD TAKE MANY ATTACKERS WITH THEM. AND THEY DID.

GINO SEEMED TO BEAR A CHARMED LIFE AS HIS CAR INCHED FORWARD SCREENING THE INFANTRY AND PRESENTING ITS THICKER FRONTAL PLATING TO THE ARMOUR-PIERCING BULLETS.
WE ARE ALMOST ON THEM.

MILES FROM THE BESIEGED VILLAGE, ANOTHER FIGHT RAGED. NOT AS MANY MEN WERE INVOLVED, BUT IT WAS JUST AS FIERCELY CONTESTED.

ONLY TWO CARS HAD SURVIVED THE SAVAGE CLASH, THOSE OF BILL 'JUMBO' ROGAN AND HANS MULLER.

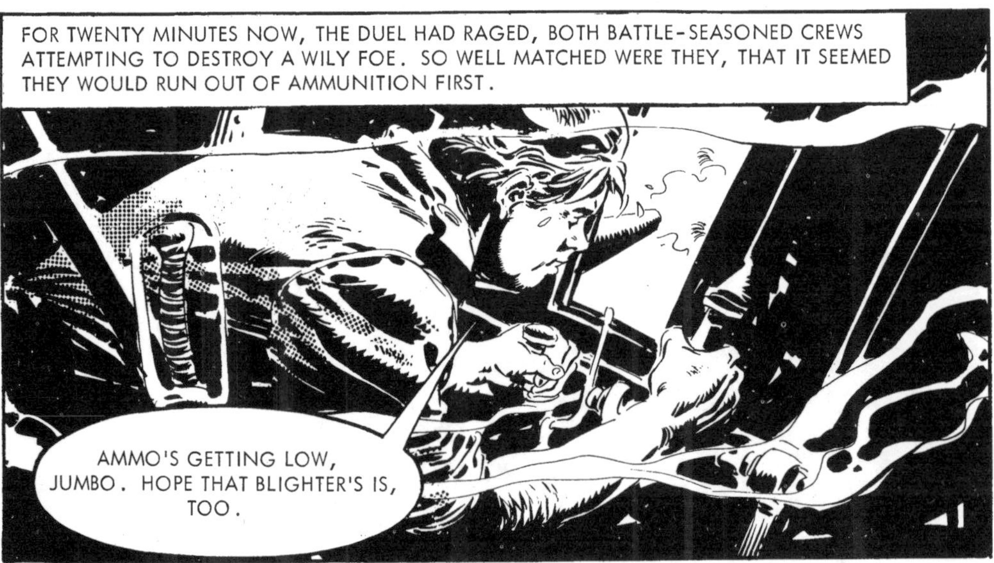
FOR TWENTY MINUTES NOW, THE DUEL HAD RAGED, BOTH BATTLE-SEASONED CREWS ATTEMPTING TO DESTROY A WILY FOE. SO WELL MATCHED WERE THEY, THAT IT SEEMED THEY WOULD RUN OUT OF AMMUNITION FIRST.
AMMO'S GETTING LOW, JUMBO. HOPE THAT BLIGHTER'S IS, TOO.

THE GERMAN CREW WERE TIRING RAPIDLY.
ARE YOU BLIND?

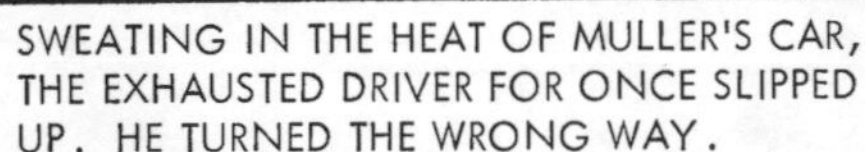
SWEATING IN THE HEAT OF MULLER'S CAR, THE EXHAUSTED DRIVER FOR ONCE SLIPPED UP. HE TURNED THE WRONG WAY.

LEFT, I SAID, FOOL! LEFT, LEFT, LEFT!

HE FLEW RIGHT INTO TUBBY'S GUNSIGHT.
STEADY, NOW. GOT HER.

THE BRITISH ARMOUR-PIERCING SHELL HIT SQUARE ON. AS HIS CAR TOPPLED, MULLER COULD HARDLY CREDIT THAT HE, HANS MULLER, HAD BEEN OUTFOUGHT.
WE ARE HIT!
THROWING HOT LEAD AND CURSES, MULLER STAGGERED TOWARDS THE BRITISH CAR.
GO ON THEN, SHOOT, YOU DOGS. SEE HOW HANS MULLER DIES FOR THE FATHERLAND. SHOOT AND GET IT DONE WITH.
MULLER WAS THE ONLY SURVIVOR OF HIS CREW.

THE ENRAGED TUBBY DROPPED A SHELL CLOSE TO MULLER.
BLAST YOU, TUBBY. YOU'VE KILLED HIM.

BUT MULLER WAS FAR FROM DEAD. HE LAY DOGGO, WHILE JUMBO APPROACHED ON FOOT.
ONE BULLET LEFT FOR YOU, BRITISHER. THAT'S IT, COME AND GET IT.

OVER EAGER, HE PLACED HIS SHOT AN INCH HIGH.

DIE, BRITISHER. HEIL HITLER!

YOU RAT!

DODGING A HURLED LUGER AND A FISTFUL OF SAND AIMED FOR HIS EYES, JUMBO TOOK THE WIND FROM MULLER'S SAILS.
I'LL KILL YOU! KILL YOU — OOOF!
YOU WANT TO USE YOUR HEAD, LIKE I DO.
MULLER'S FRANTIC STRUGGLES SUDDENLY CEASED, AND HE LAY GASPING LIKE A LANDED FISH.
YOU CAN'T DO ANYTHING WITH HIS SORT. DO THE WORLD A FAVOUR AND PUT A BULLET IN HIM.
SHUT UP, SAM. LET'S HAVE A CLOSER LOOK AT YOU, MATE.

JUMBO'S GRIN VANISHED AS HE TOOK HIS FIRST CLOSE LOOK AT HIS VICTIM.
MULLER! HANS MULLER. IT CAN'T BE!
ROGAN? SO, WE MEET AGAIN!
JUMBO, STILL TAKEN ABACK AT THE IDENTITY OF HIS PRISONER, TOOK NO CHANCES.
IT IS UNTHINKABLE THAT AN OFFICER IN THE WEHRMACHT SHOULD BE BOUND LIKE A COMMON CRIMINAL. I PROTEST STRONGLY.
ACT CIVILISED, AND YOU'LL BE TREATED AS SUCH.

BEFORE THEY LEFT, THEY CHECKED THEIR WATER SUPPLY.
WE HAVE A FULL WATER BOTTLE LEFT. SHOULD BE PLENTY TO GET US BACK TO THE VILLAGE.
WHICH IS NOW IN YOUR HANDS, NO DOUBT.
COME ON, FRITZ. OOPSY-DAISY.

THERE WAS ONLY ONE WAY TO FIND OUT WHO HAD WON THE BATTLE FOR THE VILLAGE, AND THAT WAS TO GET THERE.

COME ON, SAM. GET HER ROLLING.

SHE — SHE WON'T START!

TRY AS THEY MIGHT THE ENGINE REMAINED SILENT. IT HAD TAKEN A LOT OF PUNISHMENT IN THE BATTLE.
STUPID, USELESS HULK.
THAT WON'T HELP, MULLER. LOOKS AS IF WE WALK. WE KNOW WHICH WAY THE VILLAGE LIES.

TO AVOID ITS CAPTURE, THEY SET FIRE TO THEIR CAR.
SO LONG, OLD GIRL.
AH, THE SENTIMENTAL BRITISH. WHAT FOOLS YOU ALL ARE.
EXCEPT FOR JUMBO'S PISTOL IN ITS HOLSTER, THEY CARRIED NO WEAPONS, FOR THEY WOULD JUST BE ADDED WEIGHT.

IT WAS SAM SPOONER WHO FIRST BEGAN TO TIRE. OLDER THAN THE OTHERS, HE LACKED THEIR YOUTHFUL STAMINA.

LOOK SIR, LET'S FACE FACTS. WITH ME DRAGGING ALONG, YOU WON'T MAKE IT. CARRY ON, AND I'LL CATCH UP WHEN I GET MY WIND.

HE'S RIGHT. LEAVE HIM. HE IS HOLDING US BACK.

NOBODY GETS LEFT. IF ONE GOES, WE ALL GO.

THEY WALKED FOR HOURS. SUDDENLY, SAM BECAME DELIRIOUS AND, AS TUBBY BENT OVER HIM, THE THIRSTY MULLER SEIZED HIS CHANCE.
FOR YOU, THE END, ROGAN.

MULLER'S RED RIMMED EYES SPOTTED THE WATER BOTTLE.
WATER. I MUST HAVE IT! I MUST!
MULLER, DON'T! WAIT, YOU FOOL.

JUMBO GATHERED HIS STRENGTH FOR A LEAP THAT SENT MULLER, AND THE BOTTLE, FLYING ONTO THE SAND.
OH, NO. THE WATER. CAN'T MAKE IT.

A SMASHING RIGHT TO MULLER'S JAW ENDED THE FIGHT. GROGGILY, HE LOOKED INTO THE BARREL OF JUMBO'S REVOLVER.
PICK UP OLD SAM THERE WHEN WE MOVE, OR I SHOOT. GOT IT?
YOU'RE MAD. VERY WELL, I'LL CARRY HIM.

JUMBO DECIDED THAT THEY MUST REST FOR TEN MINUTES BEFORE CARRYING ON. EVERYBODY DID, EXCEPT MULLER.
WE ARE ALL DOOMED ANYWAY. IF — IF I COULD JUST GET THAT GUN. I WILL HAVE MY REVENGE.

INCH BY INCH, WITH STRENGTH AIDED BY HATE, MULLER DRAGGED HIMSELF OVER TO JUMBO AND EASED THE REVOLVER FROM ITS HOLSTER.
THE PLEASURE OF KILLING YOU IS MINE, NOT THE DESERT'S.
WITH A SNARL OF TRIUMPH, MULLER SQUEEZED THE TRIGGER, TO HEAR A METALLIC CLICK AS THE HAMMER FELL ON AN EMPTY CHAMBER.
IT'S EMPTY!

ONCE MORE JUMBO WAS ONE STEP AHEAD.
I THOUGHT YOU'D PULL SOMETHING LIKE THAT SO I SLIPPED THE BULLETS OUT. TIME TO BE MOVING ON, OLD SPORT.

MEANWHILE, THE VILLAGE HAD BEEN TAKEN. GINO, JUBILANT AT THE VICTORY, HAD NOT FORGOTTEN THE ARMOURED CAR BATTLE, AND HAD HURRIED BACK TO THE SCENE.

NO SIGN OF THE CREW. WHEN SHE BURNED, THEY WERE NOT IN HER.

THEY CAN'T HAVE GOT FAR. BUT WHICH WAY DID THEY GO? THE AREA IS CRISS-CROSSED WITH TRACKS. WE CAN'T FIND THEIR FOOTPRINTS.

JUMBO'S CAR WAS THE ONLY ONE WITH NO DEAD CREW INSIDE.

FOUR DIFFERENT WAYS TO GO. THREE WOULD MEAN DEATH FOR JUMBO, HIS CREW, AND MULLER. GINO CHOSE.
EAST, I THINK. NO, WAIT, DRIVE WEST. YES, WEST TOWARDS HALAFA.

THEY HEADED WEST, BUT THERE WAS NO SIGN OF ANY SURVIVORS. THEN GINO SPOTTED SOMETHING.
SOMETHING FLASHING. OVER THERE. HEAD FOR IT, MAX.

LYING IN THE SAND WERE THE DISCARDED BULLETS FROM JUMBO'S REVOLVER AND THE EMPTY WATER CANTEEN.

HANG ON, MY FRIENDS. ALL IS NOT LOST YET.

FIVE MINUTES DRIVING BROUGHT GINO TO THE EXHAUSTED PARTY.
GINO!
JUMBO, SOMEHOW I KNEW IT WAS YOU I WAS ATTEMPTING TO SAVE.
NOT BEFORE TIME. THESE DOGS ARE NOW OUR PRISONERS.

BACK AT HALAFA VILLAGE, JUMBO RECOVERED SWIFTLY. SO SWIFTLY HE WAS ABLE TO ACCEPT GINO'S INVITATION TO DINE WITH THE VICTORIOUS ITALIANS.

HERE'S TO AN END TO THE WAR. YOU AND I SHOULD FIGHT EACH OTHER ON THE TRACK, JUMBO.

I'LL DRINK TO THAT.

WHILE THEY ATE, JUMBO HEARD HOW THE BRITISH FORCE IN THE VILLAGE HAD SURRENDERED ONLY AFTER A BITTER STRUGGLE.
SO ONCE AGAIN WE OCCUPY HALAFA VILLAGE. SOON, A RELIEF FORCE WILL TAKE POSSESSION. ALREADY IT IS OVERDUE.
SHAME YOU WON'T HAVE IT LONG. OUR BLOKES WILL SOON BE ADVANCING.
NOW NOW, MY FRIEND. FOR YOU THE WAR IS ALREADY OVER, NO?

TO MULLER, THE ENEMY WAS THE ENEMY. IT WAS THAT SIMPLE. AND WHEN ONE OF THE ENEMY WAS A HATED FOE, HE COULD NOT BEAR TO SEE CHIVALRY EXTENDED.

I SEEM TO RECALL SAYING THAT THE WAR WAS OVER FOR YOU, GINO. AND LOOK WHAT HAPPENED. WHO KNOWS, I MAY DO THE SAME!

IF YOU GET THE CHANCE, JUMBO. AH, HERE IS OUR OLD FRIEND, HANS MULLER.

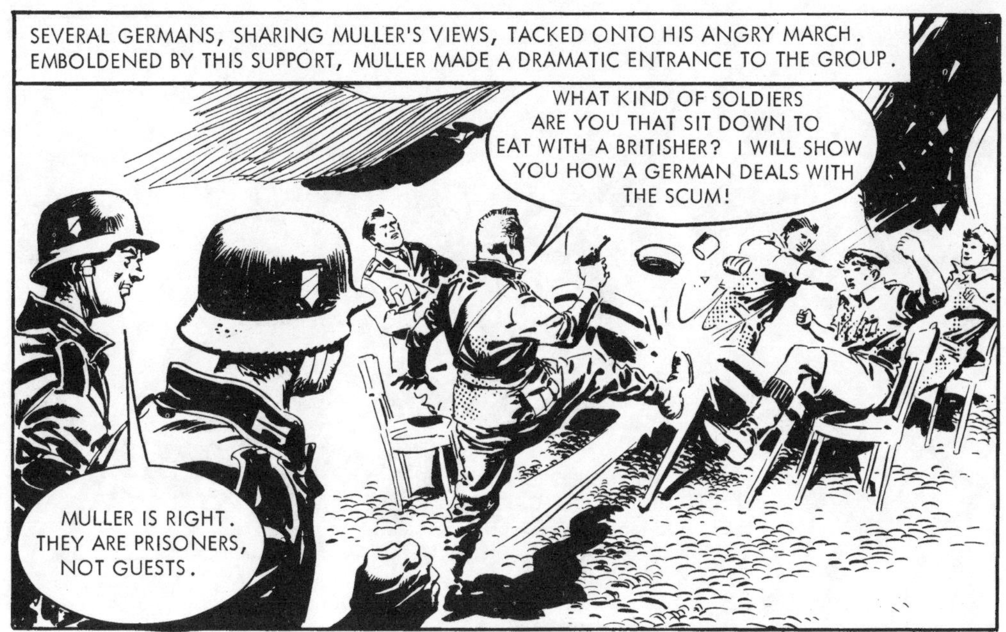
SEVERAL GERMANS, SHARING MULLER'S VIEWS, TACKED ONTO HIS ANGRY MARCH. EMBOLDENED BY THIS SUPPORT, MULLER MADE A DRAMATIC ENTRANCE TO THE GROUP.
WHAT KIND OF SOLDIERS ARE YOU THAT SIT DOWN TO EAT WITH A BRITISHER? I WILL SHOW YOU HOW A GERMAN DEALS WITH THE SCUM!
MULLER IS RIGHT. THEY ARE PRISONERS, NOT GUESTS.

MULLER WAS CRAZY WITH FURY AT THIS CALM ENGLISHMAN AND SMILING ITALIAN WHO FOR YEARS HAD TAUNTED HIM.

GET UP, ROGAN! OUT OF THAT CHAIR!
I MUST REMIND YOU, CAPTAIN MULLER, THAT LIEUTENANT ROGAN IS MY PRISONER. I WOULD ALSO ADVISE YOU TO LOOK BEHIND YOU.

ITALIAN SOLDIERS HAD APPEARED AS IF BY MAGIC. ONE WORD FROM GINO AND MULLER WOULD BE SHOT LIKE A DOG.
THE STRAIN YOUR ORDEAL IMPOSED UPON YOU, CAPTAIN MULLER, HAS MADE YOU A LITTLE EXCITED. SURELY A REST WOULD BE A GOOD IDEA?
SCOWLING, MULLER WHIRLED AND STALKED AWAY.
ONE DAY — ONE DAY I WILL HAVE MY REVENGE ON THOSE TWO.
A FEW MINUTES LATER THERE WAS ANOTHER INTERRUPTION AT THE TABLE, THIS TIME BY A YOUNG BATTLE-STAINED OFFICER.
STRONG BRITISH FORCES HAVE COUNTER-ATTACKED ALL ALONG THE LINES. THEY ARE HEADING THIS WAY. THERE WERE REPORTS OF STRONG ENEMY AIR ACTIVITY. THE RELIEVING FORCE HAS BEEN WIPED OUT.

ONCE AGAIN WAR THRUST ITSELF BETWEEN THE TWO FRIENDS. JUMBO WAS TO GO WITH THE REST OF THE BRITISH PRISONERS TO A CAMP WELL BEHIND THE FRONT.
GOODBYE, JUMBO. WE HAVE WORK TO DO HERE. AT LEAST YOU WILL BE OUT OF THE FIRING LINE.
WELL, I CAN'T WISH YOUR LOT LUCK, BUT I HOPE YOU COME OUT OF THIS OK.

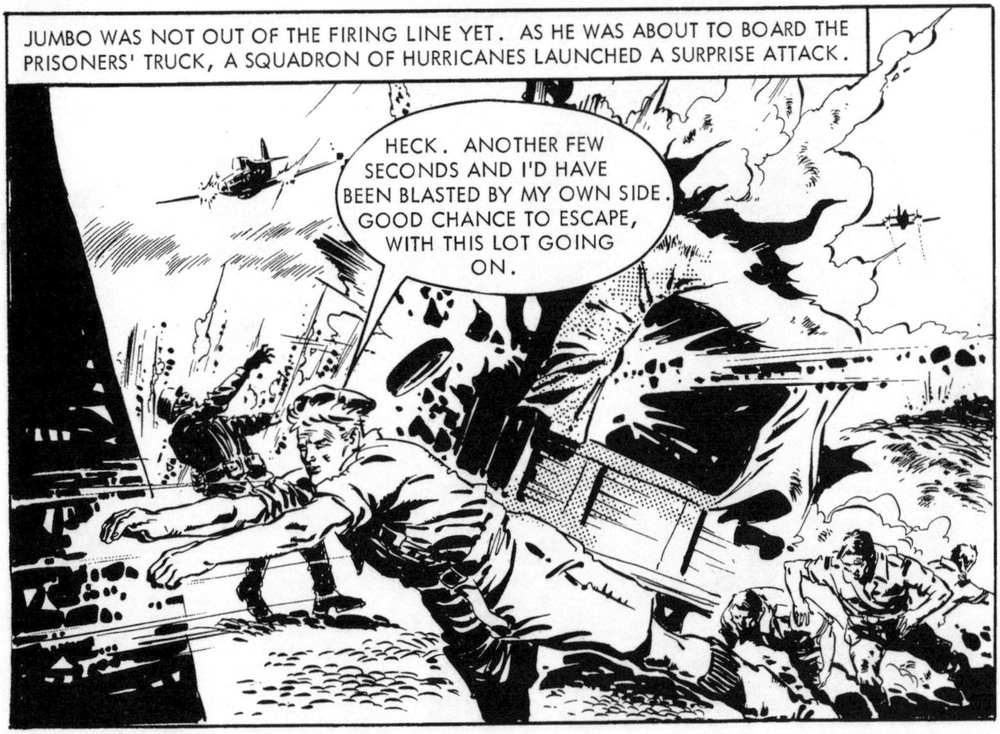

JUMBO WAS NOT OUT OF THE FIRING LINE YET. AS HE WAS ABOUT TO BOARD THE PRISONERS' TRUCK, A SQUADRON OF HURRICANES LAUNCHED A SURPRISE ATTACK.

HECK. ANOTHER FEW SECONDS AND I'D HAVE BEEN BLASTED BY MY OWN SIDE. GOOD CHANCE TO ESCAPE, WITH THIS LOT GOING ON.

HANS MULLER ALSO REALISED THAT, IN THIS BEDLAM, IT WOULD BE A GOOD CHANCE FOR THE BRITISH TO RUN FOR IT.
LOOK OUT, SCHMIDT, THAT CURSED BRITISH FIGHTER. IN HERE, QUICKLY!
IT'S SPOTTED US. I—AAAH!

JUMBO MADE A DASH FOR A GERMAN STAFF CAR, BUT HIS DESPERATE BID FOR FREEDOM WAS SPOTTED BY MULLER.

YOU WILL NOT GET FAR, ROGAN.

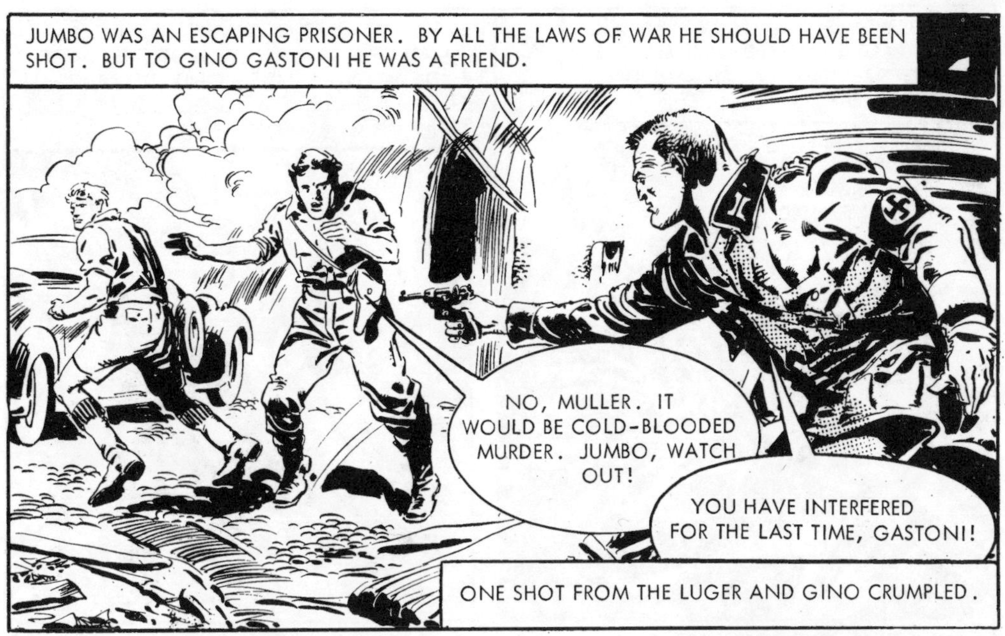
JUMBO WAS AN ESCAPING PRISONER. BY ALL THE LAWS OF WAR HE SHOULD HAVE BEEN SHOT. BUT TO GINO GASTONI HE WAS A FRIEND.
NO, MULLER. IT WOULD BE COLD-BLOODED MURDER. JUMBO, WATCH OUT!
YOU HAVE INTERFERED FOR THE LAST TIME, GASTONI!
ONE SHOT FROM THE LUGER AND GINO CRUMPLED.

WITH A SHOUT OF EVIL EXULTATION, MULLER SAW BOTH ENEMIES FALL TO HIS FLAMING WEAPON.

SO DIE ALL WHO CROSS THE PATH OF HANS MULLER.

THE HURRICANES HAD GONE, LEAVING THE VILLAGE SHATTERED. MULLER KNEW THAT BEFORE LONG BRITISH ARMOUR WOULD APPEAR.
THIS VILLAGE CANNOT BE HELD NOW. I MUST ESCAPE.

BUT MULLER HAD NOT EVEN HIT JUMBO. HE HAD HEARD GINO'S CRY OF PROTEST AND HAD FALLEN A SPLIT SECOND BEFORE MULLER FIRED. NOW HE REACHED FOR AN ABANDONED SCHMEISSER.

TO HIT HIM NOW WOULD TAKE ONE HECK OF A SHOT.

SUMMONING UP EVERY OUNCE OF CONCENTRATION, JUMBO AIMED AFTER THE FLEEING NAZI.

STEADY, JUMBO, OLD LAD. JUST LIKE BISLEY, NICE AND GENTLE SQUEEZE.

MULLER GRUNTED IN SHOCKED SURPRISE AS THE BULLET STRUCK HIM.
AS HIS HANDS LOST CONTROL OF THE WHEEL THE CAR CAME ROUND IN A WIDE CIRCLE AND HEADED BACK TO THE VILLAGE.

WHETHER JUMBO'S SHOT HAD BEEN A MORTAL ONE HE WOULD NEVER KNOW, FOR HANS MULLER AND THE CAR STRUCK A MINE.

TO JUMBO'S GREAT RELIEF, HIS FRIEND WAS NOT TO DIE BY MULLER'S BULLET. WHEN A BRITISH FORCE RE-ENTERED HALAFA GINO HAD RECOVERED ENOUGH TO MANAGE A WEAK GRIN.
MULLER IS FINISHED? DID YOU SHOOT HIM?
YES, BUT WHETHER I HURT HIM BADLY ENOUGH TO KILL HIM, I'LL NEVER KNOW. HE HIT A MINE.

GINO RECOVERED, AND WHEN THE ITALIAN PEOPLE GREW TIRED OF DICTATORS AND CAME OVER TO THE ALLIED SIDE, HE WENT INTO THE MOUNTAINS WITH THE GUERILLAS, TO FIGHT THE NAZI TROOPS.

SOON THEY WILL BE SWEPT FROM OUR SOIL, MY FRIENDS.

JUMBO AND HIS CREW SAW MUCH MORE ACTION BEFORE THE LAST GUN FIRED AND THE NAZI MENACE WAS FINALLY DESTROYED. THEN, WITH DUTY DONE, THEY WENT INTO CIVILIAN LIFE, AND PEACE. JUMBO HIRED AND TRAINED A NEW PAIR OF MECHANICS, SAM SPOONER AND TUBBY TRUBSHAW. AND THEY OFTEN MET AN OLD RIVAL OF THE DESERT WAR.

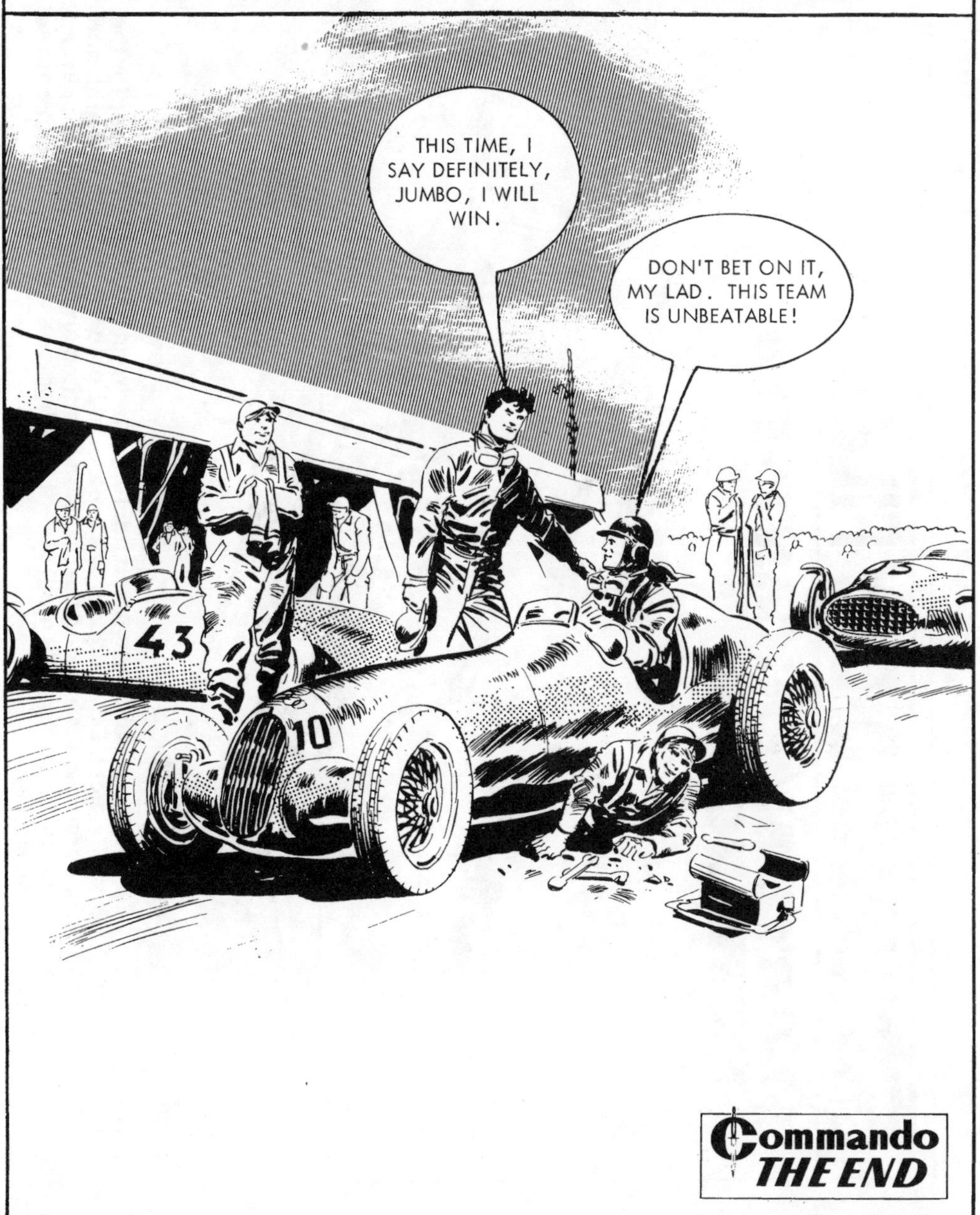
THIS TIME, I SAY DEFINITELY, JUMBO, I WILL WIN.
DON'T BET ON IT, MY LAD. THIS TEAM IS UNBEATABLE!
43
10

Commando
THE END

Commando D-DAY FILE
NORTH AMERICAN P-51B MUSTANG
B7
H
2106 992
On D-Day, 171 different Allied fighter squadrons provided air cover for the invasion fleet. Other squadrons protected bombers of the U.S. Eighth and Ninth Air Forces as they raided the invasion beaches and surrounding communications centres. Mustangs, the most potent U.S. fighters, were involved in both sets of operations.
Kennedy

MUSTANG PATROL

FLIGHT LIEUTENANT ALAN BLAKE GASPED WITH HORROR AS HIS SQUADRON LEADER'S MUSTANG CRASHED INTO THE GROUND AT OVER THREE HUNDRED MILES AN HOUR. AND WHEN HIS FELLOW PILOTS ACCUSED HIM OF CAUSING THAT MUSTANG'S FATAL DIVE, IT BROUGHT FEAR AND DOUBT THAT WOULD HAUNT ALAN THROUGH ALL THE FOLLOWING DOGFIGHTS...

AS THE SUN ROSE ON A SPRING MORNING IN 1942 THREE MUSTANGS RACED ACROSS THE CHANNEL AT LOW LEVEL, SKIMMING THE WAVE-TOPS TO AVOID DETECTION, BOUND FOR THE PORT OF ROCHEAUX.

THE MUSTANG HAD ONLY JUST COME INTO SERVICE WITH THE R. A. F. IT BORE A STRIKING RESEMBLANCE TO THE MESSERSCHMITT 109, AND THE THREE PILOTS WERE RELYING HEAVILY ON THIS SIMILARITY TO HELP THEM IN THEIR MISSION.

RADIO SILENCE WAS IN FORCE, BUT THE PILOTS HAD BEEN WELL BRIEFED. WHEN THE LEADER ROCKED HIS WINGS, FLIGHT LIEUTENANT ALAN BLAKE MOVED INTO POSITION.

THIS RUSE HAD BETTER WORK OR THERE'S GOING TO BE FIREWORKS.

ALAN HAD LEARNED HIS TRADE IN THE BATTLE OF BRITAIN AND THE FIGHTER SWEEPS THAT FOLLOWED. HE HAD TAKEN TO THE NEW AIRCRAFT AT ONCE. SUPERB AT LOW LEVEL, HEAVILY ARMED, THE MUSTANG WAS THE IDEAL GROUND-ATTACK WEAPON.

BUT THEY WERE NOT OUT TO DESTROY ANYTHING THAT DAY. EACH MACHINE CARRIED A CAMERA, WHICH WAS SET IN MOTION AS THE THREE MUSTANGS SWEPT OVER THE PORT IN A PERFECT LINE ABREAST, WATCHED CURIOUSLY BY THE GERMAN GUNNERS BELOW.

ARE THEY MESSERSCHMITTS? THEY'VE GOT THE SQUARE-CUT WINGS.
DIDN'T SEE WHICH DIRECTION THEY CAME FROM, AND THEY JUST SEEM TO BE SHOWING OFF THEIR FORMATION FLYING.

THE ARRIVAL HAD BEEN NEATLY TIMED SO THAT THE NEWLY-RISEN SUN WOULD BE IN THE EYES OF THE DEFENDERS. WITH MILITARY PRECISION, THE THREE MYSTERY AIRCRAFT TURNED AND MADE ANOTHER RUN OVER THE PORT.

WE'VE FOXED THEM PROPERLY. NOT A SHOT FIRED AT US. PITY WE CAN'T HAVE A CRACK AT THEM BEFORE WE GO.

THEIR ORDERS WERE CLEAR-CUT—GET THE PHOTOGRAPHS AND GET OUT FAST. BUT WITH THEIR MISSION COMPLETED ALAN WAS KEEN TO TRY OUT HIS NEW MACHINE IN REAL ACTION.
WELL, NOW. WHAT HAVE WE HERE?

THREE E-BOATS RETURNING FROM A NIGHT'S MARAUDING ON THE COASTAL CONVOY ROUTES WERE ALSO TAKEN IN BY THE MESSERSCHMITT-LIKE SHAPE OF THE THREE FIGHTERS.
WHAT'S THIS ONE UP TO? COMING A BIT LOW, ISN'T HE?
TRYING TO SCARE US. YOU KNOW WHAT THESE LUFTWAFFE TYPES ARE LIKE.
THE TEMPTATION HAD BEEN TOO GREAT FOR ALAN TO RESIST.

ALAN APPROACHED HEAD-ON, SO THAT THE MARKINGS ON HIS AIRCRAFT WERE INVISIBLE TO THE GERMANS. THEIR CURIOSITY TURNED TO ALARM AS HEAVY-CALIBRE BULLETS RIPPED ALONG THE LINE OF BOATS.

SURPRISE, SURPRISE, JERRIES – IT'S YOUR FRIENDLY NEIGHBOURHOOD MUSTANG.

HOLDING HIS FIRE TO THE LAST POSSIBLE MOMENT, ALAN FOUND HIS MARK WITH EVERY SHOT AS HE RAKED THE THREE TORPEDO BOATS FROM STEM TO STERN.

THE ATTACK WAS OVER IN SECONDS. ONE SHORT, MURDEROUS BURST INTO EACH E-BOAT – ALAN NEEDED NO MORE. HE WAS ACKNOWLEDGED AS THE BEST SHOT IN THE SQUADRON.

RED TWO, WHAT THE DEVIL ARE YOU PLAYING AT? REJOIN THE FORMATION.
FTOK

ALAN WINCED AS THE FLAT, TONELESS VOICE OF SQUADRON LEADER OWEN SOUNDED IN HIS HEADPHONES.

BERNARD OWEN WAS KNOWN IN THE SQUADRON AS "THE ZOMBIE". LIKE HIS VOICE, HIS FACE WAS ALWAYS UTTERLY EXPRESSIONLESS.

JUST TRYING OUT THE GUNS. THOSE POINT FIVES CERTAINLY PACK A WALLOP.

SILENCE. REPORT TO ME AS SOON AS WE LAND.

THE MOMENT THE MUSTANGS HAD COME TO REST, MECHANICS HURRIED TO TAKE OUT THE CAMERAS WITH THEIR VITAL PICTURES.

YOU HEARD THE ORDERS, BLAKE. OUR JOB WAS TO PHOTOGRAPH THE PORT, NOT GO SHOOTING UP E-BOATS. YOU JEOPARDISED THE SUCCESS OF THE WHOLE MISSION.
BUT NO HARM WAS DONE, SIR! I WAS IN AND GONE BEFORE THEY KNEW WHAT HIT THEM. THEY THOUGHT I WAS A MESSERSCHMITT.

EACH MUSTANG'S CAMERA HAD COVERED A SECTOR OF THE HARBOUR. THE THREE SETS OF PRINTS WOULD PROVIDE A DETAILED PHOTOGRAPHIC MAP OF THE AREA.

BUT IF ALAN HAD BEEN SHOT DOWN OR HIS CAMERA DAMAGED, THE MAP WOULD HAVE BEEN INCOMPLETE AND USELESS.

THE WHOLE MISSION WOULD HAVE HAD TO BE REPEATED. AND THANKS TO YOU, JERRY WON'T MISTAKE US FOR THEIR OWN AGAIN. IN FUTURE OBEY ORDERS.

VERY GOOD, SIR.

ALAN COULD NOT TRUST HIMSELF TO SAY MORE. OWEN'S PRECISE SPEECH AND LACK OF EMOTION ALWAYS ROUSED HIS UNEVEN TEMPER.

HE WAS RIGHT, MATE.
YES – HE'S ALWAYS RIGHT. IF ONLY HE'D BLOW HIS TOP ONCE IN A WHILE, INSTEAD OF ACTING LIKE A ROBOT.

THE IMPORTANCE OF THE PHOTO RECONNAISSANCE BECAME CLEAR A DAY LATER. A RAID IN FORCE WAS TO BE MADE ON THE PORT OF ROCHEAUX. MASSIVE AIR SUPPORT WAS NEEDED, AND THE MUSTANGS HAD THEIR PART TO PLAY.

WE ARE TO PATROL THE AREA BEHIND ROCHEAUX, TO WATCH FOR GERMAN REINFORCEMENTS MOVING UP. THESE MUST BE REPORTED IN DETAIL. THEN YOU MAY ATTEMPT TO DESTROY THEM, NOT BEFORE.
HE MAKES IT SOUND LIKE A PARADE GROUND MANOEUVRE.

THE MUSTANGS WERE TO WORK IN PAIRS. ALAN'S WINGMAN WAS PILOT OFFICER ROGER GROOM. FRESH FROM TRAINING, THIS WAS TO BE HIS FIRST COMBAT MISSION.

I'M LOOKING FORWARD TO THIS. MAKE A CHANGE TO SHOOT AT A REAL TARGET.
JUST REMEMBER THE TARGET WILL BE SHOOTING BACK THIS TIME. STAY CLOSE TO ME AND DO AS I TELL YOU.

AS THE MUSTANGS ARRIVED OVER ROCHEAUX THE FIRST LANDING CRAFT WERE BEACHING IN THE FACE OF HEAVY FIRE.

LOOK AT THOSE TYPHOONS GETTING STUCK IN. WISH WE COULD JOIN THEM.
DON'T WORRY, WE'LL FIND PLENTY TO DO FURTHER INLAND.

THE MUSTANGS SPLIT UP AND HEADED FOR THEIR ALLOTTED SECTORS, IN TIME TO SEE THAT THE GERMANS HAD WASTED NO TIME IN RUSHING REINFORCEMENTS TO THE THREATENED PORT.

OVER THERE, INFANTRY GUNS! HERE WE GO.
HOLD ON, HOLD ON! HAWKEYE RED TWO TO JIGSAW. SIX LIGHT INFANTRY GUNS MOVING WEST, MAP SQUARE SEVEN. RIGHT, NOW LET'S GO.

THE HORSE TEAMS LOOKED STRANGELY OUT OF PLACE, BUT THE INFANTRY GUNS THEY PULLED COULD WREAK CONSIDERABLE DAMAGE ON THE CROWDED BEACHES.

HARDLY SEEMS FAIR TO SHOOT UP THOSE NAGS. IT'S NOT THEIR WAR.
THEY'RE KICKING UP THEIR HEELS ALREADY. LET'S REALLY GET THEM GOING.

THE HORSES WHINNIED AND REARED IN TERROR AS THE TWO WINGED MONSTERS HURTLED DOWN ON THEM. NOT A SHOT WAS FIRED – THE NOISE WAS ENOUGH.
WHOA, WHOA!
IN SECONDS THE ROAD WAS A SHAMBLES OF PLUNGING, PANIC-STRICKEN HORSES, OVERTURNED GUNS AND CURSING MEN.

GRINNING AT THE FISTS SHAKEN AT THEM, ALAN AND GROOM CLIMBED AWAY, THEIR EYES SEARCHING THE ROLLING COUNTRYSIDE. TWENTY MINUTES LATER A MORE FORMIDABLE TARGET APPEARED.

SIX HALF-TRACKS TOWING FIELD GUNS, ESCORTED BY ONE ARMOURED CAR. OVER AND OUT.

THAT ARMOURED CAR'S ON THE BALL. IF WE GO TO THE OTHER END OF THE COLUMN, WHERE HE CAN'T GET AT US...

BUT THE CAR COMMANDER KNEW HIS JOB. HE MOVED HIS VEHICLE UP AND DOWN THE COLUMN AT HIGH SPEED, AND NO MATTER FROM WHICH ANGLE THE MUSTANGS APPROACHED, THEY WERE MET BY DISTURBINGLY ACCURATE FIRE.
HE'S A PERSISTENT BLIGHTER. OUR BULLETS JUST BOUNCE OFF HIM.
NOT ALL OF HIM. STAY CLEAR, I'LL HANDLE THIS.

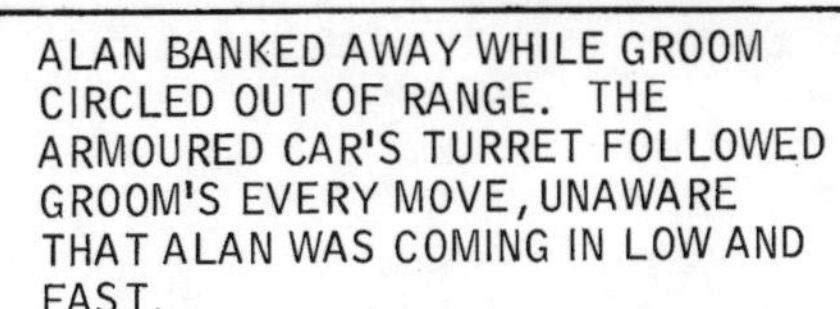
ALAN BANKED AWAY WHILE GROOM CIRCLED OUT OF RANGE. THE ARMOURED CAR'S TURRET FOLLOWED GROOM'S EVERY MOVE, UNAWARE THAT ALAN WAS COMING IN LOW AND FAST.

THIS SHOULD DO IT!

ALAN'S SUPERBLY AIMED BURST TORE THE CAR TYRES TO RIBBONS.
BULL'S-EYE! OK, RED TWO, TAKE YOUR PICK.

THE CRIPPLED ARMOURED CAR STILL SPAT DEFIANCE AT THE MUSTANGS, BUT NOW THEY COULD EASILY AVOID ITS FIRE.
EVERYBODY SEEMS TO BE SHAKING THEIR FISTS AT US TODAY.
SO WOULD I, IF I WERE HIM. I NEVER SAW SUCH SHOOTING.

A LITTLE LATER THE EXPECTED RECALL SIGNAL CAME, AND THEY HEADED FOR THE RENDEZVOUS POINT. BUT THE LANDING HAD BEEN A COSTLY FAILURE, AND THE ROCHEAUX BEACHES WERE A TERRIFYING SIGHT.
LOOKS LIKE THINGS HAVE COME UNSTUCK.

WHAT THE RECONNAISSANCE PHOTOGRAPHS HAD NOT SHOWN WAS THAT EVERY HOUSE FACING THE SEA HAD BEEN FORTIFIED AND NOW BRISTLED WITH GUNS. UNDER THIS MURDEROUS FIRE THE ASSAULT TROOPS WERE RETREATING TO THE FEW SURVIVING LANDING CRAFT. OWEN'S VOICE DRONED OUT FRESH ORDERS.

WE WILL MAKE ONE STRAFING RUN AT THE GERMAN POSITIONS, BY SECTIONS. MAKE EVERY SHOT COUNT.

TWO BY TWO, THE MUSTANGS RAKED THE FORTIFIED HOUSES. THE GERMANS HAD PLENTY OF GUNS TO SPARE, AND A CURTAIN OF FIRE AND STEEL SLASHED UP.

AT LEAST, WHAT THEY THROW AT US, THEY AREN'T USING ON THE POOR BLIGHTERS ON THE BEACH. HEY, WHERE ARE YOU GOING, GROOM?
WE'LL BE CUT TO RIBBONS!

ALAN KNEW THAT OWEN'S MAIN IDEA HAD BEEN TO DRAW SOME OF THE FIRE AWAY FROM THE BEACH, TO GIVE THE COMMANDOS A FEW MINUTES' RESPITE. BUT THE STORM OF TRACER WAS TOO MUCH FOR THE UNTRIED GROOM.

NOTHING CAN LIVE IN THAT SORT OF FIRE!
RUBBISH! YOU'RE MOVING AT OVER THREE HUNDRED MILES AN HOUR. SO DON'T LET THE FLAK SCARE YOU. YOU'LL SOON GET USED TO IT.

GROOM WAS STILL BADLY SHAKEN WHEN THE MUSTANGS LANDED AT THEIR BASE. BUT HIS ORDEAL WAS NOT OVER – HE STILL HAD TO FACE THE COLD EYES OF SQUADRON LEADER OWEN.

ONE SQUIRT OF FLAK AND YOU RUN LIKE A RABBIT. THERE IS NO ROOM FOR COWARDS ON THIS SQUADRON.
I...I'M SORRY SIR. ALL THAT TRACER COMING UP, IT JUST THREW ME FOR A MOMENT.
AH, HAVE A HEART...

WHEN I WANT YOUR ADVICE, BLAKE, I'LL ASK. NOW PULL YOURSELF TOGETHER, GROOM. OUR JOB IS TO FIGHT, NOT RUN AWAY.

WITHOUT ANOTHER WORD, OWEN WALKED AWAY, LEAVING GROOM BITTERLY DETERMINED.
A COWARD, EH? JUST WAIT...
LOOK, HE ALWAYS JUMPS ON NEWCOMERS. HE'S TOUGH... BUT HE NEVER ASKS US TO DO ANYTHING HE CAN'T DO HIMSELF.
THOUGH NO ONE LIKED OWEN, THEY ALL RESPECTED HIM.

BUT GROOM FELT BADLY ABOUT IT ALL, AND WITH THE MUSTANG MORE THAN ADEQUATELY PROVING ITS CAPABILITIES THE SQUADRON WAS SOON KEPT BUSY.
WONDER WHAT'S BREWING UP NOW? THE MECHANICS HAVE BEEN TREATING THOSE PLANES LIKE THEY WERE SICK BABIES.
SOMETHING NASTY FOR THE HUNS, I'LL WAGER – LONG-RANGE OP, PROBABLY. WE'LL FIND OUT AT THE BRIEFING.

ALAN WAS PROVED RIGHT. THE GERMANS, WELL KNOWING THE SHORT RANGE OF THE SPITFIRES AND HURRICANES USED AS ESCORTS, KEPT THEIR OWN FIGHTERS ON THE GROUND UNTIL THE ESCORTS TURNED BACK, THEN THEY CUT THE BOMBERS TO PIECES.

THE MUSTANG, AS YOU MAY KNOW, HAS A CONSIDERABLE INTERNAL FUEL CAPACITY AND A RANGE OF CLOSE ON A THOUSAND MILES. SO WE ARE TO ESCORT A BOSTON SQUADRON ON A DAYLIGHT RAID, TO BOMB THE RANZBURG-KERSTEL CANAL.

THE R. A. F. HAD GIVEN UP DAYLIGHT RAIDS ON GERMANY DUE TO HEAVY LOSSES BUT THIS WATERWAY WAS VITAL TO THE GERMAN WAR EFFORT, CARRYING COAL AND STEEL FROM THEIR INDUSTRIAL AREAS. MOST VULNERABLE WERE THE LOCKS, BUT THESE WERE SMALL TARGETS, DIFFICULT TO HIT IN DARKNESS.

THE PRIME TARGET IS THE BIG LOCK LINKING THE CANAL WITH THE KERSTEL RIVER. IT IS KNOWN TO BE HEAVILY DEFENDED. BLAKE AND MAYNARD, YOUR FLIGHTS WILL BE RESPONSIBLE FOR KNOCKING OUT THE ANTI-AIRCRAFT GUNS.
NOW YOU'LL BE ABLE TO GET YOUR OWN BACK ON THE FLAK.

AT THE FIRST STREAK OF DAWN, THE MUSTANG ENGINES CRACKLED INTO LIFE. ALAN HAD KEPT GROOM AS HIS WINGMAN, FOR HE HAD TAKEN A LIKING TO HIM.

YOU KNOW THE DRILL BY NOW. STAY CLOSE AND MAKE EVERY SHOT TELL.
DON'T WORRY, I KNOW WHAT TO DO.

ALAN EYED GROOM'S SET FACE UNEASILY, KNOWING THAT OWEN'S ACCUSATION STILL RANKLED.

THE MUSTANGS TOOK OFF, AND JOINING UP WITH THE TRIM BOSTONS, SET COURSE ACROSS THE NORTH SEA.

HURRAH FOR THE R.A.F.!

THEY MADE A BRAVE SIGHT AS THEY THUNDERED ACROSS OCCUPIED HOLLAND, THE MORNING SUN GLINTING ON THEIR WINGS. DUTCH PEOPLE, BOWED BUT UNBROKEN UNDER THE NAZI YOKE, LOOKED UP AND TOOK HEART.

NO FIGHTERS ROSE TO CHALLENGE THEM, FOR THE GERMANS WERE CONFIDENTLY WAITING FOR THE ESCORT TO TURN BACK, LEAVING THE BOMBERS AT THEIR MERCY. BUT THE MUSTANGS DID NOT TURN BACK.

THERE'S THE KERSTEL RIVER, AND THERE'S THE SIGNAL.

TWO FLIGHTS OF MUSTANGS FORGED AHEAD OF THE MAIN FORMATION, FOLLOWING THE RIVER BELOW. THE CANAL WITH ITS GREAT LOCK GATES SOON CAME INTO VIEW.

GET IN AND OUT QUICKLY, THE BOMBERS ARE ONLY MINUTES BEHIND US. THEN STAY HIGH, JERRY'LL BE HERE SOON.

THE MUSTANGS FLUNG THEMSELVES AT THE GUN EMPLACEMENTS, THEIR GUNS SPITTING HEAVY-CALIBRE BULLETS. ROGER GROOM TORE IN WITH A FEROCITY THAT FRIGHTENED ALAN.

STEADY ON, RED TWO. SAVE SOME AMMO FOR THE TRIP HOME.
NO! I'LL SHOW OWEN AND THE REST OF YOU THAT I'M NO COWARD!

UP AND DOWN OVER THE LOCK RAGED GROOM, SHOOTING AT EVERYTHING IN SIGHT IN A FRENZY OF HATE.

BANDITS, BUT THEY'VE LEFT IT JUST TOO LATE. HERE, WHERE ARE YOU GOING, RED TWO?
THERE'S ONE GUN STILL FIRING. MUSTN'T HAVE OWEN SAYING WE MESSED UP OUR JOB.

THE LONE MUSTANG SWOOPED EARTHWARDS OVER THE CANAL, TO HAMMER AT THE SURVIVING GUN. BUT GROOM HAD CROSSED THE PATH OF THE APPROACHING BOSTONS... JUST AS THEIR BOMBS BEGAN TO RAIN DOWN.

RED TWO, GET OUT OF THERE. HAVE YOU GONE CRAZY?
TS
M

HEART IN MOUTH, ALAN WATCHED AS THE DEADLY MISSILES SMASHED DOWN AROUND THE MUSTANG.

GROOM BEGAN TO TURN AWAY TOO LATE...

AAGH!

...A BOMB HAD STRUCK FULL ON THE GUN EMPLACEMENT, TOUCHING OFF THE AMMUNITION. THE COMBINED BLAST HAD BEEN ENOUGH TO TEAR THE MUSTANG ASUNDER.

THEN OWEN'S CALM VOICE ORDERED THEM TO WITHDRAW. ALAN YELLED ANGRILY –

YOU KILLED GROOM AS SURELY AS IF YOU'D PULLED THE TRIGGER – CALLING HIM A COWARD IN FRONT OF EVERY-BODY.

OWEN MADE NO ANSWER AND ALAN WAITED UNTIL THEY WERE BACK AT BASE AFTER DODGING GERMAN FIGHTERS BEFORE HE SAID ANY MORE.
GROOM WANTED TO PROVE HIMSELF AND NOW HE'S DEAD! YET YOU TAKE NO MORE NOTICE THAN IF A BUTTON HAD COME OFF YOUR TUNIC.
YOU TOLD PILOT OFFICER GROOM TO GET CLEAR WHEN THE BOMBERS ARRIVED. HE DISOBEYED ORDERS AND HAS PAID FOR IT. THERE IS NOTHING MORE TO BE SAID.
OWEN TURNED ON HIS HEEL AND STRODE AWAY, LEAVING ALAN SEETHING WITH RAGE AT THIS COLD DISMISSAL.

FOR THE REST OF THAT DAY ALAN BROODED OVER HIS FRIEND'S DEATH. THE MORE HE THOUGHT ABOUT IT, THE BLACKER HIS MOOD BECAME. SUDDENLY HE CAME TO A DECISION.
I'M GOING TO HAVE IT OUT WITH OWEN. IT'S MEN HE'S COMMANDING, NOT MACHINES.
STEADY, MAN, DON'T GO THUMPING HIM AND GETTING YOURSELF COURT-MARTIALLED. IT WON'T BRING ROGER BACK...

ALAN SHOOK OFF THE RESTRAINING HAND AND STAMPED TO OWEN'S ROOM. HE FLUNG OPEN THE DOOR, THEN STOPPED DEAD IN HIS TRACKS.
I WAS EXPECTING YOU SOONER OR LATER. COME IN AND SIT DOWN. I'M AFRAID THIS IS THE HARD PART OF COMMAND – WRITING TO THE FAMILY OF A MAN I SENT TO HIS DEATH.
ER... YES, SIR.
OWEN'S FACE WAS NO LONGER BLANK. IT REVEALED A MAN TORTURED BY GRIEF AND REMORSE. THE VOICE THAT SPOKE NOW WAS HUSKY WITH EMOTION. TAKEN ABACK BY THIS TRANSFORMATION, ALAN COULD ONLY OBEY DUMBLY.

YOU WERE RIGHT. I PUSHED GROOM TOO FAR. I'VE ALWAYS CRACKED DOWN ON ANY SIGN OF WEAKNESS, BUT THIS TIME I MISJUDGED MY MAN. BUT THAT'S NO COMFORT TO GROOM'S PARENTS.

I'M NO MONSTER. IT'S ALL AN ACT, NECESSARY IF I'M TO RUN THIS SQUADRON WELL. POPULARITY IS NO SUBSTITUTE FOR RESPECT.
YOU HAVE THAT, BUT MAYBE IF YOU COULD MIX WITH US MORE...

OWEN SHOOK HIS HEAD WEARILY.

NO, I'M
TOO FRIENDLY.
I HAVE TO GO TO
THE OTHER EXTREME
– TO GET MY ORDERS
OBEYED WITHOUT
QUESTION.
I FEEL
ABOUT TWO INCHES
HIGH, SIR. I OWE YOU
AN APOLOGY.

SHUT IN BEHIND THE BARRIER OF COLD INDIFFERENCE WAS A SENSITIVE MAN.

IT'S HELPED
TO TALK TONIGHT,
BUT NO ONE MUST EVER
HEAR OF THIS.
MY WORD
OF HONOUR,
SIR.

ALAN LEFT OWEN WITH A GREAT ADMIRATION FOR THE MAN. HE STOOD FOR SOME TIME IN THE CORRIDOR COMPOSING HIS THOUGHTS. THEN REMEMBERING HIS PROMISE TO THE LONELY OWEN, HE WALKED BACK TO THE MESS, HIS FACE BLACK AS THUNDER.

WHAT
HAPPENED? DID
YOU TELL HIM WHAT
YOU THOUGHT
OF HIM?
DIDN'T GET
THE CHANCE. HE JUST
SAT THERE WITH THAT BLANK
FACE OF HIS, TORE ME OFF SEVERAL
STRIPS THEN TOLD ME TO GET
OUT. I'LL FIX HIM ONE DAY,
THOUGH.

NOT LONG AFTER, OWEN'S SQUADRON WAS GIVEN THE TASK OF DESTROYING GERMAN RADAR STATIONS BEING BUILT ALONG THE FRENCH COASTS, USING THE NEW FIGHTER-BOMBER VERSION OF THE MUSTANG.

IF THERE'S PLENTY OF FLAK, THIS IS GOING TO BE STICKY.
THIS DARKNESS WILL HIDE US UNTIL WE'RE ALMOST OVER THEM, THOUGH.

FOR SMALL, ISOLATED TARGETS, THE FIGHTER-BOMBER WAS COMING INTO ITS OWN. AND WITH TWO BOMBS TO BACK UP ITS HEAVY ARMAMENT THE NEW MUSTANG WAS IDEAL FOR THE TASK.

NEARING THEIR TARGET, THE TWO LEADING FLIGHTS OPENED THEIR THROTTLES AND RACED AHEAD, WHILE THE REMAINDER OF THE MUSTANGS BEGAN TO GAIN HEIGHT.

RIGHT ON TARGET!
FT

THE GERMAN GUNNERS, YAWNING AND THINKING OF BREAKFAST, GOT THE SHOCK OF THEIR LIVES AS EIGHT MUSTANGS ERUPTED OUT OF THE SEMI-DARKNESS TO THE WEST. GUNS BLAZED AND BOMBS SHRIEKED DOWN.

HALF THE ANTI-AIRCRAFT GUNS WERE KNOCKED OUT IN THAT SAVAGE ATTACK, BUT THE SURVIVORS STILL HURLED DEFIANCE AT THE OTHER MUSTANGS AS THEY SWOOPED ON THE RADAR STATION.

REFORM, AND GO FOR THE GUNS AGAIN. MAKE THEM KEEP THEIR HEADS DOWN TO GIVE THE OTHERS A CLEAR RUN.

AS THEY TORE IN AGAIN, ALAN FOUND HIMSELF DIRECTLY BEHIND OWEN. THUMB ON THE GUN BUTTON, HE WAITED FOR THE SQUADRON LEADER TO PULL AWAY.

COME ON, SKIPPER, MOVE OVER. ANOTHER GUN'S STILL FIRING. WE'LL DEAL WITH HIM IN A MINUTE.

THEN IT HAPPENED. ONE STRAY BULLET PUNCHED THROUGH AND STRUCK THE CONTROL COLUMN, JERKING IT BACK IN ALAN'S HANDS AND CAUSING HIM TO OPEN FIRE ACCIDENTALLY ON OWEN'S KITE.

WHAT THE DEVIL... OH, NO!

NUMB WITH HORROR, ALAN WAITED FOR OWEN TO PULL OUT. BUT THE MUSTANG HURTLED INTO THE GROUND AT OVER THREE HUNDRED MILES AN HOUR.

YOU SHOT HIM DOWN – I SAW IT!
IT WAS AN ACCIDENT... ONLY A COUPLE OF SHOTS. I COULDN'T HAVE...

BACK AT BASE ALAN FACED THE ACCUSING EYES OF THE WHOLE SQUADRON.
HERE'S WHERE THE BULLET WENT IN. IT NICKED THE CONTROL COLUMN AND JABBED MY THUMB ON THE FIRING BUTTON. GOOD HEAVENS, I ONLY FIRED A COUPLE OF ROUNDS...
THAT'S ALL A CRACK-SHOT LIKE YOU WOULD NEED, MURDERER!

ALAN REALISED HE HAD OVERDONE THINGS WITH HIS STORY OF THE INTERVIEW WITH OWEN. THIS, COMING ON TOP OF HIS OUTBURST AFTER GROOM'S DEATH, SEEMED EVIDENCE ENOUGH OF DELIBERATE MURDER.
BE SENSIBLE, THERE WAS FLAK HOSING UP FROM THE GROUND. HE FLEW RIGHT INTO IT...
OH, DON'T WORRY, THERE'S NO PROOF THAT WOULD STAND UP AT A COURT-MARTIAL. A VERY CLEVER PIECE OF WORK, BLAKE.

FROM THEN ON, ALAN WAS SHUNNED LIKE THE PLAGUE. TO MAKE MATTERS WORSE, AS SENIOR FLIGHT COMMANDER HE HAD TO TAKE OVER UNTIL A NEW C. O. WAS APPOINTED. AND THE RAIDS ON THE RADAR STATIONS HAD TO CONTINUE...

COME ON, FORM UP. GET A MOVE ON!
FT O J

THE PILOTS OBEYED SLOWLY, SULLENLY – ALL THE CRISP EFFICIENCY THAT HAD MARKED OWEN'S COMMAND WAS GONE. SOMEHOW ALAN GOT THEM IN FORMATION AND ON COURSE FOR FRANCE.

LOOK AT THOSE BANDITS. SEEMS WE'RE EX-PECTED.
WITH ALL THE CHATTER ON THE RADIO, WHAT DID YOU EXPECT? THEY HEARD US COMING!

THERE WAS NOTHING FOR IT BUT TO JETTISON THEIR BOMBS AND MEET THE CHALLENGE OF THE MESSERSCHMITTS.

HE NEARLY HAD ME. WHERE THE BLAZES IS MY WINGMAN?

ALAN'S NUMBER TWO SHOULD HAVE BEEN GUARDING HIS TAIL, BUT HE WAS NOWHERE TO BE SEEN.

RED TWO, THIS IS RED LEADER. WHERE...WHAT THE DEVIL?

WRENCHING HIS MUSTANG OUT OF THE PATH OF THE BULLETS SNARLING PAST, ALAN SLAMMED THE PLANE ROUND IN A TIGHT TURN.

WHICH ONE FIRED? THE JERRY OR MY WING-MAN?

THIS WAS THE LAST STRAW. FOR THOUGH ALAN'S REPORT ON OWEN'S DEATH HAD BEEN ACCEPTED BY HIGH COMMAND, THE SQUADRON'S STORY WAS COMMON KNOWLEDGE AMONG MANY PILOTS. ALAN REQUESTED AN INTERVIEW WITH HIS GROUP COMMANDER.

SOMEBODY SHOT AT YOU? COME NOW, BLAKE, YOU'RE LETTING YOUR IMAGINATION RUN AWAY WITH YOU. GIVE THE LADS TIME, THEY'LL SETTLE DOWN.
NOT WITH ME AROUND. I'D LIKE A TRANSFER, SIR – AS FAR AWAY AS POSSIBLE!

THE SENIOR OFFICER COULD SEE THAT ALAN WAS ON THE VERGE OF A BREAKDOWN, AND HE TOO HAD HEARD THE WHISPERED RUMOURS.

I'LL SEE WHAT I CAN DO. A PITY – I WAS THINKING OF GIVING YOU THAT SQUADRON. YOU WON'T RE-CONSIDER...
NO, SIR. JUST SEND ME SOME PLACE WHERE I ONLY HAVE TO WATCH THE JERRIES TO STAY ALIVE.

SO ALAN FOUND HIMSELF IN NORTH AFRICA, AT A DUSTY AIRFIELD IN THE LIBYAN DESERT...

YOU'RE A SENIOR FLIGHT LIEUTENANT, ELIGIBLE FOR A SQUADRON COMMAND. WHY CHUCK IT ALL UP AND COME OUT HERE?

LET'S SAY I NEEDED A CHANGE OF SCENERY.

SQUADRON LEADER PHIL CONWAY LOOKED SHARPLY AT ALAN, WHO MET HIS GAZE STEADILY. THEN CONWAY SHRUGGED HIS SHOULDERS. HE COULD USE A FULLY-TRAINED GROUND-ATTACK PILOT.

YOU KNOW YOUR OWN BUSINESS BEST. BUT YOU'LL HAVE TO START AT THE BOTTOM AGAIN, THOUGH YOU SHOULD REALLY LEAD A FLIGHT. THE SET-UP IS ENTIRELY DIFFERENT HERE.
I REALISE THAT, SIR. CAN I HAVE A LOOK AT MY KITE?

THIS SQUADRON FLEW HURRICANE "TANK BUSTERS", WHICH CARRIED TWO 40mm CANNON, CAPABLE OF PUNCHING A HOLE IN THE THICKEST ARMOUR.
JUST LIKE OLD TIMES. I FLEW THE HURRICANE BACK IN NINETEEN-FORTY. GOOD STURDY OLD BUS.
SHE'S THAT ALL RIGHT. BUT THIS MODEL IS LOADED DOWN WITH THOSE TWO THUMPING GREAT CANNON AND EXTRA ARMOUR PLATE. SO DON'T GET CAUGHT BY A MESSERSCHMITT, OR YOU'LL BE A DEAD DUCK.

BUT ALAN QUICKLY LEARNED HIS NEW TRADE, FOR THE SQUADRON WAS OUT EVERY DAY HOUNDING THE RETREATING GERMAN FORCES.
WOW! WHAT A WALLOP THIS THING PACKS.

OUT THERE IN THE DESERT, LIVING LIKE GIPSIES, THERE WAS NO TIME FOR SPIT AND POLISH. ALAN ENJOYED THIS FREE AND EASY ATMOSPHERE AND HIS MARKSMANSHIP DID NOT GO UNNOTICED.
YOU'RE CERTAINLY PILING UP A SCORE, ALAN. HOW DO YOU DO IT... FIRE WHEN YOU SEE THE WHITES OF THEIR EYES?
WITH THESE GUNS AND TARGETS THE SIZE OF A HOUSE, I CAN HARDLY MISS!

REALISING HIS SKILL, ALAN'S FLIGHT COMMANDER TOOK HIM AS HIS WINGMAN.
KEEP HAMMERING HIM. I'LL GET THAT TANK.

THE FLIGHT COMMANDER MOVED ALONGSIDE, EDGING OVER TO BRING HIS SIGHTS TO BEAR ON THE GERMAN TANK. TO HIS AMAZEMENT ALAN SWERVED AWAY WILDLY.
WHAT'S BITING YOU?
AFTER THE DEATH OF OWEN, ALAN HAD BEEN TERRIFIED OF ANY AIRCRAFT COMING ANYWHERE NEAR HIS GUNS.

SORRY, SIR. I JUST DON'T LIKE ANYBODY GETTING IN MY WAY.
THINK I WAS GOING TO BASH INTO YOU? NO FEAR OF THAT.

AFTER THAT, CONWAY NOTICED THAT IF EVER ANOTHER HURRICANE CAME TOO NEAR, OR AHEAD OF ALAN, HE SHIED AWAY.
WHEN HE'S OUT IN FRONT, HE'LL FLY RIGHT DOWN A TANK'S GUN BARREL. IT'S NOT FLAK THAT SCARES HIM.
IT LOOKS AS IF HE'S AFRAID OF SHOOTING ONE OF OUR OWN CHAPS DOWN. YET HE'S THE BEST MARKSMAN HERE.

AND ALL THIS TIME THE BRITISH ADVANCE ROLLED ON, BUT THE AFRIKA KORPS WERE NOT TAKING DEFEAT EASILY. THEIR RESISTANCE STIFFENED AS FRESH TANKS AND MEN WERE RUSHED TO THE FIRING LINE.
MANY TANKS HAVE BEEN SPOTTED HERE. THAT'S WHY WE'VE ALL BEEN DUG OUT OF BED SO EARLY. WE'LL HIT THEM AT DAWN, BEFORE THEY DISPERSE. WE'LL ATTACK IN WAVES BY FLIGHTS...
OH, NO! THAT'S WHAT WE WERE DOING WHEN OWEN BOUGHT IT...
BUT THERE WAS NO WAY OUT OF IT FOR ALAN. WITH AN ESCORT OF SPITFIRES THE TANK-BUSTERS TOOK OFF IN THE DARK AND SET COURSE ACROSS THE DESERT. WHEN THEY TOOK UP THEIR ATTACK FORMATION, ALAN FOUND HIMSELF IN THE THIRD WAVE.
BANDITS APPROACHING FROM THE EAST.
NICE TO KNOW SOMEBODY ELSE GETS UP EARLY. NEVER MIND THEM, THE SPITS WILL SORT THAT LOT OUT.

THE HURRICANES ROARED OVER THE MASSED RANKS OF TANKS AND ARMOURED CARS, A SOLID PHALANX OF BLAZING GUNS, HURLING JAVELINS OF ARMOUR-PIERCING SHELLS – ALL EXCEPT ALAN.

WHAT'S UP, BLUE TWO? HAVE YOUR GUNS JAMMED?

ALAN SAT RIGID IN HIS SEAT, NOT DARING TO TOUCH HIS FIRING BUTTON. THE HURRICANE WAVE OF DESTRUCTION SWEPT ON, LEAVING A BURNING SHAMBLES IN ITS WAKE. THEN ALAN WENT IN ALONE –

WHERE THE DEVIL ARE YOU OFF TO?
I CAN'T WORK IN A CROWD.

ALAN RACED BACK, PICKING OUT TANKS THAT HAD ESCAPED THE ONSLAUGHT, SLAMMING HIS SHELLS INTO THEM WITH DEADLY ACCURACY.
THIS ONE IS MAD, BUT HE CAN CERTAINLY SHOOT.
HE'S MAD ALL RIGHT. HERE COME TWO MESSERSCHMITTS!

THE SPITFIRES HAD DONE A GOOD JOB HOLDING OFF THE ENEMY FIGHTERS, BUT THEY COULD NOT BE EVERYWHERE AT ONCE, AND A STRAGGLER WAS ALWAYS A FAVOURITE TARGET.
NOW I'VE LANDED MYSELF RIGHT IN THE SOUP. THE VERY THING CONWAY WARNED ME TO AVOID.

ALAN DID HIS BEST TO AVOID THE SLASHING ATTACKS, BUT LOADED DOWN WITH GUNS AND ARMOUR PLATE, THE HURRICANE WAS ABOUT AS AGILE AS A CART-HORSE.
WHAT'S THAT CLOWN DOING ON HIS OWN?
SOME OF THEM NEVER LEARN. QUICK, OR THOSE NAZIS WILL CLOBBER HIM.

THE SPITFIRES DEALT WITH HIS PURSUERS IN SHORT ORDER, AND ALAN HEAVED A SIGH OF RELIEF.
WHEW, THAT WAS CLOSE. I THOUGHT THEY HAD ME.
SERVES YOU RIGHT FOR MUCKING ABOUT. WHAT POSSESSED YOU TO LEAVE THE FORM-ATION?

SQUADRON LEADER CONWAY ASKED THE SAME QUESTION WHEN ALAN CAME LIMPING INTO THE AIRSTRIP, HIS HURRICANE VERY MUCH THE WORSE FOR WEAR.
HAVE YOU GONE MAD? YOU DON'T NEED TO PUT ON A SOLO ACT TO SHOW WHAT A WONDERFUL PILOT YOU ARE. WHAT DID YOU EXPECT, A ROUND OF APPLAUSE?
IT WASN'T THAT, SIR. I COULDN'T... LOOK, I'D BETTER TELL YOU THE WHOLE STORY.

IN HIS TENT, CONWAY LISTENED IN SILENCE WHILE ALAN EXPLAINED.

...SO I'M ALWAYS WORRIED IT MAY HAPPEN AGAIN.

NEVER! IT TAKES MORE THAN A FEW BULLETS TO DOWN A FIGHTER. I BET IT WAS THE GROUND FIRE.

CONWAY SAW THAT SYMPATHY WAS THE LAST THING ALAN NEEDED. WHAT WAS WANTED WAS A CHALLENGE, TO PUT HIM ON HIS METTLE.

RED FLIGHT COMMANDER IS LEAVING US. STOP ACTING LIKE A HYSTERICAL FOOL AND THE JOB'S YOURS. LET ME DOWN AND I'LL SKIN YOU ALIVE!

FROM THAT MOMENT ON, ALAN THREW OFF THE LAST OF HIS DOUBTS AND FEARS, AND HE WAS RIGHT THERE IN THE THICK OF IT AS THE GERMAN RETREAT BECAME A ROUT.

BLUE LEADER TO RED LEADER. LEAVE SOME FOR US!

ALAN'S SCORES, AND HIS REPUTATION, GREW AS THE ALLIED ADVANCE TORE ON, UNTIL THE ONLY GERMANS LEFT IN NORTH AFRICA WERE PRISONERS-OF-WAR.

WELL, THAT'S THAT. PERHAPS WE CAN TAKE A BREATHER NOW. THE OLD HURRICANES ARE JUST ABOUT WORN OUT.
ONLY LONG ENOUGH TO RE-EQUIP WITH NEW AIRCRAFT. ANOTHER FRIEND OF YOURS, THE MUSTANG.
RO/T 12607

THE MUSTANGS THE SQUADRON RECEIVED WERE THE SAME TYPE AS THE ONES ALAN HAD FLOWN IN EUROPE.
THE COCKPIT LAYOUT IS DIFFERENT FROM THE OLD HURRICANE. YOU CAN HELP US THERE.
IT'S STRAIGHTFORWARD ENOUGH, BUT THEY'LL BE A BIT OF A HANDFUL AFTER THE HURRICANE.
BUT WITH ALAN'S EXPERIENCE AND GUIDANCE THE SQUADRON MASTERED THEIR FIERY NEW MOUNTS IN RECORD TIME.

WITH NORTH AFRICA SECURE, SICILY WAS NEXT ON THE LIST FOR INVASION.
BANDITS TO THE NORTH.
UP AND AT 'EM, LADS.

MUCH AS HE HAD LIKED THE STAUNCH OLD HURRICANE, ALAN ENJOYED HAVING A FAST, MANOEUVRABLE AIRCRAFT UNDER HIM AGAIN. AND AS THEY SET ABOUT THE MESSERSCHMITTS, THE ALLIED INVASION FORCES BEGAN LANDING ON THE BEACH FAR BELOW.

...THIS IS JUST LIKE OLD TIMES.

SICILY FELL, AND THE ALLIED ADVANCE ROLLED ON NORTHWARDS INTO ITALY.

THE SPEARHEAD OF THE ADVANCE WAS THE FIGHTER-BOMBER, BUT THOUGH THE GERMAN AIR FORCE WAS HEAVILY OUTNUMBERED AND SHORT OF PETROL AND SUPPLIES IT WAS BY NO MEANS BEATEN...

ARE YOU HURT, SIR?
CAUGHT ONE IN THE SHOULDER. I MUST BE GETTING OLD, LETTING MYSELF BE BOUNCED LIKE THAT.

SQUADRON LEADER CONWAY REFUSED TO GO TO HOSPITAL. HE ATTENDED A CONFERENCE AT WING HEADQUARTERS AND SENT FOR ALAN ON HIS RETURN.
COME IN, ALAN. I PICK THE DARNDEST TIMES TO GET WOUNDED. THE BRASS HATS WANT US TO HIT THE CARATA DAM.
SURELY, THAT'S A JOB FOR MEDIUM OR HEAVY BOMBERS, SIR.

THE GERMANS WERE MAKING FULL USE OF THE EXCELLENT ITALIAN ELECTRIC RAILWAYS. MUCH OF THE POWER FOR THESE RAILWAYS CAME FROM THE GENERATING STATIONS HARNESSED TO THE CARATA RIVER.
THE DAM IS IN THIS VALLEY HERE, BUT THE STEEP SURROUNDING HILLS MAKE IT A DIFFICULT TARGET FOR ORDINARY BOMBERS – THOUGH WE SHOULD BE ABLE TO GET AT IT WITH NO TROUBLE.
I ASSUME THEY WANT US TO SMASH UP THE POWER STATIONS AND TRANSFORMERS, BECAUSE I CAN'T SEE OUR BOMBS CRACKING THE ACTUAL DAM.

THE PLAN CALLED FOR THE SPITFIRE SQUADRON THAT SHARED THE NEWLY-CAPTURED AIRFIELD TO ADD THEIR WEIGHT TO THE ATTACK. THEIR COMMANDER, SQUADRON LEADER VILLIERS, WAS CALLED IN AND BRIEFED.

WE'LL GO IN FIRST, WHILE YOU GIVE US TOP COVER, THEN WE'LL CHANGE ENDS. PITY YOU WON'T BE COMING, PHIL.
WOULDN'T HAVE MISSED IT FOR THE WORLD, BUT I WENT AND GOT A HOLE IN MY SHOULDER. ALAN, TAKE COMMAND FOR THIS SHOW.
SUITS ME, SIR. WE'LL LEAVE AT FIRST LIGHT IF THAT'S OK WITH YOU, SQUADRON LEADER.

THE DAM WAS NOT AS MASSIVE AS ALAN HAD EXPECTED, AND THE GERMAN ANTI-AIRCRAFT GUNNERS FIRED A FEW HALF-HEARTED SHOTS BEFORE SCUTTLING FOR COVER AS THE SPITFIRES SWOOPED.

POWER IN, CHAPS!

WASTING NEITHER TIME NOR BOMBS, THE SPITFIRES METHODICALLY REDUCED THE INSTALLATIONS TO A MASS OF RUBBLE AND TWISTED METAL.

THERE WAS PRECIOUS LITTLE LEFT STANDING WHEN THE SPITFIRES DREW AWAY...

YOUR TURN NOW.
YOU HAVEN'T LEFT US ANYTHING WORTH CLOBBERING. I'M GOING TO HAVE A CRACK AT THE DAM. IF WE CAN DAMAGE THAT, IT'LL REALLY MESS UP THE ELECTRICITY SUPPLY AROUND HERE.

ORDERING HIS SQUADRON TO WAIT, ALAN FLEW DOWN THE VALLEY THEN TURNED AND CAME RACING BACK, AIMING AT THE LIP OF THE DAM.

IT'S WEAKEST AT THE TOP. IF WE CAN CLIP A LUMP OFF THERE...

ALAN HELD HIS COURSE AS THE CONCRETE WALL LOOMED CLOSER, THEN HE PULLED BACK THE STICK AND HIT THE BOMB-RELEASE.

IT WORKS! FOLLOW ON SINGLY, AND TRY AND HIT THE SAME SPOT.

ONE BY ONE THEY HURLED THEIR BOMBS AT THE BASTION. CHUNKS OF MASONRY FLEW, BUT THE DAM STOOD FIRM.

THAT'S THE LAST. IT'LL TAKE A WHILE TO PATCH UP THOSE CRACKS ANY-WAY. LET'S GO HOME.

AS THE MUSTANGS FORMED UP FOR THE FLIGHT BACK, A YELL FROM ONE OF THE PILOTS NEARLY SHATTERED ALAN'S EARDRUMS.

WILL YOU LOOK AT THAT! ITS GOING, A WHACKING GREAT CHUNK HAS FALLEN OUT!
WELL I'LL BE... MUST HAVE BEEN THE PRESSURE OF THE WATER.

IT WOULD BE A LONG TIME BEFORE THE POWER STATIONS COULD EVER OPERATE AGAIN.

TRIUMPHANTLY THE MUSTANGS AND SPITFIRES ARRIVED BACK AT BASE.

YOU BUSTED THE THING? I DON'T BELIEVE IT!
NEITHER WOULD I, IF I HADN'T SEEN IT. LOVELY PIECE OF PRECISION BOMBING. BETTER WATCH OUT, PHIL. THIS LAD WILL DO YOU OUT OF A JOB.
COME OFF IT, YOU TWO. I WAS SURPRISED AS ANYBODY.

BUT CONWAY HAD SEEN ENOUGH OF ALAN IN ACTION TO KNOW HE HAD SHOWN ALL THE SIGNS OF A GOOD LEADER.

EUROPE WILL BE INVADED ANY DAY NOW. NEW SQUADRONS ARE FORMING IN ENGLAND AND EXPERIENCED MEN ARE NEEDED TO LEAD THEM. I THINK YOU'D DO.
ENGLAND...

ALAN HESITATED, AND CONWAY SAW IT WAS TIME TO THROW DOWN ANOTHER CHALLENGE.

DON'T START ON ABOUT OWEN AGAIN. THIS IS YOUR CHANCE TO FORGET ALL THE NONSENSE.
OK, I CAN'T RUN AWAY FOREVER. PUT MY NAME FORWARD.

TWO WEEKS LATER SQUADRON LEADER ALAN BLAKE FLEW IN TO AN AIRFIELD IN KENT TO TAKE UP HIS NEW COMMAND. HE WAS MET BY HIS ADJUTANT.
ARE THOSE MUSTANGS OURS?
YES, SIR – JUST DELIVERED. THEY'RE THE LATEST TYPE. THEY CARRY GUNS AND BOMBS OR ROCKETS. YOU NAME IT AND THEY'LL PLASTER IT.

THE ADJUTANT LED ALAN TO THE CREW ROOM WHERE HIS PILOTS WAITED TO MEET HIM. BUT AS HE ENTERED THE DOOR, ALAN FROZE IN HIS TRACKS.
WHAT'S THE MATTER, SIR? YOU'RE AS WHITE AS A SHEET.
THAT MAN... IT CAN'T BE.
STANDING THERE BEFORE ALAN WAS BERNARD OWEN – OR HIS GHOST.

NEITHER GUESS WAS QUITE CORRECT. PILOT OFFICER RALPH OWEN WAS THE DEAD SQUADRON LEADER'S YOUNGER BROTHER, BUT THE RESEMBLANCE WAS STARTLING. WITH AN EFFORT ALAN PULLED HIMSELF TOGETHER.
DELIGHTED TO BE SERVING WITH YOU, SIR. I'VE HEARD A LOT ABOUT YOU.
ER... THANK YOU.
JUST WHAT HAS HE HEARD? ALL THE STORIES ABOUT HIS BROTHER'S DEATH?
ALTHOUGH OWEN SEEMED FRIENDLY ENOUGH, ALAN FELT VERY UNEASY.

RALPH'S OUR CRACK-SHOT, YOU KNOW. KNOCK THE EARS OFF A NAZI WITHOUT RUFFLING HIS HAIR.
NOT THAT GOOD, I'M AFRAID. I HEAR YOU'RE NOT SO BAD YOURSELF, SIR.
PROVIDED THE TARGET'S BIG ENOUGH, BUT I'VE NEVER USED ROCKETS. YOU'LL HAVE TO SHOW ME THE DRILL.

THEN WHEN THE ALLIES STORMED ASHORE IN NORMANDY, WHERE THEY WERE LEAST EXPECTED, MOST OF THE GERMAN FORCES WERE FURTHER NORTH, BUT THEY IMMEDIATELY HEADED FOR THE INVASION AREA. THEY HAD TO BE STOPPED, AND THE MUSTANGS PLAYED THEIR PART.

ROCKETS AWAY!

ROCKETS GAVE A FIGHTER PLANE TREMENDOUS STRIKING POWER – CAPABLE OF REDUCING THE STRONGEST ARMOURED VEHICLE TO SCRAP IRON.

THAT BOY CAN SHOOT ALL RIGHT. THREE TANKS IN THREE SHOTS. THAT TAKES SOME DOING.

THE RAILWAYS ALSO CAME IN FOR ATTENTION. FEW TRAINS VENTURED OUT IN DAYLIGHT, AND THE SMASHING OF JUNCTIONS AND SIGNAL BOXES MADE SURE THEY NEVER REACHED THEIR DESTINATIONS. ON ONE SUCH SORTIE, ALAN HAD JUST EMPTIED HIS ROCKETS INTO THE TARGET WHEN A TRAIN CAME INTO VIEW.

TRAIN COMING. GET AFTER HIM. TALLY-HO!

AS THE MUSTANGS APPROACHED, THE TRAIN SCREECHED TO A HALT, THEN BEGAN FRANTICALLY BACKING TOWARDS THE COVER OF A TUNNEL BEHIND IT. ALAN WAS FIRST ON THE SCENE, WITH ANOTHER MUSTANG CLOSE BEHIND.

HE'S GOING TO GET AWAY. IF ONLY I HAD SOME ROCKETS LEFT...

ALAN POUNDED AT THE LOCOMOTIVE WITH HIS GUNS, BUT IT KEPT RIGHT ON GOING. THE MOUTH OF THE TUNNEL WAS LOOMING OMINOUSLY, WHEN SUDDENLY...
WHAT THE DEVIL... YOU NEARLY BLEW MY TAIL OFF!
NOT A CHANCE. YOU WERE WELL CLEAR BEFORE I FIRED.

THE VOICE THAT ANSWERED WAS RALPH OWEN'S. FEAR CLUTCHED AT ALAN'S HEART – HAD THE ROCKETS BEEN MEANT FOR HIM? BUT HE KNEW THAT OWEN WAS A CRACK-SHOT, HE ALWAYS HIT WHAT HE AIMED AT. BUT THE DOUBT PERSISTED.
HE'S ALWAYS FRIENDLY, HE'S NEVER MENTIONED HIS BROTHER'S DEATH. AM I IMAGINING THINGS... OR IS HE AS GOOD AN ACTOR AS HIS BROTHER?

AND IN THE NEXT FEW DAYS –
WHAT'S GOT INTO THE SKIPPER? HE SEEMS TO BE VERY WARY OF YOU.
SEARCH ME. HE STEERS CLEAR OF ME IN THE AIR TOO.

ALAN ALSO BECAME CARELESS. ON ANOTHER TRAIN-BUSTING MISSION THIS NEARLY PROVED FATAL. A FOCKE-WULF HAD COME IN AT TREE-TOP LEVEL, AND HAD FASTENED ON TO HIS TAIL.

I SHOULD NEVER HAVE COME THIS LOW. NO ROOM TO MANOEUVRE. HE'S GOT ME COLD.

ALAN SWEATED AS HE WAITED FOR THE INEVITABLE BULLETS, BUT INSTEAD THE IMPOSSIBLE HAPPENED – THE FOCKE-WULF'S TAIL-UNIT FLEW TO RIBBONS.

LF
WHAT A SHOT! OWEN, YOU'RE A BLOOMING MARVEL.
AH, SHUCKS, IT WAS NOTHING.
IT WAS RALPH OWEN WHO HAD SAVED HIM.

WAS THIS THE ACT OF A MAN WHO WANTED HIM DEAD?
YOU WANT TO BE MORE CAREFUL, SKIPPER.
OWEN, OF ALL PEOPLE... OR IS HE SAVING ME FOR HIMSELF? I CAN'T TAKE MUCH MORE OF THIS.

BUT HE HAD A JOB TO DO. WITH THE ALLIED FORCES FIRMLY ESTABLISHED IN FRANCE, HIS SQUADRON MOVED TO A FORWARD AIRSTRIP.
THERE'S A COLONEL FROM H.Q. TO SEE YOU IN THE BRIEFING TENT, SIR.
A BRASS HAT? BETTER NOT KEEP HIM WAITING.

THE COLONEL CAME STRAIGHT TO THE POINT. THE ADVANCE IN HIS SECTOR WAS BEING HELD UP BY A HEAVY GERMAN GUN WHICH DOMINATED A VITAL RIVER CROSSING.
THE THING'S ON A RAILWAY TRUCK IN THIS VALLEY HERE. FLAK GUNS THICKER THAN FLEAS ON A DOG'S TAIL. IF YOUR BLOKES DO MANAGE TO GET NEAR IT, IT SCOOTS INTO THE TUNNEL HERE.
THE PROBLEM IS TO TRY AND JUMP IT BEFORE IT CAN BOLT INTO ITS HOLE. QUITE A POSER.

THE COLONEL HAD SEEN THE SQUADRON IN ACTION, AND HAD HEARD OF ALAN'S DAM-BUSTING EXPLOIT IN ITALY. THAT SORT OF SKILL AND ACCURACY WAS NEEDED IF THE GIANT GUN WAS TO BE KNOCKED OUT.

OUR OWN GUNS CAN'T REACH IT. I THOUGHT A SMALL FORCE COULD SURPRISE IT, SAY AT DAWN OR DUSK...
THAT'S JUST WHEN THEY'LL BE ON THEIR TOES. THE BEST TIME TO CATCH THEM WOULD BE WHEN THE GUN IS ACTUALLY FIRING. EVERYBODY WILL BE TOO BUSY TO KEEP A PROPER LOOK-OUT, WHAT WITH THE FLASH AND SMOKE.
AND SO IT WAS DECIDED TO ATTACK AT THAT TIME.

THE SQUADRON WAS IN PERMANENT RADIO CONTACT WITH THE ARMY H.Q. A MESSAGE COULD BE FLASHED THE INSTANT THE BIG GUN OPENED FIRE.

TWO AIRCRAFT SHOULD BE SUFFICIENT. MORE WOULD ATTRACT ATTENTION. I'LL HAVE THEM READY FOR TAKE-OFF, THE MOMENT YOU GIVE THE WORD.

FAIR ENOUGH. I'LL MAKE THE NECESSARY ARRANGEMENTS MY END.

ALAN INTENDED TO LEAD THE SORTIE, BUT HE WOULD NEED A GOOD WINGMAN. ACCURATE PLACING OF THE ROCKETS WAS ESSENTIAL. HE CALLED FOR VOLUNTEERS, BUT EVERYONE WANTED TO GO.

YOU CAN'T ALL COME. SORT IT OUT AMONG YOURSELVES AND BE QUICK.
OWEN'S YOUR MAN, SIR. HE'S THE BEST SHOT ON THE SQUADRON.

THERE WAS A MURMUR OF AGREEMENT, AND THE OTHERS STOOD BACK. ALAN'S HEART SANK BUT HE COULD NOT REFUSE, FOR OWEN WAS INDEED A SUPERB MARKSMAN.

LOOKS LIKE I'M ELECTED, SIR.

VERY WELL. COME ON, I'LL SHOW YOU THE SET-UP.

NEXT DAY TWO FULLY-ARMED MUSTANGS STOOD READY AT THE END OF THE AIR-STRIP. THEY WERE NOT KEPT WAITING IDLE FOR LONG.

WELL, THIS IS IT.
AND IT'S UP TO JUST YOU AND ME.

ALAN FELT UNCOMFORTABLE AT THE THOUGHT.

THE MERLIN ENGINES ROARED INTO LIFE. ALAN PUSHED THE THROTTLE WIDE AND THE MUSTANG SWEPT INTO THE AIR.

WE'LL STAY AT LOW LEVEL ALL THE WAY. ARE YOU WITH ME, OWEN?

RIGHT HERE, BLAKE. JUST THE TWO OF US, QUITE LIKE OLD TIMES.
LOOK, IF THIS IS YOUR IDEA OF A JOKE...

ALAN'S BLOOD TURNED TO ICE AT THE SOUND OF THE FLAT, EMOTIONLESS VOICE SOUNDING IN HIS HEADPHONES. IT WAS AS IF RALPH WAS MIMICKING HIS LATE BROTHER'S TONE.

THE EXPRESSIONLESS VOICE WENT ON, JUST AS ALAN REMEMBERED IT FROM HIS DAYS WITH SQUADRON LEADER BERNARD OWEN.

YOU KNOW I NEVER MAKE JOKES, BLAKE. IT'S TIME THIS STUPID BUSINESS WAS SETTLED, ONCE AND FOR ALL.

LET'S SETTLE IT THEN. MAN TO MAN, A STRAIGHT FIGHT, NO SHOOTING IN THE BACK...

BUT AGAIN THE CHILLING VOICE CUT HIM SHORT...
YOUR TEMPER AND YOUR WILD IMAGINATION WILL BE THE DEATH OF YOU. NO ONE'S GUNNING FOR YOU ANY MORE THAN YOU WERE GUNNING FOR ANYONE BACK IN FORTY-TWO. THINK – ALL THAT GROUND FIRE COMING UP.
DON'T YOU THINK I TOLD THEM ABOUT THAT? I NEVER STOPPED TELLING THEM.

ALAN'S THOUGHTS WERE IN A TURMOIL. WHAT WAS RALPH OWEN UP TO, WHAT WAS HE TRYING TO PROVE?
YOU ALL LET YOUR IMAGINATIONS RUN AWAY WITH YOU, JUST LIKE NOW. YOU KNOW IT TAKES MORE THAN A FEW SHOTS TO KNOCK DOWN A MUSTANG. ENOUGH CHATTER NOW, WE'LL SOON BE OVER THE TARGET. GO ON IN, I'LL BE RIGHT BEHIND YOU.
SO THAT'S IT!

A COLD DETERMINATION SETTLED OVER ALAN.
MAKE ME A LAUGHING STOCK, WILL YOU? THEY'LL THINK I'VE GONE CRACKERS AND HEAR VOICES. I'LL DEAL WITH YOU AFTER I'VE CLOBBERED THAT GUN!

THE VALLEY WAS JUST WIDE ENOUGH TO TAKE THE MUSTANG. LOOMING AHEAD LIKE SOME HUGE MONSTER WAS THE MASSIVE RAILWAY GUN.
HOLD THAT LOT!
THE ROCKETS EXPLODED, TOUCHING OFF THE GIANT SHELLS THAT FED THE GREAT GUN. A TITANIC BLAST ENGULFED THE VALLEY.
HIS EARS RINGING, ALAN FOUGHT BACK ONTO AN EVEN KEEL, AND LOOKED DOWN AT THE UTTER DESOLATION.
WHAT A MESS. AND WHERE'S OWEN GOT TO? WELL, I'M NOT HANGING ABOUT FOR HIM.

WHEN ALAN LANDED, HE NOTICED THAT OWEN'S MACHINE STOOD ON THE VERY SPOT FROM WHICH THEY HAD TAKEN OFF. STRANGER STILL, THE ENGINE COWLING HAD BEEN REMOVED.

TWENTY MINUTES FOR THE WHOLE JOB. OWEN MADE GOOD TIME, BUT HE DIDN'T NEED HIS ROCKETS. AND THAT MECHANIC'S TAKING A CHANCE FIDDLING WITH A HOT ENGINE.

ALAN JUMPED FROM HIS MACHINE AND MARCHED OVER TO OWEN. THE OTHER MAN WAS LOOKING AT HIM STRANGELY.

OF ALL THE STUPID TRICKS, THIS TAKES THE CAKE. TRYING TO PUT THE WIND UP MF BY IMITATING YOUR BROTHER'S VOICE, SITTING BEHIND MY TAIL...
BEHIND YOUR TAIL? BUT I NEVER TOOK OFF – YOU WENT ON YOUR OWN. MY ENGINE WOULDN'T START. YOU CAN SEE THEY'RE STILL WORKING ON IT.

NOW IT WAS ALAN'S TURN TO LOOK BLANK. HE PUT HIS HAND ON THE OTHER MUSTANG'S ENGINE. THERE WAS NOT A TRACE OF WARMTH.
I TRIED TO RADIO YOU, BUT YOU SEEMED TO BE TALKING TO YOURSELF THE WHOLE TIME. WE THOUGHT YOU'D CRACKED UP. WHO WERE YOU TALKING TO?
YOU, OF COURSE! ARE YOU TRYING TO MAKE OUT THAT I'VE GONE POTTY? GOOD HEAVENS, I SAW YOU, AS PLAIN AS...

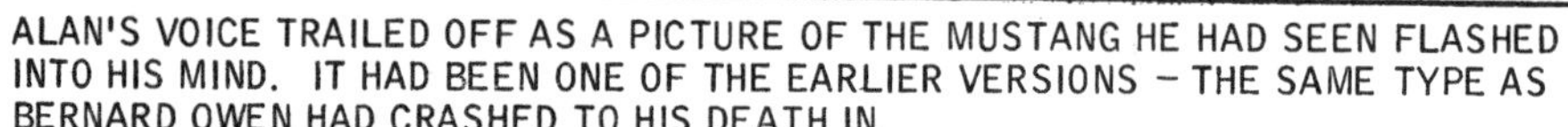
ALAN'S VOICE TRAILED OFF AS A PICTURE OF THE MUSTANG HE HAD SEEN FLASHED INTO HIS MIND. IT HAD BEEN ONE OF THE EARLIER VERSIONS – THE SAME TYPE AS BERNARD OWEN HAD CRASHED TO HIS DEATH IN.

JUST LIKE THE ONES WE HAD BACK IN FORTY-TWO. I WAS SO ANNOYED I DIDN'T NOTICE AT THE TIME, BUT NOW I'M SURE. BUT WHO...

WAS IT POSSIBLE? HAD THE GHOST OF BERNARD OWEN RETURNED FROM BEYOND THE GRAVE TO TELL ALAN HE WAS NOT TO BLAME?

HE FELT AS IF A GREAT WEIGHT HAD BEEN LIFTED FROM HIM. THE TRUTH HAD BEEN PLAIN TO SEE ALL ALONG, BUT WHERE THAT VOICE OF REASON CAME FROM, HE WOULD NEVER KNOW. ALL HE KNEW NOW WAS HIS BULLETS HADN'T CAUSED BERNARD OWEN'S DEATH...AND THAT THERE WAS A WAR TO GET ON WITH!

ARE YOU FEELING ALL RIGHT, SIR?
FINE, BETTER THAN I'VE FELT FOR A LONG TIME!
Commando
THE END

Frontline

BY AIR TO BATTLE

All the major armies of World War II used paratroopers and glider-borne troops to get their men quickly into battle with the element of surprise. Here is some of the equipment of a British paratrooper.

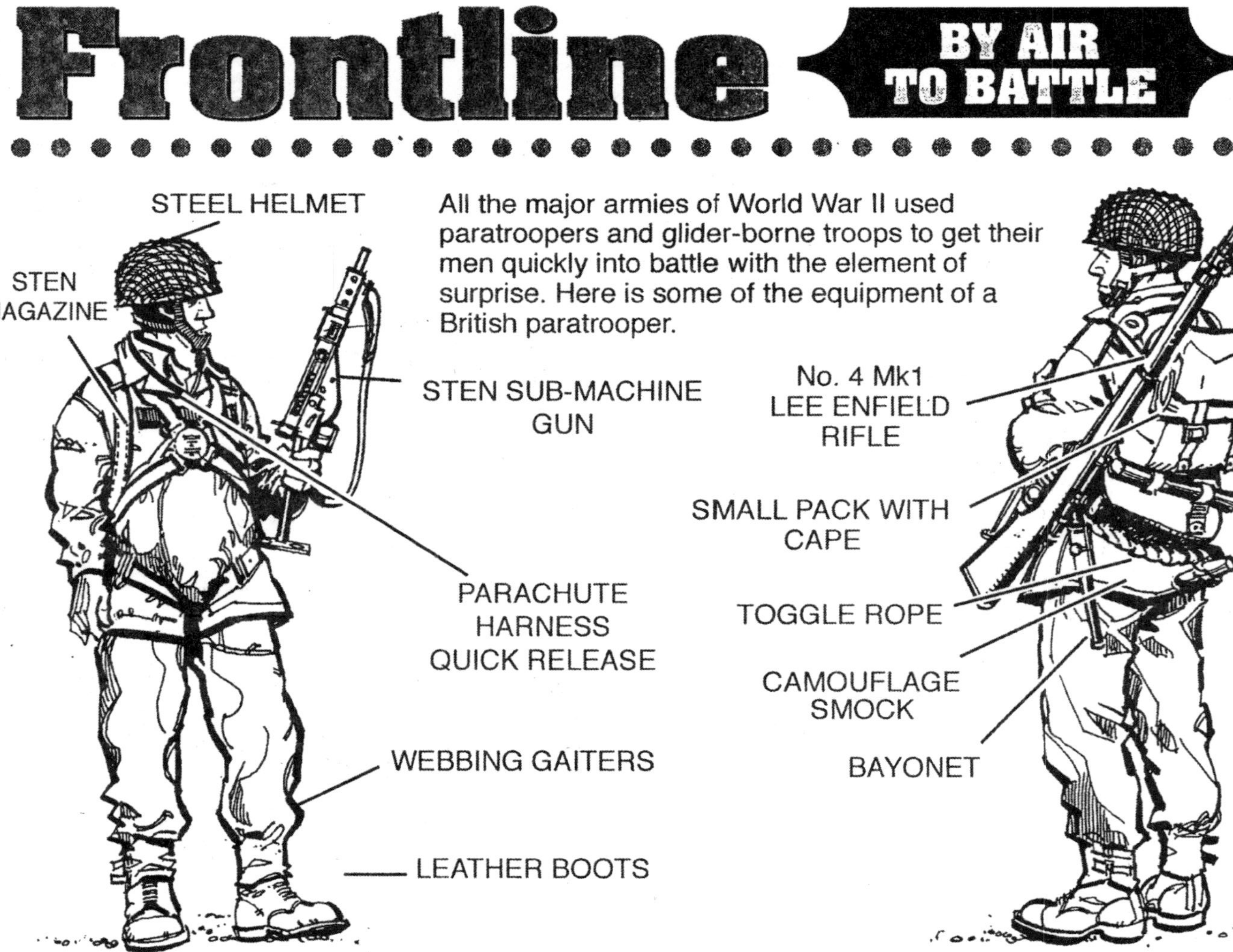
STEEL HELMET
STEN MAGAZINE
STEN SUB-MACHINE GUN
PARACHUTE HARNESS QUICK RELEASE
WEBBING GAITERS
LEATHER BOOTS
No. 4 Mk1 LEE ENFIELD RIFLE
SMALL PACK WITH CAPE
TOGGLE ROPE
CAMOUFLAGE SMOCK
BAYONET

DEATH PATROL

THE NIGHT SKY OVER THE CENTRAL MEDITERRANEAN ERUPTED INTO FLAMING DEATH. THE ALLIED INVASION OF SICILY HAD BEGUN — CODENAME, "OPERATION HUSKY"

FOR TWO MEN IN THE AIRBORNE ATTACK, "HUSKY" WAS TO POSE A TERRIFYING PROBLEM. THEY DIDN'T KNOW IT YET, BUT SOON THEY WERE TO MEET UP WITH THE DEATH PATROL!

THE TWO MEN BELONGED TO A BRIGADE H.Q. GROUP THAT WERE DROPPING WITH THE MEN TO SET UP A COMMAND CENTRE. AS A GREEN LIGHT GLOWED IN THE AIRCRAFT THAT CARRIED THE GROUP, THE BRIGADE COMMANDER'S VOICE RAPPED OUT.

AWAY YOU GO, YOUNG BOB!
I'M ON MY WAY, SIR!

BOB HANSON, A COMPETENT YOUNG LIEUTENANT, DROPPED STRAIGHT INTO A SEARCHLIGHT'S GLARE AND A SKY ABLAZE WITH FLAK.

TALK ABOUT BUTTERFLIES IN THE STOMACH! I'VE GOT A WHOLE FLOCK OF 'EM.

BOB LAID NO CLAIMS TO HEROISM. HE KNEW FEAR BUT ALWAYS FOUGHT IT WITH A TIGHT-LIPPED JEST.

BRIGADIER MULLEN, THE DARING C.O. ENTRUSTED TO SET UP H.Q., FOLLOWED BOB. BUT BEFORE THE THIRD MAN IN THE STICK COULD JUMP...
GOOD GRIEF, A DIRECT HIT! THE KITE'S HAD IT!
A SPLIT-SECOND LATER THE ALBEMARLE BLEW ASUNDER.
YE GODS!

GRIEF-STRICKEN OVER THE LOSS OF HIS PALS, BOB WAS HARDLY CONSCIOUS OF HIS OWN PERIL AS HE FLOATED INTO A SEARCHLIGHT BEAM.
USE YOUR RIGGING-LINES, LIEUTENANT — GET OUT OF THAT SEARCHLIGHT-BEAM!

BOB OBEYED MECHANICALLY. THE SEARCHLIGHT LOST HIM.
FROM WHAT I CAN SEE OF THE GROUND, IT DOESN'T LOOK MUCH LIKE THE DROPPING ZONE.

BOB AND THE BRIGADIER TOUCHED DOWN, MULLEN AWKWARDLY.

AAAAH!

BOB UNHARNESSED, AND RAN TO MULLEN.
MY ANKLE – MY FLAMING ANKLE!
HERE, LET ME UNHITCH YOUR 'CHUTE, SIR.
HE FREED THE OLDER MAN.
IT'S BROKEN. I'LL HAVE TO CRAWL.
WHERE TO? I CAN HEAR FIGHTING, BUT IN THE DISTANCE. WE'VE DROPPED IN THE WRONG PLACE.

BOB STOPPED SHORT AS HE HEARD A GRINDING AND A CLANKING FROM THE ROAD THAT PASSED CLOSE BY. NEXT SECOND HE FLUNG HIMSELF DOWN.
LIE FLAT, SIR!

SCARCELY DARING TO BREATHE, THEY WATCHED A PANZER COLUMN ROLL PAST.

JERRIES — TIGERS, AT THAT! OUR BOYS WON'T STAND A CHANCE IF THOSE MONSTERS ARE TURNED LOOSE ON THEM.

THE TIGERS DISAPPEARED, BUT THE ROAD WAS NOT LONG EMPTY.
EYETIES... SCORES OF THEM.
LUCKILY THE ITALIAN INFANTRYMEN ALSO WENT BY WITHOUT SEEING THE TWO BRITISHERS.
WE'VE GOT TO GET WELL AWAY FROM THIS ROAD BY DAY-BREAK, SIR. IF WE DON'T, WE'RE AS GOOD AS IN THE BAG.
YOU'RE RIGHT. AND IF THERE'S ONE THING I DON'T FANCY, IT'S SPENDING THE REST OF THE WAR IN A PRISON CAMP.

BOB LOOKED AROUND. A RIDGE SOME DISTANCE AWAY HELD HIS INTEREST.
I BELIEVE I SEE A CAVE. THERE, SIR — WHERE I'M POINTING. THINK YOU COULD MAKE IT BY HOPPING ON ONE FOOT, USING ME AS A CRUTCH?
I CAN'T GUARANTEE I WON'T PASS OUT. IF I DO, YOU'LL HAVE TO DRAG ME.
SURE ENOUGH, BOB HAD TO HAUL THE BRIGADIER THE LAST FIFTY YARDS.
AT LEAST WE'LL BE BETTER OFF HERE THAN WHERE WE WERE.
IN THE DARK OF THE CAVE...
I'D BEST TRY TO CATCH SOME SHUT-EYE. DAYLIGHT'S WHEN I'LL HAVE TO STAY ALERT IN CASE ANYONE COMES SNOOPING.

AT LAST BOB MANAGED TO DOZE OFF. BUT HE HAD ONLY BEEN ASLEEP A SHORT TIME WHEN A BLINDING LIGHT WAKENED HIM.

WHAT THE DICKENS?

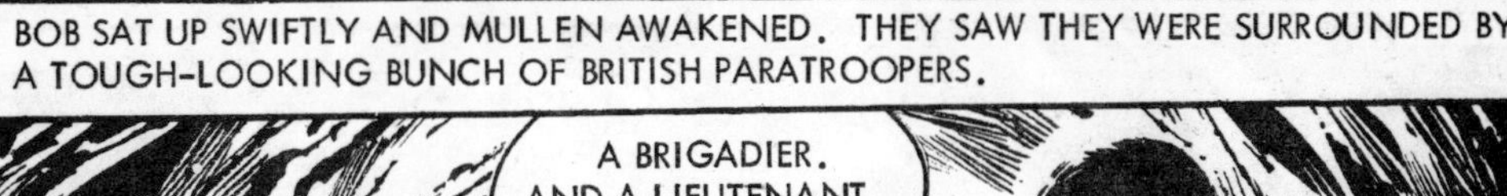
BOB SAT UP SWIFTLY AND MULLEN AWAKENED. THEY SAW THEY WERE SURROUNDED BY A TOUGH-LOOKING BUNCH OF BRITISH PARATROOPERS.

A BRIGADIER. AND A LIEUTENANT, NO LESS!

SOME OF OUR OWN LADS! THANK HEAVENS FOR THAT!

THE NAME'S BRAND, SIR — SERGEANT BRAND. THIS IS ALL THAT'S LEFT OF A WHOLE COMPANY, ELEVEN FIGHTING MEN AND A MEDICAL ORDERLY.

ONCE THE NERVOUS MEDICAL ORDERLY, PRIVATE LANG, HAD BOUND UP MULLEN'S ANKLE, BRAND AND HIS PARATROOPERS SETTLED DOWN TO PASS THE NIGHT IN THE CAVE.

WOULDN'T CARE TO BE A JERRY WITH THOSE CHARACTERS AROUND. I'VE NEVER SEEN A TOUGHER-LOOKING CREW. THAT IS, BARRING THE MEDICAL ORDERLY. HE SEEMS A BUNDLE OF NERVES, POOR KID.

THE MEDICAL ORDERLY WAS DEFINITELY ON EDGE. BOB HEARD HIM SPEAK IN A QUERULOUS UNDERTONE.
IT'S ALL RIGHT FOR YOU, SERGEANT. YOU AGREED TO THIS. BUT I WAS FORCED INTO IT.
BRAND STIFFENED. HE HISSED A SAVAGE WARNING.
SHUT UP! WHAT ARE YOU TRYING TO DO — SPOIL EVERYTHING?
THE SERGEANT LOOKED ROUND FURTIVELY. BOB WAS JUST SMART ENOUGH AND QUICK ENOUGH TO DUCK HIS HEAD.
THE BRIGADIER'S OUT COLD FROM THE PAIN-KILLER SLEEPING-TABLET YOU GAVE HIM AFTER BINDING UP HIS ANKLE. AND THE LIEUTENANT'S DOZED OFF AGAIN. BUT IT MIGHT'VE BEEN OTHERWISE!
I'M SORRY. IT'S JUST THAT I NEVER WANTED ANY PART OF THIS...

QUESTIONS COURSED THROUGH BOB'S MIND, QUESTIONS TO WHICH HE COULD FIND NO ANSWER.

WHAT IS IT LANG HAS BEEN FORCED INTO? WHY DID BRAND TELL HIM TO BELT UP? WHAT COULD LANG SPOIL BY NOT KEEPING HIS MOUTH SHUT? THERE'S SOMETHING FISHY GOING ON, BUT I'M HANGED IF I KNOW WHAT IT IS.

SPORADIC SHOOTING STILL SOUNDED FROM TIME TO TIME, BUT IT FINALLY CEASED. THEN, AT DAWN...

HERE COMES A PATROL!

WILLIE LANG PIPED UP IN AGITATION.
GERMANS?
NO, ITALIANS – FIVE OF THEM. AND I DIDN'T SEE ANYBODY ELSE IN MILES.

THE ITALIANS MOVED ABREAST OF THE CAVE, ONE OF THEM SPOTTING THE HIDDEN MEN.
BRITISH SOLDIERS!
LEAVE THEM TO ME! ONE BURST'S ENOUGH!

ONE BURST WAS ENOUGH TO WIPE OUT FOUR OF THE ITALIANS BUT THE FIFTH CHOSE TO SURRENDER.

MERCY! NO KILL, NO KILL!

BRAND'S MOUTH TWISTED INTO A COLD-BLOODED SNEER. HE EMPTIED HIS GUN INTO THE FIFTH ITALIAN BEFORE BOB COULD STOP HIM.

AARGH!
SERGEANT!

PITY FOR THE ITALIAN AND RAGE AGAINST BRAND WELLED UP IN BOB.
YOU MURDERING RAT!
THE SERGEANT EYED BOB WITH COOL INSOLENCE.
WHAT'S UP? WE CAN'T LUMBER OURSELVES WITH ANY PRISONERS. AND I COULDN'T LET HIM GO FOR HELP.
SIGNIFICANTLY, BRAND'S COMRADES GATHERED TO THEIR HULKING N.C.O. BRIGADIER MULLEN, WHO HAD AWAKENED, WATCHED UNEASILY.
ALL RIGHT, WHAT'S DONE IS DONE! JUST THE SAME, KEEP A CHECK ON YOUR TRIGGER-FINGER!
LANG APART, THEY'RE AN UGLY BUNCH. I GET THE IMPRESSION THEY'D GANG UP AGAINST YOUNG HANSON AT THE DROP OF A HAT.

THEY HID ALL DAY, THEN AT NIGHTFALL THEY LEFT THE CAVE. HEAVY GUNFIRE COULD BE HEARD.
I WONDER HOW THE SEABORNE LANDINGS WENT OFF? BETTER THAN THE AIR-DROP, LET'S HOPE. EVERYTHING SEEMED TO GO WRONG FOR US FROM THE VERY START.
MULLEN WAS BEING CARRIED ALONG ON A MAKESHIFT STRETCHER THE PARATROOPERS HAD MADE DURING THE DAY.
FOR THIS JOURNEY TO THEIR LINES, MULLEN HAD BEEN GIVEN ANOTHER TABLET TO EASE HIS PAIN. JUST AS HE WAS LOSING CONSCIOUSNESS, HE HEARD A MUMBLE OF VOICES.
HE'S NO LIGHTWEIGHT!
STOP GROUSING. HE'S OUR PASSPORT. NO ONE'S GOING TO ASK AWKWARD QUESTIONS AS LONG AS WE'RE WITH A BRIGADIER.

MULLEN BLACKED OUT, BUT REMEMBERED THAT SNATCH OF CONVERSATION WHEN HE CAME ROUND AS THEY RESTED FURTHER ON.

WE'VE STOPPED FOR A BREATHER. BRAND AND THE OTHERS ARE WATCHING THE ROAD AND KEEPING THEIR EYES PEELED FOR TROUBLE. HOW ARE YOU FEELING, SIR?
NEVER MIND HOW I'M FEELING. THERE'S SOMETHING I WANT TO TELL YOU.

HE REPEATED WHAT HE HAD OVERHEARD.

WHAT DO YOU MAKE OF IT?
I'M TYING IT UP WITH SOMETHING LANG AND BRAND SAID TO EACH OTHER IN THE CAVE...

YOUNG AS HE WAS, BOB HAD A SHREWD AND AGILE MIND.

THEY'RE DESERTERS — ALL OF THEM IN AGREEMENT EXCEPT LANG, WHO'S BEEN PRESS-GANGED INTO IT.
YOU COULD BE RIGHT. WHAT SHOULD WE DO ABOUT IT?

IT SAID MUCH FOR MULLEN'S REGARD FOR BOB THAT HE SHOULD SEEK THE LIEUTENANT'S COUNSEL.

I VOTE WE SING DUMB AND JUST KEEP ON THE ALERT, SIR.

FAIR ENOUGH. WE'LL SING DUMB — AS FROM NOW. BRAND'S STARING IN OUR DIRECTION, SUSPICIOUSLY. HE'S NO DOUBT WONDERING WHAT WE'RE TALKING ABOUT IN SUCH SECRECY.

THE MARCH WAS RESUMED UNTIL THEY REACHED A WIDE, DEEP RIVER, THE BRIDGE OVER WHICH WAS GUARDED.

THERE'S OUR ONLY WAY ACROSS — THAT BRIDGE. BUT IT'S GUARDED.
BY ITALIANS, AS FAR AS I CAN SEE.

THERE WAS EVERY POSSIBILITY OF A HARD FIGHT.

I'VE PRECIOUS LITTLE CONFIDENCE IN THIS GANG, BUT I'LL JUST HAVE TO MAKE THE BEST OF IT.

BOB WORKED OUT A PLAN OF ACTION WHICH ENTAILED CRAWLING ALONG THE RIVER-BANK. LANG SPOKE UP –

WHAT ABOUT ME, SIR?

YOU STAY PUT WITH THE BRIGADIER.

MORE THAN HALFWAY TO THE BRIDGE, BOB SIGNALLED A HALT AND BREATHED FINAL ORDERS TO BRAND.
STAY HERE WITH THREE OF YOUR MEN. THE REST OF US WILL GET CLOSE ENOUGH FOR A SURPRISE RUSH. BE READY TO COVER US IF WE'RE SPOTTED TOO SOON. IF ALL GOES WELL, DOUBLE BACK FOR LANG AND THE BRIGADIER.

BOB AND SEVEN OF BRAND'S SQUAD WORMED THROUGH SCRUB TO WITHIN A STONE'S THROW OF THE OBJECTIVE.
SO FAR, SO GOOD. BUT WILL THE SCRUFF WHO ARE WITH ME HAVE THE GUTS TO FOLLOW ME WHEN I GIVE THE WORD?
HE SPRANG UP, INSTANTLY ALERTING THE ITALIANS.
LET'S GO!
MAMA MIA!

HOT LEAD SEARED PAST BOB. THEN A GRENADE SAILED OVER HIS HEAD FROM BEHIND HIM.
DUCK, LIEUTENANT. ANY SECOND THE SHRAPNEL WILL BE COMING EVERY WAY!
SECONDS AFTER BOB HIT THE GROUND, THE GRENADE DID ITS DEADLY WORK.
AAAH!

THE ECHOES OF THE GRENADE-EXPLOSION WERE STILL SOUNDING AS BOB AND THE PARA-TROOPERS SURGED FORWARD.

WE ARE
ATTACKED!

THE ITALIANS AT THE NEAR END OF THE BRIDGE RALLIED GAMELY, BUT WERE MOWN DOWN. THEN...

HERE COME
MORE FROM THE
OTHER SIDE!

THERE WAS AN OUTBURST OF FIRING ON THE RIVER-BANK AS BRAND AND HIS TRIO WENT INTO ACTION.

WE'RE IN LUCK! THE MOON'S BROKEN THROUGH THE CLOUD AND THE EYETIES ARE CLEAR TARGETS FOR OUR GUNS.

THE ITALIANS FROM THE FAR END OF THE BRIDGE HAD SUFFERED FIFTY PER CENT CASUALTIES BY THE TIME THEY TANGLED WITH BOB'S SQUAD.

UGH!

OUT OF THE BRAWL DEATH LOOMED AT BOB.
BRITISH DOG!
A PARATROOPER APPEARED TO CUT DOWN THE ITALIAN BEFORE BOB COULD MOVE.
QUITE A FIGHT, SIR.
BOB SHUDDERED. HE KNEW THE PARA-TROOPER HAD ACTED NOT TO SAVE HIM, BUT JUST BECAUSE HE LIKED KILLING.

THE BATTLE FOR THE BRIDGE ENDED IN TOTAL VICTORY FOR THE PARATROOPERS. BRAND AND THE OTHERS ARRIVED.
ONE THING I KNOW NOW. BRAND AND HIS SQUAD ARE AS TOUGH AS THEY LOOK. WHATEVER THEY'RE DESERTING FOR, IT'S NOT BECAUSE THEY'RE SCARED TO FIGHT. BUT WHAT THE HECK IS THE REASON?

THE SERGEANT INTERRUPTED BOB'S THOUGHTS —
HAS IT OCCURRED TO YOU THERE MIGHT BE MORE ITALIANS IN THIS AREA, LIEUTENANT?
THAT'S A CHANCE WE HAD TO TAKE. WE'D BEST MAKE TRACKS FROM HERE AS FAST AS WE CAN — IF THAT'S WHAT YOU'RE DRIVING AT, BRAND.
AT THAT VERY MOMENT FIRING BROKE OUT AFRESH, BULLETS RICOCHETTING FROM BEHIND THEM.
QUICK, LET'S GET OUT OF HERE!

THEY SPED ACROSS THE BRIDGE AS THE FIRING SWELLED IN VOLUME.
COVER THE BRIGADIER. MAKE SURE HE COMES TO NO HARM.
YES, BRAND AND HIS CREW ARE CONCERNED FOR THE BRIGADIER — BUT ONLY BECAUSE HE SOMEHOW SUITS THEIR PURPOSE, WHATEVER IT MAY BE.
MACHINE-GUNS HAMMERED, RIFLES THUMPED. THE ITALIAN MILITIAMEN WERE LOW-GRADE MARKSMEN. ONLY ONE SHOT SCORED.
AAGH!
WOUNDED IN THE LEG, LANG SPRAWLED HIS LENGTH. BULLETS CHOPPED AT THE ROADWAY ALL AROUND HIM.
DON'T LEAVE ME — DON'T LEAVE ME!

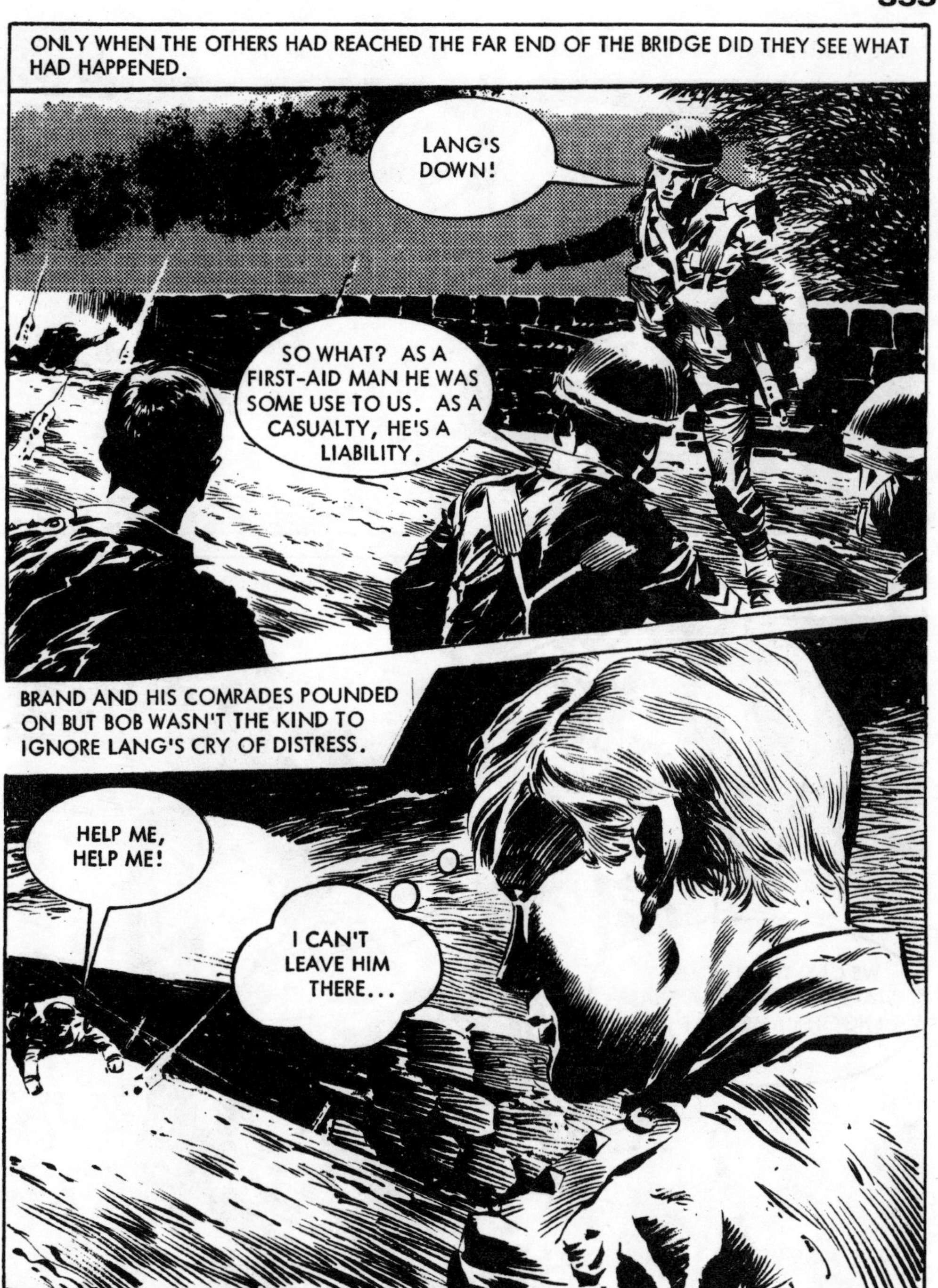

ONLY WHEN THE OTHERS HAD REACHED THE FAR END OF THE BRIDGE DID THEY SEE WHAT HAD HAPPENED.
LANG'S DOWN!
SO WHAT? AS A FIRST-AID MAN HE WAS SOME USE TO US. AS A CASUALTY, HE'S A LIABILITY.
BRAND AND HIS COMRADES POUNDED ON BUT BOB WASN'T THE KIND TO IGNORE LANG'S CRY OF DISTRESS.
HELP ME, HELP ME!
I CAN'T LEAVE HIM THERE...

BOB STARTED BACK ACROSS THE BRIDGE. THE ENEMY'S FIRE SWITCHED TO HIM.
THANKS, SIR – THANKS A MILLION!
SAVE IT, LANG. JUST KEEP YOUR FINGERS CROSSED FOR US BOTH.

HE REACHED THE WOUNDED MEDICAL ORDERLY AND HEAVED HIM ONTO HIS SHOULDER.

WE CAN THANK OUR STARS THERE'S NOT A SHARP-SHOOTER AMONG THAT LOT!

FAMOUS LAST WORDS? THEY WERE VERY NEARLY SO. BOB BIT BACK A GASP AS A BULLET BURNED HIS ARM.
YOU'RE HIT, SIR?
JUST A NICK. NOTHING TO WORRY ABOUT.

THERE WERE THICKETS ON THE FAR SIDE OF THE RIVER. BOB JOINED BRAND AND THE OTHERS THERE.

DETAIL TWO OF YOUR MEN TO TAKE CARE OF LANG. AND DON'T GIVE ME ANY OF YOUR CALLOUS ARGUMENTS!

WHATEVER YOU SAY, SIR.

FIRST LANG'S INJURY WAS BOUND UP THEN A SECOND STRETCHER WAS MADE BEFORE THEY PUSHED ON.
THEY HAVEN'T RUN THE RISK OF FOLLOWING US, IN CASE OF AN AMBUSH.
THEY WERE STILL IN WOODED COUNTRY WHEN ANOTHER DAY DAWNED.
ALL'S QUIET NEAR THE COAST. IT COULD MEAN THE SEABORNE LANDINGS HAVE BEEN SUCCESSFUL, OR THE INVASION'S BEEN REPULSED.

THEY RESTED IN COVER BESIDE A WOODLAND ROAD AND FOUND THEMSELVES WATCHING A VERY INTERESTING SHOW.

JERRIES — RETREATING NORTH. THAT MEANS THE SEABORNE INVASION'S BEEN A SUCCESS.

I THINK THE BULK OF THE ITALIANS DON'T HAVE THEIR HEARTS IN THE WAR. IF THE ISLAND HAD BEEN GARRISONED ENTIRELY BY GERMANS, THE BATTLE FOR THE BEACHES WOULD HAVE LASTED LONGER.

THEN CAME ANOTHER SOUND...THE DRONE OF AERO-ENGINES.
FIGHTER-BOMBERS — TYPHOONS! THEY'RE CIRCLING, PROBABLY ON THE PROWL FOR THAT JERRY COLUMN!
THE GERMAN COLUMN WAS SPOTTED. A TYPHOON OF THE R.A.F. SCREAMED DOWN TO RELEASE ITS BOMBS.
A BRACE OF BOMBS IS ON THE WAY, BOB.
HERE'S HOPING IT DOESN'T MISS.

THE TYPHOON PILOT WAS ON TARGET.

LOOK OUT FOR THAT TURRET — IT'S SAILING THIS WAY!

THE DISMEMBERED TANK-TURRET CRASHED TO THE GROUND.
PHEW, TALK ABOUT A CLOSE SHAVE!

MORE BOMBS FELL, WREAKING HAVOC IN THE GERMAN COLUMN. THEN, IN THE QUIET THAT FOLLOWED...

HERE COME THE FIRST OF THE JERRY FOOT-SLOGGERS. EVERYBODY KEEP WELL DOWN.

THE QUIET DID NOT LAST FOR LONG. THE TYPHOONS STRUCK AGAIN – THOUGH NOT WITH BOMBS.

THEY'RE LASHING 'EM! THE JERRIES ARE SCURRYING LIKE SCARED RABBITS.

THE NAZIS DIVED INTO THE UNDERGROWTH AT THE ROADSIDES. ONE MAN IN HIS PANIC PLOUGHED DEEPER THAN HIS COMRADES – TO FIND TROUBLE.

HIMMEL!

THE GERMAN WHIPPED ROUND TO GIVE THE ALARM. BOB POUNCED.

NO YOU DON'T, FRITZ!

HIS PISTOL-BUTT FELLED THE MAN BEFORE HE COULD ALERT HIS COMRADES.

THIS WILL PUT YOU TO SLEEP FOR QUITE A WHILE, CHUM!

THE GERMAN WENT DOWN. IN ANOTHER INSTANT BOB WAS HIS PROTECTOR.
KEEP YOUR DISTANCE, BRAND! YOU'RE NOT BUTCHERING THIS HELPLESS JERRY LIKE YOU DID THE ITALIAN WHO TRIED TO SURRENDER AT THE CAVE.
WILL HE MAKE TROUBLE FOR US? THAT'S THE QUESTION!
HE'LL MAKE NO TROUBLE. HE'S OUT COLD.
THEN YOU DON'T HAVE TO WORRY. IT'S ONLY EYETIES I CAN'T STOMACH.
BOB FELT HIS SKIN CRAWL AT THE MENACE AND INSOLENCE IN BRAND'S VOICE.

THE TYPHOONS SHEERED OFF. THE ENEMY INFANTRY REFORMED AND TRUDGED ONWARD, NONE SEEING THE HIDDEN WATCHERS.

BATTALION AFTER BATTALION OF JERRIES. I WONDER HOW LONG IT'LL BE BEFORE OUR OWN FOOTSLOGGERS BEGIN TO SHOW UP.

I'D LIKE TO STAY AWAKE FOR THE SHEER JOY OF SEEING THEM, BUT MY ANKLE'S PLAYING ME UP AGAIN. GET ME ONE OF LANG'S TABLETS, WILL YOU, BOB?

AS BOB MADE TO REACH THE HAVERSACK, LANG SUDDENLY GRABBED IT UP.
NO, NO! I'LL GET ONE FOR THE BRIGADIER.
THERE'S SOMETHING IN THERE LANG DOESN'T WANT ME TO SEE. I WONDER WHAT?

AN IDEA FLASHED THROUGH BOB'S MIND.
IF I ASKED FOR ONE OF THOSE TABLETS, I MIGHT LEARN SOMETHING THAT WOULD HELP CLEAR UP THIS MYSTERY.
HE PUT THE IDEA INTO PRACTICE, PRETEND-ING THE SLIGHT WOUND IN HIS ARM HAD STARTED TO ACHE.
THANKS, LANG. THE PAIN WILL PROBABLY HAVE WORN OFF WHEN I WAKE UP.
HE MADE A SHOW OF SWALLOWING THE TABLET, BUT SLIPPED IT FROM HIS MOUTH AS HE LAY DOWN.
I MEAN TO FIND OUT WHAT THE GAME IS. THERE'S EVERY CHANCE BRAND AND HIS CRONIES WILL GET CARELESS IF THEY THINK I'M FAST ASLEEP LIKE THE BRIG.

BOB LAY SILENT FOR A FEW MINUTES BEFORE ONE OF BRAND'S COMRADES SPOKE.
WHAT DO WE DO WITH THE BRIGADIER AND THE LIEUTENANT WHEN THEY'RE NO MORE USE TO US?
BEFORE I ANSWER THAT, LET'S BE SURE BOTH OF THEM ARE SLEEPING.
THE BRIG WAS SNORING LIKE A BUZZ-SAW. BOB BREATHED SLOWLY AND DEEPLY.
SLEEPING LIKE BABES. WHAT DO WE DO WITH THEM WHEN THEY'RE NO MORE USE TO US? THAT DEPENDS ON CIRCUM-STANCES. WE'LL MOST LIKELY KILL THEM.

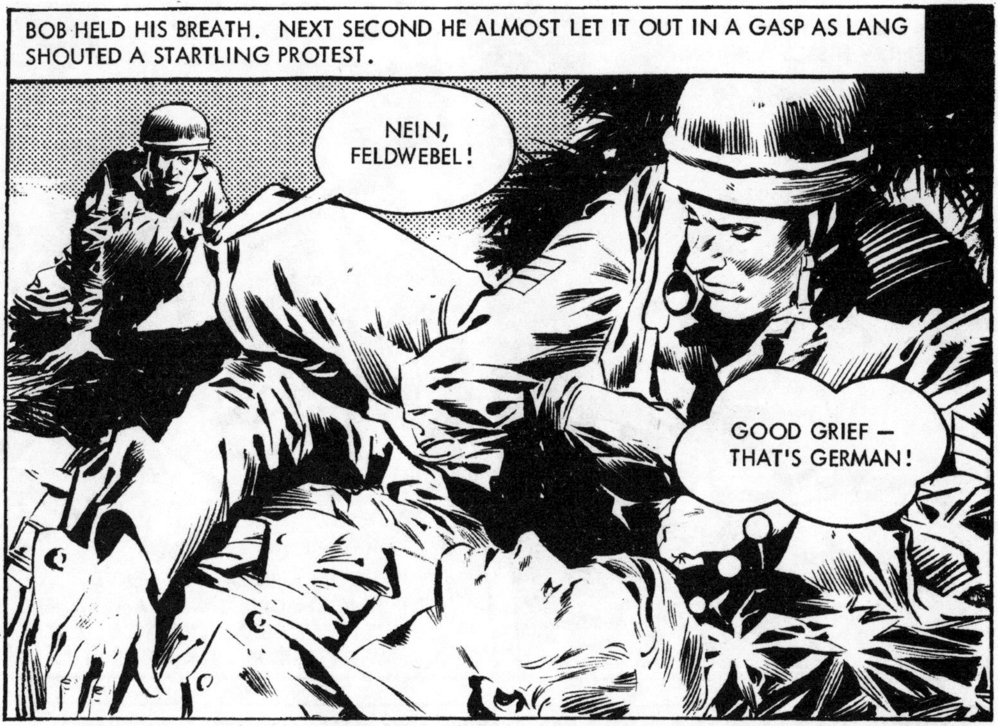

BOB HELD HIS BREATH. NEXT SECOND HE ALMOST LET IT OUT IN A GASP AS LANG SHOUTED A STARTLING PROTEST.

NEIN, FELDWEBEL!

GOOD GRIEF — THAT'S GERMAN!

THEN BOB HEARD THE VOICE OF SERGEANT BRAND, ALIAS FELDWEBEL BRAND.

SILENCE! IF YOU MUST SPEAK, USE ONLY ENGLISH! THIS AREA WILL SOON BE SWARMING WITH BRITISH TROOPS.
BOB FELT HIS SCALP PRICKLING WITH FEAR. BRAND AND HIS PARATROOPERS WERE GERMANS IN DISGUISE!

THEN SUDDENLY THE MAN POSTED AS SENTRY HISSED A WARNING.

FOUR BRITISH SOLDIERS COMING THIS WAY!

BRAND REELED OFF ORDERS.

PICK UP THE BRIGADIER, HANSON AND LANG. LEAVE THE UNCONSCIOUS GERMAN. WHEN HE REVIVES, HE MAY BE ABLE TO SLIP AWAY AND REJOIN HIS UNIT.

A MINUTE OR SO LATER, THE BOGUS PARATROOPERS WERE IN CONVERSATION WITH A FORWARD BRITISH PATROL.

THERE'S NOTHING I CAN DO. IF I STARTED ANYTHING, I'D BE SIGNING THE DEATH-WARRANTS OF THOSE FOUR OUTNUMBERED TOMMIES. I'LL HAVE TO BIDE MY TIME.

COMPLETELY UNAWARE OF THE TRUE IDENTITY OF THE PARATROOPERS, THE BRITISH CORPORAL IN CHARGE OF THE PATROL WAS PUTTING BRAND IN THE PICTURE.

WHAT YOU SAW WASN'T THE MAIN BODY OF THE JERRIES. THE BULK OF THEM RETREATED EAST OF HERE, BUT WE WERE DETAILED TO PICKET THE FLANK ON THE LEFT AS THE FIRST OF A WHOLE STRING OF PATROLS.

BRAND THEN ASKED A QUESTION. THAT GAVE BOB HIS FIRST CLUE TO THE BOGUS PARATROOPERS' PURPOSE.

SO THE SEABORNE LANDINGS WENT WELL. ARE THE ARMY COMMANDERS ASHORE YET?

YES, THE LOT — BRITISH AND AMERICAN.

SO THAT'S IT!

WITH SINKING HEART, BOB REALISED THESE NAZIS HAD BEEN GIVEN ORDERS TO ASSASSINATE THE ALLIED TOP BRASS.

BRAND AND HIS PARTY CONTINUED SOUTHWARDS. OTHER PATROLS WERE MET, BUT NONE IN GREAT STRENGTH.

BRIGADIER MULLEN, YOU SAY? WHY, OF COURSE, I RECOGNISE HIM FROM PICTURES I'VE SEEN OF HIM. BETTER GET HIM TO HOSPITAL. THERE'S ONE A FEW MILES FARTHER ON. IT'S A CIVVY SET-UP BUT WE'VE TAKEN IT OVER.

AN HOUR LATER THEY ARRIVED AT CROSS-ROADS JUST AS A BRITISH DISPATCH RIDER ON A COMMANDEERED GERMAN MOTOR-BIKE AND SIDE-CAR APPEARED.

WE'LL STOP THIS MOTOR-CYCLIST. IT'S JUST POSSIBLE HE MAY HAVE THE INFORMATION WE WANT.
THIS IS WHERE I PRETEND THAT THE EFFECT OF THE SLEEPING-TABLET'S WORN OFF...

THE MOTOR-CYCLIST, A PRIVATE MURPHY, STOPPED AT BRAND'S BIDDING.

H.Q. ALLIED COMMAND, SERGEANT? NO, I'VE NO IDEA.

BRAND AND HIS CREW ARE IN FOR A SHOCK. THIS NOTE WILL COOK THEIR GOOSE.

BOB HAD WORKED OUT A PLAN. ROUSING HIMSELF, HE ANNOUNCED HE COULD STAND UNAIDED. THEN, WHILE NO ONE WAS LOOKING, HE SCRIBBLED A HASTY NOTE.

BEFORE THE MOTOR-CYCLIST COULD THROTTLE-UP, BOB CONTRIVED TO STEP CLOSE TO HIM.
SERGEANT BRAND, WHAT'S THE LIEUTENANT UP TO?

BRAND AND HIS MEN LEAPT FORWARD. ONE SWIFT MOVEMENT, AND THE FELDWEBEL INTERCEPTED THE NOTE. HE READ IT OUT TO THE OTHERS.

"TAKE THIS MESSAGE TO THE NEAREST BRITISH UNIT. THE CHARACTERS YOU'VE BEEN TALKING TO AREN'T WHAT THEY SEEM. THEY'RE GERMANS, AND..."

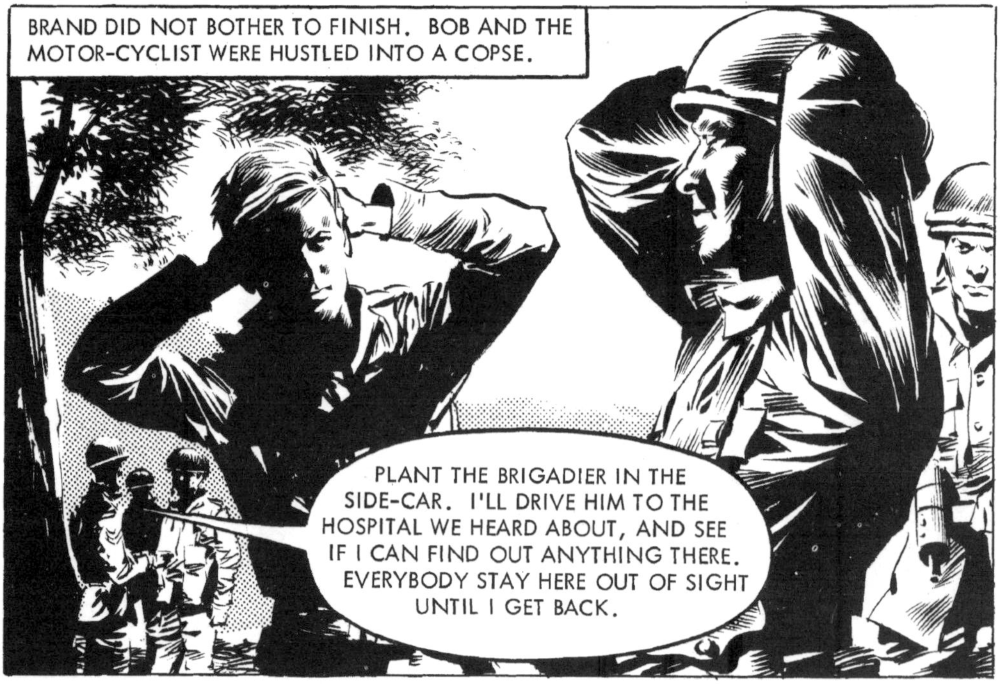

BRAND DID NOT BOTHER TO FINISH. BOB AND THE MOTOR-CYCLIST WERE HUSTLED INTO A COPSE.

PLANT THE BRIGADIER IN THE SIDE-CAR. I'LL DRIVE HIM TO THE HOSPITAL WE HEARD ABOUT, AND SEE IF I CAN FIND OUT ANYTHING THERE. EVERYBODY STAY HERE OUT OF SIGHT UNTIL I GET BACK.

IN DUE COURSE BRAND RETURNED. HE WAS IN HIGH SPIRITS.
EVERYTHING WENT LIKE CLOCKWORK. THE BRIGADIER SERVED HIS PURPOSE. AT THE HOSPITAL I WAS TREATED LIKE A HERO. ABOVE ALL, I LEARNED WHAT WE WANT TO KNOW.
BRAND WENT ON EXCITEDLY —
ALLIED COMMAND H.Q. IS AT A REQUISITIONED VILLA ON THE SIRACUSA ROAD. WE'LL START FOR IT AT ONCE.
AND NOW HE TURNED TO THE MAN WHO WAS COVERING BOB AND THE MOTOR CYCLIST.
SPENGLER, THE REST OF US WILL SCAN THE AREA FROM THAT HIGH GROUND. IF ALL'S CLEAR, I'LL WAVE. THAT WILL BE THE SIGNAL TO SHOOT THE TWO PRISONERS. THEN WAIT HERE WITH LANG UNTIL WE SHOW UP AGAIN.

THE PRISONERS WERE LEFT ALONE WITH SPENGLER AND THE INJURED LANG.

BRAND AND THE OTHERS ARE ON THE HIGH GROUND NOW. THEY'RE A LONG WAY OFF, BUT I CAN SEE THEM CLEARLY ENOUGH AGAINST THE SKYLINE. AH, THERE'S THE SIGNAL NOW!

LEERING, SPENGLER FACED BOB AND THE MOTOR CYCLIST.

NO OTHER BRITISHERS NEAR. THIS IS FOR YOU THE END OF THE WAR.

NEIN, NEIN!

SOMEHOW LANG FOUND THE COURAGE AND THE DESPERATE STRENGTH TO LUNGE AT THE KILLER.
NO, IT MUST NOT BE! THE LIEUTENANT RISKED HIS LIFE FOR ME!
LET GO OF ME, CURSE YOU!
BOB DASHED FORWARD —
HANG ON TO HIM, LANG!

LANG WAS KICKED SAVAGELY ASIDE — BUT NOT BEFORE BOB HAD GRAPPLED WITH SPENGLER.
GIVE ME THAT STEN!

THE STRUGGLE FOR THE GUN WAS BRIEF. IT ENDED AS THE STEN WENT OFF AGAIN.
AAARGH!

IT HAD ALL HAPPENED SO QUICKLY THAT MURPHY THE MOTOR-CYCLIST HAD NO CHANCE TO HELP.
IS HE DEAD, SIR?
YES. IT'S JUST AS WELL FOR HIM, MURPHY. IF HE WERE ALIVE, HE'D ONLY HAVE TO FACE A FIRING-SQUAD FOR WEARING BRITISH UNIFORM.

BOB GLANCED AT THE TERRIFIED LANG.

BRAND AND HIS MEN ARE OUT TO ASSASSINATE THE BRITISH AND AMERICAN ARMY COMMANDERS, AND THEREBY DISRUPT THE ENTIRE ALLIED SET-UP. ISN'T THAT THE DRILL? COME ON, YOU'D BETTER TALK!

JA, YOU ARE RIGHT, HERR LEUTNANT.

LANG TOLD HOW THE ENGLISH-SPEAKING MURDER SQUADS HAD BEEN FORMED IN SECRET, AND HELD READY FOR USE WHEREVER THE ALLIES MIGHT ATTACK.

BRAND AND HIS COMRADES ARE DEDICATED NAZIS. I AM NOT. UNLIKE THEM, I WAS HORRIFIED WHEN WE WERE GIVEN ORDERS TO KILL FELLOW-GERMANS TO PREVENT ANY LEAKAGE THAT MIGHT BETRAY OUR TRUE IDENTITY.

BOB HAD HEARD ENOUGH.

MURPHY, SEARCH SPENGLER FOR SPARE AMMO. THIS MAG'S EMPTY.

WHAT ABOUT ME?

HELPING LANG BACK ONTO HIS STRETCHER, BOB REASSURED HIM.

DON'T WORRY. WE'RE GOING TO LEAVE YOU HERE WHILE WE DO OUR BEST TO STOP BRAND. LET ME GIVE YOU ONE OF YOUR TABLETS...

HE REACHED FOR LANG'S HAVERSACK. LANG PROMPTLY BLURTED OUT A PROTEST.
NEIN, NEIN! I'LL GET ONE MYSELF, AND ONLY IF I NEED ONE.
HE HAS SOMETHING IN THAT PACK HE DOESN'T WANT ANYONE TO SEE. WELL, THIS IS NO TIME TO START RUMMAGING THROUGH IT.

BOB AND MURPHY MADE FOR THE MOTOR-CYCLE AND SIDE-CAR.
DO YOU KNOW WHERE THE VILLA IS?
AS A MATTER OF FACT I DO, SIR. THE ROAD TO IT IS LONG AND TWISTY. WE'LL HAVE TO GO SOME IF WE'RE TO GET THERE BEFORE THOSE NAZIS, BUT I THINK WE CAN JUST ABOUT DO IT.
THEY SET OUT ALONG A ROUTE THAT SNAKED OVER A ROCK-STREWN LANDSCAPE.
TOO BAD WE COULDN'T STRIKE ACROSS-COUNTRY LIKE BRAND AND HIS GROUP. THEY'RE HOOFING IT, SURE. BUT AT THIS RATE THEY'LL OUTSTRIP US, JUDGING BY THIS MAP.
THEY CALL ME SPEEDY, SIR, AND I'M PUSHING THIS BIKE AS HARD AS I DARE.

HARDER THAN HE DARED, IN FACT, ON SUCH A ROAD.

I CAN'T HOLD HER!

BIKE AND SIDE-CAR SHOT OFF THE ROAD.

AAAGH!

BOB, WHO WAS UNHURT, SCRAMBLED UP AND HELPED MURPHY TO HIS FEET.

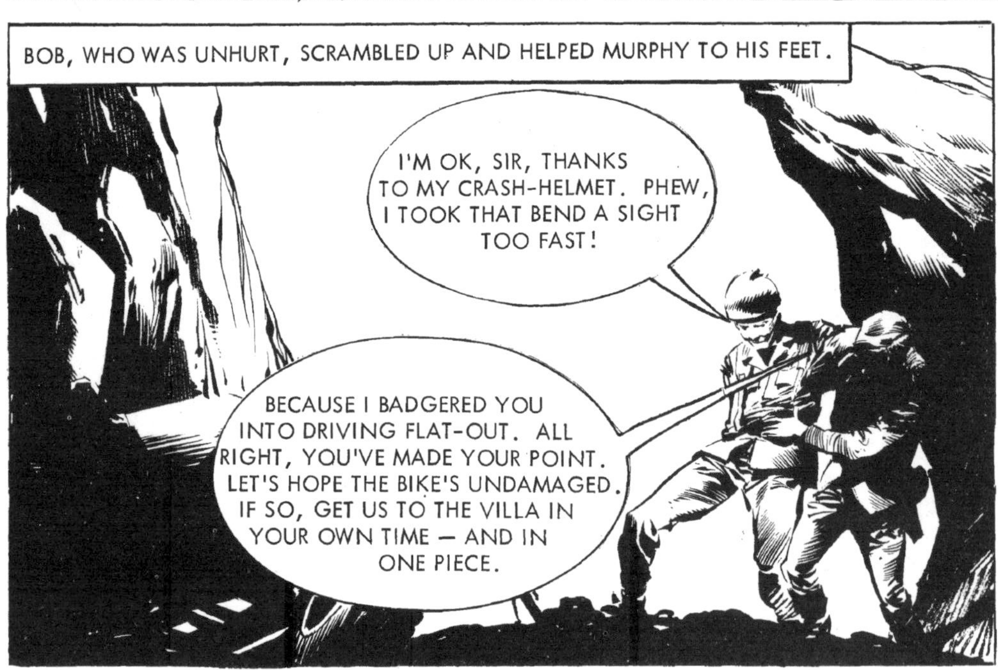
I'M OK, SIR, THANKS TO MY CRASH-HELMET. PHEW, I TOOK THAT BEND A SIGHT TOO FAST!
BECAUSE I BADGERED YOU INTO DRIVING FLAT-OUT. ALL RIGHT, YOU'VE MADE YOUR POINT. LET'S HOPE THE BIKE'S UNDAMAGED. IF SO, GET US TO THE VILLA IN YOUR OWN TIME — AND IN ONE PIECE.

THE BIKE AND SIDE-CAR COMBINATION WAS UNDAMAGED. BOB AND MURPHY WERE SOON ON THEIR WAY AGAIN.

THOSE MEN COULD BE BRAND AND HIS KILLERS. THEY'RE TOO FAR OFF FOR US TO BE CERTAIN.

IF THEY'RE THE NAZIS, SIR, I DOUBT IF WE'RE GOING TO MAKE IT TO THE VILLA AHEAD OF THEM. IT'S ONLY A FEW HUNDRED YARDS OVER THAT SKYLINE.

IT WAS BRAND AND HIS MEN. MINUTES LATER THEY WERE CROUCHED IN COVER BESIDE THE ROAD LEADING TO THE VILLA.

FELDWEBEL BRAND...
IN ENGLISH! WE WERE WARNED NEVER TO SPEAK GERMAN ON THIS MISSION IN CASE WE LAPSED INTO IT BY ACCIDENT AT THE WRONG MOMENT. IN ANY CASE, KEEP YOUR VOICE DOWN!

THE MAN WHOM BRAND HAD REBUKED WENT ON IN AN UNDERTONE.

SORRY, SERGEANT. BUT HOW DO WE GET PAST THOSE GATES?

WE STAY HERE UNTIL THEY COME OUT, THEN GET THEM ALL AT ONCE.

A MINUTE OR TWO LATER....

GOOD FORTUNE'S BEEN WITH US ALL THE WAY AND IT'S STILL SMILING ON US! THEY'RE OPENING THE GATES FOR A CAR WITH AN ESCORT THAT ONLY A GENERAL — OR GENERALS — WOULD WARRANT!

CAR AND ESCORT SWEPT THROUGH THE GATEWAY.

THERE AIN'T ANYONE TO MATCH OUR OFFICER , LIMEY.

EXCEPT THE BRITISH TOP BRASS WHO'S SHARING THAT CAR WITH HIM.

AT THE ROADSIDE, BRAND AND HIS SQUAD HAD STIFFENED. TO THE ESCORT IT NO DOUBT LOOKED AS IF THEY WERE ABOUT TO SPRING TO ATTENTION.
YOU ALL KNOW WHAT TO DO. KLAUS, SCHWARTZ, RICHTER AND I SPRAY THE CAR. THE REST OF YOU CONCENTRATE ON THE ESCORT. AFTER THE JOB'S DONE, IT'S EVERY MAN FOR HIMSELF.
JUST THEN BOB AND MURPHY SURGED INTO VIEW ROUND A TURN IN THE ROAD.
THERE'S THE GENERAL'S CAR AND THERE'S THOSE NAZI PERISHERS, ALL READY TO FIRE!
SO AM I!

THE STACCATO BLAST OF THE STEN-GUN IN BOB'S GRASP MERGED WITH THE ROAR OF THE MOTOR-CYCLE.
SHARE THIS AMONG YOU!
THERE WAS A SCREECHING OF TYRES AS STAFF-CAR AND MOTOR-CYCLES DRY-SKIDDED TO AN ABRUPT HALT.
THEY'RE NAZIS. INFILTRATORS HERE ON A MURDER MISSION!

BOB HAD EMPTIED A MAGAZINE AND WAS FITTING ANOTHER WHEN BRAND'S VOICE RANG OUT
STEADY — IT'S DO AND DIE FOR ALL OF US!
THE SURVIVORS OF THE MURDER SQUAD RALLIED FOR A SUICIDAL RUSH.
GIVE YOUR LIVES IN THE SERVICE OF THE REICH! KILL THE BRITISH AND AMERICAN GENERALS — SIEG HEIL!
DON'T LET THOSE FANATICS REACH THE CAR!

AGAIN BOB'S STEN LASHED OUT. THE GUNS OF THE ESCORT STUTTERED IN DEADLY CHORUS, CUTTING DOWN THE NAZIS.
TEUFEL!
BRAND WAS HIT, BUT DID NOT FALL. HE LURCHED TO THE CAR, AND WRENCHED OPEN A DOOR — ONLY TO BE SHOT AGAIN BY BOB.
AAGH!

BRAND'S MISSION WAS OVER. FOR HIM, LIFE ITSELF WAS OVER. BOB RUSHED OVER TO SEE IF THE TOP BRASS WERE SAFE.
ARE YOU BOTH ALL RIGHT, GENTLE-MEN?
RIGHT AS RAIN — THANKS TO YOU, IT WOULD SEEM!
BOB REMEMBERED HE WAS IN THE PRESENCE OF THE BIG GUNS. HE SNAPPED TO ATTENTION.
AT EASE, YOUNG MAN. AND LET'S HAVE THE WHOLE STORY OF THIS.
NO, NOT NOW. WE'VE MATTERS OF THE HIGHEST IMPORTANCE TO ATTEND TO. THE LIEUTENANT CAN WRITE OUT A FULL REPORT AND DELIVER IT AT H.Q. IN PERSON THIS EVENING.

THE STAFF-CAR AND ITS ESCORT MOVED OFF SHORTLY AFTER, AND BOB REJOINED MURPHY.
THE TOP BRASS WANT ALL THE FACTS. BUT BEFORE I DO THAT THERE'S SOMETHING ELSE I WANT TO DO. TAKE ME BACK TO WHERE WE LEFT LANG.

THEY ARRIVED AT THE COPSE.
THE PARATROOPER'S BODY – BUT NO LANG.
HERE'S HIS HAVERSACK.
BOB OPENED THE PACK. A BRITISH PARATROOPER'S UNIFORM HAD BEEN STUFFED INTO IT.
THIS IS THE UNIFORM HE WAS WEARING. BUT WHAT'S HE WEARING NOW?
I SAW A COUPLE OF YANK MEDICS AND THE BLOKE ON THEIR STRETCHER BACK THERE. IT COULD BE LANG.

SO THEY CHASED THE TWO AMERICAN RED CROSS MEN FROM A FORWARD DRESSING UNIT WHO HAD PICKED UP LANG.
HEY, YANKS, HOLD ON A MINUTE!

THE U.S. MEDICS LOOKED ROUND AND HALTED. LANG FELT HIS HEART SINK.
IT'S A FIRING SQUAD FOR ME, AFTER ALL. IF ONLY I COULD HAVE BEEN SWALLOWED UP AMONG ALL THE OTHER PRISONERS THE ALLIES HAVE TAKEN.

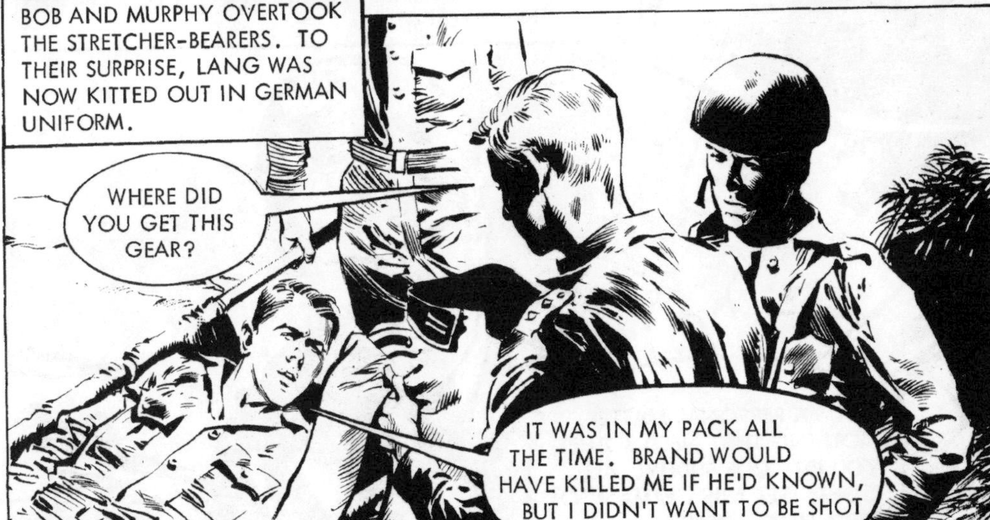
BOB AND MURPHY OVERTOOK THE STRETCHER-BEARERS. TO THEIR SURPRISE, LANG WAS NOW KITTED OUT IN GERMAN UNIFORM.
WHERE DID YOU GET THIS GEAR?
IT WAS IN MY PACK ALL THE TIME. BRAND WOULD HAVE KILLED ME IF HE'D KNOWN, BUT I DIDN'T WANT TO BE SHOT AS A SPY.

THE TWO AMERICANS SET DOWN THE STRETCHER, PUZZLED.

D'YOU MIND TELLING US WHAT THIS IS ALL ABOUT?

LANG LOOKED UP PLEADINGLY. BOB DECIDED NOT TO SATSIFY THE YANKS' CURIOSITY – OR TO MENTION LANG IN HIS REPORT.
IT'S A PERSONAL MATTER, NOTHING THAT NEED BOTHER YOU OR YOUR BUDDY. ALL RIGHT, GET THIS GERMAN TO A FIELD HOSPITAL.

AND AS THE AMERICANS LIFTED THE STRETCHER—
GOOD LUCK. I'M SURE MURPHY WILL AGREE WITH ME WHEN I SAY YOU'VE NO CAUSE FOR CONCERN.
NO CAUSE AT ALL.
THANK YOU BOTH. ESPECIALLY YOU, HERR LEUTNANT. YOU ARE A GENTLEMAN — AND A HERO.
Commando
THE END

Don't miss your next four smash-hit Commando books! They're on sale in two weeks!

"MOUNTAIN OF DEATH"
"ACE WITHOUT HONOUR"
"JUNGLE FEVER"
"DOOMED SQUADRON"

Commando **FLY PAST**

No. 117 — HANDLEY PAGE HALIFAX BVI

NP763
NOH7
H

Shown in the markings of No. 346 (Guyenne) Squadron, Free French Air Force, No. 4 Group R.A.F. Bomber Command, based at Elvington, Yorkshire, in 1944-45.

Kennedy

THE SHIP BUSTERS

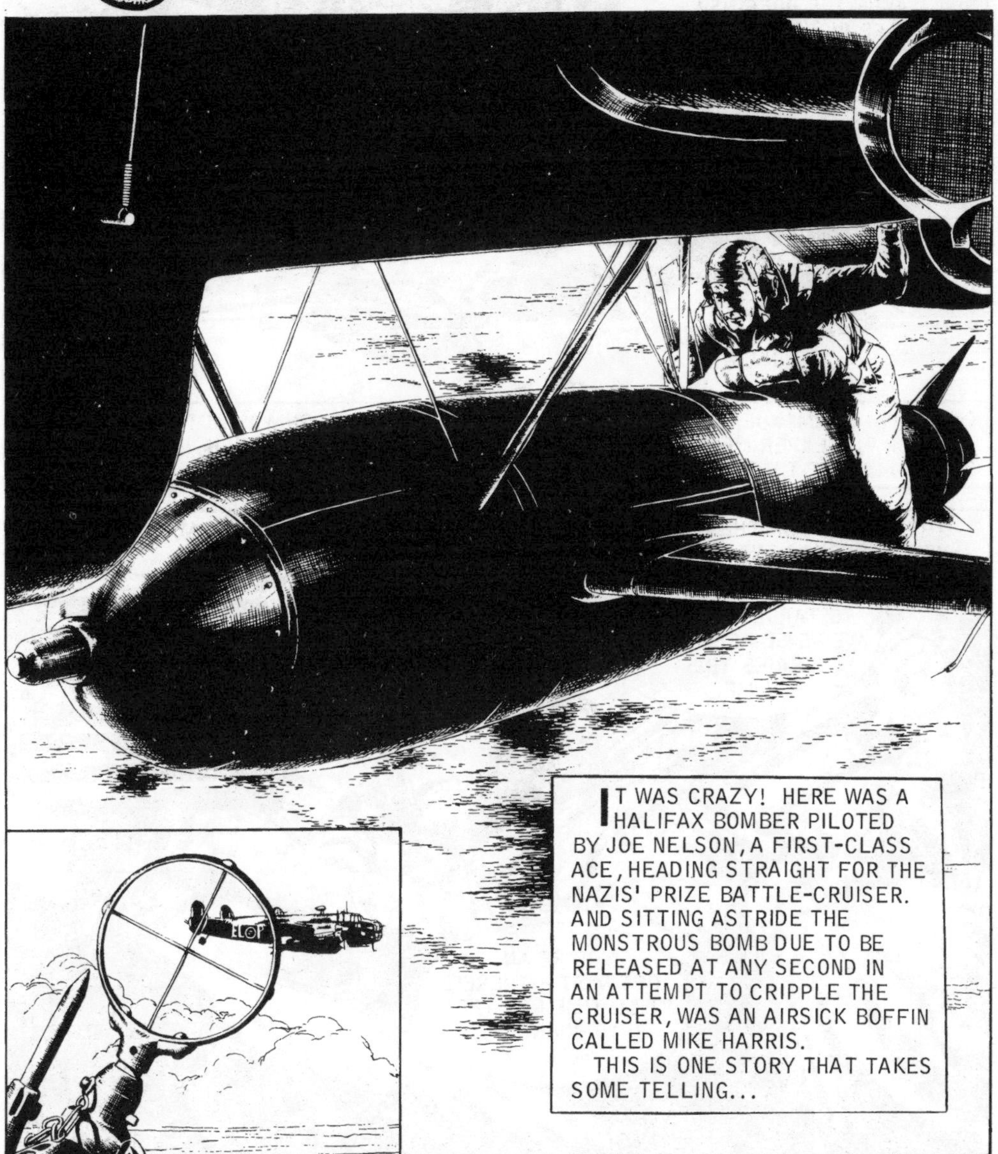
IT WAS CRAZY! HERE WAS A HALIFAX BOMBER PILOTED BY JOE NELSON, A FIRST-CLASS ACE, HEADING STRAIGHT FOR THE NAZIS' PRIZE BATTLE-CRUISER. AND SITTING ASTRIDE THE MONSTROUS BOMB DUE TO BE RELEASED AT ANY SECOND IN AN ATTEMPT TO CRIPPLE THE CRUISER, WAS AN AIRSICK BOFFIN CALLED MIKE HARRIS.
THIS IS ONE STORY THAT TAKES SOME TELLING...

IT ALL BEGAN WITH AN EXPERIMENT BY BRITISH SCIENTISTS. USING POWERFUL TRANSMITTERS THEY HOPED TO SCRAMBLE THE GERMAN RADIO FREQUENCIES AND SO DISRUPT THE NAZI FIGHTER CONTROL SYSTEM.

NO FIGHTERS AROUND, SKIPPER. MAYBE THE BOFFINS WERE RIGHT FOR ONCE.
DON'T YOU BET ON IT, NORRIE.
EL O D
EL O P
ML229

BUT WING COMMANDER JOE NELSON, WHOSE HALIFAX SQUADRON WAS ACTING AS GUINEA PIG FOR THE EXPERIMENT, HAD LITTLE FAITH IN SCIENTISTS. A TOUGH, FIERY LEADER, HE HAD LITTLE TIME FOR THOSE IN SAFE JOBS.

THE TARGET FOR THE BOMBERS WAS A MUNITIONS FACTORY IN BELGIUM. SOON THEY WERE APPROACHING IT.

TEN MINUTES TO TARGET, SKIPPER. WE'VE SLIPPED THE JERRIES THIS TIME.
YOU'RE AN OPTIMIST – THERE'S STILL TIME FOR THEM TO BOUNCE US.

JOE WAS RIGHT TO HAVE DOUBTS, FOR AT THAT MOMENT SOME YELLOW-NOSED GERMAN FOCKE-WULF FIGHTERS WERE CIRCLING ON PATROL NOT FAR AWAY.

BRITISH BOMBERS – HALIFAXES, I THINK. COME ON!

THE FOCKE-WULF FIGHTERS SWEPT IN, GUNS HAMMERING, TO CLAIM THEIR FIRST VICTIM.

BALE OUT, WE'RE ON FIRE!

THE NEXT HALIFAX TO PERISH EXPLODED IN A SHOWER OF FLAME AND SPARKS.

BAD LUCK, ENGLANDER!

JOE NELSON FACED A BITTER DECISION AS HIS LOSSES MOUNTED – EITHER RUN FOR CLOUD COVER AND ABANDON THE TARGET OR KEEP GOING AND BE MASSACRED.

JIM WHYTE'S HAD IT – THAT'S THE THIRD KITE WE'VE LOST.

BUT JOE HAD ALREADY MADE UP HIS MIND.
WE'VE GOT TO GET INTO CLOUD OR WE'RE FINISHED...
I WON'T BE SEEN OFF BY A PACK OF SQUAREHEADS. PREPARE TO DROP BOMBS.

ALMOST BRUSHING THE ROOFTOPS, JOE'S HALIFAX BORED IN TOWARDS THE TARGET.
MAKE THIS SPOT-ON, CHARLIE.
TARGET DEAD AHEAD, SKIPPER. BOMB DOORS OPEN...

THE FACTORY WAS REACHED – AND BOMBED.

BOMBS GONE.

I DON'T KNOW HOW MUCH DAMAGE IT'LL DO, BUT AT LEAST WE HIT THE TARGET.

BY CARRYING ON TO THE TARGET JOE HAD BEEN SEPARATED FROM THE REST OF HIS SQUADRON, SO THE JOURNEY HOME WAS LONG AND LONELY – BUT IT GAVE HIM TIME TO NURSE HIS DISLIKE OF SCIENTISTS.

BLASTED BOFFINS! THEY SEND US OUT ON A DAYLIGHT RAID WITH NO ESCORT TO TRY OUT SOME USELESS GADGET – AND WE GET CLOBBERED.
YOU'RE DEAD RIGHT, SKIPPER.
EL

IT WAS LATE INTO THE EVENING WHEN JOE AND HIS CREW TOUCHED DOWN. WAITING TO MEET THEM WAS THE AIRFIELD COMMANDER, GROUP CAPTAIN YOUNG. WITH HIM WAS MIKE HARRIS, ONE OF THE BOFFINS WHO HAD BEEN SENT TO EXPLAIN THE FAILURE OF THE RADIO-SCRAMBLING DEVICE.

LESS THAN HALF THE SQUADRON HAVE RETURNED. LOOK, HARRIS, I DON'T THINK IT'S WISE TO MEET JOE NELSON IN THE CIRCUMSTANCES.
I INSIST, GROUP CAPTAIN. IF I EXPLAIN WHERE WE WENT WRONG, HE'S BOUND TO UNDERSTAND.

MIKE WAS REALLY KEEN ON HIS WORK. AND HE, LIKE MANY OTHER SCIENTISTS, DID CARE WHAT HAPPENED TO THE MEN WHO TRIED OUT HIS IDEAS.

BUT JOE WAS IN NO MOOD FOR A COSY CHAT. HIS ATTITUDE TO BACK-ROOM BOYS IN SITUATIONS LIKE THIS WAS NEVER PLEASANT.
HELLO, WING COMMANDER. I'M MIKE HARRIS FROM RESEARCH AND I CAN ASSURE YOU NO ONE'S TO BLAME...
GET BACK TO YOUR LABORATORY BEFORE I BELT YOU!

OBVIOUSLY THE MEETING WAS NOT GOING TO BE A SUCCESS.

NINE CREWS LOST, AND HE SAYS IT WAS NOBODY'S FAULT? I'LL MURDER THE IDIOT!

I WARNED YOU, HARRIS.

BY MORNING JOE HAD COOLED OFF. BUT HE WAS UNREPENTANT –

I DON'T WANT AN APOLOGY, JOE. I KNOW HOW YOU FEEL. SOMETIMES THESE SCIENTISTS DON'T REALISE THE COST OF THEIR EXPERIMENTS.

THEN THEY SHOULD CHANGE PLACES WITH US, SIR. A FEW TRIPS OVER THE FATHERLAND AND THEY'D BEGIN TO SEE SENSE.

THEN GROUP CAPTAIN YOUNG GOT DOWN TO FACTS.
AS YOU KNOW, THE SQUADRON'S IN A TERRIBLE STATE AND IT'LL TAKE SOME TIME TO GET BACK INTO ACTION. NOW THERE'S A HALIFAX SQUADRON A FEW MILES AWAY WHOSE COMMANDER GOT THE CHOP RECENTLY.

I'VE RECOMMENDED YOU TO TAKE COMMAND OF THAT SQUADRON, JOE, AS A WINGCO. THEY NEED A SQUADRON LEADER TOO. IS THERE ANYONE YOU WANT TO TAKE WITH YOU?
TERRY GREAVES, SIR. HE'S A QUIET CHARACTER, BUT HE'S GOT WHAT IT TAKES.

TERRY GREAVES WAS ABOUT THE BEST FRIEND JOE HAD AND ONE OF THE BEST PILOTS TOO.

I'M TAKING OVER THIS SQUADRON, TERRY. THE JOB CARRIES WING COMMANDER'S RANK, SO I'VE ASKED FOR YOU AS SQUADRON LEADER.

THANKS, JOE. I APPRECIATE IT.

IN A FEW DAYS JOE AND GREAVES ARRIVED AT THEIR NEW AIRFIELD.

WELL, THIS IS IT.

HOME, SWEET HOME FROM NOW ON.

BUT THIS WAS NOT GOING TO BE AN EASY TASK FOR JOE. SINCE THE LAST COMMANDER HAD BEEN KILLED, MORALE AT THE AIRFIELD HAD BEEN VERY LOW.

I KNOW YOU LADS AREN'T FEELING TOO SHARP RIGHT NOW, BUT BELIEVE ME, THIS SQUADRON IS GOING TO SNAP OUT OF IT – AND QUICK!

JOE WAS TRUE TO HIS WORD. HE KEPT THE CREWS AT IT DAY AND NIGHT WITH TRAINING FLIGHTS AND GUNNERY AND BOMBING PRACTICES.

BLIMEY! IF THE BOSS SENDS US ON ANOTHER TRAINING FLIGHT IT'LL MAKE AN ALL-TIME RECORD.
DON'T WORRY, TUBBY. JOE NELSON'S JUST TRYING TO SWEAT SOME OF THE LARD OFF YOU.

AND SO IT WENT ON, BUT JOE'S TOUGH TACTICS WERE PAYING OFF. BY THE TIME OPERATIONS BEGAN AGAIN, THE SQUADRON WAS NEEDLE-SHARP AND READY FOR ANYTHING.

THE MORALE IN NELSON'S SQUADRON SEEMS EXCELLENT. I'VE NEVER SEEN MEN SO KEEN.

THE WAY JOE HAS THEM TRAINED, THEY'D FOLLOW HIM ANYWHERE.

JOE WAS DEVELOPING A NEW TECHNIQUE – LOW-LEVEL SHIPPING ATTACKS, THAT WERE USUALLY THE WORK OF TORPEDO BOMBERS. AT LEAST UNTIL NOW...

THERE'S OUR LITTLE PIGEON!
THE NASTY GERMANS ARE FIRING NASTY BULLETS AT US.
MU P

RIGHT. NOW IT'S OUR TURN!

AND BELOW...
THE MANIACS HAVE NO FEAR.
THEY'LL TOSS THOSE BOMBS RIGHT DOWN OUR FUNNELS. THEY'RE TOO CLOSE TO MISS!

IT WAS A DARING PLOY, AND ONE THAT ONLY PILOTS AS WELL-TRAINED AS JOE'S COULD GET AWAY WITH.
THERE'S EGG ON YOUR FACE, JERRY!
MU P

THE METHOD WAS EFFECTIVE ALTHOUGH JOE, LEADING THE ATTACKS, SELDOM ESCAPED DAMAGE –
FLAK DAMAGE ON THE PORT OUTER ENGINE, SKIPPER. THE OIL PRESSURE'S FALLING FAST.
RIGHT, WE'LL FEATHER THE PROP. ANYWAY, IT'S TIME WE WERE GOING HOME.

BEFORE LONG JOE'S PILOTS HAD BUILT A REPUTATION FOR THEMSELVES AS A CRACK OUTFIT AND THIS HAD NOT GONE UNNOTICED IN HIGH PLACES.
NOTICES
DATE AUGUST
SERVICE DUTY
CREWS
JOE NELSON'S MOB TOPS THE CHARTS AGAIN THIS MONTH. AND THEY'VE THE LOWEST CASUALTY FIGURES, AS WELL.
PITY THEY'RE NOT STAYING WITH US. UNFORTUNATELY, RESEARCH HAS A SPECIAL JOB FOR THEM – I JUST GOT THE DETAILS TODAY.

WHEN JOE RETURNED THAT AFTERNOON FROM ONE OF HIS ENDLESS TRAINING FLIGHTS, HE WAS SURPRISED TO HEAR THE AIR COMMODORE WANTED TO SEE HIM –

IT'S AN IMPORTANT JOB, JOE – TESTING A NEW WEAPON. BUT IT MEANS MOVING THE SQUADRON TO AN AIRFIELD IN SCOTLAND.
BUT WE'RE DOING A GOOD JOB HERE, SIR, IN ACTION. WE'D BE WASTING OUR TIME ON THESE EXPERIMENTS.

JOE PROTESTED, BUT HE COULD NOT ARGUE WITH ORDERS AND EXPECT TO WIN.

I'M SORRY, NELSON, BUT RESEARCH ASKED SPECIALLY FOR YOUR SQUADRON. YOU'LL MOVE OUT TOMORROW TO YOUR NEW BASE – AND YOU'LL GET TO HEAR ABOUT THIS BOMB WHEN YOU ARRIVE.
VERY WELL, SIR, BUT I HOPE WE SHAN'T BE OUT OF THE WAR FOR LONG.

THE NEXT DAY THE SQUADRON FLEW TO A REMOTE AIRFIELD AND TEST RANGE IN THE NORTH OF SCOTLAND.
GLAD TO MEET YOU, NELSON. IF YOU COME OVER TO MY OFFICE I'LL INTRODUCE YOU TO OUR SCIENTIFIC ADVISER.
LET'S HOPE HE'S BETTER THAN SOME I'VE MET. THEY'RE AN ODD BUNCH, THESE SCIENTISTS.

IN THE STATION COMMANDER'S OFFICE JOE STARED IN ASTONISHMENT AT THE MAN WITH WHOM HE WAS SUPPOSED TO WORK.
THIS IS DOCTOR MIKE HARRIS, A RADIO EXPERT. YOU'LL BE CO-OPERATING ON THE BOMB PROJECT.
WE'VE MET BEFORE. I HOPE YOU WON'T LET PERSONAL FEELINGS INTERFERE WITH THE JOB, NELSON.

BUT RIGHT FROM THE BEGINNING IT LOOKED AS THOUGH JOE HAD DECIDED THAT THE PROJECT WAS A WASTE OF TIME. HE DID VERY LITTLE TO HIDE HIS CONTEMPT OF MIKE AND HIS IDEAS.
THIS IS THE BOMB. IT WORKS LIKE A GLIDER BUT CAN BE STEERED BY THE BOMB-AIMER RIGHT TO THE TARGET.
PROVIDING IT WORKS. THESE FANCY GADGETS HAVE BEEN KNOWN TO GO WRONG...

THE GLIDER-BOMB WAS MIKE'S PRIDE, AND HE REACTED VIOLENTLY TO CRITICISM.
IT WILL WORK IF IT'S USED INTELLIGENTLY.

JUST HOW DO WE USE IT THEN?
IT IS DROPPED LIKE A NORMAL BOMB, AND AS IT GLIDES DOWN YOU GUIDE IT TO THE TARGET BY REMOTE CONTROL.

THE FIRST TRIALS BEGAN, WITH JOE FLYING A SPECIALLY-MODIFIED HALIFAX WITH A DUMMY GLIDER-BOMB WHICH WAS MINUS ANY EXPLOSIVES. THE FLIGHT WAS JUST TO TEST HOW WELL IT COULD BE CONTROLLED AFTER RELEASE.

BOMB GONE, SKIPPER. AND I'VE SWITCHED ON THE CONTROL PANEL.
SURELY IT'LL WORK BETTER THAN THAT HALF-BAKED RADIO SCRAMBLER IDEA DID.
MU

THE BOMB FLEW DOWN TOWARDS ITS TARGET.

THIS TAKES A BIT OF GETTING USED TO...

BUT EVEN JOE HAD TO ADMIT, GRUDGINGLY, THAT THE BOMB COULD BE CONTROLLED ACCURATELY.

BULL'S-EYE! IT REALLY WORKS.
MAYBE, BUT THIS IS JUST A TEST TARGET.
MU

AS JOE POINTED OUT WHEN THEY LANDED, THE BOMB HAD TO BE DROPPED FROM HIGH ALTITUDE TO BE EFFECTIVE.

YES, IT HAS TO BE DROPPED FROM A HIGH ALTITUDE – TO GIVE THE BOMB AIMER TIME TO MAKE CORRECTIONS. WHAT'S WRONG WITH THAT?
NOTHING IF YOU'RE PLANNING IT IN AN OFFICE. BUT WHAT HAPPENS WHEN THE FLAK'S AS THICK AS PEA SOUP AND YOU'RE GETTING TOSSED UP AND DOWN?

ONCE AGAIN MIKE'S TEMPER FLARED AT WHAT HE THOUGHT WAS UNFAIR CRITICISM.
YOUR TROUBLE, NELSON, IS THAT YOU DON'T WANT IT TO WORK. YOU'VE NO TIME FOR BOFFINS OR ANY NEW IDEAS.

MIKE STALKED OFF IN A FURY AS JOE SHOUTED AFTER HIM.

NO, HARRIS, I JUST LIKE RESULTS – AND I DON'T LIKE MY MEN RISKING THEIR LIVES TO TEST YOUR STUPID GADGETS!

DESPITE THE SUCCESSFUL TEST OF THE GLIDER-BOMB, JOE'S SENTIMENTS HAD SPREAD THROUGH THE SQUADRON. THE MEN FELT OUT OF THE WAR AND AS USELESS AS IF THEY HAD BEEN GROUNDED.
CAREFUL WITH THAT. THERE ARE DELICATE VALVES IN THAT TAIL.
SORRY, SIR. WE'RE NOT USED TO DUMMY BOMBS WITH FRAGILE WIRELESS GADGETS IN 'EM.

TERRY GREAVES BEGAN TO FEEL SORRY FOR MIKE WHO WAS WORKING UNDER DIFFICULT CONDITIONS.

CAN I GIVE YOU A LIFT, MIKE? ISN'T THERE ANY TRANS-PORT TO BRING YOU FROM THE HANGARS?
NELSON SAID HE WOULD ARRANGE SOME BUT I DON'T THINK HE HAS MUCH TIME FOR CIVILIANS.

TERRY SAID NOTHING BUT HE DIDN'T LIKE THE WAY JOE WAS TREATING MIKE.

THEN MIKE OFFERED TO AIM THE BOMB HIMSELF ON ONE OF THE TESTS. THIS TIME THE BOMB WAS NO DUMMY AND THE TARGET WAS A ROTTING OLD HULK OF A COASTER.

RIGHT, HARRIS, HERE'S YOUR CHANCE.
IF YOU'D KEEP THIS PLANE LEVEL I MIGHT BE ABLE TO HIT THAT TARGET!

MIKE WAS PRONE TO AIRSICKNESS AND JOE HAD BEEN FAR FROM GENTLE IN HIS HANDLING OF THE BOMBER.

THE BOMB FLEW DOWNWARDS AND MISSED. IT EXPLODED ON THE SURFACE OF THE WATER STILL FIFTY YARDS FROM THE TARGET. AND IT GAVE JOE THE OPPORTUNITY TO VOICE HIS HATRED OF ALL THIS.
ANOTHER FAILURE! HARRIS, YOU SHOULD GET OUT OF THIS BUSINESS AND TAKE UP GARDENING.
OH, SHUT UP!

BACK AT BASE –
I THOUGHT YOU SAID IT WAS EASY TO CONTROL THE BOMB.
CONFOUND IT, THERE'S NOTHING WRONG WITH THE BOMB!

JOE'S CREW WERE NOT IMPRESSED EITHER.
AND "BRAINS" WAS GOING TO SHOW US HOW TO DO OUR JOB.
THE SKIPPER GAVE HIM A ROUGH RIDE, THOUGH – I HEAR HE GETS AIRSICK IF HE GOES UPSTAIRS ON A BUS.

BY THE TIME OF THE NEXT TEST, JOE HAD WITHDRAWN HIS SERVICES AND IT WAS LEFT TO TERRY GREAVES AND MIKE TO PROVE THE BOMB.
MAYBE THIS CREATES INTERFERENCE AT THE MOMENT OF RELEASE. SUPPOSE WE DELAY THESE RELAYS?
IT MIGHT WORK...AND I THINK I'LL FLY WITH YOU, TERRY, AND TRY AGAIN.

WITH THE TWO MEN WORKING TOGETHER MOST OF THE SNAGS WERE IRONED OUT.
IT'S PERFECT, TERRY. IT'S GOING TO BE A DIRECT HIT.
WELL DONE, DOC. AND YOU HAVEN'T EVEN BEEN AIRSICK!

BY THE TIME THE INITIAL TESTS ENDED MIKE AND TERRY GREAVES WERE GOOD FRIENDS. BUT SOON THE FLYING BOMB WOULD HAVE TO DO ITS STUFF BEFORE A HIGH-RANKING AUDIENCE.
SO TOMORROW'S THE FINAL TEST WITH A LIVE BOMB. I'LL FLY THAT – I'D HATE ANYTHING TO GO WRONG.
YOU MEAN YOU'LL MAKE SURE IT DOES! LOOK, THERE WILL BE A LOT OF BRASS-HATS WATCHING. IT ISN'T FAIR TO WRECK MIKE'S PROJECT.

TERRY GREAVES THOUGHT HE KNEW WHAT WAS IN HIS COMMANDER'S MIND.

YOU'D DO ANYTHING TO GET YOUR OWN BACK FOR THE TIME MIKE'S RADIO SCRAMBLER FLOPPED! CAN'T YOU FORGET THE PAST?

NO, NOT WHEN I THINK OF ALL THOSE LIVES THAT WERE WASTED.

TERRY WAS TOO WORKED UP NOW TO RESPECT DIFFERENCES IN RANK.

YOU'RE AFRAID THAT IF THE BOMB WORKS MIKE WILL GET ALL THE CREDIT, AND YOU'LL ONLY HAVE BEEN THE DRIVER.

I'LL FORGET YOU SAID THAT, TERRY, AND IF WE MISS THE TARGET TOMORROW IT WON'T BE THE DRIVER'S FAULT.

MIKE WAS UNDERSTANDABLY NERVOUS WHEN THE TEST BEGAN, AND JOE WASN'T ALL THAT REASSURING.
I WISH I COULD AIM THE THING MYSELF, NELSON, BUT I'D PROBABLY MAKE A MESS OF IT. DON'T LET ME DOWN.
LOOK, IF THAT CONTRAPTION OF YOURS IS ANY GOOD WE'LL CONVINCE THE BRASS HATS.

FOR CONVINCING PROOF THE BOMB WAS RELEASED AT ITS MAXIMUM RANGE FROM THE TARGET.

THAT THING'S GOING TO FALL SHORT BY A MILE.
GIVE IT TIME. IN A MOMENT YOU'LL SEE IT CHANGE DIRECTION... I HOPE.

THE BOMB DID CHANGE COURSE AND NOW IT FLEW SWIFTLY TOWARDS ITS TARGET.

THERE SHE GOES NOW!

THE RESULT WAS ALL THE DISTINGUISHED AUDIENCE COULD HAVE WANTED.

SUPERB! A DIRECT HIT.

WE MADE IT, MIKE!

IT'S AMAZING, HARRIS. HOW SOON CAN WE BLAST THE JERRIES WITH THESE BOMBS?
WELL, IT'LL TAKE US A WHILE TO REACH FULL PRO-DUCTION.

BUT IT TOOK MORE TO CONVINCE JOE THAT THE "HARRIS BOMB" WAS WORTH ALL THE TROUBLE.

LOOKS LIKE THE DOC'S BOMB IS A WINNER, SKIP.
WHEN IT STARTS KILLING JERRIES, I'LL BELIEVE IT.

AFTER THAT FINAL LIVE TEST MIKE MOVED BACK DOWN SOUTH WITH THE SQUADRON. BUT HIS HOPES OF AN EARLY TRIUMPH SOON FADED.

THIS CONFOUNDED WAITING! HOW MUCH MORE TIME MUST WE WASTE UNTIL SOMEONE FINDS US A TARGET?

SPEAK FOR YOURSELF, OLD BOY. JUST BECAUSE MY HALIFAXES HAVE BEEN ADAPTED TO TAKE YOUR GLIDER-BOMB HASN'T KEPT THEM OFF ORDINARY MISSIONS.

IT HAD BEEN DECIDED THAT THE GLIDER-BOMBS WERE STILL TOO PRECIOUS TO WASTE ON INDUSTRIAL TARGETS. ENEMY SHIPPING WAS TO BE THEIR PRIME TARGET.

BUT HOW OFTEN ARE WE LIKELY TO GET THE CHANCE TO ATTACK JERRY SHIPS? WE MIGHT WAIT FOR MONTHS.
THAT WAS THE MINISTRY'S DECISION, NOT MINE. WHEN THE OPPORTUNITY COMES, WE'LL BE READY.

BUT JOE WAS OBVIOUSLY TOO PLEASED TO BE BACK IN THE WAR TO BOTHER ABOUT MIKE'S INVENTION.

MEANWHILE JOE'S BOYS WERE ONCE AGAIN MAKING A NAME FOR THEMSELVES. BUT ON THIS RAID, TERRY GREAVES WAS IN CHARGE WHILE JOE STAYED BACK HOME.
BANG ON!
RIGHT, LADS, LET'S GO HOME. THE WEATHER'S GETTING DIRTY.
AS THE SQUADRON CROSSED THE NORTH SEA, GREAVES SAW A WALLOWING GREY SHAPE IN THE MIST.
LOOK – A DIRTY GREAT JERRY TANKER SNEAKING DOWN THE COAST – YOU GOT ITS POSITION, JIM?
GOT IT, SKIPPER. I'LL SEND A REPORT TO BASE.

HE FOUND JOE WAITING FOR HIM WHEN HE LANDED – DRESSED IN HIS FLYING-KIT.

I'VE JUST HAD ORDERS TO ORGANISE ANOTHER OPERATION IMMEDIATELY. WHAT CLOT REPORTED THAT JERRY TANKER?
I DID. SHE'S A WHOPPING GREAT PRIZE TOO.

FURIOUSLY JOE EXPLAINED THAT HE HAD BEEN ORDERED TO TRY THE GLIDER-BOMBS.

DOES MIKE KNOW ABOUT THIS?
NO, HE'S IN LONDON TRYING TO DRUM UP SOME ACTION FOR HIS BOMBS. WELL, HE'S GOT IT NOW.
RAF

DETAILS OF THE RAID WERE SWIFTLY ARRANGED.

ONLY THREE KITES ARE FITTED WITH THE BOMBS. I'M TAKING TWO OF THE STAND-BY CREWS WITH ME AND I'LL LEAVE YOU IN CHARGE, TERRY.
RIGHT, SIR, AND GOOD LUCK.

MIKE GOT BACK JUST IN TIME TO SEE THE BOMBERS TAKE OFF.

THEY'RE CARRYING MY BOMBS! WHERE ARE THEY GOING... WHY WASN'T I TOLD?

THERE WAS NO TIME FOR DETAILED PLANNING, MIKE. THE ORDERS CAME WHEN YOU WERE ON YOUR WAY BACK FROM LONDON.

JOE LED HIS FORCE OF THREE OUT TO SEA AT LOW LEVEL, INTO THE MIST THAT WAS STILL THICKENING.
KEEP IN CLOSE, CHARLIE, WE DON'T WANT TO LOSE CONTACT IN THIS FOG.
WE MAY RUN OUT OF IT SOON.

BUT VISIBILITY ONLY GREW WORSE.

FIVE MINUTES TO THE TANKER, SKIP. THAT'S IF SHE'S WHERE SHE OUGHT TO BE.

TOO TRUE. AND UNLESS THIS FOG LIFTS WE WON'T BE ABLE TO BOMB.

BUT UNKNOWN TO THEIR CREWS THE THREE BOMBERS PASSED WITHIN LESS THAN A MILE OF THEIR TARGET.

SOUND OF HEAVY AIRCRAFT TO PORT, HERR KAPITÄN. THEY ARE VERY CLOSE.

TORPEDO BOMBERS, PERHAPS. ALTER COURSE TO STARBOARD.

AT THE ESTIMATED TARGET POSITION, WELL AWAY FROM WHERE THE TANKER REALLY WAS, JOE BEGAN A SWEEPING RUN.

NO SHIP IN SIGHT, SKIPPER. BUT IT'S HARDLY SURPRISING. I CAN ONLY JUST SEE THE SURFACE.

WE'LL SEARCH FOR TEN MINUTES, THEN WE'LL HAVE TO PACK IN AND GO HOME.

THERE WAS NO FURTHER SIGN OF THEIR TARGET. AT A SAFE HEIGHT JOE ORDERED THE BOMBS TO BE JETTISONED.
OK, GET RID OF THE BOMBS AND LET'S GO.
MU

BACK IN THE OPERATIONS ROOM AT THE AIRFIELD JOE'S ORDER TO JETTISON THE BOMBS WAS RELAYED OVER THE TANNOY.

NORTH SE
Dogger Bank
MUST BE PRETTY ROUGH OUT THERE FOR JOE TO TURN BACK.
ROUGH? DO YOU REALISE THAT FLAMING IDIOT HAS CHUCKED AWAY BOMBS I'VE SPENT YEARS MAKING?

MIKE WAS FURIOUS. HE'D SEEN JOE OBSTRUCT HIM AT EVERY TURN AND NOW THIS LATEST ACTION SEEMED TOO MUCH.

THE HALIFAXES TOUCHED DOWN ONLY MINUTES BEFORE FOG CLOSED THE AIRFIELD. AND MIKE WAS WAITING FOR THEM.

SORRY ABOUT THAT, HARRIS, BUT IT'S MURDER FLYING IN THIS FOG. EVEN THE BIRDS ARE WALKING.
YOU JETTISONED THOSE BOMBS TO SABOTAGE MY PROJECT. YOU KNEW HOW PRECIOUS THEY WERE.

ANGER WAS BLINDING MIKE'S REASON, BUT JOE REMAINED CALM.
THERE'S A STANDING ORDER THAT NO AIRCRAFT BRINGS BACK ITS BOMBS – ESPECIALLY YOURS.

JOE'S RIGHT, MIKE. IT WOULD BE VERY TRICKY TRYING TO LAND WITH A HUGE BOMB HANGING UNDER YOUR BELLY.
STUFF AND NONSENSE! NOBODY SAID ANYTHING ABOUT IT TO ME. I'LL COMPLAIN TO THE MINISTRY!

MIKE, ANGRY AT JOE, CARRIED OUT HIS THREAT, AND REPORTED THE INCIDENT TO HIS SUPERIORS. SO JOE HAD SOME EXPLAINING TO DO.
...SO THAT'S HOW IT WAS, SIR. WE DID OUR BEST, BUT THE WEATHER BEAT US.
HARRIS MAY BE A BRILLIANT SCIENTIST, BUT OTHERWISE THE MAN'S A COMPLETE FOOL. HE HAS POWERFUL FRIENDS, HOWEVER, AND I'VE BEEN TOLD TO GET SOME RESULTS, JOE.

ONCE AGAIN THE WAITING BEGAN, THIS TIME WITH THE SQUADRON EXCUSED NORMAL OPERATIONS.

POOR OLD MIKE WILL WEAR OUT THE GRASS. I'LL BET HE EVEN TALKS OF SHIPPING RAIDS IN HIS SLEEP.

HUH, THE MAN'S A SNEAKING TELL-TALE.

JOE'S DISTRUST OF SCIENTISTS HAD NOW BECOME AN OBSESSION.

THEN ONE MORNING, AS A SUNDERLAND PATROLLED LEISURELY ABOVE THE NORTH SEA—

LOOK OVER THERE!
IT'S A BATTLE-CRUISER. MAYBE IT'S THE SIEGREICH — WE WERE TOLD TO LOOK OUT FOR HER.

ABOARD THE GERMAN BATTLE-CRUISER "SIEGREICH" THEY WERE NOT EVEN AWARE THAT THEY HAD BEEN SIGHTED.
I THOUGHT I SAW AN AIRCRAFT. IT MUST HAVE BEEN A SEA-BIRD.
MORE THAN LIKELY, BUT KEEP THE LOOKOUTS ALERT.

WHEN THE NEWS REACHED HIM, MIKE THOUGHT HIS PRAYERS HAD BEEN ANSWERED.

THERE ARE SIX KITES STANDING BY WITH GLIDER-BOMBS ON BOARD. WILL THAT BE ENOUGH?

NO, TERRY, I'VE ALREADY ORDERED ANOTHER THREE TO BE LOADED WITH ORDINARY BOMBS. WE'LL NEVER GET A BETTER CHANCE THAN THIS TO HIT THE SIEGREICH.

THEN MIKE BUTTED IN.
I SUPPOSE YOU'LL BE LEADING THE ATTACK. WHAT HAPPENS IF YOU DON'T FIND THE TARGET – AGAIN?
AS A MATTER OF FACT, TERRY WILL LEAD THE SIX AIRCRAFT CARRYING YOUR BOMBS.

JOE EXPLAINED –
I SHALL TAKE THREE HALIFAXES WITH ORDINARY BOMBS IN FIRST – JUST TO CREATE A DIVERSION AND TO GIVE THE OTHERS A CHANCE. THE FLAK WILL BE MURDEROUS.

WHILE THE AIRCRAFT WERE MADE READY, TERRY REASSURED MIKE.
WE'LL DO OUR BEST FOR YOU, MIKE. BUT YOU WERE WRONG ABOUT JOE, HE'S TAKING THE BIGGEST RISK.
I SUPPOSE SO. BUT I'M STILL GLAD IT'S YOU WHO'S DROPPING THE BOMBS.

ENGINES THUNDERING, THE LUMBERING AIRCRAFT SET OFF.

WELL, THEY'RE OFF. WE MAY AS WELL GO AND LISTEN IN THE OPS ROOM, HARRIS.

I WISH I COULD HAVE GONE WITH THEM, THOUGH...

HUGGING THE SURFACE, JOE'S TIGHT FORMATION SKIMMED ABOVE THE DANCING WAVES.

WE'RE DRAWING AHEAD OF THE OTHER SIX, SKIPPER. THOSE BOMBS ARE SLOWING THEM UP.

THAT'S THE GENERAL IDEA!

TERRY GREAVES WAS THE FIRST TO REALISE WHAT JOE WAS PLANNING.

NELSON'S FORMATION IS ALMOST OUT OF SIGHT. THEY'RE IN A HURRY TO GET TO THE PARTY.

THE CUNNING BLIGHTER INTENDS TO SETTLE FOR THE NAZIS WITH ORDINARY BOMBS BEFORE WE EVEN GET THERE.

A SHORT TIME LATER JOE SIGHTED HIS TARGET ON THE DISTANT HORIZON.

THERE SHE IS! ATTACK INDIVIDUALLY AT LOW LEVEL.

A STREAM OF FIRE FROM THE GERMAN GUNS FILLED THE AIR AS THE BOMBERS BEGAN THEIR RUN.
COME ON, SCHWEINHUNDS. WE ARE READY FOR YOU.
THE FIRST HALIFAX ROARED OVER THE WARSHIP'S MASTS, BUT THE BOMBS WERE NOT ON TARGET.
WE MISSED!
NEVER MIND. THE OTHERS WILL GET HER.

BUT THE SECOND AIRCRAFT RAN INTO A CURTAIN OF FLYING STEEL AS IT APPROACHED.

YOU SHOULD HAVE KNOWN BETTER THAN TO ATTACK US, ENGLANDER!

AFTER TWO UNSUCCESSFUL ATTEMPTS, IN CAME JOE'S HALIFAX, ALL HER CREW DESPERATELY HOPING FOR A HIT.

HERE COMES NUMBER THREE.

WE CAN DEAL WITH THIS ONE LIKE THE OTHERS, HERR KAPITÄN.

JOE DID MANAGE TO SCORE ALTHOUGH THE EFFECT ON THE SIEGREICH WAS SMALL, AND SHE WAS CERTAINLY FAR FROM BEING SUNK.

WE GOT HER THAT TIME.
DON'T KID YOURSELF. I'LL BET WE HARDLY SCRATCHED THE PAINT.

BITTERLY JOE REALISED HE HAD RUINED THE MISSION.

IF GREAVES AND HIS MOB SUCCEED IT'LL LOOK EVEN WORSE FOR ME. I'LL HAVE TO THINK OF SOMETHING...

JOE RADIOED TERRY GREAVES WHOSE FORMATION WAS NOT YET IN SIGHT OF THE GERMAN SHIP, THE FLYING-BOMBS HAVING SLOWED THEIR SPEED GREATLY.
NELSON HERE – JETTISON BOMBS AND RETURN TO BASE. WE HIT SIEGREICH BUT THE SHIP'S TOO FAR OUT BY NOW FOR YOU TO ATTACK.
I DON'T RECKON SHE'LL BE THAT FAST OFF THE MARK...

BUT JOE WAS IN NO MOOD FOR ANYONE ELSE'S OPINIONS.
WHEN I SAY TURN BACK, IT'S AN ORDER. I DON'T WANT A DEBATE ON THE SUBJECT!

SO TERRY SAID NO MORE.
I'LL BET NELSON'S MADE A MUCK OF IT AND DOESN'T WANT MIKE'S BOMBS TO GRAB ALL THE GLORY.

JOE'S HALIFAX AND THE OTHER SURVIVING BOMBER SOON OVERTOOK TERRY AND HIS FORMATION ON THE WAY BACK.

GET RID OF THOSE BOMBS NOW – YOU KNOW THE ORDERS.

MU P

FIVE GLIDER-BOMBS PLUNGED HARMLESSLY INTO THE SEA BUT TERRY MADE NO MOVE TO RELEASE HIS.
WHAT ABOUT OUR BOMB, SKIPPER? SHALL WE DITCH IT?
NO, DON'T WASTE IT. WE'LL TAKE IT HOME WITH US.
IT WAS A BRAVE DECISION TO ATTEMPT TO LAND WITH THE BOMB STILL ATTACHED.

WHEN JOE LANDED THE FIRST PERSON TO MEET HIM WAS THE GROUP CAPTAIN.

I'VE LEFT HARRIS IN THE OPS ROOM. HE'S HOWLING FOR BLOOD. HE HAD A FIT WHEN GREAVES' LOT DUMPED THEIR BOMBS.

THERE WAS NO USE GOING AFTER THE SHIP. THEY WOULD NEVER HAVE MADE IT.

JOE EXPLAINED WHY HE HAD ATTACKED FIRST.

THE GLIDER-BOMB MAKES THE AIRCRAFT CARRYING IT TOO SLOW AND CLUMSY. WE COULD HAVE LOST FOUR OR FIVE CREWS IN THAT ATTACK. THEY WOULD HAVE BEEN SITTING DUCKS.

I AGREE. BUT I STILL DON'T ENVY YOU THE JOB OF EXPLAINING THAT TO HARRIS.

AS THEY SPOKE THE REMAINING AIRCRAFT WERE LANDING.

TERRY GREAVES WILL AGREE WHEN HE GETS DOWN, I'M SURE.

HE'S COMING IN NOW, I THINK.

GREAVES WAS ABOUT TO LAND, BUT NOT BEFORE HIS CREW BALED OUT. HE WAS STILL DETERMINED TO LAND WITH HIS BOMB INTACT.

THE LADS AREN'T HAPPY ABOUT BAILING OUT AND LEAVING YOU TO LAND ALONE, SKIPPER.
TELL THEM TO BALE OUT – THAT'S AN ORDER!

AS HE SAW THE PARACHUTES OPEN JOE REALISED WHAT WAS HAPPENING.

LOOK, IT'S GREAVES! THE FOOL'S STILL GOT HIS BOMB!

HE'LL NEVER MAKE IT. THAT BLASTED BOMB WILL WEIGH HIM DOWN.

TERRY GUIDED IN THE HALIFAX GENTLY, BUT AS THE WHEELS TOUCHED THE RUNWAY IT DESCENDED WITH A SICKENING THUMP.

THE UNDER-CARRIAGE HAS PACKED UP – HE'LL PRANG!

THE BOMBER CARTWHEELED ACROSS THE RUNWAY, AND BROKE UP AS IT WENT.

GOOD GRIEF! HE'LL BE LUCKY TO GET OUT OF THAT ONE.

THE RESCUE TEAMS WERE SOON INTO ACTION.
HE'S UNHURT AS FAR AS WE CAN TELL, BUT HE'S TRAPPED IN THE WRECKAGE.
BUT WE CAN'T USE CUTTING TORCHES TILL THAT BOMB IS DEFUSED.

A JEEP PULLED UP WITH A SQUEAL OF BRAKES, AND MIKE BOUNDED OUT.
KEEP CLEAR, THIS IS NO PLACE FOR YOU.
OUT OF MY WAY, I'VE GOT TO DEAL WITH THAT BOMB.

FOR LONG, NERVE-RACKING MINUTES MIKE WORKED AMONG THE WRECKAGE.
CAN I HELP YOU AT ALL?
YES, BY NOT ASKING SILLY QUESTIONS. I KNOW WHAT I'M DOING, THANK YOU.

AT LAST HE SCRAMBLED FROM BENEATH THE FUSELAGE.
THE BOMB'S SAFE NOW. I'VE REMOVED THE MAIN FUSES.
IT TOOK COURAGE TO GET UNDER THERE...

JOE STARED IN EXASPERATION AS MIKE IGNORED HIS OUTSTRETCHED HAND.
THAT CONFOUNDED MAN. HE WON'T EVEN LET ME BE CIVIL TO HIM...
HAVE THE BOMB TAKEN TO A HANGAR WHERE I CAN CHECK IT.
BUT ALL ELSE WAS FORGOTTEN AS TERRY WAS BROUGHT CLEAR OF THE WRECKAGE ONLY SLIGHTLY INJURED.

TERRY SPENT THE NEXT COUPLE OF DAYS IN SICK BAY. AND AS JOE TOLD HIM WHEN HE VISITED, HE HAD NO INTENTION OF ALLOWING TERRY'S EFFORTS TO SAVE THE REMAINING BOMB TO BE WASTED.
MAYBE YOU WERE RIGHT, TERRY. I'VE BEEN A BIT UNFAIR TO HARRIS, AND I RECKON IF WE CAN GET THE SIEGREICH WITH THE BOMB YOU BROUGHT BACK, HIS PROJECT WILL STAND A CHANCE.
WELL, I HOPE NOTHING GOES WRONG, BECAUSE IF THIS BOMB FAILS IT WILL BE THE END OF THE EXPERIMENT.

THEN ONE WEEK LATER THE SIEGREICH WAS SPOTTED AGAIN BUT MIKE WAS SCEPTICAL WHEN HE HEARD THAT JOE WAS TAKING THE REMAINING GLIDER-BOMB.
WE'RE TAKING THREE MORE AIRCRAFT, LOADED WITH CONVENTIONAL BOMBS. WE ATTACK IF THEY MISS.
I SEE. MY BOMB IS A LAST RESORT IF ALL ELSE FAILS.

JOE CONTROLLED HIS TEMPER WITH DIFFICULTY AND HIS ANSWER SENT MIKE'S PULSE RACING.
WE'VE A FEW MINUTES BEFORE TAKE-OFF. IF IT MAKES YOU FEEL ANY HAPPIER, GRAB SOME FLYING GEAR AND COME WITH US.
I'LL DO JUST THAT!

JOE'S HALIFAX TOOK OFF AND BEGAN TO CLIMB WITH ITS EXTRA CREW MEMBER ON BOARD.

ACCORDING TO REPORTS THE SIEGREICH'S BEEN JOINED BY TWO DESTROYERS. IT SHOULD BE QUITE A PARTY!

I'M SURE. NOW, IF YOU DON'T MIND, I'LL GO BACK. I DON'T FEEL WELL.

MIKE WAS CURSED WITH HIS AIRSICKNESS DURING THE LONG FLIGHT TO THE TARGET.

HAVE A DRINK OF THIS, SIR, IT'LL BUCK YOU UP.

THANK YOU. FLYING REALLY DOESN'T SUIT ME.

AS JOE HAD THOUGHT, THE FLAK WAS HEAVY AND ACCURATE – LONG BEFORE THEY WERE WITHIN BOMBING RANGE.
A WARM WELCOME. OK, LADS, MAKE THIS GOOD.
MU

THE FIRST RUN PRODUCED A HIT. ONE OF THE TWO DESTROYERS FLANKING THE SIEGREICH WAS BLOWN OUT OF ACTION.

SMACK ON THE NOSE!

ONE DOWN, TWO TO GO!

BUT THE BIG PRIZE, THE SIEGREICH, REMAINED UNTOUCHED.
FOOLS! OUR GUNNERS WILL BLAST YOU FROM THE SKY.
I WISH I SHARED YOUR OPTIMISM, VOORMAN.

AND IT WAS NOT LONG BEFORE THE GERMAN GUNNERS SCORED A HIT ON JOE'S KITE TOO.

AAGH!
GREAT SCOTT, HE'S WOUNDED!
FLIGHT SERGEANT ERIC PAIGE, THE TOP GUNNER, SLUMPED BACKWARDS WITH A STRANGLED CRY.

MIKE BURST INTO THE COCKPIT, HORRIFIED BY HIS FIRST TASTE OF WAR.
THE GUNNER'S BEEN HURT – AND THERE'S A FIRE!
GET A GRIP ON YOURSELF. THIS ISN'T A PLEASURE FLIGHT.

YOU'D BETTER GET BACK AND FIGHT THAT FIRE THEN.
YES... OF COURSE.

THEN ONE OF THE TWO BOMBERS WHICH WERE ATTACKING THE SECOND GERMAN DESTROYER STOPPED A DIRECT HIT.
AAGH!
SAMMY'S BOUGHT IT. I HOPE JOE AND HIS BOMB CAN FINISH THE JOB.

JOE KNEW IT WAS NOW UP TO HIM TO GET THE SIEGREICH AND HE WAS READY TO TRY, BUT UNFORTUNATELY THE BOMB WAS NOT.
SOMETHING'S UP WITH THE BOMB, SKIPPER. IT'S NOT RESPONDING TO THE CONTROLS.
THE FLAK MUST HAVE DAMAGED IT. GET HARRIS TO LOOK AT IT. QUICK!

DESPITE HIS NERVOUSNESS MIKE WAS HELPING WITH THE FIRE-FIGHTING.
THE SKIPPER WANTS YOU TO LOOK AT THE BOMB, SIR. THERE'S SOMETHING WRONG WITH THE DROP MECHANISM.
WE CAN MANAGE HERE, SIR. THE FIRE'S OUT NOW.

MIKE CLAMBERED THROUGH TO THE BOMB-BAY AND STRADDLED THE MIGHTY GLIDER-BOMB, FUMBLING FOR A SCREWDRIVER. THE BOMB-AIMER WATCHED IN AWE, FOR ONE SLIP MEANT A DROP TO DEATH IN THE SEA BELOW.

RATHER HIM THAN ME!
THE DIRECTIONAL SYSTEM IS INTACT. IT JUST NEEDS A START...

AS THEY PASSED OVER THE SIEGREICH, JOE BANKED AWAY FROM HIS COMPANIONS.

WE'VE SPENT OUR BOMBS, SKIPPER. THERE'S NOTHING MORE WE CAN DO.
OK, YOU BLOKES, GET GOING. WE'LL STICK AROUND FOR A BIT.

CIRCLING OUT OF FLAK RANGE, THEY WAITED ALONE AS THE SECONDS TICKED BY. JOE LEFT THE SECOND PILOT IN CHARGE AND CAME TO SEE FOR HIMSELF.

TIME'S RUNNING OUT. THE JERRY SHORE-BASED FIGHTERS WILL BE AFTER US SOON.

GIVE ME ANOTHER TWO MINUTES. WE MUST MAKE IT WORK!

MIKE WORKED LIKE A MAN POSSESSED AND EVENTUALLY HE FOUND THE SOLUTION, BUT IT WAS A DESPERATE ONE.
IT'LL WORK IF I HOLD THESE WIRES TOGETHER JUST LONG ENOUGH TO RELEASE IT. TELL THE BOMB-AIMER TO GET READY.
DON'T BE CRAZY. WE CAN'T DROP THE BOMB WITH YOU ON IT.

BUT MIKE WOULD NOT BE DISSUADED.

DO AS I SAY. I'LL GET OFF IN PLENTY TIME.

OK, IF THAT'S THE WAY YOU WANT IT.

AND JOE HURRIED TO THE CONTROLS.

WITH MIKE GRIMLY CLINGING TO THE BOMB AND HOLDING THE DAMAGED WIRES IN PLACE, THE HALIFAX BORED IN THROUGH A CURTAIN OF FLAK.
RIGHT. I'M GOING TO DROP HER. PASS THE WORD TO THE BOFFIN...

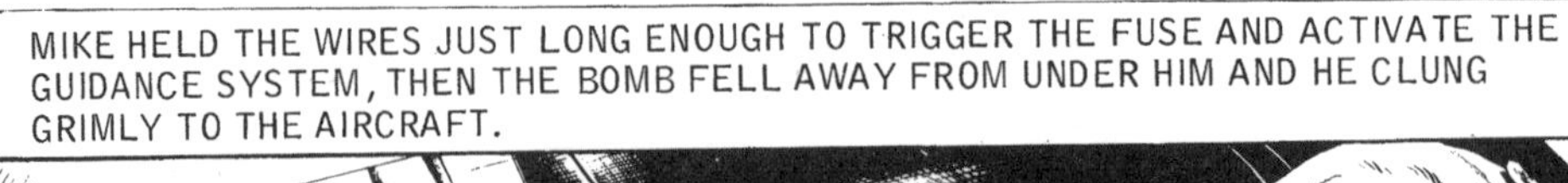
MIKE HELD THE WIRES JUST LONG ENOUGH TO TRIGGER THE FUSE AND ACTIVATE THE GUIDANCE SYSTEM, THEN THE BOMB FELL AWAY FROM UNDER HIM AND HE CLUNG GRIMLY TO THE AIRCRAFT.

THERE SHE GOES!
GREAT STUFF, SIR! I'LL SOON HAVE YOU IN...
A HEFTY PULL AND MIKE WAS SAFELY INSIDE THE BOMBER.

THE BOMB-AIMER TOOK OVER AND THE GLIDER-BOMB WAS GUIDED STRAIGHT TOWARDS THE SIEGREICH.

GOTT IN HIMMEL! THAT BOMB HAS CHANGED COURSE TO COME AT US.

TWIST AND TURN AS SHE MIGHT, THE HUGE WARSHIP COULD NOT ESCAPE. THE BOMB STRUCK HER AMIDSHIPS AND BLASTED A GAPING HOLE IN THE HULL.

RIGHT ON TARGET!

THE GIANT SHIP KEELED OVER ON ITS SIDE AS THE SURVIVORS SCRAMBLED FREE TO BE PICKED UP BY THE OTHER DESTROYER.

GOOD SHOW, MIKE. YOU DID IT AFTER ALL.
WE DID IT, JOE. ALL OF US.

HUGGING THE SURFACE THEY RACED FOR HOME BEFORE JERRY FIGHTERS COULD INTERCEPT THEM.

I NEVER THOUGHT A BACK-ROOM BOFFIN WOULD HAVE MORE GUTS THAN ALL OF US PUT TOGETHER.

WE JUST LIKE TO GIVE GOOD AFTER-SALES SERVICE.

MIKE AND JOE ARRIVED BACK HOME, ALL ENMITY GONE.

THANKS FOR THE TRIP, JOE. IF THAT HASN'T CURED MY AIR-SICKNESS, NOTHING WILL.

IT'S BEEN A PLEASURE. IF EVER YOU WANT TO CHANGE YOUR JOB, I'LL BE HAPPY TO HAVE YOU IN THE CREW.

AND THAT FROM JOE WAS PRAISE INDEED.

THEN, BECAUSE IT MADE THE AIRCRAFT CARRYING IT TOO VULNERABLE, THE GLIDER-BOMB WAS EVENTUALLY SCRAPPED. BUT MIKE WENT ON TO DO INVALUABLE RESEARCH WORK – AND JOE DID HIS SHARE OF WINNING THE WAR IN HIS OWN WAY!
Commando
THE END

WHEELS OF WAR

TRUCKS OF THE SECOND WORLD WAR

Trucks like these and their drivers played a vital military role. They transported supplies and equipment, bringing soldiers to the action — or helping to evacuate them in any retreat.

BEDFORD (3 TON)

Instantly recognisable to all British soldiers, this type of truck was the most used in the British army of the time. There were almost 400,000 in service by the end of the war, and they had more than proved their worth.

SIX-CYLINDER ENGINE 72hp **WEIGHT — 2690kg**
TOP SPEED — about 40mph

BATTLE-WAGON
THEIR JOB WAS VITAL. WITHOUT THEM EVEN THE FINEST TROOPS IN THE WORLD COULD NOT HOLD THEIR POSITIONS. WHATEVER THE ODDS AGAINST THEM MIGHT BE — BAD WEATHER, TREACHEROUS ROADS, THE DESPERATE EFFORTS OF THE ENEMY — THE SUPPLY DRIVERS OF THE ROYAL ARMY SERVICE CORPS ALWAYS GOT THROUGH. CORPORAL MIKE MAGUIRE WAS NO EXCEPTION.

ITALY, 1943. WITH NARROW MOUNTAIN ROADS BEING POUNDED BY ENEMY ARTILLERY, THE PROBLEM OF GETTING SUPPLIES THROUGH WAS A NIGHTMARE FOR EVERY FIELD COMMANDER.
GRUB AND AMMO AT LAST! WHAT WOULD WE DO WITHOUT THESE SUPPLY BOYS?
THEY'RE JUST IN TIME, SERGEANT. WE COULDN'T HAVE HELD OUT ANOTHER TWENTY-FOUR HOURS.

WITH THE APPALLING ROADS AND WEATHER CONDITIONS, IT WAS A JOB FOR ONLY THE BEST AND TOUGHEST DRIVERS. AND THE TEN-MAN SECTION OF CORPORAL MIKE MAGUIRE WERE CONVINCED THEY WERE THE BEST.
MOUNT UP AND GET 'EM ROLLING!
RASC
COME ON, LADS, NOBODY BEATS MIKE MAGUIRE'S BOYS.

BUT THERE WAS ANOTHER SECTION ON THAT FRONT THAT HAD DIFFERENT IDEAS, AND THAT WAS AN EQUALLY TOUGH, EQUALLY SKILFUL GANG OF DRIVERS UNDER BIG BILL BRAGG.

YOU'RE WASTING YOUR TIME, JERRIES! WE'RE BIG BILL'S BOYS AND THEY DON'T COME ANY TOUGHER THAN US!

THE RIVALRY BETWEEN THESE TWO OUTFITS WAS SO INTENSE THAT SOME SAID IT WAS WORSE THAN THE WAR AGAINST THE NAZIS. ONE DAY, WHEN THEY MET UP BACK AT THEIR BASE, WHICH WAS A LARGE FOREST CLEARING –

SUPPLY DRIVERS – YOU MAKE ME LAUGH. BESIDE US YOU'RE JUST A BUNCH OF AMATEURS.
WHY DON'T YOU GUYS ADMIT YOU'RE IN THE WRONG BUSINESS? THIS IS A MAN'S GAME AND YOU'RE JUST A CROWD OF BOY SCOUTS.
R.A.S.C

THE PERSONAL RIVALRY BETWEEN THE TWO CORPORALS, MIKE AND BIG BILL, WAS THE FIERCEST OF ALL.
I WAS DRIVING TRUCKS WHEN YOU WERE ONLY A SCHOOLBOY, MAGUIRE.
MAYBE YOU WERE, GRANDAD, BUT YOU HAVEN'T LEARNED MUCH IN ALL THOSE YEARS, HAVE YOU?
MIKE MAGUIRE WAS THE SON OF A GARAGE OWNER. HIS FIRST LOVE WAS DRIVING, HIS SECOND FIGHTING. MANY SAID THAT GIVEN A BREAK FROM DRIVING DUTIES HE COULD HAVE BECOME THE ARMY HEAVYWEIGHT CHAMPION.
BILL BRAGG, A TRUCK DRIVER SINCE HIS TEENS, HAD LEARNED HIS FIGHTING IN THE DOCKLAND OF LIVERPOOL. WHAT HE LACKED IN SCIENCE HE MADE UP WITH HIS ENORMOUS STRENGTH.
WHY DON'T YOU MOVE OVER BEFORE YOU GET HURT? DON'T YOU KNOW IT'S DANGEROUS TO ARGUE WITH SOLDIERS?
WHY DON'T YOU TRY TO STOP US, MAGUIRE? THEN WE'LL SOON SORT OUT THE MEN FROM THE BOYS.

BILL'S CHALLENGE WAS ALL THAT WAS NEEDED. IN AN INSTANT, THE FOREST CLEARING WAS A MASS OF STRUGGLING, FIGHTING MEN.
RIGHT, PAL —
GET 'IM, JOCK!
WATCH YOUR BACK, SCOUSE!
IT HAPPENED TO BE THE MOMENT WHEN LIEUTENANT-COLONEL WAINWRIGHT, COMMANDER OF THE SUPPLY UNITS IN THE AREA, CAME TO PAY A ROUTINE VISIT. WITH HIM WAS THE ADJUTANT, CAPTAIN SINCLAIR, WHO NEVER MISSED AN OPPORTUNITY TO SHOW HIS AUTHORITY.
THIS IS DISGRACEFUL. STOP IT! DO YOU HEAR ME? STOP IT AT ONCE!

BUT THE DRIVERS WERE TOO BUSY TO HEAR SINCLAIR'S ANGRY SHOUTS.
I'M SORRY, SIR. I'LL MAKE SURE THE RINGLEADERS ARE PUNISHED.
I SHOULDN'T BOTHER, SINCLAIR. LET THEM FIGHT IT OUT, AND THEN SEND MAGUIRE AND BRAGG WITH THEIR MEN TO MY HEADQUARTERS THIS AFTERNOON.

AND SO, LATER THAT DAY...
WHAT'S THE MATTER WITH YOU? AREN'T YOU GETTING ENOUGH ACTION FIGHTING THE GERMANS? OR HAVEN'T YOU REALISED YOU'RE BOTH ON THE SAME SIDE?

YOU CAN'T TELL ME WHAT A TOUGH JOB SUPPLY-DRIVING IS – I WAS A DRIVER MYSELF ONCE. BUT WHILE I CAN WINK AN EYE AT A LITTLE STEAM BEING WORKED OFF, YOU AND YOUR MEN CAUSE TROUBLE EVERY TIME YOU MEET. SO IT SEEMS THERE IS ONLY ONE THING I CAN DO WITH YOU...

OUTSIDE THE OFFICE, THE DRIVERS LISTENED WITH BATED BREATH.
FROM NOW ON, YOU AND YOUR SECTIONS ARE GOING TO OPERATE IN DIFFERENT SECTORS OF THE FRONT. AND AS FAR AS I'M CONCERNED, THE FARTHER YOU ARE KEPT APART THE BETTER. THAT'S ALL. DISMISS.

THERE'S ONE THING — IT'LL BE A RELIEF NOT TO HAVE YOUR UGLY MUG AROUND ANY LONGER, BRAGG.

IT'S A BREAK FOR YOU, ISN'T IT, MAGUIRE? NOW THERE'LL BE NO ONE ABOUT TO SHOW YOU UP!

ASC

COLONEL WAINWRIGHT AND THE ADJUTANT WATCHED THE TWO GROUPS DRIVE OFF.

I'M GLAD YOU GAVE THEM A TALKING-TO, SIR. THEY CERTAINLY DESERVED IT.

PERHAPS THEY DID, SINCLAIR. PERHAPS THEY DID.

CAPTAIN SINCLAIR NEVER TIRED OF MAKING HIS VIEWS KNOWN — ESPECIALLY ON DISCIPLINARY MATTERS.

THEY'VE BEEN A BAD EXAMPLE TO EVERYONE. NOW THEY'RE SEPARATED WE MIGHT GET SOME PEACE.
I THINK YOU'VE RATHER MISSED ONE POINT, SINCLAIR.

THOSE MEN ARE THE BEST I'VE GOT. MANY A BATTALION WOULD HAVE GONE UNDER IF THEY HADN'T RISKED THEIR LIVES GETTING THROUGH. YOU CAN'T EXPECT MEN LIKE THAT TO BE MEEK AND MILD OFF DUTY — THEY'RE TOUGH AND THEY LIVE TOUGH. I'M SEPARATING THEM BECAUSE I DON'T WANT THEM INJURING ONE ANOTHER.

AND SO PEACE OF A SORT CAME TO THE ITALIAN FRONT...
...FOR AS LONG AS MIKE AND BILL STAYED APART, SUPPLIES RAN SMOOTHLY UP TO THE FRONT LINES.
TO KEEP THIS PEACE, COLONEL WAINWRIGHT'S JUNIOR OFFICERS MADE CERTAIN THE TWO CREWS DID NOT MEET — EVER. 
RASC
YOU CAN'T SEND MAGUIRE'S MEN ON THAT ROUTE — AT THIS POINT THEY'D RUN RIGHT INTO BRAGG'S OUTFIT.
WELL, YOU KNOW WHAT THE C.O. SAID. WE'LL HAVE TO FIND ANOTHER ROUTE FOR HIM —
ITALY

SEPARATED AS THEY WERE, MIKE AND BILL BEGAN TO GET SECRET DOUBTS OF THEIR OWN SUPERIORITY AS REPORTS OF THE OTHER'S SUCCESSES REACHED THEM.
HAVE YOU HEARD THE NEWS, SKIPPER? BILL BRAGG'S OUTFIT KNOCKED OUT TWO TANKS LAST WEEK.
I'D NEVER SAY IT OUT LOUD, BUT BRAGG'S PRETTY GOOD!

I'VE HEARD MAGUIRE'S BEEN MENTIONED IN DISPATCHES, CORP.
AGAIN? HE'S DOING OK. BUT WE'RE STILL THE TOP OUTFIT — NO ONE CAN DENY THAT!

HAD IT NOT BEEN FOR THE GERMANS, THE EVENTUAL SHOWDOWN BETWEEN THE TWO CRACK SUPPLY SECTIONS MIGHT NEVER HAVE HAPPENED. BUT THE NAZIS WERE DETERMINED TO HAMMER THE BRITISH FOR ONCE AND FOR ALL.
FIRE!
THIS IS THE ATTACK THAT WILL THROW THE BRITISH BACK INTO THE SEA.

THE CRUSHING NAZI ATTACK TOOK THE ALLIED TROOPS BY SURPRISE.
THEY'RE COMING OUT OF THE MIST IN THOUSANDS, SIR!
WE'RE BEING OVERRUN! WE'LL HAVE TO PULL OUT!

THE OFFENSIVE WAS SUCCESSFUL ALONG THE WHOLE FRONT EXCEPT AT ONE HILLTOP OUTPOST, AT CARPIO, A TINY VILLAGE IN A VERY ADVANTAGEOUS POSITION.
LET 'EM HAVE IT!
AGAIN AND AGAIN THE NAZIS SLOGGED GRIMLY UP THE STEEP SLOPE, ONLY TO BE BEATEN BACK TIME AFTER TIME.

BUT THE ATROCIOUS WEATHER WAS IN FAVOUR OF THE BRITISH.
DO YOU THINK WE CAN HOLD THEM, SIR?
WE'VE A GOOD CHANCE, BOB, AS LONG AS OUR AMMO HOLDS OUT. WE'RE IN A STRONG POSITION, AND THEY'RE FINDING THAT HILL DIFFICULT IN THIS WEATHER.
THE C.O. AT CARPIO WAS MAJOR MACKAY, A TOUGH, EXPERIENCED VETERAN.
EVEN THE TANKS SUFFERED IN THE SLIPPERY, CLINGING MUD.
HIMMEL, WILL THIS RAIN NEVER STOP? GET ON THE STONIER GROUND OVER THERE!

WITH THE HEROIC RESISTANCE HOLDING UP THEIR OFFENSIVE, THE GERMANS THREW EVERYTHING THEY HAD INTO THE ATTACK.

WE'RE TAKING HEAVY LOSSES, HERR MAJOR!

NEVER MIND THAT — OUR WHOLE OFFENSIVE IS IN DANGER. WE MUST TAKE THIS POSITION AT ALL COSTS.

FOR THIRTY-SIX SAVAGE HOURS THE ISOLATED GARRISON HELD OUT. THEN AN URGENT CALL REACHED BRITISH H.Q.
IT'S THE OUTPOST AT CARPIO AGAIN, SIR. MAJOR MACKAY WANTS TO SPEAK TO YOU.

AS THE PHONE CRACKLED FRANTICALLY, THE GENERAL'S FACE TURNED STERN.

YOU'VE SPLIT THE ENTIRE GERMAN ATTACK BY DENYING THEM THAT ESCARPMENT — WHILE YOU HOLD IT THEY CAN'T BRING THEIR FULL STRENGTH UP AGAINST US. HOLD ON FOR ANOTHER DAY, AND YOU'LL HAVE SAVED THE ENTIRE SECTOR. YOU MUST DO IT, MACKAY.

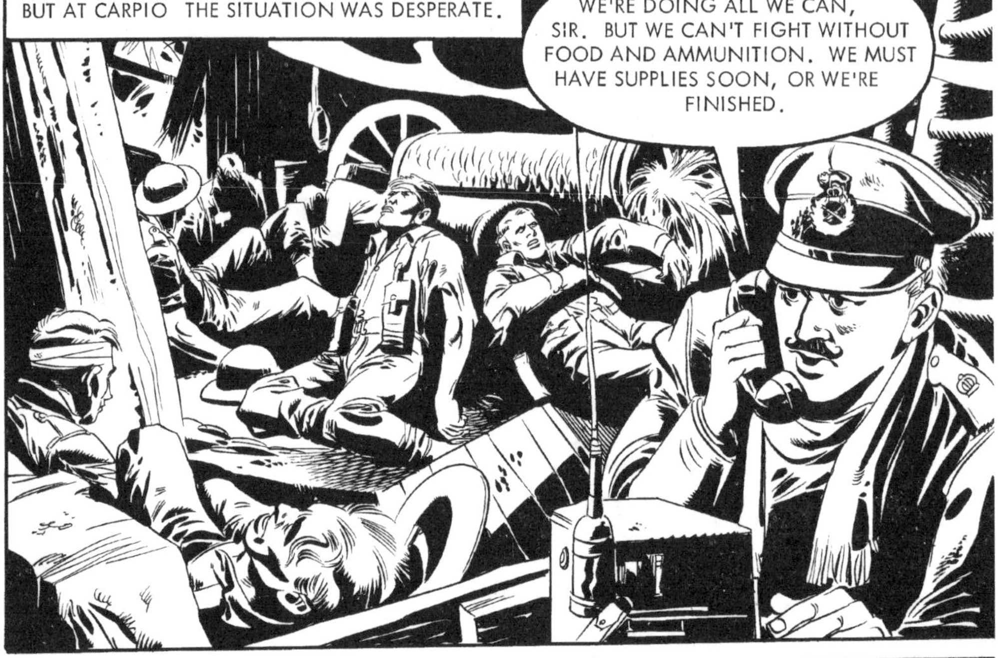

BUT AT CARPIO THE SITUATION WAS DESPERATE.
WE'RE DOING ALL WE CAN, SIR. BUT WE CAN'T FIGHT WITHOUT FOOD AND AMMUNITION. WE MUST HAVE SUPPLIES SOON, OR WE'RE FINISHED.
BACK AT COMMAND HEADQUARTERS, THE GENERAL TURNED TO WAINWRIGHT, WHO HAD JUST COME IN. 
WELL, WAINWRIGHT – YOU'RE THE SUPPLY MAN. WHAT CAN YOU DO TO HELP THESE CHAPS AT CARPIO?
WE CAN'T AIR-DROP TO THEM BECAUSE OF THE WEATHER, BUT THERE ARE SUPPLY COLUMNS TRYING TO REACH THEM BY ROAD AT THIS MOMENT.

BUT KNOWING THE IMPORTANCE OF KEEPING SUPPLIES FROM THE MAROONED OUTPOST, THE GERMANS WERE READY. THE SUPPLY TRUCKS DID NOT HAVE A CHANCE.
THE BRITISH WILL GET NO HELP FROM THIS CONVOY, HANS.
YOU'RE RIGHT. IT'S A MASSACRE!

NEWS OF THE AMBUSH CAUSED CONSTERNATION AT HEADQUARTERS.

EVERY TRUCK WAS WIPED OUT, SIR! THERE WASN'T A SINGLE SURVIVOR!

THAT'S THE SECOND CONVOY WE'VE LOST IN TWENTY-FOUR HOURS.

NEVER MIND ABOUT YOUR LOSSES. IF THAT GARRISON AT CARPIO HAS TO SURRENDER I MIGHT LOSE THOUSANDS OF MEN. WHAT DO YOU INTEND TO DO NOW, WAINRIGHT?

AS ALL EYES TURNED ON WAINRIGHT, HE GAVE A SUDDEN START. HE TURNED TO SINCLAIR.
GET HOLD OF MAGUIRE AND BRAGG. TELL THEM I WANT THEM AND THEIR SECTIONS HERE AS FAST AS THEY CAN TRAVEL.

IT WAS THE ADJUTANT'S TURN TO START.
BOTH OF THEM, SIR? TOGETHER?
DON'T BE A FOOL, MAN! THE WAR IS MORE IMPORTANT THAN THEIR PRIVATE QUARRELS. GET THEM HERE, QUICKLY!

AND SO, AT DUSK THAT SAME DAY, BILL BRAGG AND HIS MEN ARRIVED.
WHAT'S THE IDEA OF GETTING US HERE, BILL?
SIMPLE, DAVE. THEY'VE GOT A TOUGH JOB AND THEY KNOW THE RIGHT OUTFIT TO DO IT.

A MOMENT LATER BILL'S JAW DROPPED.
I DON'T BELIEVE IT! IT'S MAGUIRE AND HIS OUTFIT!
HEY, THAT'S BILL BRAGG. SOMEONE MUST HAVE GOT HIS LINES CROSSED.

AS THE TWO OUTFITS MOVED AGGRESSIVELY TOWARDS ONE ANOTHER, THE DOOR OF THE COMMAND POST OPENED SHARPLY.

HOLD IT! THE FIRST MAN TO START TROUBLE WILL WISH HE'D NEVER BEEN BORN. MAGUIRE AND BRAGG — IN MY OFFICE, ON THE DOUBLE!

GRIMLY COLONEL WAINRIGHT STATED THE FACTS.

THE GERMANS HAVE ALL THE ROADS TO CARPIO BLOCKED AND WE CAN'T SUPPLY BY AIR BECAUSE OF THE WEATHER. BUT IF WE DON'T GET SUPPLIES THROUGH, OUR WHOLE FRONT IS IN DANGER. UNDERSTOOD SO FAR?

RASC

RASC

AS THE TWO CORPORALS, SILENT FOR ONCE, NODDED THEIR HEADS, WAINRIGHT WENT ON QUIETLY.
BECAUSE IT'S YOUR BOAST YOU ALWAYS GET THROUGH, I THOUGHT YOU MIGHT VOLUNTEER. WOULD YOU PREFER TO TALK TO YOUR MEN FIRST?

I DON'T NEED TO TALK TO MINE, SIR. WE'RE READY TO GO NOW.
WE'RE MORE THAN READY, SIR. AND NOBODY WILL STOP US, EITHER.

WAINRIGHT COULD NOT HIDE A SMILE AS THE TWO MEN SCOWLED AT EACH OTHER.

THAT'S THE ANSWER I EXPECTED. ALL RIGHT — THIS IS MY PLAN. YOU'LL BOTH TAKE DIFFERENT ROUTES TO CARPIO — NOT TO KEEP YOU APART, BUT TO GET THE GERMANS TO CONCENTRATE ON ONE COLUMN AND SO GIVE THE OTHER ONE A CHANCE OF GETTING THROUGH.

THERE ARE YOUR ROUTES. MAGUIRE WILL TAKE THE NORTHERN ONE, BRAGG THE SOUTHERN. YOU'LL MOVE OFF AT FIRST LIGHT. ANY QUESTIONS?
WE'LL BE OK, SIR.

AS THE TWO CORPORALS LEFT THE COMMAND POST, THEIR DRIVERS CLUSTERED ROUND ANXIOUSLY.

LET'S HAVE IT STRAIGHT, SKIPPER. WE'RE NOT WORKING WITH BRAGG'S COWBOYS AGAIN, ARE WE?

WHAT'S THE SCORE, BILL? WHAT ARE MAGUIRE'S MOB DOING HERE?

IT'S ALL RIGHT, BOYS — THE C.O. HAS GIVEN US A CHANCE AT LAST TO PROVE WHICH IS THE BEST OUTFIT. WE'RE GOING TO TAKE SUPPLIES THROUGH TO CARPIO. THE OTHER CROWD ARE COMING ALONG, BUT ONLY TO MAKE UP THE NUMBERS.

BILL HAD HEARD MIKE'S CONTEMPTUOUS COMMENT. HE STRODE OVER ANGRILY.
THAT'S A LAUGH. WE'LL DROP OUR SUPPLIES AND BE ON OUR WAY BEFORE YOU'RE THROUGH THE FIRST ROAD BLOCK!
YOU THINK SO? OK, LET'S MAKE THIS THE SHOWDOWN! WHOEVER GETS THE MOST TRUCKS THROUGH TO CARPIO IS THE BEST — KING OF THE ROAD. NO ARGUMENT. WILL YOU TAKE IT ON, OR ARE YOU SCARED OF LOSING?
SCARED? THAT'S THE FUNNIEST THING I'VE HEARD IN YEARS!

OK, IT'S A DEAL, BOY BLUE. AND THIS TIME TOMORROW YOU'LL BE WISHING YOU'D KEPT YOUR BIG MOUTH SHUT.
PERHAPS IT'S WRONG OF ME TO USE THEIR RIVALRY LIKE THIS. BUT IT'S MY ONLY CHANCE OF GETTING SUPPLIES THROUGH TO CARPIO!
RASC

FIRST LIGHT NEXT MORNING FOUND THEM HAMMERING DOWN THE ROAD. RIVALRY WAS AT FEVER PITCH, AND THE WEATHER WAS FOUL.

WELL, THIS IS WHERE WE SPLIT UP. NOW WE'LL SEE WHO'S BEST.

SPEEDING ALONG THE SOUTHERN ROUTE, BILL'S OUTFIT SOON HEARD HEAVY GUN-FIRE.
IT WON'T BE LONG BEFORE THEY SPOT US!

BILL WAS ONLY TOO RIGHT. SHELLS BEGAN TO LAND ROUND THE SPEEDING TRUCKS.
THEY'VE GOT THE ROAD ZEROED IN! HANG ON, TED, WE'RE TAKING OFF!

TO THE SURPRISE OF HIS FELLOW-DRIVERS, BILL SWUNG HIS WHEEL HARD OVER AND ROARED OFF THE ROAD.

RASC

BILL'S GOING OFF INTO THE BUSH! FOLLOW HIM UP!

ONLY THE STRONGEST AND MOST SKILFUL DRIVERS COULD HAVE HELD THE TRUCKS AS THEY BUCKED AND LEAPT OVER THE SCRUB.

FOR PETE'S SAKE, BILL, MIND THE SPRINGS!

CALM DOWN, MATE. THESE TRUCKS ARE BUILT TO TAKE THIS. AND WE'RE OUT OF THE JERRIES' SIGHT, TOO.

SKIRTING THE BARRAGE, BILL LED HIS TRUCKS BACK ONTO THE ROAD. HIDDEN IN THE MIST AHEAD, HOWEVER, WAS ANOTHER HAZARD — A GERMAN ANTI-TANK BATTERY HAD BLOCKED THE ROAD.

I CAN HEAR THEIR ENGINES. GET READY TO FIRE!

AS BILL SWUNG HIS TRUCK ROUND A SHARP BEND, THE MIST LIFTED FOR A MOMENT...
LOOK OUT! ROAD BLOCK!
STOP! REVERSE BACK ROUND THE BEND!
OUT OF SIGHT OF THE GERMANS, THE DRIVERS SAW BILL LEAVE THE ROAD AGAIN.
STICK TIGHT — I'LL BE BACK IN A COUPLE OF MINUTES.
WHAT'S HE UP TO NOW?

ONCE MORE THE TANTALISING MIST HID FROM THE GERMANS WHAT BILL WAS DOING. HIS OWN DRIVERS WERE EQUALLY AT A LOSS AS HE URGED HIS HEAVY TRUCK UP THE STEEP HILL.

HAS HE GONE CRAZY?
NOT BILL. HE MIGHT LOOK LIKE A BRUISER BUT HE'S AS CRAFTY AS A FOX. HE'S GOT SOME TRICK UP HIS SLEEVE.

WORKING HIS WAY ALONG THE FLAT-TOPPED HILL, BILL POSITIONED HIS TRUCK, WITH ITS LOAD OF EXPLOSIVES, OVER THE GERMAN ROAD BLOCK. THEN HE JUMPED.

I NEVER THOUGHT I'D EVER BE IN THE ARTILLERY BUSINESS, BUT THERE'S ALWAYS A FIRST TIME.

THE MASSIVE TRUCK, PACKED WITH HIGH EXPLOSIVES, CRASHED DOWN INTO THE PASS.
HIMMEL... LOOK OUT!
BUT THE SOLDIER'S WARNING CAME TOO LATE. THE THREE TONS OF EXPLOSIVES IN BILL'S TRUCK CUT SHORT HIS FRENZIED SHOUT.
AAAAGH!

FIVE MINUTES LATER, THE COLUMN WAS ON THE MOVE AGAIN. BILL HAD TAKEN OVER THE LEADING TRUCK.
GREAT WORK, BILL!
ANOTHER FOUR MILES AND WE'LL BE AT THE BRIDGE. AND THEN, FIRST STOP CARPIO.
BUT THE GERMANS HAD THEIR EMERGENCY PLANS TOO. FOUR MILES FARTHER ON, DEMOLITION ENGINEERS WORKED FEVERISHLY TO STOP THE SPEEDING CONVOY.
I'VE SUDDENLY LOST CONTACT WITH ROAD BLOCK ONE, SIR. THE BRITISH MUST HAVE BROKEN THROUGH.
YOU KNOW WHAT TO DO. HURRY — YOU ONLY HAVE A FEW MINUTES LEFT.

AS BILL AND HIS OUTFIT SWEPT INTO SIGHT OF THE BRIDGE, THE NAZIS REDOUBLED THEIR EFFORTS.
THEY'RE GOING TO BLOW THE BRIDGE! WE'VE GOT TO MOVE!
HERE THEY COME! HURRY!

WITH ENGINES SCREAMING, BILL'S TOUGH DRIVERS RACED DOWN INTO THE NARROW GORGE, THEIR CO-DRIVERS FIRING AS THEY HURTLED DOWN THE NARROW ROAD.

BLOW IT UP BEFORE THEY CAN CROSS!

AAAAGH!

AS THE SERGEANT COLLAPSED, THE GERMAN OFFICER, A BRAVE MAN, RAN OUT INTO THE HAIL OF FIRE. ALTHOUGH HE WAS HIT, HIS FALLING BODY DROPPED ON TOP OF THE PLUNGER.

AAH!

A SECOND LATER, THE BRIDGE DISAPPEARED IN A THUNDEROUS EXPLOSION. FOR THE SECOND TIME THAT DAY, BILL AND HIS DRIVERS LEAPT ON THEIR BRAKES.

THAT'S TORN IT! WE'LL NEVER GET ACROSS NOW!

WITH THE GORGE AN UNSURMOUNTABLE OBSTACLE BEFORE THEM, THE DRIVERS GATHERED ROUND BILL. BUT BILL HAD ANOTHER TRICK UP HIS SLEEVE.
WHAT'S THE SCORE, BILL? DO WE TURN BACK?
ONLY AS FAR AS THIS TURN-OFF, A COUPLE OF MILES BACK. THEN WE'RE HEADING NORTH, ON TO MAGUIRE'S ROUTE. I SAID WE'D GET TO CARPIO AND THAT'S WHERE WE'RE GOING.

AND SO A FEW MINUTES LATER THEY WERE ON THE MOVE AGAIN, HAMMERING BACK THE WAY THEY HAD COME.

MAGUIRE'S NOT GOING TO LIKE THIS, BILL.

WHO CARES WHAT THAT CREEP LIKES? IF HE STARTS ANYTHING WE'LL JUST PUSH HIM OFF THE ROAD.

AFTER A FEW MILES BILL'S COLUMN RAN OUT INTO A WIDE VALLEY. INSTANTLY HIS CO-DRIVER POINTED TO SOME VAGUE SHAPES AMONG THE TREES.

THERE'S SOMETHING MOVING BEHIND THOSE TREES, BILL.

LET'S STOP AND TAKE A LOOK.

THEY CREPT UP TO THE TREES AND PEERED STEALTHILY THROUGH THE UNDERGROWTH.
IT'S JERRY HALF-TRACKS, AND THEY'RE GOING IN OUR DIRECTION.
YES, THEY'RE BEING SENT TO HEAD OFF MIKE. LET'S SEE IF WE CAN STOP THEM.

BILL GOT TWO OF HIS MEN TO ROLL A PETROL DRUM ON TO A TRUCK TAILBOARD.
OK, BILL, WE'RE READY.
THE REST OF YOU WAIT UNTIL THE FUN STARTS, THEN COME OUT SHOOTING.

WORKING HIS WAY THROUGH THE TREES, BILL BURST OUT SUDDENLY AMONG THE STARTLED GERMANS, PETROL STREAMING FROM THE DRUM ON THE TAILBOARD.

ACHTUNG, ACHTUNG! KEEP TOGETHER!

IT'S SO CRAZY IT MIGHT JUST COME OFF!

AS BILL SCREAMED ROUND IN A HALF-CIRCLE IN FRONT OF THE HALF-TRACKS, ONE OF HIS MATES IN THE BACK OF HIS TRUCK DROPPED A GRENADE INTO THE SPILLED PETROL – WITH SPECTACULAR RESULTS.

HIMMEL, RUN FOR YOUR LIVES!

THE BEWILDERED GERMANS GOT ANOTHER SHOCK WHEN THE REST OF BILL'S OUTFIT CHARGED THROUGH THE TREES, FIRING AS THEY CAME.

THIS IS THE STUFF, LADS! GIVE IT TO 'EM!

IN A FEW MINUTES IT WAS ALL OVER. THE SURVIVING GERMANS, COMPLETELY ROUTED, FLED INTO THE MIST.

BACK, BACK!

BILL'S GANG WERE JUBILANT AS THEY SET OFF ONCE MORE.

GREAT WORK, BILL. IF THEY'D GOT THROUGH TO MAGUIRE THEY MIGHT HAVE FINISHED HIM OFF.

LET'S GO AND TELL HIM THAT. HE CAN'T BE FAR AWAY NOW.

AND MIKE MAGUIRE WAS, IN FACT, ONLY A FEW MILES AHEAD. HIS MEN HAD ALREADY FOUGHT TWO DESPERATE BATTLES OF THEIR OWN, BUT NOW THEY WERE UNEASY.

WHY HAVE THEY STOPPED SHELLING US?

IT MEANS THEY'RE SENDING TROOPS IN TO GET US. KEEP YOUR EYES SKINNED!

MIKE HAD ALREADY FINISHED SPEAKING WHEN HIS CO-DRIVER LET OUT A YELL.

JERRIES! AHEAD, AMONG THOSE TREES!

RASC

RASC

OK, LET 'EM HAVE IT.

BUT AS MIKE'S BOYS OPENED UP —

FOR PETE'S SAKE! HAVEN'T YOU GOONS LEARNED WHAT JERRIES LOOK LIKE YET?
HOLD IT, IT'S BILL BRAGG!

AN ANGRY SCENE FOLLOWED IN WHICH BILL EXPLAINED HIS PRESENCE. MIKE WAS FAR FROM HAPPY TO SEE HIM.

OK, IF YOU'VE KNOCKED OUT THOSE HALF-TRACKS I SUPPOSE WE'LL PUT UP WITH YOU. BUT DON'T GET ANY IDEAS ABOUT DRIVING IN FRONT OF ME, MATE.

RASC

BILL QUICKLY MADE HIS PLANS PLAIN.
DON'T COME THAT WITH ME, MAGUIRE. YOU KNOW I'LL GET THERE FIRST EVEN IF I GIVE YOU A DAY'S START.

AS THE TWO OUTFITS THUNDERED ON TOGETHER, THE GERMANS REDOUBLED THEIR EFFORTS TO DESTROY THEM. FROM CUNNINGLY-PLACED OBSERVATION POSTS MESSAGES CRACKLED URGENTLY OVER THE AIR.
ACHTUNG! THE ENEMY SUPPLY TRUCKS ARE PASSING BENEATH ME NOW.

AND LESS THAN TWO MILES AHEAD, THE MESSAGE WAS BEING ACTED ON.

IT'S BORMAN, SIR. HE SAYS THE ENGLANDERS STILL HAVE NINE TRUCKS ON THE ROAD.

TEUFEL! IF IT WERE NOT FOR THIS MIST WE COULD STRAFE THEM FROM THE AIR.

IF IT WASN'T FOR THE MIST THE R.A.F. WOULD BE STRAFING US TEN TIMES AS HARD!

THEY MUST BE STOPPED AT ALL COSTS. CALL UP THE PANZERS AS WELL!

FIRE!

THIS TIME THE SHELLING WAS DEADLY ACCURATE.
THAT'S TWO TRUCKS GONE — ONE OF OURS AND ONE OF BILL'S.
STEP ON IT! THIS PATH IS A DEATH-TRAP! 
THE TOUGH DRIVERS PUT THE FOOT DOWN HARD, AND THE SEVEN TRUCKS HURTLED FORWARD THROUGH THE SMOKE OF THE BURSTING SHELLS.
THEY MUST HAVE RANGED ON THE ROAD BEFORE THE MIST CAME DOWN. THAT MEANS THEY'RE SHOOTING BLIND — WE'LL SOON BE OUT OF IT.

BUT MOMENTS LATER A BLINDING FLASH AND A DEAFENING EXPLOSION MADE MIKE'S TRUCK SWERVE VIOLENTLY.

THAT'S EIGHTY-EIGHTS AGAIN! WHERE THE HECK'S IT COMING FROM?

IT WAS SOON TO BE OBVIOUS WHERE IT WAS COMING FROM. FOUR TIGER TANKS HAD BEEN CUTTING LOOSE WITH THEIR BIG GUNS, AND WERE NOW RUMBLING INTO AN AMBUSH POSITION ROUND A SHARP BEND.

I WANT THEM BLASTED OFF THE ROAD COMPLETELY, UNDER-STAND?
JAWOHL, HERR HAUPTMANN.

AS MIKE AND BILL ROARED ROUND THE BEND, THERE WAS THE SUDDEN HARSH SCREAMING OF BRAKES...

PANZERS! GET BACK ROUND THE BEND, ON THE DOUBLE.

WE'RE TRAPPED! THERE'S ONLY ONE THING TO DO!

MIKE'S REACTION WAS LIGHTNING FAST. PUSHING HIS CO-DRIVER OUT OF THE CAB, HE SLAMMED IN HIS GEARS AND HEADED STRAIGHT FOR THE ENEMY TANKS.
MIKE, IT'S SUICIDE. COME BACK!
HIMMEL, THE ENGLANDER HAS GONE MAD!
YOU CRAZY FOOL! WHAT DO YOU THINK YOU'RE DOING?

TAKEN BY SURPRISE, THE TIGER CREWS TOOK A MOMENT TO OPEN FIRE. BUT THEN THEY LET LOOSE WITH EVERYTHING THEY HAD.
KEEP FIRING! BLAST HIM OFF THE ROAD!

CROUCHING IN COVER OF NEARBY ROCKS, BIG BILL LOOKED ON IN HORROR.
HE'S ON FIRE! THAT AMMO HE'S GOT IN THE BACK WILL BLOW HIM TO PIECES.

CROUCHED DOWN INSIDE THE DOOMED TRUCK, MIKE WAS COUNTING OFF THE SECONDS.
EIGHT, NINE, TEN....TIME TO GO!

SWINGING THE WHEEL HARD OVER, HE DIVED OUT.
HERE YOU ARE, FRITZ, A PRESENT FROM BRITAIN.
WITH A GRINDING CRASH, THE TRUCK SLAMMED INTO THE ROCKS. MIKE TURNED AND SPRINTED AWAY.

GRITTING HIS TEETH, HE RACED BACK ALONG THE ROAD. BULLETS SPLATTERED INTO THE GROUND ALL ROUND HIM.
IT'S GOT TO WORK, OTHERWISE WE'VE ALL HAD IT.

SECONDS LATER, THE TRUCK'S PETROL TANK EXPLODED, TAKING MIKE'S LOAD OF SHELLS WITH IT.

HE'S DONE IT, BILL — THE SHELLS ARE EXPLODING!

A SUDDEN OMINOUS RUMBLE OVERHEAD ALERTED THE GERMAN TANK CREWS. THEY LOOKED UP IN HORROR, BUT IT WAS TOO LATE.

AAAAGH!

REVERSE, QUICKLY!

SO THAT'S WHAT HE WAS AFTER! HE'S BROUGHT THE OVERHANG DOWN ON THEM!

HUNDREDS OF TONS OF PLUNGING ROCK SWEPT THE TANKS OFF THE ROAD AS IF THEY HAD BEEN TOYS.

ALL RIGHT, YOU GUYS — YOU CAN OPEN YOUR EYES NOW. JERRY'S BEEN TAKEN CARE OF, AND WE'RE ON THE MOVE AGAIN.

AS HIS TRUCK REACHED MIKE, BILL LEANT OUT, GRINNING.

GREAT WORK, MAGUIRE. REMIND ME TO PUT YOU UP FOR A MEDAL. BUT DON'T FORGET OUR BET'S STILL ON — AND THAT LITTLE STUNT COST YOU ANOTHER TRUCK.
RASC
RASC

GUIDED BY BILL, THE TRUCKS STARTED TO BYPASS THE BLOCKED ROAD. IT WAS JUST AS TRICKY AS IT LOOKED.

COME ON, YOU CAN DO IT IF YOU TAKE IT SLOWLY.

BUT BEHIND THE BRITISH COLUMN, THE GERMANS HAD NOT GIVEN UP THE CHASE.
MORE JERRIES, SKIPPER! COMING UP FAST BEHIND US!
THERE THEY ARE! FASTER!

GET IN, SKIPPER! THEY'LL BE HERE IN A COUPLE OF MINUTES.

NO, I'LL HANG ON FOR A WHILE. GET AROUND THAT BLOCKED ROAD AS FAST AS YOU CAN.

KNOWING THE MORE MANOEUVRABLE HALF-TRACKS WOULD SOON CATCH THE TRUCKS UNLESS THEY WERE HELD OFF, MIKE RAN BACK TO THE ROCKS LEFT BY THE AVALANCHE AND DROPPED AMONG THEM.
FASTER! THEY MUST NOT GET THROUGH.
STEP ON IT, TOSH. THEY'RE RIGHT BEHIND US.
BUT AS THE HALF-TRACKS PREPARED TO FOLLOW THE COLUMN DOWN THE SLOPE, MIKE LET FLY WITH HIS TOMMY GUN.
TEUFEL! THEY'VE LEFT A REAR-GUARD TO COVER THEM!

UNABLE TO ADVANCE PAST MIKE'S ACCURATE FIRE, THE GERMANS WERE FORCED TO TAKE COVER ROUND THE BEND. A PARTY WAS QUICKLY ORGANISED TO SURROUND HIM.

GET THE ENGLANDERS OUT OF THERE QUICKLY! THERE IS NO TIME TO LOSE.

ON THE OTHER SIDE OF THE BLOCKED ROAD, BILL BRAGG, UNAWARE OF WHAT WAS HAPPENING, WAS FRANTICALLY URGING THE TRUCKS ON.
C'MON, YOU LOT, STEP ON IT, OR THOSE HALF-TRACKS WILL GET US!

THEN HE HEARD THE RATTLE OF GUNFIRE.

WHAT'S GOING ON BACK THERE? WHO'S FIRING?

IT'S MIKE. HE'S STAYED ON THE ROAD TO HOLD THE JERRIES BACK.

MAGUIRE? ON HIS OWN? THAT'S CRAZY.
MAYBE, BUT HE'S GIVING US A CHANCE TO ESCAPE.

DARN HIM — WHAT'S HE WANT TO DO THAT FOR? IT'S PUTTING ME IN HIS DEBT.

BACK ALONG THE BLOCKED ROAD, THE ODDS AGAINST MIKE WERE NOW OVER-WHELMING.
HURRY, YOU FOOLS! THE BRITISH TRUCKS ARE ESCAPING!
WELL, LOOKS LIKE I'VE HAD IT, BUT I'LL TAKE PLENTY OF THEM WITH ME.
AS THE GERMAN ASSAULT PARTY SWARMED DOWN ON HIM, MIKE JUMPED TO HIS FEET AND FACED THEM, HIS TOMMY GUN STUTTERING DEFIANTLY.
FAN OUT!
HE DOES THIS FOR HIS COMRADES? HE IS A BRAVE MAN.

THE UNEQUAL FIGHT COULD HAVE ONLY ONE ENDING. MIKE LURCHED BACK WITH A CRY AS A GERMAN BULLET WHACKED INTO HIS ARM.
AAAAAGH!
BUT A MOMENT LATER THE GERMANS HAD A SHOCK. WITHOUT WARNING, A SUDDEN GUST OF FIRE SCYTHED INTO THEIR RANKS.
HIMMEL, WHAT'S HAPPENING? AAAGH!

THE SURVIVING GERMANS BROKE AND RAN AS BILL CAME CHARGING AT THEM.

YOU LOUSY SQUAREHEADS — YOU'VE KILLED THE BRAVEST GUY IN THE BRITISH ARMY.

MIKE, WHO HAD ONLY RECEIVED ARM WOUNDS, ROSE TO HIS FEET WITH A SHAKY GRIN.
THANKS FOR THE COMPLIMENT! I SEE THE TRUTH'S SUNK IN AT LAST!
YOU'RE ALIVE! THAT'S THE KIND OF LOW TRICK YOU WOULD PULL, MAGUIRE.

SORRY TO DISAPPOINT YOU. NOW, HOW ABOUT GETTING ON WITH THE WAR? THOSE HALF-TRACKS MUSTN'T CATCH UP WITH OUR COLUMN.

AND UP AHEAD, THE CONVOY STILL SPED ON.
THEY'RE DOING A GREAT JOB, DUSTY. THERE'S STILL NO SIGN OF THE JERRIES.
YEAH — I HOPE THEY GET OUT ALL RIGHT.
NOTHING WOULD STOP THEM NOW.
ONLY TWO MORE MILES TO CARPIO, MAC.
YES. THANKS TO MIKE AND BILL WE OUGHT TO MAKE IT NOW.

AHEAD, ON THE BESIEGED ESCARPMENT OF CARPIO, THERE WAS GREAT EXCITEMENT AS THE TRUCKS CAME INTO VIEW IN THE DISTANCE.

TRUCKS COMING OUR WAY — HEY, THEY'RE OURS!

SO IT WAS THAT THE SUPPLY COLUMN FINALLY REACHED THEIR TARGET.

YOU'VE JUST MADE IT IN TIME, MATE! WE'RE DOWN TO OUR LAST ROUND.

NEVER MIND THE CONGRATULATIONS — TIME FOR THAT LATER. GET THE STUFF UNLOADED BEFORE JERRY HITS US AGAIN.

THE C.O. AT CARPIO, MAJOR MACKAY, WAS MORE THAN PLEASED.
PUT ME THROUGH TO COMMAND HEADQUARTERS. I WANT TO SPEAK TO THE GENERAL.
BACK AT HEADQUARTERS, THE NEWS BROUGHT EQUAL JOY AND RELIEF.
CONGRATULATIONS, WAINWRIGHT. YOUR MEN HAVE GOT THROUGH. MAJOR MACKAY SAYS HE CAN HOLD THE POSITION.
THAT'S WONDERFUL NEWS, SIR. WILL YOU ASK THEM WHAT CASUALTIES MY MEN HAVE SUFFERED?

ONLY SIX. ALTHOUGH I'M AFRAID TWO CORPORALS WERE AMONG THEM.
THE COLONEL'S EXPRESSION CHANGED, AND WITHOUT REPLYING HE WALKED ACROSS TO THE WINDOW. THE GENERAL FOLLOWED.
CHEER UP, WAINWRIGHT! SURELY SIX MEN'S A CHEAP PRICE TO PAY FOR SAVING OUR ENTIRE FRONT?
YOU DIDN'T KNOW MAGUIRE AND BRAGG.
COLONEL WAINWRIGHT'S FEELINGS WERE SHARED AT CARPIO.
AND WHAT ARE YOU GUYS LOOKED SO MISERABLE ABOUT? YOU'VE DONE THE IMPOSSIBLE AND GOT THROUGH, AND YET YOU ALL LOOK AS IF IT'S THE END OF THE WORLD.
WHAT HAVE WE TO BE HAPPY ABOUT? WE'VE LOST BILL, THE BEST N.C.O. ANY SUPPLY OUTFIT EVER HAD.
AND WE'VE LOST MIKE — THE GREATEST DRIVER IN THE BUSINESS.

AS THE INFANTRYMEN SYMPATHISED WITH THE DRIVERS THERE WAS A YELL FROM A NEARBY LOOK-OUT.

THERE'S ANOTHER TRUCK COMING IN!
IT'S BILL'S! HE MUST HAVE GOT AWAY!

THE RELIEF AMONG BILL'S MEN WAS IMMENSE.

GOOD OLD BILL. HE'S MADE IT!
THAT GIVES US THREE TRUCKS THROUGH AS WELL.

BUT THEN, AS THE TRUCK DREW NEARER, THE SERGEANT SPOKE AGAIN.
THERE ARE TWO MEN IN THE CABIN. DOES HE HAVE A CO-DRIVER WITH HIM?
NO, I'M HIS CO-DRIVER. HE MADE ME RIDE ON WHILE HE WENT BACK.
THEN WHO'S THAT WITH HIM? A PRISONER?

THE MYSTERY WAS SOLVED A FEW SECONDS LATER, WHEN THE TRUCK ROLLED TO A HALT BESIDE THE FARMHOUSE.

THEY'RE BOTH IN THERE – BILL AND MIKE!

YOU HEAR THAT, YOU GUYS! MIKE'S MADE IT AS WELL!

ARE BOTH OF YOU WOUNDED?
YES. I GOT IT IN THE ARMS AND BILL GOT IT IN THE LEGS.
SO WE DROVE THE TRUCK BETWEEN US.

HOW MANY TRUCKS GOT THROUGH?
THREE EACH, COUNTING YOURS, BILL.

WELL, THAT MAKES US DEAD LEVEL, MATE.
FAIR ENOUGH, I GUESS.

AT THAT MOMENT OF VICTORY, MUTUAL ADMIRATION FOR THE OTHER'S COURAGE BROUGHT PEACE BETWEEN THE TWO OUTFITS...

YOU KNOW, FOR A KID YOU DIDN'T DO A BAD JOB OUT THERE, MAGUIRE.

I WAS GOING TO SAY THE SAME THING ABOUT YOU, GRANDAD. IF YOU KEEP IT UP YOU COULD BECOME A SUPPLY DRIVER AFTER ALL!

TWO WEEKS LATER, HOWEVER, THE BATTERED CREWS WERE WELL ON THEIR WAY TO RECOVERY, AND THE GENERAL DECIDED TO VISIT THEM IN HOSPITAL.
NOW THAT THE FRONT IS STABILISED AGAIN, I HAD TO COME AND THANK YOUR MEN PERSONALLY. THEY DID A MAGNIFICENT JOB, WAINWRIGHT.
THANK YOU, SIR. I KNOW THEY'LL APPRECIATE YOUR VISIT.

BUT AS THE OFFICERS APPROACHED THE WARD, THE PEACE OF THE AFTERNOON WAS SHATTERED.

SOMEONE GET THE M.P.'s, QUICK. I CAN'T CONTROL THEM.

CAN'T CONTROL WHO? WHAT'S GOING ON?

THE THREE OFFICERS RUSHED INSIDE. FROM THE SCENE OF CHAOS, IT WAS EVIDENT THAT THE DRIVERS WERE ACTING TRUE TO FORM ONCE MORE.

THEY'RE AT IT AGAIN. I THOUGHT IT WOULDN'T BE LONG!

DISGRACEFUL! ABSOLUTELY DISGRACEFUL!

BILL AND MIKE WERE UNABLE TO TAKE PART — BUT THEIR INTENTIONS WERE OBVIOUS.

YOU WOULDN'T USE THAT BIG MOUTH SO MUCH IF I COULD TAKE A SWING AT YOU!
YOU'RE FULL OF FIGHT WHEN YOU KNOW I CAN'T CHASE YOU, MATE.

CAPTAIN SINCLAIR, AS USUAL, TRIED TO TAKE OVER.

STOP IT AT ONCE!
I WOULDN'T BOTHER, SINCLAIR. THEY CAN'T HEAR YOU IN ANY CASE. LEAVE THEM TO IT.

THE GENERAL, HIS GREY EYES TWINKLING WITH AMUSEMENT, LED THE SHOCKED CAPTAIN SINCLAIR OUTSIDE...

BUT IT'S TERRIBLE, SIR. PARTICULARLY AFTER YOU CAME ALL THIS WAY TO SPEAK TO THEM. AND THEY'RE WRECKING THE WARD!

NEVER MIND, SINCLAIR, IT'S A SMALL PRICE TO PAY FOR BREAKING THE GERMAN OFFENSIVE!

AND SO THE TOUGH CREWS OF BILL BRAGG AND MIKE MAGUIRE NEVER DID HEAR THE CONGRATULATIONS OF THEIR HIGH COMMAND.
THANK YOU FOR BEING SO UNDERSTANDING, SIR. I'M AFRAID THOSE ARE TWO OUTFITS I'LL NEVER BE ABLE TO CHANGE.
I SHOULDN'T TRY, WAINWRIGHT. THEY'RE BORN FIGHTERS – PARTICULARLY THEIR TWO CORPORALS. THAT'S HOW THEY GOT THROUGH TO CARPIO. AS LONG AS WE'VE MEN LIKE THAT IN OUR COMMAND WE NEED NEVER BE AFRAID OF LOSING THE WAR.
Commando
THE END

Don't miss your next four all-action Commando books — They're on sale in two weeks! Ask for —

"LAIR OF THE LEOPARDS"
"BEWARE THE CAT"

"TELL NO TALES"
"THE LONG CHASE"

QUICKFIRE!

SUB-MACHINE-GUNS OF WORLD WAR II

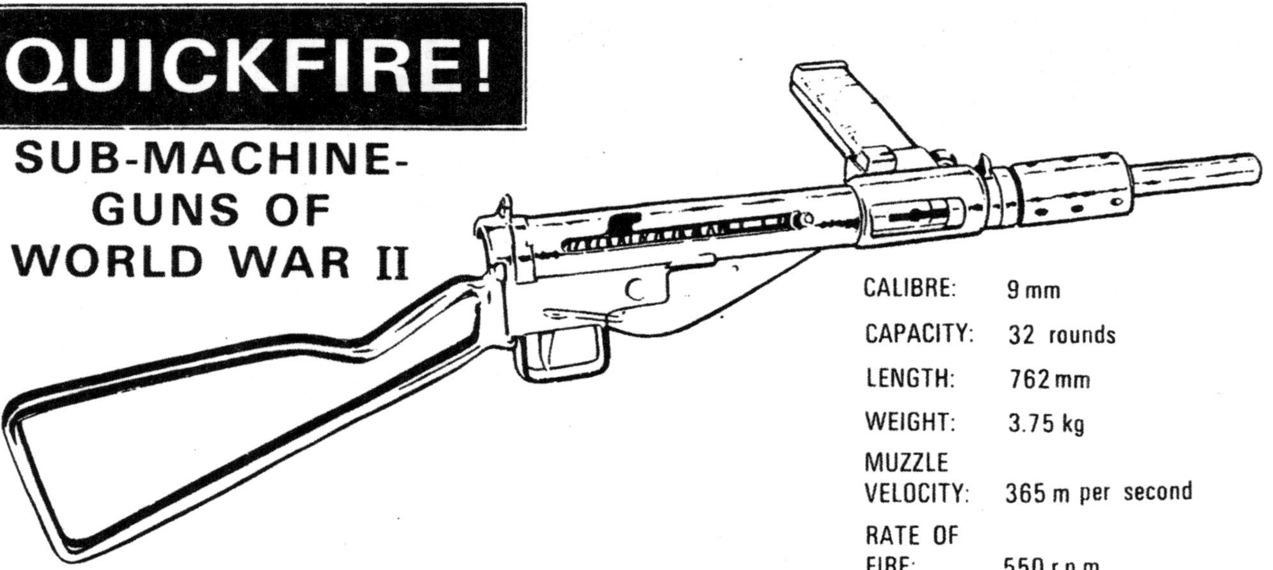

CALIBRE:	9 mm
CAPACITY:	32 rounds
LENGTH:	762 mm
WEIGHT:	3.75 kg
MUZZLE VELOCITY:	365 m per second
RATE OF FIRE:	550 r.p.m.

No.1 — STEN MkII: This well-known British weapon was first manufactured in 1941 and by 1945 nearly 4,000,000 had been made, over half of these being the MkII shown here. It was a favourite fire-arm with paratroopers and commandos, and it was dropped into many occupied countries to arm resistance fighters who liked it because it could be quickly stripped down and easily concealed. Despite its tendency to jam due to poor feed from the magazine, the Sten was popular—it was light, simple to use, and cheap and easy to manufacture. A special version, the MkIIS, was fitted with a silencer. Using this, the only sound heard a few metres away was the movement of the bolt!

THREE... TWO...ONE... ZERO!
1
2
3
4
5
6
IT WAS A COMBAT SCHOOL, A TRAINING GROUND FOR SABOTEURS AND RAIDERS – A REMOTE, HEAVILY-GUARDED AREA OF THE SOUTHERN ITALIAN COAST UNDER CONTROL OF THE ALLIES. AND FROM HERE BRAVE MEN LEFT ON HAZARDOUS MISSIONS, KNOWING THEY HAD VERY LITTLE CHANCE OF SURVIVING. THIS IS THE STORY OF ONE VERY SPECIAL MISSION...

EXPERTS IN ALL ASPECTS OF WARFARE TAUGHT AT THE SCHOOL, ALL OF THEM SEASONED FIGHTERS – LIKE ROYAL MARINE SERGEANT BERT ANDREWS, INSTRUCTOR ON THE FROGMEN'S COURSE.
HUH, I DIDN'T JOIN UP TO BE A FLAMIN' INSTRUCTOR TO A BUNCH OF KIDS!

BUT BERT WAS TOO GOOD A SOLDIER TO COMPLAIN. THE SKILLS TAUGHT BY HIM AND THE OTHER INSTRUCTORS WERE LEARNED BY AN EQUALLY MIXED BODY OF PUPILS WHO HAD BEEN HAND-PICKED FROM VARIOUS ARMIES THROUGHOUT THE WORLD.
THEY WERE ALL HERE –INDIANS, AUSTRALIANS, AND EVEN YUGOSLAVIAN GUERILLA FIGHTERS.

TWO OF THE PUPILS DREW PARTICULAR ATTENTION.

LOOK AT THOSE TWO YUGOSLAVS, BERT. FEROCIOUS, AIN'T THEY?

FEROCIOUS MY EYE! THOSE CHARACTERS ARE ALL SHOW.

BERT WAS A SOLDIER OF THE OLD SCHOOL. HE OBJECTED TO THE TRAINEES' COLOURFUL STYLE OF DRESS AND GENERAL ATTITUDE.
IT'S A PITY THEY'RE NOT ON THE FROGMEN'S COURSE — I'D SOON MAKE REAL SOLDIERS OF THEM.
DISCIPLINE AND UNIFORM AIN'T EVERYTHING, COBBER.

THE AUSTRALIAN WAS RIGHT, AND BERT COULDN'T HAVE BEEN MORE WRONG. THE TWO MEN WERE IN FACT VETERAN YUGOSLAV PARTISANS WHO WERE BEING GIVEN SPECIAL TRAINING IN COMMANDO ARTS.

ANOTHER JOKE, EH? SORRY, MATE, I DON'T SAVVY THE LINGO.

IN THE MOUNTAINOUS WILDS OF YUGOSLAVIA, SUCH MEN, POORLY EQUIPPED AND HEAVILY OUTNUMBERED, MANAGED TO PIN DOWN SEVERAL GERMAN DIVISIONS...

NOW, MY BROTHERS, WE HAVE THEM!

...DIVISIONS THAT WOULD OTHERWISE BE FIGHTING THE ALLIED ARMIES.

THIS FACT WAS ABOUT TO BE DRIVEN HOME TO CAPTAIN SAM COLWELL OF THE ROYAL MARINES – THE MAN IN CHARGE OF THE FROGMEN'S COURSE AND BERT'S SUPERIOR OFFICER.

SOUNDS LIKE SOMETHING BIG IS BREWING UP...

HQ

HE HAD BEEN ORDERED TO A MEETING WITH THE C. O. ,MAJOR HENRY WALKER.
YUGOSLAVIA
ADRIATIC SEA
AH,COME IN, COLWELL. EVER HEAR OF THE KUBRAN DAM? NO?WELL,IT'S HERE IN THE MOUNTAINS OF YUGO-SLAVIA,AND IS A VITAL SOURCE OF ENERGY TO THE GERMAN WAR EFFORT.

SAM WAS USED TO HIS C.O.'s BRUSQUE, DIRECT BRIEFINGS. HE LISTENED INTENTLY –

THE DAM IS VERY HEAVILY DEFENDED AND OUR YUGOSLAV ALLIES HAVE BEEN UNABLE TO DESTROY IT. THEY REQUESTED OUR HELP, AND WE FEEL THAT YOUR SPECIAL SKILLS ARE CALLED FOR SINCE THE R.A.F. BOMBERS CAN'T GET NEAR THE PLACE.

SAM WAS GIVEN AN EASY CHOICE.

A JOB FOR TWO MEN, I THINK. ANY IDEAS WHO ELSE?
NO DOUBT ABOUT THAT, SIR. SERGEANT ANDREWS.

SO SAM TOLD BERT ABOUT THE MISSION.

HOW DO YOU FEEL ABOUT IT?
WELL, I'LL BE GLAD TO GET BACK INTO ACTION, SIR. BUT AS FOR THOSE PARTISANS...

SAM SMILED. HE KNEW HIS SERGEANT WAS ANXIOUS TO GET BACK INTO ACTION, EVEN IF IT MEANT LIAISING WITH IRREGULAR RESISTANCE UNITS.

NEVER MIND, BERT – AT LEAST YOU'LL BE ABLE TO SHOW THEM HOW A REAL MARINE BEHAVES.

YES, BUT... AW, WHAT'S THE USE?

BERT HAD NO LOVE FOR ROMANTIC, FREEDOM-FIGHTING PARTISANS WHO CARED LITTLE FOR DISCIPLINE AND THE LIKE.

AND SO TWO NIGHTS LATER, TWO HEAVILY-BURDENED AND FULLY-BRIEFED MEN PARACHUTED FROM AN R.A.F. WELLINGTON INTO THE SKIES ABOVE WAR-TORN YUGOSLAVIA.

IMAGINE HAVING TO WORK WITH UNWASHED, SCRUFFY NATIVES? A BLOKE...

THE LANDING WAS SAFELY MADE. AS SAM UNCLIPPED HIS HARNESS HE CALLED IN A WHISPER –

OK?

YES, EVERYTHING'S OK.

THE MARINES HURRIEDLY BUNDLED UP THEIR CHUTES AND BURIED THEM IN THE SNOW ALONG WITH THE CHUTES AND SUPPLY CANISTERS WHICH WERE ALREADY EMPTIED.

HUH, I WOULDN'T WANT TO COME HERE FOR A HOLIDAY. WHERE'S THE RECEPTION COMMITTEE?
I DON'T KNOW, BERT, BUT THE PILOT WOULDN'T HAVE DROPPED US IF HE HADN'T SEEN THE RE-COGNITION SIGNAL.
BUT THEIR DROP HAD BEEN OBSERVED ALL RIGHT...

...OBSERVED BY MORE THAN ONE WATCHER UNFORTUNATELY, FOR A GERMAN ALPINE KORPS PATROL WAS ALSO ON THE SCENE.
SO, ENGLANDERS... WHY ARE THEY HERE?

A CRACK OF A TWIG SENT THE TWO MARINES FOR THEIR GUNS, BUT TOO LATE. A HUGE FIGURE STOOD OVER THEM, SNARLING IN HEAVILY-ACCENTED ENGLISH.
HAH! LIKE CHILDREN! CAUGHT IN THE OPEN WITHOUT GUNS. HEY, PIETRO, COME AND SEE WHAT CHILDREN THEY HAVE SENT TO HELP.
FROM HIS ACCENT, BOTH THE MARINES REALISED THAT THE GIANT WAS A YUGOSLAV, AS WAS HIS COMPANION, PIETRO, WHO JOINED HIM ALMOST AT ONCE.

BERT ANDREWS WAS NOT ONE TO BE INSULTED WITH IMPUNITY.

LOOK, MATE. CREEPING UP ON US IS ONE THING, BUT SO HELP ME, I'LL...

HOLD IT, BERT. THEY'RE SUPPOSED TO BE OUR ALLIES.

A PUZZLED EXPRESSION FILLED THE YUGOSLAV'S FACE AS HE ASKED SAM A QUESTION.

WHERE IS THE REST OF YOUR FORCE? WE HAVE ASKED FOR HELP TO BLOW UP THE KUBRAN DAM, AND WE GET SOFT-SKINNED BOYS!
NOW THEN, WHOEVER YOU ARE, WE ARE TRAINED MARINES, EXPERTS...

HE COULD NOT BELIEVE THAT SAM AND BERT WERE ALONE.

BAH! IT IS NOT POSSIBLE. THREE TIMES I, SANDRO, HAVE LED MY MEN AGAINST THE DAM, AND EACH TIME HAVE BEEN DRIVEN BACK. WE ASK FOR MANY TRAINED MEN, NOT CHILDREN WHO PLAY WITH TOYS!

BOTH THE MARINES HAD BEEN SENT ON THIS MISSION TO HELP THE LOCAL PARTISANS, AND IF THEY WERE TO WORK TOGETHER, ARGUING AND CYNICAL REMARKS WERE NOT GOING TO HELP THEIR RELATIONSHIP ANY.
WE'RE ALL YOU'RE GOING TO GET, CHUM, SO FORGET THE INSULTS AND TAKE US TO THE DAM. LET'S GET THIS OVER AND DONE WITH SO WE CAN GET OUT OF HERE AS SOON AS WE CAN.
YES, AWAY FROM YOU FANCY-DRESS GORILLAS!

NOW IT WAS PIETRO'S TURN TO LOSE HIS TEMPER...

ENGLISHMAN, I WILL BREAK YOUR BACK LIKE A TWIG.

GARN, YOU'RE AS THICK AS THE MOUNTAINS YOU RUN AROUND IN, SUN-SHINE!

BEFORE ANY MORE INSULTS COULD BE TRADED, THERE WAS AN INTERRUPTION AS ANOTHER PARTISAN APPEARED.

SANDRO — GERMANS! A SKI-PATROL OF ABOUT SIX MEN. THEY MUST HAVE SEEN THE PARACHUTES FROM THE TOP OF THE HILL.
QUICK! RUN FOR THOSE TREES. TAKE YOUR EQUIPMENT.

THE TWO MARINES STRUGGLED THROUGH THE SNOW, LADEN WITH THEIR GEAR. BERT LOOKED BACK, BUT THE PARTISANS HAD DISAPPEARED.

THEY'VE FLAMIN' ABANDONED US!

LEAVE THE GEAR AND RUN!

LIKE EAGLES, THE GERMAN PATROL SWOOPED DOWN ACROSS THE WHITE SNOW TOWARDS THEIR PREY.
ACHTUNG! ZWEI ENGLANDER...

SUDDENLY THE SNOW ERUPTED AND THE GERMANS WERE FACED WITH THREE HUGE, BEAR-LIKE FIGURES, THEIR GUNS SPITTING DEATH.

DIE, NAZI!

IT WAS A NEAT TRICK. THE PARTISANS HAD STAYED HIDDEN BELOW WHITE SHEETS FROM THEIR PACKS, MAKING THEM MERGE COMPLETELY WITH THE SNOWSCAPE.

THE FIGHT WAS FAST AND FURIOUS. THE PARTISANS HAD THE ELEMENT OF SURPRISE, AND WITHIN SECONDS ALL BUT ONE OF THE GERMANS WERE DEAD...

HA, HE FLIES! WHERE HE GOES NOW, HE CANNOT FLY WITHOUT SINGE-ING HIS WINGS!
AAARGH!

BERT ANDREWS FELT THE FIRST STIRRINGS OF RESPECT FOR THESE STRANGE ALLIES AS HE AND SAM WALKED BACK TO THE SCENE.

PHEW, I TAKE BACK THE BIT ABOUT "FANCY DRESS".

SAM WAS VERY IMPRESSED.
THAT WAS QUITE A TRICK BACK THERE.
AN OLD ONE, BUT IT ALWAYS WORKS. THERE IS NO BETTER SNOW CAMOUFLAGE THAN A SIMPLE WHITE SHEET.

MINUTES LATER, IT WAS TIME TO GO.
COME, WE MUST HURRY!
WHERE TO?

AS THEY TURNED FROM THE DEAD GERMANS, SANDRO ANSWERED SAM AS THEY TRUDGED ALONG.

TO OUR CAMP. WE WILL WAIT THERE FOR THE REST OF YOUR PARTY.

LOOK, PAL. I'VE TOLD YOU, THERE'S JUST THE TWO OF US. WE'RE ALL THE HELP YOU'RE GETTING.

THE TWO MARINES WERE NOT USED TO TRAVEL IN SNOW, AND THEY WERE SOON A LITTLE WEARY.

HOW MUCH FURTHER?
NOT FAR. OUR CAMP IS IN THE VALLEY BEYOND.

A FEW MINUTES LATER, SANDRO SAW A YOUNG TREE BENT INTO A PECULIAR POSITION...

WHAT IS IT?
A TREE BENT LIKE THIS MEANS DANGER. IT IS A WARNING.

SANDRO MADE PLANS TO DISCOVER WHAT THE WARNING SIGNAL COULD MEAN.

YOU TWO STAY HERE WITH JOSIP. PIETRO AND I WILL GO ON AHEAD TO SEE WHAT IS WRONG.

REAL CLOAK-AND-DAGGER STUFF!

IT WAS SOME TIME BEFORE SANDRO AND PIETRO RETURNED. WHEN THEY DID, THEY HAD A THIRD MAN WITH THEM.
PHEW, ABOUT TIME. I THOUGHT WE'D BEEN ABANDONED.
YEAH, I'M QUITE SURE THAT HE WOULD LIKE THAT TO HAPPEN.

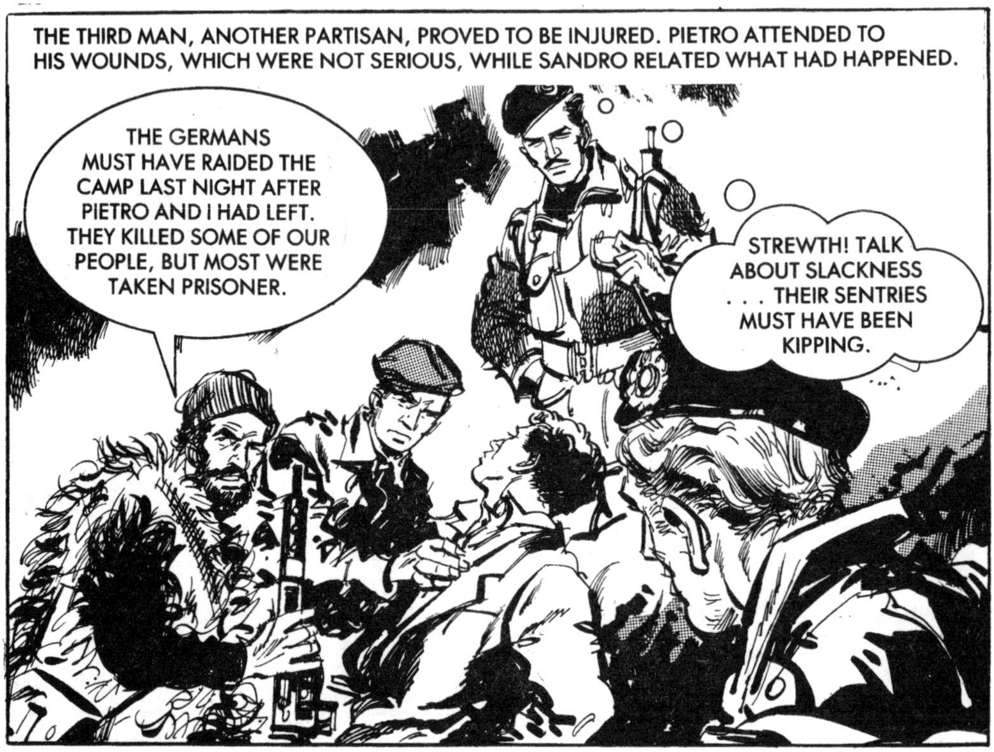

THE THIRD MAN, ANOTHER PARTISAN, PROVED TO BE INJURED. PIETRO ATTENDED TO HIS WOUNDS, WHICH WERE NOT SERIOUS, WHILE SANDRO RELATED WHAT HAD HAPPENED.

THE GERMANS MUST HAVE RAIDED THE CAMP LAST NIGHT AFTER PIETRO AND I HAD LEFT. THEY KILLED SOME OF OUR PEOPLE, BUT MOST WERE TAKEN PRISONER.

STREWTH! TALK ABOUT SLACKNESS . . . THEIR SENTRIES MUST HAVE BEEN KIPPING.

LATER THE PARTY MOVED DOWN INTO THE RUINED CAMP, SANDRO CONTINUING WITH HIS EXPLANATION OF THE EVENTS.
THEY HAVE TAKEN OUR PEOPLE TO THE CASTLE IN THE LAKE.
THE CASTLE IN THE LAKE?
SOUNDS LIKE SOMETHING FROM A FAIRY TALE!

SANDRO TOOK SAM AND THE OTHERS TO A VANTAGE POINT AND SHOWED THEM WHAT HE MEANT.
LOOK – THE LOCAL GERMAN ARMY H.Q. IS BASED IN THAT OLD CASTLE ON THE ISLAND IN THE LAKE. THE PLACE IS IMPREGNABLE. THERE IS ONLY ONE WAY IN, AND THAT IS ACROSS THE BRIDGE.
SWIFTLY SAM SIZED THE PLACE UP.
VERY WELL, WE WILL HELP YOU TO RESCUE YOUR COMRADES – BUT ONLY AFTER WE COMPLETE WHAT WE CAME HERE TO DO.
YOU! HOW CAN YOU HELP?

SAM ALREADY HAD A FEW THOUGHTS ON HOW HE AND BERT WOULD BE ABLE TO HELP, BUT HE WASN'T READY TO DISCLOSE THEM YET.
I'LL EXPLAIN LATER. BUT FIRST, TAKE US TO THE DAM – COME ON, SERGEANT, LET'S GET GOING.
CAUTIOUSLY THEY APPROACHED THE KUBRAN DAM, SOURCE OF SO MUCH POWER AND A GERMAN STRONGHOLD.
SO THAT'S IT. WE'LL WAIT UNTIL DARK BEFORE WE ATTACK.
HA! HOW CAN TWO MEN MAKE AN ATTACK ON A CONCRETE MONSTER LIKE THAT?

SANDRO WAS STILL BEMUSED. HE COULD NOT UNDERSTAND HOW TWO CRAZY, MAD ENGLISHMEN COULD POSSIBLY DESTROY THE DAM THEMSELVES.

LISTEN, MATE, WE'VE TOLD YOU ALREADY THAT WE'RE HERE TO DO THE JOB, AND —

NEVER MIND, SERGEANT. HE'LL FIND OUT SOON ENOUGH THAT A BATTALION ISN'T NEEDED FOR THIS.

WHEN DARKNESS FELL THE TWO MARINES UNPACKED THEIR DIVING GEAR. SANDRO REALISED FOR THE FIRST TIME THAT THEY WERE FROGMEN.
SO, WE GO UNDER THE WATER!
WELL DONE, MATE. TEN OUT OF TEN AND A GOLD STAR TO YOU!

AS HE AND BERT SET THEIR EXPLOSIVE CHARGES, SAM EXPLAINED WHAT THEY INTENDED TO DO.

THE WALLS OF THE DAM WILL BE TOO THICK, SO WE WILL BLOW UP THE SLUICE GATES. THE DAM WILL BE OUT OF ACTION FOR MONTHS.

GET THE PICTURE NOW, MATE?

SANDRO'S MANNER WAS NOW A LITTLE MORE RESPECTFUL, THOUGH HE STILL HAD HIS DOUBTS.

THIS IS LIKELY TO BE A LONG JOB. WAIT FOR US, WON'T YOU?
OF COURSE – IN CASE ANYTHING GOES WRONG.

THE ATTACK WAS ON, AND THE TWO FROGMEN SWAM TO THEIR TARGET IN THE DARK, ICY DEPTHS.
IT'S SO DARK, WE'LL ONLY KNOW WE'VE REACHED THE DAM WHEN WE BUMP INTO IT!
THE DAM WAS REGULARLY PATROLLED, BUT THE GUARDS WERE NOT EXPECTING AN ATTACK.
LIEBER GOTT! IT IS SO COLD TONIGHT... MY BLOOD FREEZES.
YET IT WAS A HAZARDOUS RAID. BELOW THE SURFACE, THE TWO MARINES WERE ONLY TOO AWARE THAT IF THEIR AIR-BUBBLES WERE SEEN...
... A HAND GRENADE THROWN INTO THE WATER WOULD MEAN CERTAIN DEATH.

TO THE WATCHERS ON THE BANK, THE WAITING SEEMED A LIFETIME.

THEY HAVE BEEN GONE LONG NOW...

IT SEEMS LIKE ETERNITY.

BUT AT LAST THE EXHAUSTED DIVERS RETURNED, AND WERE HAULED ONTO THE BANK BY ANXIOUS HANDS.

ALL WENT WELL?
VERY WELL. THE CHARGES SHOULD GO OFF AT DAWN.
YEAH, THEN YOU'LL SEE SOMETHING.

DAWN CAME...AND WENT.
PAH, NO BANG! DID YOU SET THE CHARGES TO GREENWICH MEAN TIME, EH?
IN THAT CASE, WE HAVE A LONG WAIT!

BUT THE MARINES WERE UNCONCERNED.
AW, BELT UP, YOU GREAT HAIRY OX! ANY MINUTE NOW...

SECONDS LATER THE PARTY WERE ABLE TO ADMIRE THE RESULTS OF THE NIGHT'S EFFORTS AS A VIOLENT BLAST TORE AT THEIR TARGET.
WILL YOU LOOK AT THAT EXPLOSION?
THAT SHOULD PUT THE KUBRAN DAM OUT FOR QUITE A WHILE.
MEIN GOTT, WAS GIBT?
SO GREAT WAS THE CONFUSION AS THE PRECIOUS WATER DRAINED AWAY THAT NO NAZIS CAME SEARCHING FOR THE SABOTEURS.

SAM AND BERT WERE NOW READY TO HELP IN THEIR PROMISED TASK OF HELPING IN THE RESCUE OF THE CAPTURED PARTISANS.

AND NOW...
LEAD ON, MACDUFF. WHICH WAY BACK TO THE CASTLE IN THE LAKE?

SANDRO LED THEM TO THE SPOT, AND THE TWO FROGMEN EXAMINED THE TASK THEY HAD SET THEMSELVES.

WHAT ABOUT IT, THEN, SKIPPER?
JUST AS I HOPED. YES, WE SHOULD BE ABLE TO HELP.

WHAT SAM HAD NOTICED WAS THE SENTRY BOXES—

THE SENTRIES ARE FACING OUT THE WAY TO PROTECT THE CASTLE . . . THEY WON'T EXPECT ANY ATTACK FROM BEHIND.

SO ONCE MORE THE TWO MARINES RETURNED TO THE ELEMENT THEY WORKED SO WELL IN.

THE GUARDS DID NOT IN FACT EXPECT DANGER FROM THIS QUARTER.
THOSE GOONS ARE IN FOR A NASTY SURPRISE.

IT WAS A MOMENT'S WORK TO OVERPOWER THE UNSUSPECTING DEFENDERS OF THE CASTLE.

TIE THEM UP AND STRIP THEM OF THEIR GREATCOATS, BERT.

UURGH!

WITH BOTH GUARDS RENDERED UNCONSCIOUS, SAM AND BERT PUT ON THE SENTRIES' GREAT-COATS AND HELMETS OVER THEIR STILL WET SUITS.

READY, BERT?
YEAH, WON'T BE A MINUTE.

WHEN THEY WERE BOTH READY, SAM PREPARED TO SEND A PREARRANGED SIGNAL TO THE WAITING PARTISANS ON THE SHORE OF THE LAKE.

ALL SET, SKIPPER. THIS JERRY GEAR AIN'T NEAT, IS IT?

WE'RE NOT HERE FOR A MANNEQUIN PARADE, BERT! NOW FOR THE SIGNAL TO SANDRO.

SOON THE TWO MARINES WERE JOINED BY THEIR PARTISAN ALLIES. THE NEXT STEP TOWARDS THE RESCUE OF THE CAPTURED YUGOSLAVS LAY AHEAD.

WELL DONE, MY FRIENDS, YOU HAVE PROVED YOURSELVES THIS NIGHT.
NOW IT'S YOUR TURN, MATE!

SAM DECIDED TO ACCOMPANY THE PARTISANS ON THEIR DESPERATE TASK, AS HIS FLUENT GERMAN MIGHT HELP HIM BLUFF THEIR WAY INTO THE CASTLE. HE LEFT INSTRUCTIONS WITH HIS TOUGH SERGEANT –

IF ANYONE TRIES TO CROSS, DELAY THEM AS LONG AS POSSIBLE. I'LL BE BACK AS SOON AS I CAN.

OK, SKIPPER. MAYBE NOW I'LL GET ME FEET UP AND GET A BREATHER!

MINUTES LATER, ONLY ONE SENTRY STOOD BETWEEN THE RAIDING PARTY AND THE INTERIOR OF THE CASTLE.

LEAVE HIM TO ME, SANDRO.
WELL...OK, BUT MY MEN ARE TRAINED IN DOING THIS. YOU ARE A MERE FROGMAN...
SAM SHRUGGED OFF THIS COMMENT. HE BECKONED THE HUGE YUGOSLAV TO FOLLOW. HIS HELP WOULD BE NEEDED.

THE SENTRY WAS NOT AT ALL SUSPICIOUS OF SAM — AFTER ALL, YOU DON'T EXPECT ONE OF "YOUR OWN MEN" TO DO ANYTHING UNTOWARD.
ACH, WHAT A NIGHT. ANOTHER TEN MINUTES AND I WILL BE OFF DUTY.
JA, THIS WAR DOES NO ONE ANY FAVOURS!

A STRANGLED GASP TOLD SAM THAT THE WAY TO THE DUNGEONS WAS CLEAR.

UURGH!

WELL, NOW IT'S UP TO YOU. I'LL GO BACK AND KEEP BERT COMPANY.

SANDRO AND HIS COMPANIONS FOUND THEIR WAY TO THE DUNGEONS OF THE OLD CASTLE EASILY ENOUGH.
IT IS GOOD, THERE ARE ONLY TWO OF THEM. NOW WE SHOW THESE MARINES HOW IT IS DONE!

THE TWO DUNGEON GUARDS HAD BEEN HAVING A PEACEFUL GAME OF CARDS WHEN THE PARTISANS SWOOPED.

HA, YOUR GAMES ARE OVER FOR THE NIGHT!

GOTT IN HIMMEL... AAARGH!

PIETRO THEN GRABBED A BUNCH OF KEYS, AND THE LIBERATION OF THE CAPTURED PARTISANS MOVED ONE STAGE FURTHER.

MEANWHILE ON THE BRIDGE, THE TWO MARINES WERE ABOUT TO HAVE THEIR DISGUISES PUT TO A SEVERE TEST AS A CAR APPROACHED FROM THE SHORE.

HEY, SIR. LOOKS LIKE WE'VE GOT VISITORS.
JUST SALUTE AND LET THEM PAST, BERT.

THEIR ONLY CHANCE WAS TO BLUFF THEIR WAY THROUGH, AND ACT AS NORMAL SENTRIES WOULD.

THE GERMAN STAFF CAR CARRIED TWO SENIOR OFFICERS RETURNING LATE TO H.Q. FROM A NIGHT OF REVELRY IN THE LOCAL INN.

WE WILL SOON BE BACK IN THE WARM, EH, SCHMIDT?

JAWOHL, HERR OBERST, AND MAYBE SOME MORE SCHNAPPS, HEIN?

THE GERMANS RETURNED THE MARINES' SALUTE, AND ALL LOOKED WELL AS THE CAR PASSED ON TO THE CASTLE.

PHEW, SO FAR SO GOOD.
JUST KEEP ON GOING, FRITZ.

IT LOOKED AS IF THE RUSE HAD BEEN COMPLETELY SUCCESSFUL, UNTIL –
HIMMEL, STOP THE CAR! THERE WAS SOMETHING ABOUT THOSE MEN...

THE OFFICER HAD SEEN SAM'S BREATHING APPARATUS WHICH HAD NOT BEEN PROPERLY CONCEALED.

LOOKS LIKE THE GAME'S UP. WHEN I GIVE THE WORD, LET 'EM HAVE IT!

FOR SAM AND BERT, THEIR MASQUERADE AS GERMAN SOLDIERS WAS OVER.
YOU MEN, LOWER YOUR GUNS!
CERTAINLY, COLONEL!

AND LOWER THEM THEY DID — INTO A FIRING POSITION — FAR TOO QUICKLY FOR THE ENEMY TO REACT.

IT'S LIKE BEING AT THE FAIR!

I HOPE THAT SANDRO'S FINISHED HIS WORK BY NOW.

MEIN GOTT . . .

THE YUGOSLAVS WERE ALMOST READY. THE SOUND OF GUNFIRE FROM THE BRIDGE ALERTED THEM TO THE DANGERS THAT LAY IN WAIT FOR THEM OUTSIDE THE CASTLE WALLS.
GUNFIRE!
COME, EVERYONE, WE MUST HURRY. RUN FOR YOUR LIVES!

AS BERT STRIPPED THE CAR OF ITS MACHINE GUN, SAM REALISED THE VEHICLE COULD BE USED AS A MEANS OF ESCAPE.

SANDRO, GET YOUR PEOPLE INTO THE CAR. BERT AND I WILL HOLD OFF ANY PURSUIT.

HUH, FLAMIN' HEROES TO THE END!

THE GERMAN GARRISON, NOW AWARE OF WHAT WAS GOING ON, BEGAN TO THROW THEMSELVES INTO ACTION AS THE CAR LOADED WITH PARTISANS PREPARED TO MOVE OFF.

BLITZEN! WE MUST KILL THE SCHWEIN BEFORE IT IS TOO LATE.
PIETRO, YOU DOLT. THIS IS NOT A HORSE YOU DRIVE – A CAR HAS GEARS!

AS THE CAR SCREAMED OFF THE BRIDGE, SAM AND BERT PREPARED TO HOLD UP THE GERMAN ADVANCE AND ALSO MADE READY FOR THEIR ESCAPE.

KEEP THEIR HEADS DOWN, BERT, UNTIL I CAN GET CHANGED.

THAT I WILL. COME ON, THEN, NASTIES, HAVE I GOT A SURPRISE FOR YOU!

AS THE GERMANS CAME POURING OUT OF THEIR CASTLE, THE TWO MARINES WERE READY FOR THEM – AS THE GERMANS COULD TESTIFY AS BULLETS CRACKED PAST THEM VICIOUSLY.
THAT SHOULD KEEP THEM QUIET – I 'OPE!

THE GERMAN FIRE BECAME MORE ACCURATE AS SAM LOOKED AROUND TO SEE IF THE CAR WAS CLEAR.

FLAMIN' HECK! THINGS ARE GETTING A LITTLE HOT HERE. IS IT TIME TO MOVE YET, SKIPPER?

OK, BERT. THEY'RE CLEAR NOW. LEAVE THE GUN!

FOR THE TWO FROGMEN, THEIR ESCAPE WAS TO BE UNDERWATER.
LET'S GO!
LAST ONE IN BUYS THE DRINKS!

SO BEGAN THEIR SHORT BUT PERILOUS SWIM TO THE OPPOSITE BANK.
PHEW, TRAINING WAS NEVER LIKE THIS!

THEY EVENTUALLY CAME ASHORE AT THE SPOT THEY HAD LEFT SOME TIME PREVIOUSLY TO AN ECSTATIC WELCOME FROM SANDRO.

WELL DONE, MY FRIENDS. THE CAR HAS TAKEN MY MEN TO SAFETY. YOU COME WITH ME!
GLADLY, AS SOON AS WE DITCH THESE DIVING SUITS AND GET CHANGED INTO SOMETHING MORE COMFORTABLE.

LATER IN A CAVE DEEP IN THE MOUNTAINS, SANDRO INTRODUCED TWO OF HIS COMRADES WHO WOULD ACT AS GUIDES THROUGH THE HILLS TO THE SEA AND TO THE M. T. B. THAT WAITED FOR THE MARINES.

THIS IS NIKI AND MIKHAIL. THEY WILL GUIDE US TO THE BOAT THAT WAITS FOR YOU.
US?

SANDRO HAD DECIDED THAT HE TOO WAS GOING TO ACCOMPANY THE MARINES TO THE COAST.
YES, THE GERMANS WILL BE ALERTED NOW AND THERE WILL BE MUCH DANGER ON THE JOURNEY. I THINK MAYBE YOU WILL NEED ME.
I DON'T SEE WHY, MATE. WE'VE MANAGED WELL ENOUGH WITHOUT YOU SO FAR!
AND SO THE SMALL PARTY SET OUT ON THEIR HAZARDOUS JOURNEY.
THE WAY THROUGH THE FOREST IS LONGER, BUT IT SHOULD BE SAFER.
YES, THE ROADS WILL BE SWARMING WITH GERMANS AFTER LAST NIGHT.

BUT IT WAS NOT ONLY THE ROADS THAT WERE BEING WATCHED.

ACH, THE LEUTNANT MUST HEAR OF THIS. THEY COULD BE RESPONSIBLE FOR LAST NIGHT'S FIASCO.

THE EAGER YOUNG N.C.O. REPORTED BACK TO THE PATROL LEADER. AND AS THE YUGOSLAVS AND MARINES TRUDGED ON, AN ORDER WAS GIVEN.
SO, SCHMIDT WAS RIGHT. FEUER!

FORTUNATELY THE FIRST BURST OF BULLETS WAS INACCURATE.
TAKE COVER!

THE SMALL PARTY WAS SPLIT UP INTO TWO GROUPS.
WHERE ARE THE OTHERS? ARE THEY HIT?
I DON'T KNOW. I THINK THEY ARE OVER THERE!

NIKI AND MIKHAIL WERE WHERE SANDRO HAD POINTED, BUT THEY HAD NO INTENTIONS OF SITTING STILL, SINCE THEY HAD FOUND A WAY TO OUTFLANK THE GERMANS.
COME, WE CAN REACH THEM THIS WAY.

MEANWHILE, NOT KNOWING WHAT WAS GOING ON, SAM ATTEMPTED TO FIRE AT THE GERMAN POSITION.

PHEW, THIS ISN'T VERY HEALTHY.

CAN'T THESE YUGOSLAVS DO ANYTHING RIGHT? NOW THEY'VE MADE ANOTHER MESS OF IT AND LED US INTO AN AMBUSH!

AT THAT MOMENT, NIKI AND MIKHAIL JUMPED OUT FROM COVER AND CHARGED THE GERMAN SKI-TROOPS.

COME, MIKHAIL. AVENGE OUR PEOPLE!
DEATH TO THE NAZIS, DEFILERS OF OUR COUNTRY!

AND THEN SANDRO LET OUT AN EAR-SPLITTING BELLOW AND CHARGED TO HELP HIS COMRADES.

THE TWO PARTISANS PRESSED HOME THEIR ATTACK, AND IN A CONCERTED EFFORT KILLED THE GERMANS – BUT NIKI WAS HIT.

AAGH!

I COME, MY BROTHERS! FIGHT ON!

AAIEE!

SANDRO WAS TOO LATE. NIKI WAS DEAD, AND NOW BERT'S OPINIONS OF HIS ALLIES WERE CHANGING.
A GOOD MAN. I HAVE KNOWN HIM MANY YEARS.
AND A BRAVE ONE TOO.

AFTER BURYING THEIR COMRADE, THE FOUR MEN CONTINUED THEIR URGENT RACE TO THE M.T.B.

SOON THE GERMANS WILL KNOW EXACTLY WHAT ROUTE WE ARE TAKING.

WELL, IT'S TOO LATE TO CHANGE IT NOW IF WE WANT TO CATCH OUR BOAT TONIGHT.

THROUGHOUT THE DAY THE PARTY MADE GOOD TIME, AND IN THE LATER AFTERNOON, MIKHAIL CALLED A HALT.

HALT! LOOK, THERE!
WHAT'S HE SEEN?
SMOKE! IT CAN ONLY BE THE GERMANS. WE MUST TAKE ANOTHER ROUTE.

BUT ONCE AGAIN, THEY HAD BEEN SEEN BY ONE OF THE MANY SKI-PATROLS SEARCHING THE AREA.

GUT! THERE THEY ARE. MULLER, RADIO IN THEIR POSITION.

FORTUNATELY SANDRO HAD SPOTTED THE DANGER, BUT DESPITE THAT, THINGS DID NOT LOOK GOOD.
THE SKIS WILL SLOW THEM DOWN WHILST THEY CLIMB, BUT ONCE THEY REACH THE TOP...

THE GAP BETWEEN THE TWO FACTIONS CLOSED TO A DANGEROUSLY SHORT DISTANCE.

COME ON!

WE CAN HOLD THEM OFF FOR A WHILE AT THAT GULLEY.

SANDRO AND MIKHAIL HAD PLANS TO SLOW DOWN THEIR PURSUERS.
HERE, TAKE THIS EXPLOSIVE – YOU KNOW WHAT TO DO.
YES, LEAVE IT TO ME.

THE OTHERS PREPARED TO GIVE MIKHAIL COVERING FIRE AS HE PLACED HIS EXPLOSIVE CHARGES.

HERE COMES THE FIRST OF THEM — READY?

READY AS WE'LL EVER BE, CAPTAIN.

HIS CHARGES SET, HE SIGNALLED TO SANDRO THAT ALL WAS READY, JUST AS THE GERMANS BEGAN TO REGROUP.

IT IS DONE. WHEN I GIVE THE ORDER, FIRE.

SECONDS LATER, SANDRO'S DEEP, BULL-LIKE VOICE ECHOED ACROSS THE MOUNTAINSIDE.

THE GERMANS COULD NOT SEE MIKHAIL – THEY WERE TOO BUSY KEEPING THEIR HEADS DOWN.

WE CAN KEEP THEM PINNED DOWN HERE FOR HOURS, BUT HOW WILL MIKHAIL GET CLEAR?

HAVE NO FEAR. HE KNOWS WHAT HE MUST DO.

SECONDS LATER MIKHAIL DETONATED THE EXPLOSIVES, KNOWING FULL WELL THAT HE HAD NO CHANCE OF GETTING CLEAR AS TONS OF SNOW AND ICE THUNDERED DOWN, WIPING OUT THE NAZI PATROL.

MIKHAIL!
AAIEE!

THE MARINES RAN FORWARD TO SEE IF THEY COULD SAVE MIKHAIL.

WHERE IS HE? WE MUST FIND HIM.

NO, HE KNEW WHAT HE WAS DOING. WE MUST NOT WASTE THE TIME HE HAS WON FOR US.

GRIMLY THEY PRESSED ON, USING THE TIME MIKHAIL HAD BOUGHT FOR THEM WITH HIS LIFE.

MEANWHILE THE FUGITIVES' POSITION HAD BEEN PINPOINTED. WOULD THEY BE ABLE TO WIN THE RACE TO THE SEA BEFORE NIGHT FELL AND BEFORE THEIR GERMAN PURSUERS CAUGHT UP WITH THEM?
THEY MUST BE MAKING FOR THE SEA. MOVE UP MEN HERE, AND HERE. RADIO FOR AN E-BOAT TO CUT OFF THEIR ESCAPE!

NOW THE THREE MEN WERE ALMOST IN SIGHT OF THEIR GOAL.
IT IS MUCH FURTHER?
NO, WE SHOULD BE ABLE TO SEE THE SEA FROM THE TOP OF THIS HILL.

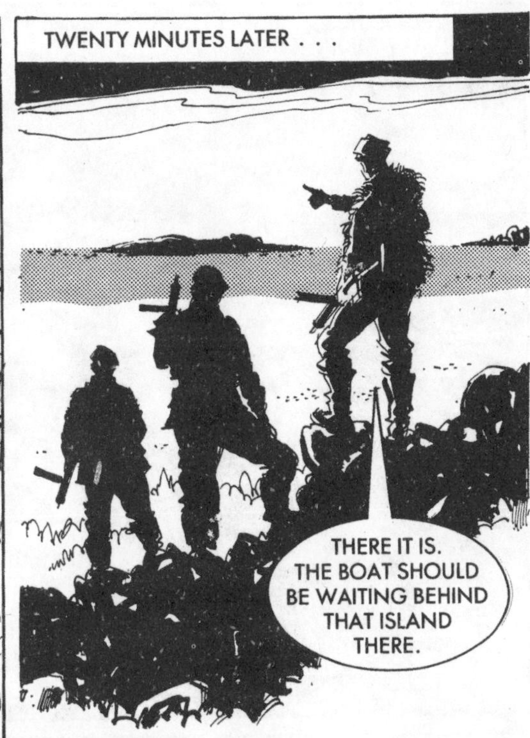
TWENTY MINUTES LATER . . .
THERE IT IS. THE BOAT SHOULD BE WAITING BEHIND THAT ISLAND THERE.

THE MOTOR TORPEDO BOAT WAS THERE, AND READY TO TAKE THEM AWAY.
THIS IS LIKELY TO BE A LONG NIGHT, NUMBER ONE . . . I HOPE OUR PASSENGERS MAKE IT ALL RIGHT.

AS DARKNESS CREPT IN, SANDRO MADE THE PRE-ARRANGED SIGNAL FROM THE ROCKY SHORE-LINE.

WE WILL SOON KNOW IF THEY ARE THERE.

TOO BAD IF THEY'RE NOT – I'VE A FUNNY FEELING WE'RE BEING FOLLOWED AGAIN!

BUT ALL WAS WELL. THE SIGNAL WAS SEEN, AND THE NEXT PHASE OF THE OPERATION BEGAN ON BOARD THE M.T.B.

SIGNAL FROM THE SHORE, SIR!
LOWER THE DINGHY!

BERT HAD BEEN RIGHT. THE FIRST OF THE PURSUING GERMANS MADE CONTACT WITHIN MINUTES OF SENDING OFF THE SIGNAL.

HERE THEY COME, BOYS!

LET THEM HAVE IT!

THE DINGHY FROM THE M.T.B. ARRIVED TO TAKE AWAY THE TWO MARINES AS THE SKIRMISH REACHED ITS PEAK.

HERE IT COMES. OVER HERE, MATE – BEHIND THIS ROCK!

THE MARINES PREPARED TO SAY FAREWELL TO THEIR COMRADE, SANDRO.

ARE YOU SURE YOU WON'T COME WITH US?

SURE. I WILL EASILY BE ABLE TO SLIP AWAY ALONG THE COAST IN THE DARKNESS.

NOW THE TIME HAD COME FOR BERT TO SET THE RECORD STRAIGHT.
SANDRO, WHEN I STARTED OUT ON THIS MISSION I DIDN'T HAVE MUCH OF AN OPINION OF YOUR PEOPLE, BUT . . .
SAY NO MORE, MY FRIEND, I FEEL MUCH THE SAME WAY!

AS HE LOOKED BACK, SAM SAW FROM THE GUN FLASHES THAT SANDRO WAS SURROUNDED AND THAT ESCAPE AS HE INTENDED WOULD BE IMPOSSIBLE.
HE'S SURROUNDED! YOU CARRY ON, I'M GOING BACK!

SANDRO WAS HARD-PRESSED BY THE TIME SAM RETURNED.
SANDRO! YOU'LL HAVE TO COME WITH US. YOU'RE SURROUNDED!
NO, LEAVE ME AND ESCAPE YOURSELVES!

HIS REASON FOR NOT ESCAPING BY SEA SOON BECAME APPARENT.
YOU MUST COME, THERE'S NO HOPE FOR YOU HERE!
I CAN'T COME! YOU SEE, I CAN'T... I CAN'T SWIM!

THEN BERT CAME SPLASHING OUT OF THE NIGHT. HE WAS UNABLE TO ABANDON HIS COMRADES-IN-ARMS, AND SAM SOON EXPLAINED THEIR PREDICAMENT.
WE'VE A BIT OF A PROBLEM — SANDRO CAN'T SWIM.
BLAST! I'VE JUST TOLD THE DINGHY TO GO BACK TO THE BOAT — I SAID WE WOULD SWIM OUT.
BUT SAM HAD SEEN SOMETHING THAT HE KNEW WOULD BE USEFUL.
WHERE ARE YOU OFF TO, SIR?
HANG ON, I'VE GOT AN IDEA. COVER ME!

WHEN SAM RETURNED, BERT AND SANDRO COULD NOT UNDERSTAND WHAT HE WAS PLAYING AT.

WHAT ON EARTH...

LOOK, THE LOG WILL FLOAT. IF SANDRO HOLDS ON TO IT, WE CAN PULL HIM THROUGH THE WATER!

IT WAS A CRAZY IDEA, BUT THEY HAD TO TRY SOMETHING. NEITHER MARINE WAS PREPARED TO LEAVE BEHIND THIS MAN WHO HAD FOUGHT LIKE A TIGER FOR THEM.

AT LAST THE THREE WERE READY TO MOVE OFF. SANDRO HELD ON TO THE LOG AS IF HIS LIFE DEPENDED ON IT – AND IT DID.
THE WATER, IT IS SO COLD!
BERT! GIVE 'EM ONE LONG BURST AND THEN JOIN US!
BERT OBLIGED, AND HOT SEARING LEAD FLEW THROUGH THE AIR TOWARDS THE REMAINS OF THE GERMAN PATROL.

THE SCHEME WORKED AND THEY SOMEHOW MANAGED TO SLIP AWAY UNDER THE VERY NOSES OF THE GERMANS.

IT LOOKS LIKE WE'LL MAKE IT OK.

THIS WATER'S FREEZING. NOW I KNOW WHAT A COD FILLET FEELS LIKE!

AT LAST THE THREE COMPANIONS WERE HAULED OUT OF THE ICE-COLD WATER AND ONTO THE DECK OF THE WAITING M.T.B.
HERE YOU COME, MATE.
THANKS, PAL. ANY CHANCE OF A MUG OF TEA?

THE M.T.B. GATHERED SPEED AND LEFT THE LAND BEHIND AS IT PREPARED FOR ITS DASH ACROSS THE ADRIATIC SEA TO THE COMPARATIVE SAFETY OF ITALY.
FULL SPEED AHEAD, NUMBER ONE. LET'S HEAD FOR THE OPEN SEA.
AYE, AYE, SIR!

THE THREE COMRADES RETURNED TO THE DECK, DRY AND WARM, ONLY TO HEAR THE NEWS THAT THEY WERE NOT YET OUT OF DANGER.

VESSEL BEARING GREEN FIVE-OH, SIR. LOOKS LIKE AN E-BOAT.

READY THE TORPEDO TUBES!

THE LOOK-OUT WAS RIGHT. IT WAS AN E-BOAT, LARGER AND MORE POWERFUL THAN THE M.T.B. – A DANGEROUS OPPONENT, EVEN ALTHOUGH THE BRITISH HAD SURPRISE ON THEIR SIDE.
IT LOOKS AS IF OUR HOPE OF A CLEAN RUN FOR IT IS DONE FOR. WE'LL HAVE TO FIGHT HIM!
THE M.T.B. RACED ALONG IN A STRAIGHT LINE FOR THE GERMAN WARSHIP. THE COMMANDER MADE READY TO FIRE HIS TORPEDOES.
STEADY, STEADY – FIRE!
OUT LANCED THE TWO TWIN MESSENGERS OF DEATH, AIMED EXACTLY AT THE TARGET.

THE TORPEDOES STRUCK HOME WITH DEVASTATING EFFECT. THE E-BOAT WAS BLOWN APART INSTANTLY.

BULL'S-EYE!

WHAT AN EXPLOSION! YOU CERTAINLY PACK SOME PUNCH!

SANDRO, WHO NOW THOUGHT HE WAS SAFE, WANTED TO REJOIN HIS PEOPLE ON SHORE...
CAN YOU PUT ME ASHORE SOMEWHERE DOWN THE COAST?
I'M SORRY, THAT'S FAR TOO DANGEROUS. YOU'LL HAVE TO COME ALL THE WAY WITH US TO ITALY.

SANDRO TRIED TO ARGUE, BUT TO NO AVAIL.

I CANNOT RISK THE BOAT BY CLOSING WITH THE COAST ONCE MORE.

DON'T WORRY, SANDRO. IF I KNOW OUR PEOPLE, THEY'LL HAVE YOU BACK IN YUGOSLAVIA IN NO TIME.

HE EVENTUALLY RECONCILED HIMSELF TO THE INEVITABLE.

VERY WELL, IF I MUST GO, THEN I MUST.
ANYWAY, YOU CAN TAKE THE OPPORTUNITY TO HAVE A HOLIDAY. AFTER ALL, IT'S MUCH WARMER IN ITALY!

SO SAM, BERT AND SANDRO SPED OFF ACROSS THE SEA TO ITALY, AND A WELL-DESERVED REST BEFORE RETURNING TO ACTION ONCE AGAIN.
BESIDES, PAL, I WILL PERSONALLY TAKE THE TIME TO TEACH YOU TO SWIM!
WELL, WELL — BERT REALLY HAS CHANGED HIS TUNE!
Commando
THE END

Don't delay — order the next four Commando books now! On sale in two weeks are —

"FIGHTING TEAM"
"SABOTAGE MISSION"
"GUILT AND GLORY"
"THE FINAL COUNTDOWN"

WEIRD WEAPONS of World War II

No. 13: Fascine/Mortar Tank

During the war the British had more specialised tanks than any other nation. Many types were operated by men of the Engineers, and were called AVREs — Armoured Vehicle Royal Engineers. Their job was to clear the way for other vehicles and infantry, and that included bridging rivers, filling in broad ditches and so on.

This one, a converted Churchill tank, carried a huge bundle of split chestnut staves called a fascine which it could release into a ditch or a shell-hole in the road so that other tanks or trucks could drive on over it. Afterwards it was free to use its mortar which fired an enormous bomb specially designed to shatter pill-boxes and concrete defence-walls.

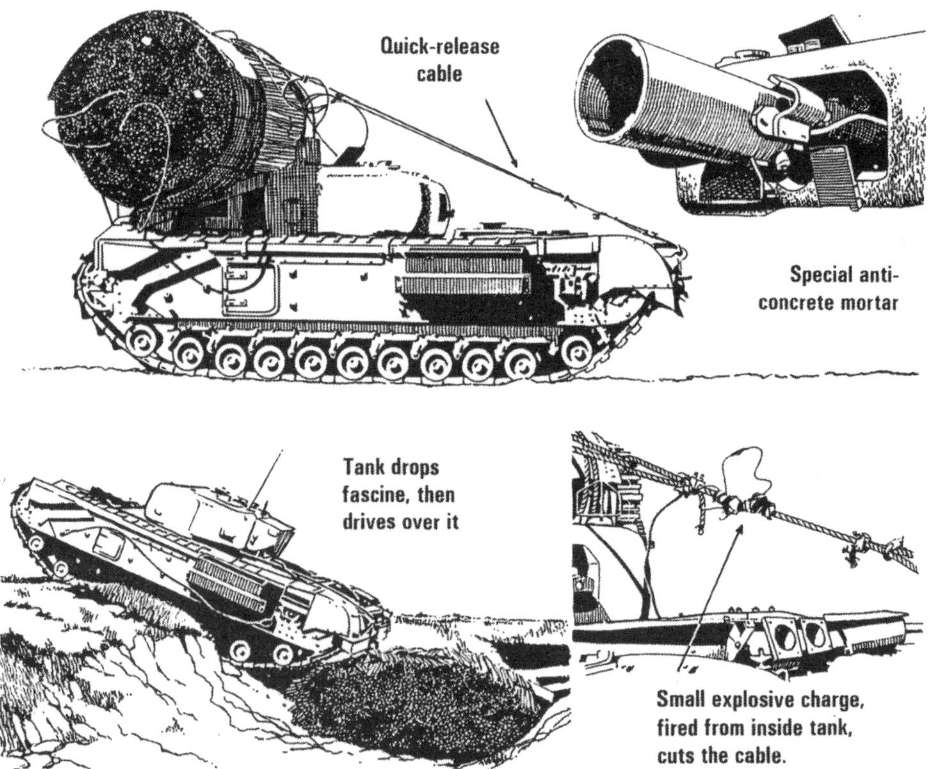
Quick-release cable
Special anti-concrete mortar
Tank drops fascine, then drives over it
Small explosive charge, fired from inside tank, cuts the cable.

MARCH OF THE MONSTERS

LCT

THEY WERE CALLED "THE FUNNIES", THE WEIRD ARMOURED VEHICLES DEVELOPED FOR THE D-DAY LANDINGS. BUT LIEUTENANT DICK MURRAY DIDN'T SEE THE JOKE IN THE SPRING OF 1944 WHEN HIS BRIGADE WAS SENT TO ITALY TO DEMONSTRATE THE TANKS TO THE TOP BRASS.

IT MEANT THEY'D MISS OUT ON THE BATTLE FOR FRANCE, AND DICK DIDN'T LIKE THAT AT ALL. AFTER MONTHS AND MONTHS OF TOUGH TRAINING HE WANTED SOME REAL ACTION. WELL, HE WAS GOING TO GET IT. IN FACT HE WAS GOING TO BE STARTING HIS OWN PRIVATE WAR!

AS HE GLOOMILY SET SAIL, DICK HAD COMMAND OF A SCORPION, A PETARD, A CROCODILE AND A BOBBIN – FOUR SPECIALIST TANKS DESIGNED FOR THEIR OWN VERY PARTICULAR JOB.

BEATS ME WHY THEY BOTHERED TO GIVE US LIVE AMMUNITION, SIR! WE AIN'T LIKELY TO MEET ANY JERRIES.

AT LEAST IT WILL PROVE THAT THE FUNNIES WILL BE OF USE.

LIEUTENANT HUBERT STREED, SKIPPER OF THE LCT, OR "LANDING CRAFT, TANK", THOUGHT THE WHOLE EXERCISE A WASTE OF TIME.

YOU TANK BOYS SHOULD BE FIGHTING, NOT PLAYING SOLDIERS FOR THE H.Q. STAFF!
I COULDN'T AGREE MORE. BUT THE G.O.C. GIVES THE ORDERS, NOT ME!

AND HUBERT HAD A POOR OPINION OF THE ARMY, PARTICULARLY OF THE GENERAL STAFF.

WHAT YOU BROWN-JOBS NEED IS SOME NAVAL EFFICIENCY.
JUST MY LUCK TO GET A POMPOUS NIT-WIT WHO FANCIES HIMSELF AS AN ADMIRAL.

TO HUBERT'S FURY HIS ENGINES BEGAN TO GIVE TROUBLE AND HE WAS FORCED TO DROP BEHIND.

SIGNAL FROM COMMODORE, ASKING IF WE NEED ANY PADDLES!

AND SOON, TO DICK'S AMUSEMENT, THE REST OF THE CONVOY WAS OUT OF SIGHT.

BLIMEY, EVEN THE STAR-FISH ARE OVERTAKIN' US! DO YER RECKON WE SHOULD GET OFF AN' PUSH?
TAKE THAT MAN'S NAME AND PUT HIM ON A CHARGE FOR IN-SOLENCE!
LCT 10853

DICK WAS QUICK TO COME TO THE SOLDIER'S AID. HIS SHARP REPLY WAS INTERRUPTED BY A WARNING SHOUT FROM THE LOOKOUT.

I DIDN'T HEAR HIM SAY ANYTHING. ANYWAY, AT LEAST OUR TANK ENGINES WORK.

AIRCRAFT APPROACHING FROM THE STARBOARD BEAM, SIR!

THE NEW ARRIVAL PUT AN IMMEDIATE END TO THE ARGUMENT – FOR IT WAS A JUNKERS 88.
ENEMY AIRCRAFT. GUN CREW TO ACTION STATIONS.
WE MAY AS WELL LEND A HAND, BUSTER. TELL THE BLOKES TO GET SOME TOMMY GUNS ON DECK.

DISREGARDING THE FIRE FROM THE TWO OERLIKONS THE JUNKERS SWOOPED DOWN AND RELEASED A STICK OF BOMBS.

MOVE OVER, THAT JERRY'S GOT OUR NUMBER ON IT!

THE LITTLE SHIP QUIVERED AS A NEAR-MISS RIDDLED THE HULL WITH SPLINTERS.

YOU CAN BET HE'LL COME ROUND AGAIN!
LCT 10853

BUT THIS TIME DICK'S TROOP SERGEANT, BUSTER HUCKLE, HAD A RECEPTION COMMITTEE READY.

WE GOT 'EM! WE COPPED THE ENGINE!

WE SURE DID! LOOK AT THAT.

AND SUDDENLY THE JUNKERS DIPPED AND PLUNGED INTO THE SEA.
AAGHH!

ALMOST IMMEDIATELY AN ARGUMENT BEGAN OVER WHO HAD FIRED THE FATAL SHOT.

IT WAS OURS! THEM PEA-SHOOTERS OF YOURS WOULDN'T KNOCK DOWN A FLY.

WHAT? YOU WERE RELOADIN' WHEN WE PUT HIM INTO THE SEA!

BUT HUBERT HAD NO HESITATION IN CLAIMING THE KILL FOR HIS OWN MEN.
I'LL CLAIM IT FOR THE NAVY. BUT OF COURSE I'LL MENTION IN MY REPORT THAT YOUR CHAPS HELPED.
THAT'S BIG OF YOU! LET'S JUST HOPE YOU GET A CHANCE TO MAKE YOUR REPORT.

DICK WAS RIGHT TO BE WORRIED, FOR THE ENGINES HAD STOPPED.
...AND I'M AFRAID OUR WIRELESS HAS HAD IT COMPLETELY.
THEN SHALL I TRY TO SEND A MESSAGE ON ONE OF THE TANK RADIOS?

HUBERT REJECTED THE OFFER IRRITABLY, CLAIMING THAT A WIRELESS SIGNAL MIGHT BRING MORE ENEMY BOMBERS.
WE DON'T NEED ANY ASSIS-TANCE FROM OUR PASSENGERS.
YOU MEAN YOU DON'T WANT US TO PULL YOUR CHESTNUTS OUT OF THE FIRE FOR YOU!

BUT AS THE HOURS PASSED THE ENGINES STUBBORNLY REFUSED TO START.
THEY AIN'T 'AVIN' MUCH LUCK, SIR! THAT JUNKERS DID MORE DAMAGE THAN WE THOUGHT.
AND THE SEA'S GETTING ROUGHER — I RECKON THERE'S A STORM BLOWING UP.

BY NIGHTFALL THE LCT WAS ROLLING UNCOMFORTABLY, AND HUBERT HAD TO ADMIT THEY WERE IN TROUBLE.

PERHAPS WE'D BETTER TRY YOUR WIRELESS, JUST AS A PRE-CAUTION.

I THOUGHT YOU MIGHT SEE IT MY WAY.

BUT HE HAD LEFT IT TOO LATE, FOR ATMOSPHERICS NOW MADE IT IMPOSSIBLE TO MAKE CONTACT.
IT'S NO USE, SIR. IT'S THE BLOOMIN' STORM.
ALL RIGHT, DON'T WASTE THE BATTERIES. WE'LL TRY AGAIN LATER.

ALTHOUGH HE WAS RELUCTANT TO ADMIT IT, HUBERT WAS A VERY WORRIED MAN.

THE STORM'S MAKING THINGS DIFFICULT. WE CAN'T GET A STAR SIGHT AND THERE'S NO WAY OF ESTIMATING OUR DRIFT.

IN OTHER WORDS, YOU DON'T KNOW WHERE WE ARE! WHAT WERE YOU SAYING EARLIER ABOUT NAVAL EFFICIENCY?

BUT THE WEATHER CONDITIONS WERE NOT HUBERT'S FAULT, AND AFTER A FEW HOURS ONE OF THE ENGINES WAS REPAIRED.

IT SHOULDN'T BE LONG BEFORE THE OTHER ONE'S WORKING NOW.

NO LONGER DRIFTING WITH THE WIND, THE LCT HEADED IN THE DIRECTION OF ITALY.

JUST WHEN THEIR PROSPECTS WERE BEGINNING TO LOOK BRIGHTER, THE LOOKOUT GAVE A STARTLED YELL.

LOOK, HUGE WAVES AHEAD!
FULL ASTERN — EMERGENCY!

BUT THE STRAIN WAS TOO MUCH FOR THE SINGLE OVERWORKED ENGINE. IT GAVE OUT WITH A TORTURED GURGLE, AND THE HORRIFIED MEN FELT THE WALLOWING CRAFT FLUNG SHOREWARDS BY THE HOWLING WIND. WITH A GRINDING CRASH THEY GROUNDED ON A SLOPING SANDY BEACH, AND STUCK FAST.

BLIMEY, WE'VE REACHED ITALY.
WE MADE BETTER TIME THAN I THOUGHT!

NEXT MORNING, WHEN SEVERAL ATTEMPTS TO BACK OFF HAD FAILED, HUBERT ORDERED THE VEHICLES ASHORE TO LIGHTEN THE SHIP.

ARE YOU CRAZY? WE'RE PROBABLY BEHIND THE GERMAN LINES!
NONSENSE! GET EVERYTHING ASHORE, LIEUTEN-ANT.

HUBERT'S WORD WAS LAW ON BOARD, SO THE FOUR TANKS AND DICK'S JEEP WERE DRIVEN ASHORE, LEAVING THE TWO LORRIES ON BOARD WITH THE SPARE FUEL AND AMMUNITION.

DON'T SEEM TO 'AVE DONE NO GOOD, SIR. THEY'RE STILL STUCK.

I RECKON WE'LL BE HERE FOR A WHILE.

WITH HIS MEN STILL WORKING ON THE SECOND ENGINE, HUBERT DECIDED THERE WAS LITTLE TO WORRY ABOUT.
WHEN IT'S A BIT CALMER WE'LL TAKE A KEDGE ANCHOR OUT IN THE DINGHY, AND USE IT TO WINCH OURSELVES OFF THE BEACH.

DICK DECIDED TO TRY AND FIND OUT WHERE THEY HAD LANDED, BUT THE SUGGESTION ANNOYED HUBERT.
THERE'S NO NEED, WE'LL ONLY DRAW ATTENTION TO OUR-SELVES. YOU CAN GET YOUR VEHICLES BACK ON BOARD WHILE WE'RE WAITING.
NOT UNTIL I KNOW IF WE'RE IN FRIENDLY TERRITORY. WE WON'T BE ABLE TO DEFEND OURSELVES FROM INSIDE YOUR SHIP.
AND DICK WASN'T UNDER NAVAL ORDERS WHILE ON SHORE, SO HE AND BUSTER WENT FOR A CAUTIOUS STROLL.
LIEUTENANT STREED SEEMS PRETTY SURE WE'RE BEHIND OUR OWN LINES, SIR. I SUPPOSE HE WANTS TO SNEAK OFF BEFORE ANYONE KNOWS HE'S RUN AGROUND.
THAT'S RIGHT, BUT I WANT TO FIND OUT FOR SURE BEFORE WE PUT OUR STUFF ON BOARD AGAIN.

THEY MOVED STEALTHILY, ALERT FOR DANGER – THEN SUDDENLY BUSTER HISSED A WARNING.

WE GOT OUR ANSWER, SIR – THEY'RE JERRIES!

THEN LET'S GRAB THEM. THEY MIGHT BE ABLE TO TELL US WHERE WE ARE.

THE UNSUSPECTING GERMANS DIDN'T STAND A CHANCE AGAINST THEIR TWO WELL-TRAINED OPPONENTS.
OK, FRITZ, SLEEPY TIME.
UNGHHH!

THE TWO GERMANS WERE SENT SPRAWLING ON THE GROUND, LEAVING THE THIRD TO FUMBLE FOR HIS RIFLE.

HE ALMOST MANAGED TO LEVEL IT, BUT DICK WAS TOO QUICK FOR HIM.
KAMERAD! DON'T HIT ME.
YOU AREN'T EXACTLY THE BRAVEST, ARE YOU?

SOON THEY RETURNED TO THE SHIP WITH THEIR PRISONERS.
WE...ER... MUST HAVE DRIFTED FURTHER NORTH THAN I THOUGHT.
THIS ONE SPEAKS A LITTLE ENGLISH – I'M SURE HE'LL TELL US WHERE WE ARE.

THE HELPFUL GERMAN NOT ONLY TOLD WHERE THEY WERE, HE SHOWED THEM ON THE MAP.
VE HAF ONLY RESERVE TROOPS IN DER AREA. SEE, I SHOW YOU WHERE!
WE'VE GOT A RIGHT LITTLE HERO HERE. I'LL MAKE NOTES AS WE GO ALONG.

AND AS DICK LISTENED HE SAW A WAY OF IMPROVING THEIR CHANCE OF EVADING CAPTURE.

THE COUNTRY FOR A FEW MILES AROUND US IS SWAMPY AND THERE ARE ONLY THREE WAYS IN. A ROAD BRIDGE, A RAIL BRIDGE, AND A MOUNTAIN TRACK. IF WE BLOCK ALL THREE, WE CAN WAIT HERE UNTIL WE'RE READY TO LEAVE!

BUT WHAT ABOUT THE TROOPS IN THE VILLAGE?

WE'LL MOP UP THEIR TROOPS FIRST! IF WE MUST SIT HERE UNTIL THE WEATHER BREAKS AT LEAST WE'LL DO IT IN COMFORT.
I CAN'T ORDER YOU TO STAY HERE, BUT I SHALL MAKE AN ENTRY IN THE LOG THAT I ADVISED YOU NOT TO GO.

DICK IGNORED HUBERT'S OBJECTIONS, FOR HE KNEW THAT BY MORNING THE GERMANS WOULD BE OUT LOOKING FOR THE MISSING PATROL.

I RECKON HE'D LIKE TO PUT US ALL ON A CHARGE, SIR! GOOD JOB HE AIN'T THE BOSS!

AND IT'S LUCKY THAT WE'VE GOT LIVE AMMUNITION AND OUR OWN WEAPONS, BUSTER.

WITH THE FOUR TANKS FOLLOWING HIS JEEP, DICK LED THE WAY TO THE FIRST VILLAGE OUTPOST.

THE JERRIES HAVE TAKEN OVER THE SCHOOL, SO WE'LL FIND THEM EASILY ENOUGH.

THE GERMANS HAD NO SENTRIES POSTED, FOR THEY WERE NOT EXPECTING TROUBLE.

DO WE CHUCK IN A GRENADE, SIR?

WE DON'T WANT TO MAKE TOO MUCH NOISE. TELL CORPORAL CRISP TO BRING THE PETARD CLOSER.

DICK KNOCKED BOLDLY AT THE DOOR — AND THE GERMAN N. C. O. WHO ANSWERED STARED IN AMAZEMENT.

THE WAR'S OVER, CHUM. SURRENDER OR WE'LL BLOW YOU TO BLAZES!
ACH, NEIN, WE SURRENDER! WAIT, I CALL THE OTHERS.

CORPORAL CRISP'S PETARD, AN ULTRA-HEAVY MORTAR, QUICKLY PUT PAID TO ANY HEROIC IDEAS AS THE GERMAN SAW ITS HUGE BARREL YAWNING IN FRONT OF HIM.

WITHIN SECONDS A STREAM OF BEWILDERED PRISONERS EMERGED FROM THE SCHOOL WITHOUT A SHOT BEING FIRED.

TELL CORPORAL NOBBS TO ESCORT THEM BACK TO THE LCT AND MEET UP WITH US AT THE NEXT VILLAGE.

RIGHT, SIR. HE CAN TAKE A COUPLE OF TOMMY GUNS WITH HIM IN CASE OF TROUBLE.

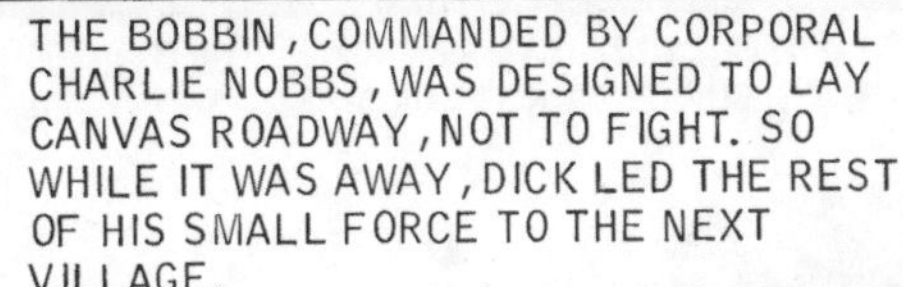
THE BOBBIN, COMMANDED BY CORPORAL CHARLIE NOBBS, WAS DESIGNED TO LAY CANVAS ROADWAY, NOT TO FIGHT. SO WHILE IT WAS AWAY, DICK LED THE REST OF HIS SMALL FORCE TO THE NEXT VILLAGE.

THE GERMANS HAD SOME MACHINE GUNS AND WERE PREPARED TO FIGHT – UNTIL THE TANKS BEGAN TO SHOOT, THAT WAS!

HIMMEL, WE CAN'T FIGHT TANKS WITHOUT ANTI-TANK GUNS!

WHEN THE PETARD ALSO TOOK A HAND, A WHITE FLAG WAS WAVED HURRIEDLY FROM AN UPPER WINDOW.

THEY'RE PACKING IT IN, SIR!

RIGHT, COVER THEM AS THEY FILE OUT. AND WE'LL COLLECT THEIR WEAPONS.

THE PRISONERS CREATED A PROBLEM, FOR DICK COULDN'T SPARE ANY MEN TO ESCORT THEM TO THE LCT. BUT THEN THEY SAW THE BOBBIN TRUNDLING UP, FESTOONED WITH GUN-TOTING SAILORS.

THE NAVY'S SENT US SOME ESCORTS, SIR. MAYBE THEY'RE HOPIN' TO GET SOME SOUVENIRS!
PROBABLY LIEUTENANT STREED WANTS TO SHARE ANY CREDIT THAT'S GOING.

BUT DICK WAS GLAD OF THE EXTRA ASSISTANCE, EVEN THOUGH HE SUSPECTED HUBERT STREED'S MOTIVES.

THE OTHER TWO GARRISONS WILL BE ALERT BY NOW, SO WE'VE GOT TO MOP THEM UP QUICKLY BEFORE THEY CAN BE REIN-FORCED.

THE GERMANS IN THE THIRD VILLAGE WERE WAITING, AND NARROWLY MISSED DICK'S JEEP AS HE APPROACHED.

THIS ONE WON'T BE A PUSHOVER, SIR!
WE'LL HAVE TO RUSH THEM, AND RELY ON OUR FIREPOWER. WE CAN'T AFFORD TO HANG AROUND.

HE CALLED HIS COMMANDERS TOGETHER FOR A HURRIED CONFERENCE.

WE'LL BASH STRAIGHT IN, BUT WATCH OUT FOR ANTI-TANK GUNS. BETTER NOT USE THE FLAME-THROWER IN CASE THERE ARE ITALIAN CIVILIANS IN THE VILLAGE.

WE'LL JUST ROLL STRAIGHT OVER THE JERRIES, SIR. THEY WON'T KNOW WHAT'S HIT 'EM!

CORPORAL JIM STEEL OF THE FLAME-THROWING CROCODILE HAD ENOUGH CONFIDENCE TO TAKE ON THE WHOLE GERMAN ARMY.

GET THAT UNARMED SARDINE CAN OUT OF MY WAY. I'LL SHOW YOU HOW REAL TANKIES OPERATE.
GO BOIL YOUR HEAD, JIM. I'LL BE RIGHT BEHIND YOU WHEN YOU HIT TROUBLE.

WITH THE CROCODILE LEADING THEY RACED INTO THE MAIN STREET, RELYING ON THEIR SPEED TO HELP THEM.

TRAVERSE LEFT, GUNNER, MORE JERRIES IN THAT WHITE HOUSE ON THE CORNER.

AAAAGHH!

THE VICIOUS BARK OF AN ANTI-TANK GUN ALERTED STEEL TO A NEW DANGER.
HECK, THAT WAS CLOSE! WHERE ARE THEY?

JIM STEEL WAS THE FIRST CASUALTY – BUT NOT THROUGH ENEMY ACTION.
AAAAGHH! WE'VE GONE INTO SOMEONE'S CELLAR!

THE CROCODILE WAS A HELPLESS TARGET – BUT CHARLIE NOBBS WAS CLOSE BEHIND IN THE BOBBIN.

ACH, WHAT IS IT? SOME NEW SECRET WEAPON?

GET THE CARPET DOWN, FRED, WE'VE GOT COMPANY!

THE STARTLED GERMANS FOUND THEMSELVES IN TROUBLE AS THE BOBBIN'S ROLL OF ROADWAY DROPPED OVER THEIR POSITION, FOLLOWED BY THE VEHICLE ITSELF.
WAS IST DAS?
NIP OVER THE BACK AND KEEP 'EM COVERED, FRED. WE'LL GET A CABLE ON THE CROCODILE TO TOW IT OUT.

JIM STEEL FOUND HE HAD TO ACCEPT A TOW FROM THE DESPISED BOBBIN IN THE MIDDLE OF THE BATTLE.

I GOT TO HAND IT TO YOU, JIM, YOU TANKIES CERTAINLY HAVE SOME CLEVER TRICKS!

AW, DON'T RUB IT IN, CHARLIE. I'LL NEVER LIVE THIS DOWN...

MEANWHILE THE SCORPION WAS DEALING WITH THE OPPOSITION IN ITS OWN WAY. ITS CHAIN FLAILS, DESIGNED TO BEAT A PATH THROUGH MINEFIELDS, WERE EQUALLY GOOD AT FLUSHING OUT CONCEALED INFANTRY.

AAAGHHH, RUN!

THAT'LL TEACH 'EM NOT TO TRY AND HIDE IN LONG GRASS!

AND THE PETARD HADN'T BEEN LEFT OUT EITHER – EVERY TIME IT FIRED, A FORTY-POUND CHARGE WHISTLED INTO THE GERMAN POSITIONS.

LEFT A BIT, AND UP TWENTY YARDS.

I'LL BET THE JERRIES DIDN'T EXPECT TO BE SHELLED BY RE-MOTE CONTROL!

MEANWHILE DICK AND BUSTER WERE HAVING THE TIME OF THEIR LIVES WITH THE JEEP AND SOME GRENADES.
NICE WORK, SIR! SAVE ONE FOR THAT HOUSE AT THE END. I JUST SAW A JERRY POP HIS HEAD OUT.

IT WAS NOT LONG BEFORE THE GERMAN OFFICER IN CHARGE DECIDED HE HAD HAD ENOUGH.

AAAAGHH!

ACH, WE SHALL DIE FOR NOTHING. THERE MUST BE DOZENS OF BRITISH TANKS IN THE VILLAGE.

AND SOON ANOTHER GROUP OF PRISONERS WAS READY TO MARCH BACK TO THE LCT.
TAKE THEM BACK TO THE SHIP, NOBBS, AND THEN MEET UP WITH US AT THE NEXT VILLAGE.

MEANWHILE BACK AT THE BASE, HIGH RANKING OFFICERS HAD GATHERED ON THE BEACH TO WATCH THE DEMONSTRATION THEY'D BEEN PROMISED.

COME ALONG NOW, COMMANDER – WHERE'S THIS LANDING CRAFT WITH THE NEW TANKS?

ER – I'M SORRY, SIR. IT SEEMS TO HAVE GOT LOST FROM THE CONVOY.

LOST? PAH! THEY'RE PROBABLY PICNICKING SOMEWHERE.

BUT PICNICKING WAS FAR FROM DICK'S MIND AS HE PRESSED ON TO THE OTHER GERMAN-OCCUPIED VILLAGE.
THE TRACK MIGHT BE MINED – THEY'VE HAD PLENTY OF TIME. SO YOU'D BETTER TAKE THE LEAD, BANE.
RIGHT, SIR. WE'LL SOON CLEAR A WAY THROUGH.

THERE WERE NO MINES, BUT THE GERMANS LISTENED FEARFULLY TO THE NOISY CLATTER OF THE SCORPION'S FLAIL.
THERE MUST BE A WHOLE ARMOURED BRIGADE COMING!
YES, COLLECT EVERY-THING WE CAN CARRY. WE'LL WITHDRAW ACROSS THE RIVER.
AND AS DAWN BROKE DICK AND HIS MEN DROVE THEIR TANKS INTO A DESERTED VILLAGE.
THEY'VE GONE, SIR.
THEN WE'D BETTER SECURE THE APPROACHES BEFORE THEY MOUNT A COUNTER-ATTACK.
DICK BRIEFED HIS MEN SWIFTLY, KNOWING THAT EVERY MOMENT WAS PRECIOUS.
THE CROCODILE WILL COVER THE ROAD BRIDGE, THE PETARD THE RAIL BRIDGE, AND THE SCOR-PION THE PASS. THE BOBBIN WILL RETURN TO THE LCT IN CASE THERE ARE ANY URGENT MESSAGES.
BLIMEY, JUST MY LUCK! MISSING THE SCRAP TO ACT AS A MOBILE TELEPHONE EXCHANGE.

DICK ACCOMPANIED JIM STEEL IN HIS JEEP, FOR HE KNEW THE FIERY CORPORAL TENDED TO BE RECKLESS.

THE BRIDGE IS JUST BEYOND THAT CREST. I'LL GO AHEAD IN THE JEEP AND SEE IF IT'S GUARDED.

OK, SIR. BUT WATCH OUT FOR AMBUSHES.

IT WAS FORTUNATE THAT DICK WAS ALERT, FOR HE CAME UNDER FIRE THE MOMENT HE REACHED THE CREST.

FIRE!
BACK, DRIVER, THEY'VE SEEN US.

THE GERMANS, ASSUMING A FULL-SCALE INVASION HAD TAKEN PLACE, WERE DEFENDING THE RIVER IN FORCE.

HERE COMES THE FIRST TANK! ALERT THE REST OF THE POSTS ALONG THE RIVER.

AS A SHELL PASSED DANGEROUSLY CLOSE, JIM STEEL WITHDREW THE CROCODILE INTO COVER.

THAT EIGHTY-EIGHT NEARLY COPPED ME, SIR! SHALL WE TRY A DASH THROUGH A SMOKE SCREEN?
NO, TOO RISKY. BUT WE SHOULD BE ABLE TO SNEAK UP TO THE RIVER THROUGH THE SCRUB. LET'S HAVE A TRY ANYWAY.

DICK CIRCLED ROUND AND THEN THROUGH THE THICK UNDERGROWTH, WITH THE CROCODILE CLOSE BEHIND.

WE CAN'T BE SEEN NOW, BUT THE BRIDGE IS NOT FAR DOWNSTREAM. AND IT'S MADE OF WOOD, SO WE'LL TRY TO BURN IT!

BUT IT'S OUT OF RANGE, SIR.

BUT DICK HAD A PLAN.

WITHIN SECONDS JIM STEEL HAD SET ABOUT CARRYING OUT DICK'S PLAN.

WE'LL FLOAT BURNING LIQUID FROM THE FLAMETHROWER DOWNSTREAM.
IT'S FLOWING DOWN NICE AND SLOWLY. NOW SEE WHAT HAPPENS.

THE GERMANS WATCHED IN DISMAY AS THE FLAMES NEARED THE BRIDGE – THEN THE BONE-DRY WOODWORK CAUGHT FIRE.
MEIN GOTT – THE BRIDGE!
THERE ARE DEMOLITION CHARGES UNDER IT, TO HALT THE IN-VADERS. RUN!

AND AS THE FLAMES REACHED THE EXPLOSIVES, THE BRIDGE DISAPPEARED WITH A THUNDEROUS ROAR.

AAGHH!

ONE THING'S FOR SURE, SIR, NO-BODY WILL CROSS THAT FOR A FEW DAYS.

YOU'D BETTER FIND SOME COVER AND KEEP AN EYE ON THINGS. I'LL GO AND SEE HOW THE OTHERS ARE GETTING ON.

WHEN DICK ARRIVED AT THE RAIL BRIDGE HE FOUND THAT JOE CRISP HAD BEEN USING HIS INITIATIVE.
THERE WERE ONLY A FEW JERRY SENTRIES AROUND, SO WE KNOCKED THEM OFF.
LOOKS AS IF YOU TORE UP THE TRACK JUST IN TIME. HERE'S A TRAIN COMING!

A SHOT FROM THE PETARD HALTED THE TRAIN AS IT CAME INTO RANGE.
STOP THE TRAIN. WE ARE BEING ATTACK-ED!

AS THE TRAIN SHUDDERED TO A HALT, TROOPS BEGAN TO POUR OUT OF THE TRUCKS, AND DICK WATCHED APPRE-HENSIVELY.

IF THEY CROSS FURTHER UPSTREAM THEY'LL CUT US OFF, SIR!

WE'LL HANG ON UNTIL WE SEE WHAT THEY'RE PLANN-ING. BUT THEY'RE LAYING A SMOKE SCREEN.

BUT THE GERMANS HAD NO INTENTION OF CROSSING THE RIVER. UNDER COVER OF THE SMOKE THEY PLACED CHARGES ON THE BRIDGE.
THEY BLEW THE BRIDGE THEM-SELVES, SIR.
THEY MUST THINK WE'VE IN-VADED IN FORCE AND THEY'RE TRYING TO DELAY US. IF ONLY THEY KNEW!

LEAVING JOE CRISP TO KEEP WATCH, DICK HEADED FOR THE PASS TO SEE HOW BUSTER HUCKLE WAS GETTING ON.
LOOKS AS IF THEY'RE HAVING TROUBLE. STAY HERE, I'LL GO AHEAD ON FOOT.
BETTER WATCH YOUR STEP, SIR. THE SCORPION'S BEING SHELLED FROM BEYOND THAT RIDGE.

DICK FOUND A PUZZLED BUSTER TRYING TO WORK OUT WHY THE GERMANS WERE NOT ADVANCING.

WE BULLDOZED ROCKS INTO THE PASS TO BLOCK IT. BUT THEY HAVEN'T TRIED TO GET THROUGH.

I DON'T THINK THEY WILL, BUSTER. IT LOOKS AS IF THEY'RE WAITING.

THEN WE'LL BE ABLE TO SIT TIGHT UNTIL THE LANDING CRAFT HAS BEEN REFLOATED. WHAT A BIT OF LUCK!
SO LONG AS THE WEATHER DOESN'T IMPROVE, THEY CAN'T SEND A RECCE AIR-CRAFT OVER. IF THEY DO, WE'RE SUNK.
MEANWHILE, AS DICK HAD SUSPECTED, THE GERMANS WERE IN UTTER CONFUSION. OBERST ENGEL, THE AREA COMMANDER, RECEIVED NEWS OF THE "INVASION" AT DAWN.
SO, THE ENEMY HAS REACHED THE RIVER AT TWO POINTS AND A THIRD COLUMN HAS GOT TO THE PASS. AND OUR MEN HAVE WITH-DRAWN TO THE RIVER DEFENCE LINE.
JAWOHL, HERR OBERST. BUT THE ORDERS STATE THAT SUCH ACTION IS ONLY TO BE TAKEN IN THE EVENT OF A FULL-SCALE INVASION!

LEUTNANT ZELLER, THE COLONEL'S DEPUTY, WAS NO FOOL, AND HE HAD READ ALL THE REPORTS.

THERE WAS A LOT OF CONFUSION LAST NIGHT, HERR OBERST, AND NO-BODY HAS YET CON-FIRMED THE ENEMY STRENGTH.

THAT CAN WAIT. I'LL PHONE HEADQUARTERS, THEN WE'LL GO AND HAVE A LOOK AT THE ENEMY.

THE GENERAL COMMANDING HAD NO DOUBT THAT THE INVASION WAS GENUINE.
IT'S AN ATTEMPT TO RELIEVE THE PRESSURE AT ANZIO AND DRAW OFF OUR DIVISIONS. I'LL GIVE YOU ALL THE REINFORCEMENTS I CAN SPARE. YOU MUST HOLD ON AT ALL COSTS.
JAWOHL, HERR GENERAL, WE SHALL GIVE OUR LIVES BEFORE WE RETREAT.

ALREADY COLONEL ENGEL COULD SEE PROMOTION GLITTERING IN THE FUTURE – IF ONLY HE COULD HOLD THE BRITISH.

I MUST DO NOTHING RASH, NOTHING THAT WILL WEAKEN OUR POSITION. THEN PERHAPS I WILL BE "GENERAL" ENGEL!

DRIVING TO THE RIVER, HE FOUND HIS MEN WATCHING THE RAIN-SWEPT DESERTED COUNTRYSIDE.
IT'S HARD TO BELIEVE THAT THE ENEMY HAD ONE OR MORE DIVISIONS OVER THERE.
THEIR CAMOUFLAGE DRILL MUST BE VERY EFFECTIVE. NOT A SINGLE UNIT HAS SHOWN ITSELF SINCE DAWN.
THE SITUATION WAS LAUGHABLE. THE CHAOS CAUSED BY THE FOUR TANKS HAD REALLY SHAKEN THE NAZIS INTO BELIEVING A LARGE INVASION FORCE WAS ON THE RAMPAGE.

BUT JOE CRISP HAD ALSO BEEN WATCHING, AND THE STAFF CAR PROVIDED A TEMPTING TARGET.
THAT SHOULD MAKE 'EM SIT UP! LET'S MOVE OUT OF HERE BEFORE THEY TOSS A FEW BRICKS BACK!

AND THE SMOKING WRECK OF HIS CAR CONVINCED THE COLONEL THAT THE COUNTRYSIDE WAS NOT EMPTY.
WE HAVEN'T ENOUGH MEN HERE TO STOP A DETERMINED ATTACK, WE NEED ARTILLERY SUPPORT. GET ME THE GENERAL ON THE RADIO.

WITH THE PROMISE OF ARTILLERY SUPPORT THE COLONEL FELT MUCH HAPPIER.
THE GENERAL AGREES. IF WE GIVE THE MAP CO-ORDINATES OF EVERY LIKELY FORMING-UP POINT, THEY WILL BE SHELLED BY OUR LONG-RANGE ARTILLERY!
WHY NOT LET ME TAKE A PATROL ACROSS THE RIVER, HERR OBERST? I COULD PIN-POINT THE ENEMY FORMATIONS THEN.

LEUTNANT ZELLER'S SUGGESTION WAS MET WITH AN ANGRY REBUKE.

NOBODY CROSSES THE RIVER! IF THE ENEMY TAKE A PRISONER THEY MAY DISCOVER HOW WEAK OUR DEFENCES ARE – AND ATTACK!

AND SO, BY A FORTUNATE COMBINATION OF BAD WEATHER WHICH PREVENTED AIR RECONNAISSANCE, AND OBERST ENGEL'S CAUTION, DICK'S SMALL FORCE REMAINED UNDISTURBED.

BUT AS RESERVE UNITS WERE RUSHED INTO POSITION TO PREVENT ANY BREAK-OUT FROM THE BEACH, THE LONG-RANGE ARTILLERY BEGAN TO POUND THE AREA.

AS THE SHELLING INCREASED, DICK SAW ANOTHER WAY TO ADD TO THE CONFUSION.

THEY'RE PLASTERING EVERY LIKELY HIDING PLACE, SIR! GOOD JOB WE HAVEN'T A COUPLE OF DIVISIONS HERE!

BUT THE JERRIES THINK WE HAVE. SO WE'D BETTER PROVIDE THEM WITH SOME EVIDENCE.

DICK ORDERED JIM STEEL TO MOVE AROUND AND START FIRES WITH HIS FLAMETHROWER.
GOOD JOB THE JERRIES SEEM TO HAVE EVACUATED THE EYETIE PEASANTS. WE'D BETTER MOVE ON BEFORE THEY PUT DOWN ANOTHER BARRAGE AROUND OUR EARS.

MEANWHILE DICK, AWARE THAT THE ENEMY WOULD BE LISTENING, WAS KEEPING THE RADIO BUSY.

BAKER FIVE FROM SUN-RAY, HOLD THE SECOND BRIGADE IN POSITION. FOR-WARD DIVISION IS HAVING HEAVY CASUALTIES FROM SHELLING, OVER.

LET ME 'AVE A GO, SIR. I'VE ALWAYS WANTED TO BE A GENERAL!

LATER HE RETURNED TO THE BEACH, WHERE HUBERT HAD GOT A KEDGE ANCHOR OUT BUT WAS STILL HAVING TROUBLE.
WE'VE TRIED TO WINCH HER OFF, BUT IT'S NO GOOD. IF ONLY WE HAD MORE MEN TO DIG AROUND THE HULL.
WHY NOT USE THE JERRY PRISONERS? THERE'S CERTAINLY ENOUGH OF THEM.

HUBERT WAS A STICKLER FOR CONVENTION, AND HE LOOKED SCORNFUL AT DICK'S SUGGESTION.

NO! PRISONERS MUST NOT BE USED FOR MILITARY PURPOSES.

IT'S OK IF THEY VOLUNTEER. HANG ON A MINUTE, I'LL HAVE A WORD WITH THEM.

DICK SUSPECTED THAT MANY OF THE GERMANS WOULD WELCOME A CHANCE TO GET AWAY TO SAFETY.

AND WE ALL KNOW WHAT WILL HAPPEN TO THEM IF THEIR GENERAL DISCOVERS THEY SURRENDERED TO A HANDFUL OF BRITISHERS.
ACH, THEY WOULD BE SHOT! I WILL EXPLAIN THAT IF THEY VOLUNTEER TO HELP, THEY WILL GO TO ENGLAND.

AND HE WAS RIGHT, FOR THEY VOLUNTEERED WILLINGLY.

WELL, THAT'S SETTLED. NOW I'LL GET MY SPARE AMMUNITION UNLOADED. WE MAY NEED IT LATER.

I'VE ALREADY HAD EVERYTHING DUMPED ON THE BEACH TO LIGHTEN SHIP. YOU'LL FIND IT OVER THERE.

TWENTY OF THE ITEMS UNLOADED WERE "SNAKES" – STEEL TUBES PACKED WITH EXPLOSIVES, USED FOR CLEARING MINEFIELDS.

I HOPE YOU HANDLED THEM CAREFULLY? IF THEY EXPLODED THEY WOULD WIPE OUT EVERYTHING WITHIN FIFTY YARDS.
WHAT? PEOPLE HAVE BEEN TRIPPING OVER THEM ALL DAY.

LEAVING THE NAVAL OFFICER FUMING, DICK RETURNED TO HIS MEN AND SPENT THE DAY MAINTAINING HIS WAR OF NERVES AGAINST THE GERMANS WITH FIRES AND FAKE WIRELESS MESSAGES. THEN, AT DUSK, HE BEGAN TO WITHDRAW HIS TANKS.

IT'S TIME WE MOVED OUT DOWN TOWARDS THE BEACH.

BUT AS THE SCORPION BEGAN TO WITHDRAW IT WAS SPOTTED BY A SHARP-EYED GERMAN ARTILLERY OBSERVER.

LOOK OUT, SIR, THEY'VE SEEN US.

AND THAT GROUND'S GIVING WAY UNDER THE SCORPION'S WEIGHT.

AND AS THE HILLSIDE CRUMBLED THE SCORPION SLID INTO THE VALLEY AND OVERTURNED.
SEEMS LIKE EVERYONE'S OK, SIR, BUT WE'LL NEVER SHIFT THE OLD GIRL NOW.
NO, WE'LL HAVE TO DESTROY HER AND GO BACK IN THE JEEP. PUT A MATCH TO THE FUEL TANKS.

AS THEY DROVE AWAY, THE SCORPION BURNED AMONGST A HAIL OF ENEMY SHELLS.

THEY WON'T GET MUCH INFORMATION FROM THAT. THEY'RE SHELLING IT TO BLAZES.

THEY PROBABLY THINK THEY'VE HIT A WHOLE SQUADRON.

BUT UNKNOWN TO DICK, LEUTNANT ZELLER HAD DECIDED TO INVESTIGATE THE OTHER BANK OF THE RIVER FOR HIMSELF.
NO SIGN OF THE ENEMY, HERR LEUTNANT. THEIR OUTPOSTS MUST BE NEARER THE COAST.
JA, OUR GUNS HAVE HELD THEM BACK. BUT WE MUST GO CAREFULLY FROM NOW ON.

OUR GUNS ARE ENGAGING A TARGET OVER THERE.
WE'LL KEEP AWAY AND TRY TO GET A PRISONER FROM A QUIETER AREA.

AND AT THE BEACH, HUBERT WAS GROWING INCREASINGLY DESPERATE AT THEIR FAILURE TO REFLOAT THE LCT.

IF ONLY WE'D HAD MORE MEN DIGGING THIS EVENING, I'M SURE WE'D HAVE FLOATED OFF. THOSE TRENCHES MUST BE DEEPENED!

TURNING AWAY FROM THE LANDING CRAFT HE SAW CORPORAL CHARLIE NOBBS AND THE CREW OF THE BOBBIN.

GET YOUR MEN OUT OF THAT TANK, CORPORAL, AND START DIGGING. THIS ISN'T A PICINC!
BETTER DO AS HE SAYS. I DON'T SUPPOSE THE PRISONERS WILL RUN AWAY.

BUT ONE GERMAN NOTICED THE EMPTY VEHICLE AND HAVING DRIVEN GERMAN TANKS, FELT HE WOULD HAVE LITTLE DIFFICULTY IN OPERATING THE BOBBIN.

IF I CAN GET BACK AND REPORT THAT THERE IS NO REAL INVASION, I SHALL BE PROMOTED. IT'S WORTH THE RISK.

AND DICK RETURNED JUST AS THE BOBBIN ROARED AWAY INTO THE DARKNESS.

A PRISONER'S JUST STOLEN THAT TANK. IF HE GETS AWAY AND REPORTS, WE'RE FINISHED!
COME ON, BUSTER, WE MIGHT CATCH HIM. A GRENADE IN THE DRIVING HATCH WILL SOON STOP HIS TRICKS.

BUT AS HE RACED AFTER THE BOBBIN, IT WAS ALREADY HEADING INTO TROUBLE.

IT'S A
BRITISH TANK!
FIRE, YOU CAN'T
MISS.

AND THE ROAR OF THE PANZERSCHRECK PUT AN END TO THE ESCAPE BID.

BUT THE FLAMES FROM THE BURNING TANK BROUGHT AN IMMEDIATE RESPONSE FROM THE GERMAN ARTILLERY.

AAIIEE!
CURSE IT,
OUR GUNS MUST
BE CLOSING IN READY
FOR THE COUNTER-
ATTACK AT
DAWN.

THE JEEP SLITHERED TO A STOP AT THE FIRST SIGN OF TROUBLE ,AND DICK REALISED IMMEDIATELY WHAT HAD TAKEN PLACE.

WHAT HAPPENED ,SIR? THE BOBBIN BLEW UP BEFORE THE SHELLIN' STARTED!

IT WAS AMBUSHED. THE JERRIES MUST HAVE PUT A PATROL ACROSS THE RIVER. WE'VE GOT TO STOP THEM REACHING THE BEACH!

RETURNING TO THE BEACH HE GATHERED HIS MEN TOGETHER AND BRIEFED THEM SWIFTLY.

THE MEN CAN RIDE IN THE JEEP AND ON THE CROCODILE. HOW'S THE FLAME-THROWER?
WE NEED ANOTHER NITROGEN CYLINDER ,SIR. BUT THE SEVENTY-FIVE STILL HAS A FEW SHELLS.

LEAVING JOE CRISP AND THE PETARD TO DEFEND THE LANDING CRAFT, DICK HURRIED TO SET A COUNTER-AMBUSH.
SPREAD OUT UNDER COVER, AND OPEN FIRE WHEN I GIVE THE ORDER. AND MAKE SURE NOBODY GETS AWAY!
ONLY A SMALL PATROL, SIR, WE SHAN'T NEED THE CROCO-DILE.
JUST AS WELL. THE SEVENTY-FIVE ISN'T MUCH USE AGAINST INFANTRY IN THE DARK.
THE INTRUDERS WERE MET BY A HAIL OF FIRE FROM THE SHADOWS.
AAGHH!
ACHTUNG, AN AMBUSH!

LEUTNANT ZELLER, WHO HAD ESCAPED THE FIRST DEADLY VOLLEY, SNATCHED A FLARE PISTOL FROM HIS BELT.
THAT WILL BRING DOWN A BARRAGE, AND WE MAY BE ABLE TO ESCAPE IN THE CONFUSION.
THE ARTILLERY RESPONSE WAS SWIFT – AND THE CROCODILE WAS THE FIRST THING THAT GOT HIT.
ONLY ONE CASUALTY, SIR. WE GOT OUT JUST IN TIME.
RIGHT, PUT HIM UNDER COVER AND HELP US TO ROUND UP THE JERRY SUR-VIVORS.

THE GERMAN ARTILLERY OBSERVERS, ON A CREST BEYOND THE RIVER, CONCENTRATED THEIR FIRE ON THE FLAMES OF THE BURNING CROCODILE.

BANG GOES THE JEEP, SIR!

LET'S GET OUT OF HERE – WE'RE A SITTING TARGET FOR THEIR GUNS.

BUT AS THEY CALLED THEIR MEN TOGETHER, DICK AND BUSTER HEARD A TRIUMPHANT SHOUT.
I CAUGHT THIS ONE TRYIN' TO GET AWAY, SIR! HE'S THE JOKER WHO FIRED THAT FLARE.
GOOD, BRING HIM ALONG. WE'LL QUESTION HIM WHEN WE GET TO THE BEACH.

ZELLER WAS DEFIANTLY SULLEN – THAT WAS UNTIL THEY REACHED THE BEACH.

WHERE ARE THE REST OF YOUR TANKS – AND YOUR INVASION FLEET?

THIS IS ALL THERE IS, CHUM. WE CERTAINLY HAD YOU FOOLED, EH?

FOR A MOMENT HE LOOKED STUNNED, THEN HE BURST INTO A BELLOW OF LAUGHTER.
ACH, IT IS MAGNIFICENT! MY DEAR COLONEL WILL PROBABLY BE SHOT FOR THIS – WHILE I'LL BE SAFE IN A PRISON CAMP.
PROVIDING WE CAN GET AWAY. HOW LONG WILL IT BE BEFORE YOUR CHAPS MOUNT A COUNTER-ATTACK?

THE LEUTNANT WAS QUITE PREPARED TO TALK, FOR HE REALISED DICK'S LITTLE FORCE WAS NO THREAT.

TWO DIVISIONS ARE MOVING UP TO ATTACK AT DAWN, WITH ASSAULT CRAFT TO CROSS THE RIVER. SO YOU'D BETTER NOT BE HERE THEN.

I'LL DO MY BEST TO MAKE SURE WE'RE NOT AROUND.

HUBERT, WHO REALISED THE DESTRUCTION OF THE BOBBIN WAS HIS FAULT, WAS IN A SUBDUED MOOD WHEN DICK CONSULTED HIM.
THE DIGGING IS FINISHED, SO WE SHOULD BE ABLE TO FLOAT THE LANDING CRAFT.
FIRST, I'M GOING TO PREPARE A LITTLE SURPRISE FOR THE JERRIES.

DICK USED HIS REMAINING TANK, THE PETARD, TO TOW THE EXPLOSIVE SNAKE AWAY FROM THE BEACH.
WE'LL LEAVE THE SNAKE ACROSS THE VALLEY BEHIND US, AND PARK THE PETARD HERE ON THE RIDGE. THERE'S NO AMMUNITION LEFT, BUT THE SIGHT OF IT MIGHT SLOW THE NAZIS DOWN.

HAVING UNLOADED THE SNAKES THE PETARD CREW RETURNED TO THE LANDING CRAFT, LEAVING DICK WITH THE PETARD. TO DICK'S SURPRISE BUSTER RETURNED HALF AN HOUR LATER.

I BROUGHT SOME GRUB, SIR, IT'LL BE A LONG WAIT.

THEN, NEXT DAY, AS DAWN APPROACHED, THEY SAW FLARES SPARKLING ON THE HORIZON.
WHAT'S HAPPENIN', SIR? THE BARRAGE SEEMS TO BE GETTING CLOSER.
THE JERRIES ARE CROSSING THE RIVER, EXPECTING TO MEET HEAVY OPPOSITION. WON'T BE LONG NOW...

IT WAS NOT LONG BEFORE THE LEADING GERMAN TANKS WERE SWEEPING ACROSS THE COUNTRYSIDE.

HERE THEY COME!

ENEMY ARMOURED VEHICLE, RANGE TWO THOUSAND! FIRE!

AND THE LAST OF THE FUNNIES EXPLODED AS SHELLS RIPPED INTO ITS HULL.
COME ON, WE'VE GOT TO GET TO THE NEXT RIDGE BEFORE THEY SEE US!

THE GERMAN TANKS MOVED CONFIDENTLY PAST THE BURNING PETARD, AND DIPPED INTO THE VALLEY.

I CAN ONLY JUST SEE THE SNAKE, BUT I CAN'T AFFORD TO MISS IT.

GOOD LUCK, SIR.

IT WAS QUITE A GAMBLE – ATTEMPTING TO DETONATE THE SNAKE WITH A .303 RIFLE BULLET.

DICK'S AIM WAS TRUE – AND THE SNAKE EXPLODED WITH A DEVASTATING ROAR.
AAGHH!
HIMMEL. WHAT WEAPON IS THIS?

JA, THE BRITISH HAVE WITHDRAWN, BUT THEY HAVE LEFT STRANGE WEAPONS. WE NEED ENGINEERS TO CLEAR THEM. WE'RE NOT MOVING FORWARD UNTIL THEY ARRIVE!

DICK AND BUSTER HEADED FOR THE BEACH, WHERE TO THEIR DELIGHT THEY SAW THAT THE LANDING CRAFT WAS AFLOAT.

COME ON, SIR, YOU NEARLY MISSED THE BOAT.

WE HAD SOME UNFINISHED BUSINESS TO ATTEND TO!

HUBERT EXPLAINED THAT THE TRENCHES DUG AROUND THE HULL, COMBINED WITH THE KEDGE ANCHOR, HAD DONE THE TRICK.

WHAT WAS THAT EX-PLOSION?
WE CLOBBERED SOME JERRY TANKS, TO DISCOURAGE THEM FROM CHASING. THEY WERE HEADING FOR THE BEACH.

FOR A MOMENT THE NAVAL OFFICER WAS SILENT – THEN ABRUPTLY HE THRUST OUT HIS HAND.

I'M SORRY. I'VE BEEN A POMPOUS IDIOT. YOU AND YOUR MEN HAVE SAVED OUR NECKS ON THIS TRIP – AND I'D LIKE TO THANK YOU.

IT'S ALL IN A DAY'S WORK, CHUM. AND REMEMBER WE'RE STILL RELYING ON YOU TO GET US HOME.

AND AS THE FIRST ENEMY INFANTRY REACHED THE BEACH, THE LCT WAS GLIDING AWAY INTO THE MORNING MISTS.

TOO LATE, JERRY, YOU SHOULD GET UP EARLIER!

A FEW HOURS LATER OBERST ENGEL REPORTED TO HEADQUARTERS.

YOU'LL BE INTERESTED TO KNOW THAT BECAUSE OF YOUR BLUNDER TWO DIVISIONS WERE WITHDRAWN FROM ANZIO — AND THE BRITISH ARE BREAKING OUT! NO DOUBT YOU'LL HAVE AN EXPLANATION FOR THE COMMANDER-IN-CHIEF.

PERHAPS, IF I AM VERY LUCKY, THE WAR WILL BE OVER BEFORE I AM SHOT.

BUT BY THAT TIME DICK AND HUBERT WERE APPROACHING NAPLES, AND THEY RECEIVED A STARTLED WELCOME FROM EVERYONE WHO HAD ASSUMED THEY WERE DEAD.
QUITE A RECEPTION! I'LL BET THEY WERE SURPRISED TO HEAR WE'D BEEN SIGHTED ENTERING HARBOUR.
THEY'LL BE EVEN MORE SURPRISED IN A MINUTE — THEY THINK WE'VE GOT FOUR TANKS AND A JEEP ON BOARD.

AS THE RAMP WENT DOWN AND THE PRISONERS STREAMED ASHORE, A CHEER WENT UP FROM THE ASSEMBLED SPECTATORS AND THERE WERE CONGRATULATIONS FROM THE SENIOR NAVAL AND ARMY OFFICERS. THE FUNNIES HAD GONE — BUT THEY HAD MORE THAN PROVED THEIR VALUE IN BATTLE.
SO MUCH FOR THE NAZI SUPERMEN!
THEY'RE PRETTY MEEK. MIND YOU, THEY GOT QUITE A SHOCK SEE-ING YOU AND YOUR MAD TANKS!
Commando
THE END

Four all-action Commando books are coming your way in just two weeks!
Keep a look-out for: —

"THE FIGHTING FOOLS" **"WIN OR LOSE . . ."**

"INLAND NAVY" **"SOUND THE ALARM!"**

THOMPSON SUB-MACHINE GUN

Equipment of the Second World War — No. 8

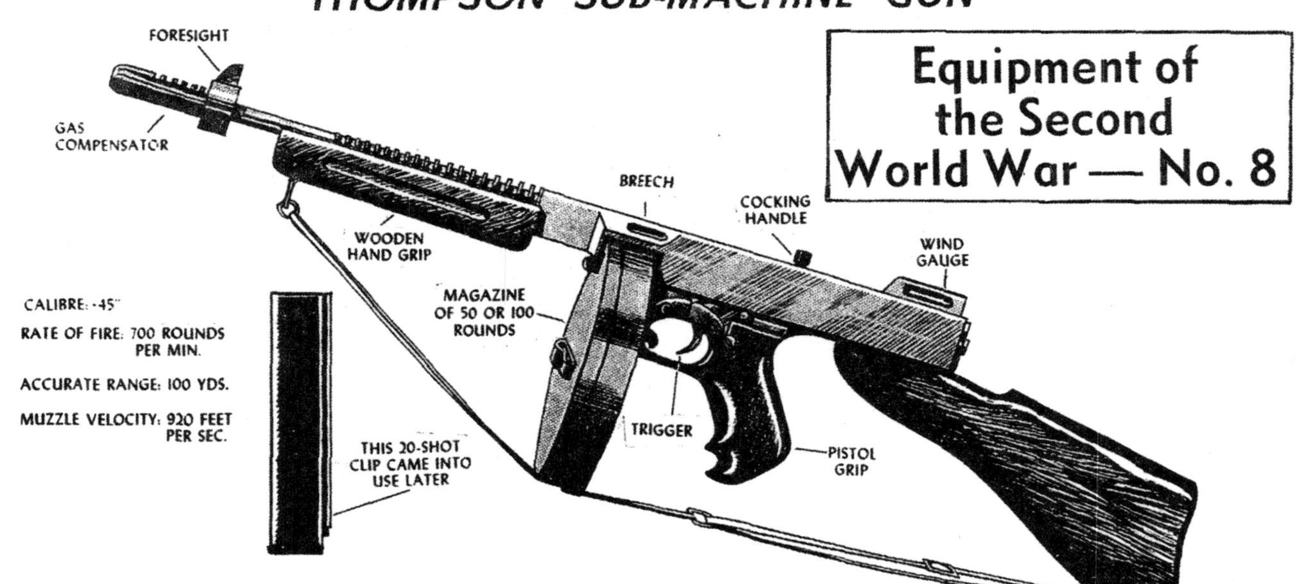
FORESIGHT
GAS COMPENSATOR
WOODEN HAND GRIP
BREECH
COCKING HANDLE
WIND GAUGE
MAGAZINE OF 50 OR 100 ROUNDS
TRIGGER
PISTOL GRIP
THIS 20-SHOT CLIP CAME INTO USE LATER

CALIBRE: ·45"

RATE OF FIRE: 700 ROUNDS PER MIN.

ACCURATE RANGE: 100 YDS.

MUZZLE VELOCITY: 920 FEET PER SEC.

THE American, J. T. Thompson, who invented the Tommy-gun, got the idea when he saw how effective the spray of lead from a sawn-off shotgun was. He adapted this idea, and America's gangsters soon made his gun famous—or infamous.

Hundreds were shipped to Britain at the outbreak of the war as an anti-Nazi paratrooper weapon.

British soldiers didn't like them at first because of their short range, but once the Commandos and the Parachute Regiment came into being, the Tommy-gun was the ideal close-combat weapon, replacing the rifle and bayonet. Its light weight and deadly spraying action made it a favourite with these crack troops. A hit almost anywhere on the body with its .45 slug will stop an enemy.

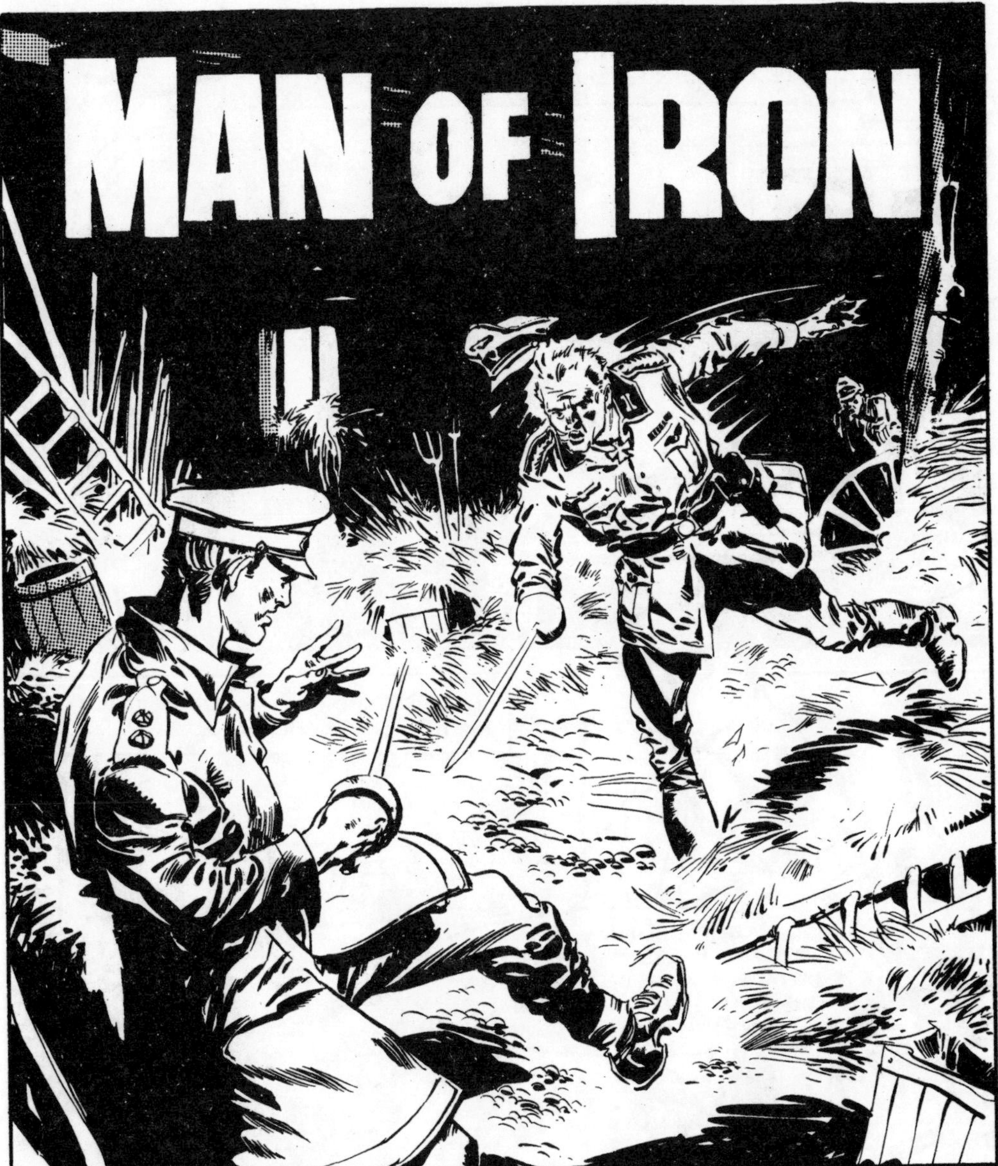
MAN OF IRON

LIEUTENANT BERT ROGAN WAS A ROUGH, TOUGH FIGHTER WHO COULDN'T CARE LESS ABOUT OFFICERS. AND THAT LANDED HIM IN DEEP TROUBLE — WITH BRITISH AND GERMAN OFFICERS ALIKE!

THE GERMANS SAID — WHAT KIND OF GENTLEMAN WOULD FIGHT WITH BOOTS AND FISTS?

THE BRITISH ASKED — WHAT KIND OF MAN WOULD SHOOT A PRISONER IN THE BACK?

THIS IS BERT'S STORY...

THE OFFICERS' MESS OF THE LENNOX RIFLES WAS ONE OF THE MOST EXCLUSIVE IN THE BRITISH ARMY, UNTIL ONE DAY IN 1944 A BREATH OF RAW COLD AIR BLEW IN, IN THE SHAPE OF LIEUTENANT BERT ROGAN.
GOOD HEAVENS! WHO'S THIS?
MIND YOUR BACKS, LADS!
BERT HURLED HIS KIT-BAG DOWN ON TOP OF A BEAUTIFULLY POLISHED TABLE.
I SAY! YOU CAN'T PUT THAT THERE! WHO ARE YOU?
ROGAN'S THE NAME, BERT ROGAN. I'VE BEEN WITH THE THIRD BATTALION IN THE DESERT AND NOW THEY'VE POSTED ME HERE. WHAT'S IT LIKE HERE? GOOD GRUB?
I'LL SHOW YOU YOUR QUARTERS. TAKE THAT KIT-BAG OFF THE TABLE. YOU SHOULDN'T HAVE ONE ANYWAY – AND WHY DIDN'T YOU GET ONE OF THE MEN TO CARRY IT?

I ALWAYS USE A KIT-BAG. YOU CAN CRAM MORE INTO IT. AND WHY SHOULD I MAKE ONE OF THE LADS CARRY MY KIT? I'M NOT A CRIPPLE.

GOOD GRIEF, THE MAN'S COMPLETELY UNCOUTH. HOW ON EARTH DID HE GET A COMMISSION?

HE WEARS A MILITARY MEDAL RIBBON — THAT SHOWS HE'S COME UP FROM THE RANKS. THINGS MUST HAVE BEEN PRETTY DESPERATE IN THE DESERT IF THEY PICKED HIM FOR AN OFFICER.

BERT'S BEHAVIOUR HAD MADE HIM TWO ENEMIES — THE ARISTOCRATIC CAPTAIN ROGER JENKINS AND LIEUTENANT JOHN PHIBBSON.

AT DINNER THAT EVENING...
JUST LOOK AT HIM EAT. MANNERS OF A PIG.
SOMEBODY SHOULD SAY SOMETHING.
IT WAS THE C.O., LIEUTENANT COLONEL ROBINSHAW, WHO SPOKE FIRST.

ON BEHALF OF THE MESS I WANT TO WELCOME YOU HERE, ROGAN. I UNDERSTAND YOU WERE IN THE DESERT AND PROVED YOURSELF A FIRST-RATE SOLDIER. I'M SURE YOU'LL BE A MOST VALUABLE MEMBER OF OUR TEAM.
ALWAYS TRIED TO GIVE SATISFACTION, SIR. I HOPE AS HOW WE GET ON ALL RIGHT.

THEN BERT LEANED TOWARD THE TWO SNOBS.
I HEARD WHAT YOU TWO WERE SAYING. THINGS WERE DESPERATE IN THE DESERT ALL RIGHT. TIME YOU GOT OUT THERE AND HAD A LOOK FOR YOURSELVES!
NOW, NOW, GENTLEMEN. THERE WILL BE NO MORE ARGUING.
THANKS TO LIEUTENANT-COLONEL ROBINSHAW, THE INCIDENT DID NOT DEVELOP FURTHER.

THE FOLLOWING DAY BERT THREW HIMSELF INTO THE TRAINING PROGRAMME.

PICK 'EM UP, YOU SHOWER OF OLD MEN! YOU'RE A BUNCH OF IDLE LAYABOUTS! COME ALONG THERE — MOVE!

DID YOU EVER HEAR AN OFFICER BAWLING AT HIS MEN LIKE THAT? THAT'S THE N.C.O.'s JOB.

YES I KNOW. THIS IS BECOMING RIDICULOUS. THE MAN HAS NO SENSE OF DIGNITY AT ALL.

BERT FINALLY HANDED OVER AGAIN TO SERGEANT BLACK.

I DON'T KNOW ABOUT THE LADS, BUT I ENJOYED THAT, SARGE. CAN'T BEAT IT FOR EXERCISING THE LUNGS. TELL THEM I'LL POP IN TO SEE THEM LATER IN THE BILLET.

THE IDEA OF AN OFFICER HOB-NOBBING WITH THE MEN IN THEIR BILLETS WAS UNKNOWN TO THE LENNOX RIFLES.

I KNOW YOU LADS ARE BORED STIFF WITH THE TRAINING AND CAN'T WAIT TO HAVE A CRACK AT JERRY. MY GUESS IS YOU WON'T HAVE LONG TO WAIT – AND THEN YOU'LL BE GLAD OF EVERY MINUTE YOU SPENT TRAINING.

BUT THE REGIMENT'S TWO SNOBS, PHIBBSON AND JENKINS, WERE ALREADY PROTESTING TO THE COLONEL.
DON'T YOU THINK IT'S WRONG, SIR, THE WAY ROGAN HOB-NOBS WITH HIS MEN?
THAT SORT OF THING WILL DISRUPT DISCIPLINE THROUGHOUT THE WHOLE REGIMENT.
HIS METHODS ARE UNUSUAL, I AGREE, BUT THEY SEEM TO WORK. BY THE WAY, I'VE LEARNED HOW HE GAINED HIS COMMISSION. I HEARD IT FROM TUBBY MASTERS OF THE THIRD BATTALION...
THE COLONEL TOLD THEM HOW, WHEN BERT WAS A SERGEANT, HIS UNIT WAS TAKEN PRISONER DURING THE BITTER FIGHTING IN THE DESERT. THE PRISONERS WERE HAVING A TOUGH TIME UNTIL...
MOVE MORE QUICKLY, ENGLISH PIG!
AW, GO AND MAKE SAND-PIES, YOU SQUARE-HEAD!

YOU WILL LEARN TO RESPECT US, CORPORAL!
HEY — LAY OFF HIM, FRITZ!

AS THE GUARD RAISED HIS RIFLE, BERT PUSHED AGAINST HIM.
I'VE GOT A KNIFE AGAINST YOUR RIBS. DROP THE RIFLE OR YOU'RE DEAD. I'M NOT JOKING!
BERT HAD KEPT A SMALL KNIFE HIDDEN IN HIS BOOT. HE HAD BEEN WAITING FOR THIS OPPORTUNITY.

AS THE RIFLE FELL TO THE GROUND, BERT MOVED LIKE LIGHTING, SNATCHING IT UP.
RUN FOR IT, LADS! I'LL HOLD 'EM!

THEN THE GERMAN GUARDS DECIDED TO SHOOT IT OUT WITH BERT. BUT THEY WEREN'T QUICK ENOUGH FOR THIS MAN OF IRON.
AARGH!
GRAB THEIR GUNS AS I DROP THEM!
THE PRISONERS REGAINED THEIR WITS FIRST, AND IT WAS JUST AS WELL FOR BERT THEY DID. 
NO YOU DON'T, JERRY!

THEY SNATCHED UP THE GERMANS' RIFLES AND BERT LED THEM INTO THE SAND HILLS.
WHERE ARE WE GOING, SARGE?
BACK TO OUR OWN LINES, OF COURSE. HOW CAN THEY WIN THIS WAR WITHOUT US?

THEY FOUGHT AND STOLE THEIR WAY TO THE BRITISH LINES, PICKING UP STRAGGLERS ON THE WAY. BERT LED THEM WITH RUTHLESS EFFICIENCY.

THEY DREW NEAR TO A MAIN ROAD — AND CAME UPON A SCENE BERT WAS TO REMEMBER FOR A LONG TIME.

WE CANNOT WASTE TIME ON USELESS PIGS LIKE THESE. SHOOT THEM — AND GET YOUR MEN TO THE FRONT LINE WHERE THERE IS REAL WORK TO BE DONE.
BUT THEY ARE PRISONERS OF WAR, HERR MAJOR. WE ARE TAKING THEM BACK TO THE PRISON CAGE.
DO NOT ARGUE WITH ME, SERGEANT — THAT IS AN ORDER. THEY ARE NO USE TO US. 
JAWOHL, HERR MAJOR.

THE GERMAN MAJOR ROARED OFF.

BERT AND HIS MEN HEARD EVERY WORD. AS THE EXECUTION SQUAD RAISED THEIR RIFLES...
AAAAH!
A SERIES OF SHOTS ECHOED FROM THE HILLS.

WITHIN SECONDS THE GERMANS WERE WIPED OUT.

BLIMEY! ARE WE GLAD TO SEE YOU! THOSE JERRIES —

GET IN THE LORRY. WE'VE GOT TO GET OUT OF HERE QUICKLY.

AS THEY REACHED THE BRITISH LINES THEY RAN SMACK INTO A GERMAN ARTILLERY BARRAGE.

DON'T SHOOT! WE'RE ON YOUR SIDE!

WHERE IN THE DICKENS DID YOU LOT COME FROM?

THEY WERE AT THE EXTREME FLANK OF THE BRITISH FRONT LINE, WHICH WAS UNDER HEAVY ATTACK.

CAPTAIN CRAIG, THE OFFICER IN CHARGE OF THIS SECTION, WAS DESPERATE FOR HELP.

CAN YOU HOLD THIS POSITION? THE JERRIES ARE THROWING EVERYTHING THEY'VE GOT INTO THE ATTACK AND WE'VE LOST A LOT OF MEN.

JUST GIVE US ENOUGH RIFLES AND BRENS AND LEAVE IT TO US, SIR. COME ON, LADS!

WITH CALM AUTHORITY BERT PLACED HIS MEN IN POSITION.

ARMING THEMSELVES WITH BRENS AND RIFLES, BERT AND HIS MEN WERE SOON IN THE THICK OF IT.
WHERE ARE THEY ALL COMING FROM?
THIS IS NO GOOD. WE'VE GOT TO GET THEM ON THE DEFENSIVE. WE'RE GOING TO ATTACK THEM, LADS!

BERT HAD REALISED THEY HAD THE SUN BEHIND THEM, AND THE THICK SMOKE AND DUST WERE ALSO ON THEIR SIDE.
THE BRITISH ARE ATTACKING! BUT WE WERE TOLD THIS WAS A WEAK PART OF THE LINE!
THE SURPRISE OF THE BRITISH ATTACK WAS AS EFFECTIVE AS THEIR BULLETS — NOT ONE OF WHICH WAS WASTED.

THE GERMAN INFANTRY STARTED RETREATING — AND THREW OUT OF GEAR THE CAREFULLY-CALCULATED THRUST BY THE TANKS.
GET OUT OF THE WAY! LET US PAST!
THE DELAY WAS FATAL — IT GAVE THE BRITISH ARMOUR TIME TO REACH THE SCENE.

THE GERMANS NEVER REGAINED THE INITIATIVE. THE BRITISH ARMOUR SOON HAD THEM ON THE RUN.
THAT'S THAT. NOT BAD FOR A BUNCH OF ESCAPED PRISONERS.

AFTER THAT, ROBINSHAW TOLD THEM, THERE WAS A SERIOUS SHORTAGE OF OFFICERS. BERT WAS GIVEN A TEMPORARY COMMISSION.

I'VE NOT HEARD ANY REPORT OF HIM HAVING DISGRACED IT — EXCEPT POSSIBLY BY HIS TABLE MANNERS. AND I'LL OFFER HIM A FRIENDLY WORD OF ADVICE CONCERNING THOSE. GOOD DAY, GENTLEMEN.

BUT SIR — THERE'S STILL A CERTAIN STANDARD —

BUT THE COLONEL WASN'T INTERESTED ANY MORE. PHIBBSON AND JENKINS WERE LEFT FUMING.

THEN CAME THE DAY THEY'D ALL BEEN WAITING FOR — D-DAY. AND THE LENNOX RIFLES WERE AMONG THE FIRST ASHORE.
THERE'S FRANCE — AND THERE'S JERRY, WAITING FOR US.
I LEFT FROM DUNKIRK FOUR YEARS AGO. IT'S GOOD TO BE BACK.
HITTING A BLOOD-SPATTERED BEACH UNDER A HAIL OF HOT STEEL WAS A TEST OF COURAGE, AND THE LENNOX RIFLES PASSED THE TEST.

BERT HEADED STRAIGHT FOR A PILL-BOX WHICH WAS PINNING DOWN TROOPS ON A LARGE AREA OF BEACH.

HOW DO WE GET INTO THIS THING? SERGEANT BLACK — I WANT A DIVERSION SO I CAN SLIP ROUND TO THE TRADESMEN'S ENTRANCE.

I'LL MAKE SOME SMOKE TO BLIND 'EM, SIR.

AS SERGEANT BLACK DROPPED TWO SMOKE BOMBS BELOW THE GUN SLITS, BERT SLID ROUND TO THE BACK OF THE PILL-BOX AND BURST IN THROUGH THE DOOR.
AAARGH!
WHAT IS GOING ON OUT THERE? I CANNOT SEE.
YOU'VE BEEN CAUSING TOO MUCH TROUBLE, GENTS!
CLEARING THE PILL-BOX GAVE BERT'S BATTALION THE CHANCE TO FIGHT CLEAR OF THE BEACH. THE INVADERS SLOGGED THEIR WAY INLAND AND THEN BEGAN THE LONG BATTLE THROUGH FRANCE.

THE BATTALION REGROUPED AT A FARM.

BREW UP NOW, LADS, AND GET SOME KIP. WE'RE GOING TO BE BUSY TOMORROW. AND SAVE A CUP OF CHAR FOR ME.

ROGAN — THE COLONEL WANTS ALL OFFICERS IN THE BARN FOR A CONFERENCE.

WE'VE TO CAPTURE THE CHATEAU WHICH LOOKS DOWN ON OUR MAIN ADVANCE ROUTE. IT'S OCCUPIED BY S.S. MEN.
THAT MEANS WIPING THE LOT OUT. THEY'LL NEVER SURRENDER.
THE S.S. BATTALIONS WERE THE FINEST, MOST RUTHLESS TROOPS ON THE GERMAN SIDE.

WE'LL ATTACK FROM THE NORTH JUST BEFORE DAWN. THEN THE REAL STRIKING FORCE WILL COME UP THE OTHER SIDE AND HIT THE CHATEAU. LIEUTENANT ROGAN, YOU WILL COMMAND THIS STRIKING FORCE.

LATE THAT NIGHT, BERT AND HIS MEN TOOK UP THEIR POSITIONS.

WHY CAN'T THE R.A.F. BOYS CLEAR THEM OUT, SIR?

NO USE. PILES OF RUBBLE MAKE IT EASIER FOR THE DEFENDERS. ANYWAY, THE CHATEAU HAS DEEP CELLARS THAT BOMBS CAN'T TOUCH. RIGHT — HERE WE GO!

AT ZERO-HOUR THE STRIKING FORCE SILENTLY CLIMBED UP THE HILL AT THE BACK OF THE CHATEAU.
THE FRONTAL ATTACK SEEMS TO BE DOING WELL, SIR. THEY'VE FOUGHT THEIR WAY ALMOST TO THE TOP.
BUT IT'S OUR ATTACK THAT COUNTS. THEY'LL NEVER DISLODGE THE JERRIES FROM THE FRONT.
BUT AS BERT'S MEN PREPARED TO CHARGE IN THROUGH THE REAR DOOR, A VOICE CALLED OUT FROM THE FRONT OF THE CHATEAU.

WHERE'S ROGAN'S MEN? THEY SHOULD HAVE REACHED THE BACK BY NOW!

HIMMEL! COVER THE BACK DOOR!

THE GERMAN DEFENDERS REALISED WHAT WAS HAPPENING AND RUSHED TO THE BACK OF THE CHATEAU.

BERT'S ATTACK WASN'T THE SURPRISE IT SHOULD HAVE BEEN.
WHO WAS THE IDIOT WHO GAVE US AWAY?

HE DISPOSED OF ONE GERMAN WHILE SERGEANT BLACK TOOK CARE OF THE OTHER TWO.

TAKE A SEAT, MATE! RIGHT, LADS, IT'S TIME WE HELPED THE OTHERS AT THE FRONT.

THEY FINALLY REACHED THE MAIN TARGET — THE GROUND FLOOR DEFENDERS.
BUT SO FIERCE WAS THE FIGHTING THAT NONE OF THEM HAD TIME TO GLANCE UP THE STAIRCASE DOWN WHICH TWO NAZIS WERE CREEPING.

BUT AS HE REACHED FOR ANOTHER MAGAZINE, BLACK GLANCED UP, NOT A MOMENT TOO SOON.
LOOK OUT!
THE S.S. MEN WERE ALREADY TAKING AIM...

...WHEN THE FRONT DOOR BURST OPEN TO ADMIT THE OTHER BRITISH RAIDING FORCE LED BY JENKINS.
OK, I'VE GOT 'EM!
IN A COUPLE OF MINUTES THE BATTLE WAS OVER. THE CHATEAU WAS IN BRITISH HANDS.

AS THE SURVIVING HANDFUL OF PRISONERS WAS LED AWAY, JENKINS SPOKE UP.
MADE RATHER A MESS OF THINGS, DIDN'T YOU, ROGAN? YOU SHOULDN'T HAVE NEEDED US TO SAVE YOUR SKINS.
IT WAS ONE OF YOUR CLOWNS WHO GAVE THE GAME AWAY BY SHOUTING. I'D LIKE TO GET MY HANDS ON HIM!
FORGET IT. WE'VE ACCOMPLISHED OUR OBJECTIVE, AND THAT'S WHAT MATTERS.
BUT BERT WAS SEETHING INSIDE. HE COULD ALMOST SWEAR THE VOICE THAT HAD CALLED OUT WAS PHIBBSON'S.
ONE OF THE PRISONERS, MAJOR KURNITZ, WAS BROUGHT BEFORE ROBINSHAW.
I THOUGHT I'D KEEP HIM BACK IN CASE YOU WANTED TO INTERROGATE HIM, SIR.
AS YOU KNOW, I CAN ONLY GIVE YOU MY NAME, RANK AND NUMBER.
WE'LL GET NOTHING OUT OF HIM, PHIBBSON. TAKE HIM AWAY. WE'LL USE THIS AS A TEMPORARY H.Q. AND MESS. SEND A MAN TO THE CELLARS AND SEE IF THERE'S ANY FOOD AND DRINK.

BUT AS A SOLDIER WENT TO OPEN THE CELLAR DOOR —
STOP! DON'T GO DOWN THERE!
WHAT'S THE MATTER?

I DO NOT WANT ANY MORE UNNECESSARY BLOODSHED. THERE ARE SOME S.S. MEN IN THE CELLAR. THEY WOULD SHOOT YOUR MAN AS SOON AS HE WENT DOWN.
IS THAT SO? PHIBBSON — SEND A DETAIL DOWN TO FLUSH 'EM OUT.

AS SOON AS THEY OPENED THE CELLAR DOOR, THE S.S. MEN FIRED AT THEM.
THE BRITISH TROOPS CUT LOOSE IN REPLY, KILLING ALL THE NAZIS.

COLONEL ROBINSHAW HAD MIXED FEELINGS ABOUT THE GERMAN MAJOR. HE HAD SAVED BRITISH LIVES — BUT WHAT SORT OF OFFICER GAVE AWAY HIS OWN MEN?
PLEASE REMEMBER, I AM A GERMAN ARMY OFFICER. WE HAVE NO TIME FOR THE S.S. — BRUTES AND SAVAGES!
I GUESSED YOU WERE A REGULAR OFFICER — YOU HAVE SABRE SCARS, I NOTICE.
I SUGGEST, SIR, THAT WE INTERROGATE MAJOR KURNITZ DURING DINNER.

THE COLONEL WAS DOUBTFUL.

THIS MAN IS A PRISONER.

I GIVE YOU MY WORD AS AN OFFICER THAT I WILL NOT ATTEMPT TO ESCAPE WHILE HERE.

THAT SETTLED IT. PHIBBSON AND JENKINS RECOGNISED THE GERMAN MAJOR AS A GENTLEMAN LIKE THEMSELVES.

HALF AN HOUR LATER THEY WERE HAVING THEIR MEAL WHEN THE DOOR FLEW OPEN AND BERT CAME IN.
THERE YOU ARE, ROGAN. COME AND HAVE A BITE TO EAT.
THANKS SIR. BLIMEY — WHO'S THAT?
BERT STOPPED IN HIS TRACKS AS HE SAW THE GERMAN MAJOR, AND SLID HIS REVOLVER OUT OF ITS HOLSTER.

FORGET YOUR GUN, ROGAN. HE'S A GUEST IN THE MESS.

GUEST? I KNOW THIS BLOKE — HE'S A BLOOMIN' MURDERER!

STEADY ON, ROGAN — YOU CAN'T SAY THAT.

I SAW YOU IN THE DESERT — YOU ORDERED YOUR MEN TO KILL BRITISH PRISONERS!

I DO NOT KNOW WHAT YOU'RE TALKING ABOUT.

YOU MUST BE MISTAKEN, ROGAN. MAJOR KURNITZ HAS ALREADY SHOWN US HE'S NOT THAT TYPE AT ALL.

THEY TOLD BERT HOW KURNITZ HAD WARNED THEM OF THE S.S. MEN. BUT BERT WASN'T IMPRESSED.

KURNITZ HAD MADE THAT MOVE, BERT SAID, SIMPLY TO GAIN THEIR CONFIDENCE.

THE MAJOR SAYS HE WAS NEVER IN THE DESERT. AND I DOUBT VERY MUCH IF YOU COULD RECOGNISE HIM AS SOMEONE YOU ONLY CAUGHT A FLEETING GLIMPSE OF, A YEAR AGO.

THAT'S A FACE I'LL NEVER FORGET. I'D SHOOT THE RAT ON THE SPOT, GIVEN HALF A CHANCE. I'M CERTAINLY NOT GOING TO EAT WITH HIM — I PREFER THE COMPANY OF MY OWN MEN.

BERT STORMED OUT THE DOOR, LEAVING THE OTHERS TO APOLOGISE FOR HIS BEHAVIOUR.

NEXT MORNING THE BATTALION RECEIVED ORDERS TO MOVE ON.

WHAT DO WE DO WITH THE PRISONER, SIR?

HE'LL HAVE TO BE TAKEN BACK UNDER ESCORT. GET LIEUTENANT JOHNSON TO ARRANGE IT.

TEN MINUTES LATER, PHIBBSON RETURNED WITH DISQUIETING NEWS.

JOHNSON'S BEEN TAKEN SICK, SIR. WHO'S GOING TO ESCORT THE PRISONER?

BLAST! PHIBBSON, GET ANOTHER LIEUTENANT TO TAKE HIM BACK.

THE ONLY OTHER LIEUTENANT THAT PHIBBSON COULD FIND WAS BERT.

THE JOB OF ESCORTING KURNITZ HAD FALLEN TO THE MAN WHO HATED HIM MOST.
THE SLIGHTEST HINT OF ANY FUNNY BUSINESS, AND I'LL RIDDLE YOU!

WHEN THEY HAD BEEN TRAVELLING FOR HALF AN HOUR, THE RADIATOR BEGAN TO BOIL.
WE NEED SOME WATER. WE'LL CALL AT THE FARMHOUSE OVER THERE.

THE OLD FARMER WHO LIVED THERE ALONE WILLINGLY GAVE THEM WATER.

I'LL WANT TO TOP UP THE JERRICANS TOO, IF YOU DON'T MIND.

HELP YOURSELF.

AS BERT FILLED THE LAST OF THE CANS...
KURNITZ IS GETTING VERY MATEY WITH THE FARMER. WHAT'S HE UP TO?

BERT WALKED QUIETLY ACROSS...
I'LL GIVE YOU MY GOLD WATCH FOR THE RIFLE.
NO YOU WON'T!

BERT HAD STOPPED KURNITZ ONLY JUST IN TIME.
THOUGHT YOU'D QUIETLY GET HOLD OF THE RIFLE AND USE IT ON ME, EH? I'LL LOOK AFTER THIS WATCH — SO YOU WON'T BE TEMPTED TO USE IT AS A BRIBE AGAIN. YOU CAN HAVE IT BACK LATER.

BUT AS THEY SET OFF AGAIN, A LONE MESSERSCHMITT SPOTTED THEM CROSSING A BRIDGE.
A BRITISH JEEP! I'LL GIVE THEM SOMETHING TO THINK ABOUT!

BERT NOTICED THE MESSERSCHMITT AND SLAMMED THE JEEP TO A HALT AT THE FAR SIDE OF THE BRIDGE.

LET'S GET TO SOME SHELTER!

THE BULLETS LASHED OVER THEIR HEADS AND CUT THROUGH THE TREES.

THE BULLETS MISSED THE TWO MEN — BUT A HEAVY BOUGH FROM ONE OF THE TREES TRAPPED BERT.
HERE — HELP ME OUT!
HELP YOU? OH NO — THAT WOULD BE VERY FOOLISH OF ME!
KURNITZ'S WHOLE ATTITUDE CHANGED. NO LONGER WAS HE A FRIENDLY OFFICER AND GENTLEMAN.
THE NAZI TOOK BERT'S GUN AND LEAPT INTO THE JEEP.
YOU'VE GOT THE UPPER HAND NOW, BUT YOU'LL BE PICKED UP IN NO TIME.
I DO NOT THINK SO. WITH THE HELP OF YOUR GUN I CAN GET A GOOD START.
AND KURNITZ SPED BACK TOWARDS THE FARMHOUSE.

A MINUTE LATER, AS BERT WAS STILL STRUGGLING TO GET CLEAR, THERE WAS A BURST OF FIRING.
THE MURDERER – HE MUST HAVE SHOT THAT OLD FARMER!

LEAVING THE FARMER FOR DEAD, KURNITZ TOOK HIS CLOTHES AND MADE HIS ESCAPE.

IF — IF I CAN FIND STRENGTH ENOUGH TO REACH MY BOAT, I CAN GET HELP DOWNSTREAM.

THE OLD FARMER REACHED HIS BOAT BUT FELL DEAD BESIDE IT.

WITH A DESPERATE JERK, BERT FINALLY DRAGGED HIMSELF CLEAR OF THE BRANCH.
NOW TO GET AFTER KURNITZ. I'LL HEAD TO-WARDS OUR ADVANCE.

BUT THE BRANCH WAS LYING ON A BEND IN THE ROAD, SO HE TUMBLED IT INTO THE RIVER.

BETTER MOVE THIS BEFORE A VEHICLE RUNS INTO IT.

THEN HE SPOTTED A JEEP APPROACHING.

IT WAS JENKINS AND PHIBBSON, ON THEIR WAY TO G.H.Q. TO PICK UP SEALED ORDERS.
ROGAN, WHAT ARE YOU DOING HERE — WHERE'S YOUR PRISONER?
YOUR GENTLEMAN FRIEND BROKE HIS WORD. HE ESCAPED.
MAJOR KURNITZ? I DON'T BELIEVE IT!
BERT SAW THE TWO OFFICERS LOOK POINTEDLY AT EACH OTHER.

IT'S A LONG STORY...
WHERE'S YOUR GUN?
AS BERT PULLED OUT HIS HANDKERCHIEF TO MOP HIS BROW, KURNITZ'S WATCH FELL TO THE GROUND.

YOU'VE DROPPED YOUR WATCH, ROGAN.
I'VE SEEN THAT WATCH BEFORE – MAJOR KURNITZ WAS WEARING IT!
I HAD TO TAKE IT OFF HIM. LOOK, COME OVER TO THE FARM AND I'LL SHOW YOU WHAT HE DID.

THEY REACHED THE FARMHOUSE BUT BERT GOT A SHOCK WHEN THEY FOUND IT EMPTY.
BUT THE OLD FARMER SHOULD BE HERE! I HEARD KURNITZ SHOOTING HIM!
THERE'S NO ONE HERE, ROGAN.
BUT THERE ARE FRESH BLOODSTAINS ON THE FLOOR.
BERT'S TOMMY GUN WAS ALSO THERE ON THE FLOOR.

I SEE YOUR GUN'S BEEN FIRED RECENTLY, ROGAN.
I TOLD YOU — KURNITZ USED IT TO KILL THE FARMER. THE BLOODSTAINS ARE ON THE FLOOR...
SOMEONE'S BLOODSTAINS ARE. LISTEN, ROGAN, YOU'D BETTER COME BACK TO THE BATTALION WITH US.
BERT GOT A SUDDEN COLD FEELING INSIDE HIM. EVERYTHING THAT HAD HAPPENED BEGAN TO LOOK UNREAL — AND THERE WAS A DISBELIEVING LOOK IN THE EYES OF HIS FELLOW OFFICERS.

THEY TRAVELLED IN SILENCE BACK TO THE BATTALION. THERE BERT TOLD HIS STORY TO COLONEL ROBINSHAW.

SO THAT'S WHAT HAPPENED, ROGAN?

SIR, WE FIND IT HARD TO BELIEVE THAT MAJOR KURNITZ SHOULD BREAK HIS SOLEMN WORD AND ATTEMPT ESCAPE.

JUST WHAT ARE YOU IMPLYING, PHIBBSON?

PHIBBSON MADE IT QUITE CLEAR WHAT HE WAS GETTING AT.
YOU TOLD US YOU'D KILL KURNITZ IF YOU GOT THE CHANCE. YOU LEFT HERE ALONE WITH HIM — AND HE'S VANISHED. YOU HAD HIS WATCH IN YOUR POCKET, AND YOUR GUN HAD BEEN FIRED.
THAT'S ALL TRUE. I'VE EXPLAINED IT TOO. AND RIGHT NOW KURNITZ IS PROBABLY BACK OVER ON HIS OWN SIDE.

WHEN WE APPROACHED, ROGAN, YOU WERE TIPPING SOMETHING INTO THE RIVER. IT COULD HAVE BEEN A BODY.

THAT WAS THE BRANCH THAT FELL ON ME! OK, YOU THINK I KILLED KURNITZ AND YOU'LL TWIST EVERYTHING TO PROVE IT.

I'M SORRY, ROGAN — I'LL HAVE TO TAKE ACTION TO SORT THE TRUTH OUT. IF WHAT YOU SAY IS TRUE, THEN YOU HAVE NOTHING TO FEAR.

BUT BERT DIDN'T SHARE THE COLONEL'S CONFIDENCE. HE KNEW THAT EVERYBODY WOULD SEE THINGS JUST AS JENKINS AND PHIBBSON HAD.

BERT WAS SENT UNDER ESCORT BACK TO G.H.Q. WHERE A COURT MARTIAL WOULD BE ARRANGED.
KURNITZ WOULD LAUGH HIMSELF SILLY IF HE COULD SEE ME NOW!. AND I'LL BET HE'S BEING GREETED LIKE A HERO.

THEY FINALLY REACHED THE G.H.Q. IN A SMALL FRENCH TOWN.

WHY THE HECK AM I LETTING THEM DO THIS TO ME?

BERT BRIEFLY LOOKED AT THE DOORWAY AHEAD, A DESPERATE PLAN FORMING IN HIS MIND.

AS HE WALKED THROUGH THE DOORWAY, BERT KICKED SHUT THE DOOR BEHIND HIM.
PARDON MY MANNERS.
HEY! WHAT –
PHASE ONE OF BERT'S PLAN HAD WORKED, ALTHOUGH HE STILL WASN'T FREE.

AS BERT HOPED, THERE WAS A BOLT ON THE INSIDE.
HE'S BOLTED IT!
GET ROUND TO THE BACK!

WITHOUT PAUSING, BERT WENT STRAIGHT TO THE BACK OF THE BUILDING AND DIVED THROUGH THE WINDOW AHEAD OF HIM.

THE M.P.'s REACHED THE BACK OF THE BUILDING JUST IN TIME TO SEE BERT DISAPPEARING.

THERE HE IS — AFTER HIM!

BERT DIVED INTO THE FIRST OPEN DOORWAY HE SAW.
I'LL ONLY BE HERE A MINUTE OR SO.
THEY THINK I'M CRAZY — MAYBE I AM!
HE STOOD LISTENING AS THE M.P.'s RACED PAST, THEN HE EMERGED AND HEADED FOR THE MAIN ROAD.

BERT FOUND HIS RANK USEFUL IN GETTING A LIFT.

HOP IN, SIR. I'M GOING TO CHERBOURG.

THANKS. DROP ME AS NEAR THE QUAY AS YOU CAN.

THE DRIVER ATTEMPTED TO MAKE CONVERSATION ON THE JOURNEY, BUT BERT KEPT SILENT.

AT CHERBOURG, A HOSPITAL SHIP WAS TAKING ON WOUNDED MEN.
WELL THAT'S THAT, BUT NOW WHAT? I MAY AS WELL TRY MY LUCK WITH A BIT OF BLUFF.

I'M LOOKING FOR A DESERTER WHO MAY BE POSING AS WOUNDED. HAVE YOU A MAN CALLED BROWN GOING ABOARD?
BROWN? YOU MUST BE JOKING. THERE ARE DOZENS OF THEM.

BERT DIDN'T WAIT TO DISCUSS THE MATTER.
I'LL TAKE A QUICK LOOK ROUND AND SEE IF I CAN SPOT HIM.
CARRY ON. I'M TOO BUSY TO LOOK FOR DESERTERS.

WHEN THE SHIP PULLED OUT, BERT WAS STILL ON BOARD.
HERE YOU ARE, LADS. ANYONE WANT ANYTHING ELSE?
WELL, AT LEAST I'M ON MY WAY BACK TO ENGLAND.
BETTER THAN A NURSE, YOU ARE, SIR!

WHEN THEY REACHED BRITAIN, BERT STAYED WITH THE WOUNDED MEN AND BOARDED THE TRAIN FOR LONDON.
NO SIGN OF ANY M.P.'s ON THE LOOK-OUT FOR ME. THEY MUST THINK I'M STILL IN FRANCE.

ONLY WHEN HE REACHED LONDON DID BERT HAVE TIME TO STOP AND THINK CLEARLY.

UNDERGR

WAIT A MINUTE, WHAT AM I DOING HERE? I DON'T WANT TO DESERT — I WANT TO FIGHT THOSE LOUSY JERRIES, IF PEOPLE WOULD LET ME!

Three

BUT TO DO THAT, BERT HAD TO TAKE ONE IMPORTANT STEP — LOSE HIS IDENTITY.

HE FINALLY MADE CONTACT WITH THE BLACK MARKET, WHERE ANYTHING WAS AVAILABLE AT A PRICE — INCLUDING IDENTITY CARDS.

THERE YOU ARE. YOUR NAME IS BERT RITCHIE NOW, AND YOU'RE A CIVILIAN.

THERE'S YOUR CASH. NOW TO BUY SOME CIVVY CLOTHES.

NEXT DAY HE REGISTERED FOR MILITARY SERVICE.
BEATS ME, RITCHIE, HOW WE HAVEN'T CALLED YOU UP BEFORE NOW. NEVER MIND. YOU'LL FIND YOURSELF IN UNIFORM BEFORE YOU CAN TURN AROUND.
I'LL FEEL A LOT BETTER ONCE I'M BACK AT THE FRONT WITH THE OTHER BLOKES.
BY THE END OF THE WEEK, HE WAS AT AN ARMY TRAINING CAMP.

THEN BERT STARTED FROM SCRATCH TO LEARN TO BE A SOLDIER AGAIN, WITH THE CAMSHIRE REGIMENT. HIS PREVIOUS EXPERIENCE MARKED HIM OUT RIGHT AWAY FOR PROMOTION. AT THE END OF HIS TRAINING, HE FOUND HIMSELF SEWING ON HIS SERGEANT'S STRIPES.

SHORTLY AFTER, THE CAMSHIRES JOINED THE ALLIED FORCES IN EUROPE. THEY WERE MOVED UP TO THE FRONT RIGHT AWAY. THE GERMANS HAD LAUNCHED A MASSIVE OFFENSIVE THROUGH THE ARDENNES FOREST AND THE ALLIES THREW IN EVERYTHING THEY HAD TO HOLD BACK THE TIDE.
THERE ARE JERRIES ALL OVER THIS FOREST. WATCH OUT FOR SNIPERS.
IF THEY'RE ANY GOOD, YOU WON'T SEE THEM ANYWAY.

AT THAT MOMENT RIFLE SIGHTS WERE TRAINED ON THE LIEUTENANT.

ANOTHER BRITISH OFFICER'. GUT. IF WE WIPE THEM OUT, THE BRITISH FORCES WILL SOON BE IN CONFUSION'.

A SINGLE SHOT RANG OUT AND THE LIEUTENANT FELL.
AAARGH'.
DOWN, EVERYBODY! DROP'.

THEY WAITED FOR A WHILE, BUT THERE WERE NO MORE SHOTS.
THE IDEA THOSE SNIPERS HAVE IS TO KILL OFF ALL THE OFFICERS. THEY WON'T WASTE A BULLET ON US. WE'VE GOT TO GET THIS BLOKE TO SHOW HIMSELF.
HOW DO WE DO THAT, SARGE?

BERT PUT ON THE DEAD OFFICER'S COAT AND HAT.
I'M GOING FORWARD AS BAIT. HE'LL SHOOT AT ME IN THIS UNIFORM — KEEP YOUR EYES PEELED FOR THE FLASH FROM HIS RIFLE. AS SOON AS YOU SEE IT, GET HIM.
BUT HE'LL GET YOU FIRST, SARGE.
BERT SHRUGGED. HE HOPED TO BE ONE JUMP AHEAD OF THE SNIPER.

HE MARCHED FORWARD TO THE SAME SPOT WHERE THE LIEUTENANT HAD BEEN HIT.
THEY SAY LIGHTNING NEVER STRIKES TWICE IN THE SAME SPOT, BUT A SNIPER MIGHT. THIS IS PROBABLY THE ONLY PLACE HE CAN GET HIS SIGHTS CLEARLY ON HIS TARGET — ME.
HIS MUSCLES TENSED AS HE WENT FORWARD.

BERT DIDN'T WAIT FOR THE SHOT. HE DROPPED AS SOON AS HE REACHED THE CRUCIAL SPOT. AT THAT SECOND, A BULLET ZIPPED OVER HIS HEAD, MISSING HIM NARROWLY.

IT WORKED'. LETS HOPE THE LADS SPOTTED HIM.

THEY DID AND THE GERMAN SNIPER STOOD NO CHANCE UNDER THE HAIL OF FIRE.
AAARGH'.

AT THE MOMENT TWO BRITISH SOLDIERS MADE THEIR WAY THROUGH THE FOREST TOWARDS BERT.

WHERE ARE YOU MEN FROM?

LENNOX RIFLES, SIR. JERRY IS REALLY HAMMERING US ON THE ROAD THROUGH THE FOREST. WE NEED HELP.

BERT LED HIS MEN TOWARDS THE SOUND OF FIRING.

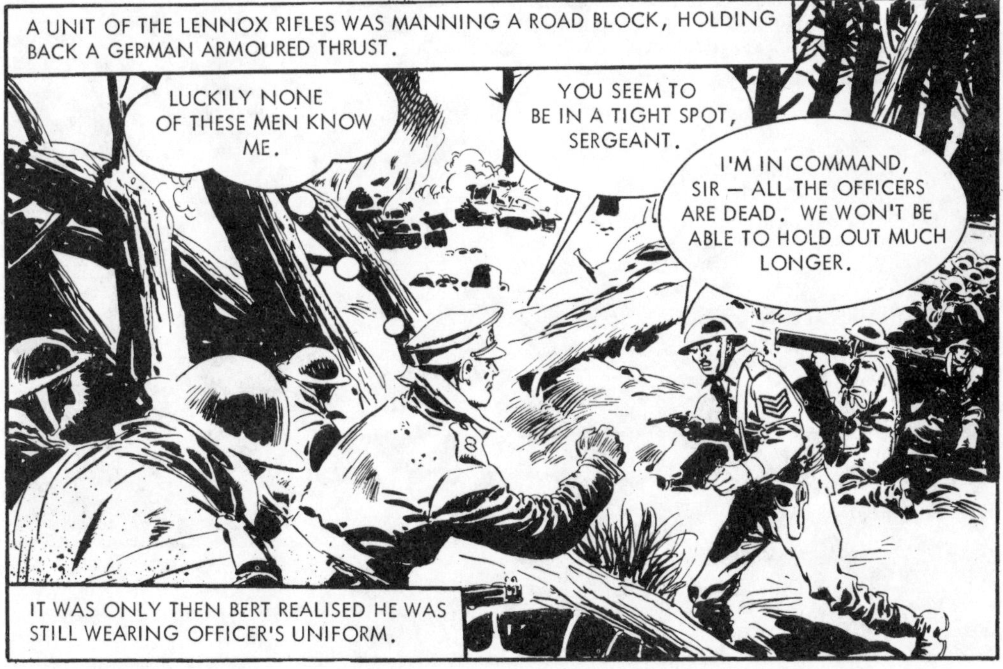
A UNIT OF THE LENNOX RIFLES WAS MANNING A ROAD BLOCK, HOLDING BACK A GERMAN ARMOURED THRUST.
LUCKILY NONE OF THESE MEN KNOW ME.
YOU SEEM TO BE IN A TIGHT SPOT, SERGEANT.
I'M IN COMMAND, SIR — ALL THE OFFICERS ARE DEAD. WE WON'T BE ABLE TO HOLD OUT MUCH LONGER.
IT WAS ONLY THEN BERT REALISED HE WAS STILL WEARING OFFICER'S UNIFORM.

A DISABLED TANK MADE AN EFFECTIVE ROAD BLOCK — FOR A WHILE.

THEY'RE TRYING TO PUSH IT CLEAR FROM BEHIND! GIVE ME THAT BAZOOKA!

WITH THE SERGEANT, BERT EDGED ROUND THE TREES BY THE DISABLED TANK.

ONE SHOT FROM THE BAZOOKA TURNED THE SECOND TANK INTO AN INFERNO.
IT'S GOING TO TAKE 'EM A HECK OF A TIME TO CLEAR THE TWO OF THEM. LET'S GET BACK.
AS THEY REJOINED THE REST OF THE DEFENDERS, THE GERMAN INFANTRY DOUBLED THE FURY OF THEIR ATTACK.

FOR AN HOUR THEY HELD OUT. THEN –
WE'VE NO AMMO LEFT.
THIS IS NO GOOD, LADS, WE DON'T STAND A CHANCE. WE'LL HAVE TO SURRENDER. AT LEAST WE'VE HELD THEM UP FOR A WHILE.
THEY HAD SUCCEEDED IN THEIR MAIN OBJECTIVE – DELAYING THE GERMAN ARMOUR.
MARCH THESE MEN AWAY. BUT TAKE THE OFFICER STRAIGHT TO H.Q. FOR INTERROGATION.
ME? BUT I'M NOT...

BERT TRIED TO EXPLAIN.
THIS ISN'T MY UNIFORM...
YOU THINK WE'RE FOOLS? YOU CAN'T AVOID INTERROGATION THAT WAY. TAKE HIM AWAY!
HE WAS BUNDLED INTO A SCOUT CAR AND TAKEN TO THE GERMAN H.Q.

THE GERMANS HAD TAKEN OVER A FARM.
WELL, I ESCAPED FROM THE BRITISH H.Q., BUT I WONDER WHAT MY CHANCES ARE HERE?

THE INTERROGATION STARTED IMMEDIATELY, CONDUCTED BY A GERMAN MAJOR.
NAME?
RITCHIE. AND IF YOU'RE AFTER ANY TOP SECRET INFORMATION YOU'RE WASTING YOUR TIME, BECAUSE I HAVEN'T GOT ANY.
IT WAS THEN THAT BERT SAW ANOTHER GERMAN OFFICER COME IN.

KURNITZ! YOU MURDERING RAT — I KNEW I'D MEET UP WITH YOU SOME DAY!
SILENCE! DO NOT TALK OF A GERMAN OFFICER IN THAT WAY!

HE'S AN OFFICER ALL RIGHT — BUT HE'S NO GENTLE-MAN! THIS IS THE BLOKE WHO GAVE HIS WORD NOT TO ESCAPE — THEN BROKE IT AND KILLED A HELPLESS CIVILIAN.
BE QUIET. TAKE THIS SCHWEIN AWAY!
AT BERT'S OUTBURST, A GLEAM OF INTEREST CAME INTO THE MAJOR'S EYES.

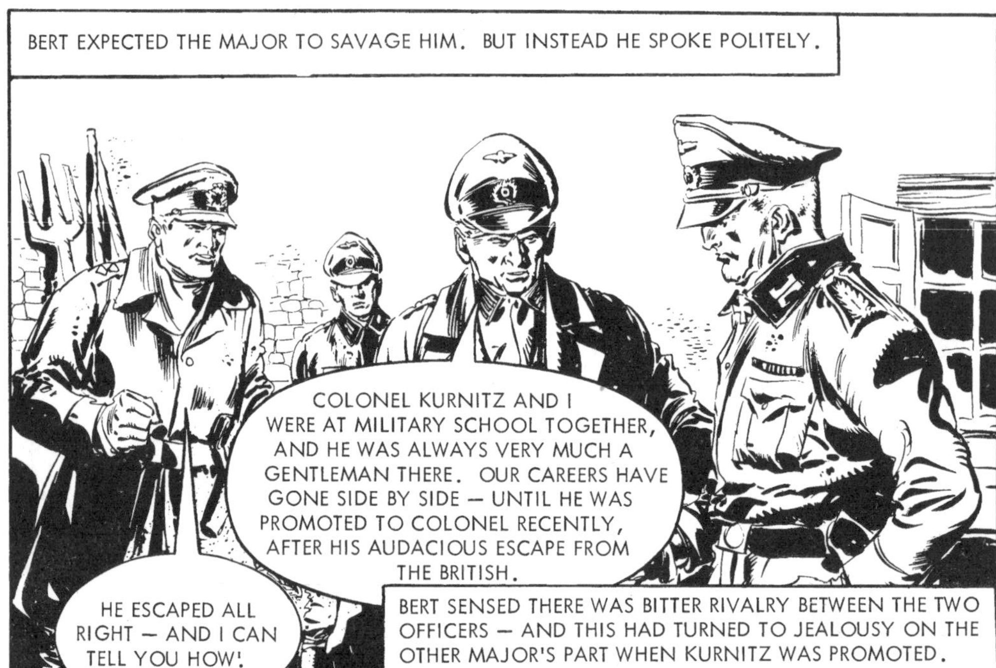
BERT EXPECTED THE MAJOR TO SAVAGE HIM. BUT INSTEAD HE SPOKE POLITELY.
COLONEL KURNITZ AND I WERE AT MILITARY SCHOOL TOGETHER, AND HE WAS ALWAYS VERY MUCH A GENTLEMAN THERE. OUR CAREERS HAVE GONE SIDE BY SIDE — UNTIL HE WAS PROMOTED TO COLONEL RECENTLY, AFTER HIS AUDACIOUS ESCAPE FROM THE BRITISH.
HE ESCAPED ALL RIGHT — AND I CAN TELL YOU HOW!
BERT SENSED THERE WAS BITTER RIVALRY BETWEEN THE TWO OFFICERS — AND THIS HAD TURNED TO JEALOUSY ON THE OTHER MAJOR'S PART WHEN KURNITZ WAS PROMOTED.

BERT SET OUT TO NEEDLE KURNITZ IN FRONT OF THE OFFICER.
KILLER KURNITZ — A MASTER AT KILLING OLD MEN AND STEALING CIVILIAN CLOTHES! YOUR NAME STINKS, KURNITZ!
I WILL NOT STAY AND LISTEN TO THIS.
I ASSUME THIS IS ALL UNTRUE, COLONEL?
THE TONE OF THE MAJOR'S WORDS STUNG KURNITZ INTO ACTION.

JUST WHAT DO YOU MEAN BY THAT?
I WAS SIMPLY THINKING — IF ANYONE HAD MADE SUCH ACCUSATIONS TO ME, I WOULD DO SOMETHING ABOUT IT.
THE MOCKERY IN THE MAJOR'S VOICE WAS CUTTING. BERT SENSED THAT THE REAL HATRED WAS NOT BETWEEN HIM AND THE GERMAN OFFICERS, BUT BETWEEN THE OFFICERS THEMSELVES.

BRITISH PIG! YOU HAVE QUESTIONED MY HONOUR. GUARD! TAKE HIM AWAY... NO,WAIT. I'VE A BETTER WAY TO SETTLE THIS...I CHALLENGE YOU TO A DUEL.

THEY WENT STRAIGHT ACROSS TO A BARN.
I TAKE IT YOU CAN USE A SABRE, BRITISHER?
I'M WILLING TO HAVE A GO.
CRIKEY! WHAT HAVE I LET MYSELF IN FOR?

KURNITZ'S ORDERLY CAME IN WITH TWO SABRES AND HANDED THEM OVER.

BEGIN, GENTLEMEN.

WELL, HERE GOES!. I ONLY HOPE KURNITZ ISN'T TOO GOOD AT THIS GAME.

BUT KURNITZ WAS GOOD. RIGHT AWAY BERT COULD SEE HE WAS HOPELESSLY OUTCLASSED.
I'VE GOT TO KEEP DODGING HIM.
I AM GOING TO KILL YOU, ENGLANDER!

IT WAS ONLY NIMBLE FOOTWORK THAT ENABLED BERT TO SURVIVE THE FIRST FEW MINUTES.
STAND STILL AND FIGHT!
NOT BLOOMING LIKELY!

THEN KURNITZ'S SABRE SLASHED BERT'S LEFT ARM.
HE'S GOING TO CUT ME TO RIBBONS IF I LET HIM!
BERT, KNOWING HE HAD NOTHING TO LOSE, DECIDED TO ATTACK.

THE FEROCITY OF HIS ATTACK SURPRISED KURNITZ, FORCING HIM OFF BALANCE.
THIS IS NOT HOW TO USE A SABRE!
IT'S HOW I USE IT, MATE!

BUT, JUST AS IT LOOKED AS IF BERT MIGHT WIN, HIS SABRE SHATTERED ON KURNITZ'S BLADE.

ROTTEN GERMAN WORKMANSHIP — CAN'T EVEN MAKE A DECENT SABRE!

BUT THAT WASN'T THE END OF THE DUEL.

KURNITZ MEANT TO HAVE HIS KILL.

KURNITZ — THE MAN IS DISARMED!

NO MORE WILL I TAKE YOUR SNEERS!

BERT ACTED QUICKLY, TEARING OFF HIS COAT...
FIGHT YOUR WAY OUT OF THAT ONE!

KURNITZ WENT PURPLE WITH RAGE — NOT AT WHAT BERT HAD DONE, BUT AT WHAT WAS SHOWING ON HIS SLEEVES.
THIS MAN — HE IS ONLY A SERGEANT! I HAVE BEEN TRICKED!
DON'T LET IT WORRY YOU, KURNITZ. THERE'S WORSE TO COME.

AS KURNITZ RANTED AND RAVED, BERT SENT THE OIL LAMP FLYING.
LET'S BRIGHTEN UP THE PROCEEDINGS!

THE OIL SET THE STRAW BLAZING. IN THE CONFUSION, ONLY BERT KNEW WHAT HE WAS DOING.
GET MOVING, KURNITZ, WE'RE LEAVING!
HE FORCED THE COUGHING, SPLUTTERING GERMAN OUT OF THE BARN AND NO ONE COULD SEE THEM THROUGH THE SMOKE.

ONCE OUTSIDE, BERT QUICKLY TOOK POSSESSION OF KURNITZ'S LUGER.
GET INTO THAT CAR AND START DRIVING WEST. DON'T HESITATE, KURNITZ — I'M JUST LOOKING FOR AN OPPORTUNITY TO KILL YOU!

AS THEY SPED TOWARDS THE FRONT LINE...
YOU CANNOT GET AWAY WITH THIS. SEE — SOME GERMAN SOLDIERS ARE APPROACHING.
JUST CARRY ON, MATE!

THE MEN WERE, IN FACT, BRITISH PRISONERS UNDER GUARD. AND BERT RECOGNISED THE SURVIVORS OF HIS OWN UNIT AND THE LENNOX RIFLES WHO HAD SURRENDERED IN THE FOREST. HE ORDERED KURNITZ TO STOP.
SEE THIS LOT, KURNITZ? I WANT YOU TO ORDER THE GUARDS TO RELEASE THEM.
I SHALL NOT!
BUT BERT POKED THE GUN INTO KURNITZ'S RIBS IN A WAY WHICH SHOWED HE MEANT BUSINESS.

RELUCTANTLY KURNITZ OBEYED BUT BERT REALISED THE GUARDS WERE CONFUSED BY THE SITUATION AND WENT INTO ACTION.
JUMP THEM, LADS! I'LL GET YOU OUT OF HERE!
IT'S SERGEANT RITCHIE! COME ON, BOYS!
BEFORE THE SURPRISED GUARDS COULD MOVE, THEY WERE SET UPON.

IT WAS OVER IN A MATTER OF SECONDS. AS A GERMAN LORRY APPROACHED BERT GAVE ORDERS FOR IT TO BE SEIZED.

YOU HAVE SUCCEEDED SO FAR, BUT YOU WON'T GET AWAY WITH THIS.

YOU'RE WRONG, KURNITZ. AND YOU'RE COMING BACK WITH ME!

PILING INTO THE LORRY THEY HEADED FOR THE BRITISH LINES. THE DRIVER PUT ON A GERMAN CAP TO PREVENT THEM LOOKING TOO CONSPICUOUS.

JUST KEEP YOUR BOOT RIGHT DOWN, DRIVER.

BERT TOOK THEM ON A RECKLESS RACE THROUGH THE GERMAN LINES, THE SHEER NERVE OF THE VENTURE CARRYING THEM THROUGH.
KEEP DOWN, KURNITZ! I WANT YOU ALIVE. I'M GOING TO SHOW YOU TO SOME-ONE.
THEY FINALLY MET UP WITH A BRITISH PATROL, WHICH DIRECTED THEM BEHIND THE LINES.

THE FOLLOWING EVENING, THERE WERE TWO SURPRISE VISITORS IN THE TEMPORARY OFFICERS' MESS OF THE LENNOX RIFLES.
WHO IS THIS SERGEANT BARGING INTO THE MESS?
IT'S ROGAN — GET HIM!
DON'T WORRY, I'M NOT RUNNING AWAY!

IT'S KURNITZ — THE MAN ROGAN WAS ACCUSED OF KILLING!
IT'S KURNITZ ALL RIGHT — YOUR GENTLEMAN COLLEAGUE! I RECKON THIS CALLS FOR CERTAIN PEOPLE TO TAKE BACK SOME THINGS THEY'VE SAID.
I DON'T BELIEVE IT.
BUT THEY HAD TO BELIEVE IT. HOW COULD A MAN BE CHARGED WITH MURDER WHEN HE PRODUCED THE VICTIM ALIVE AND UNHARMED?
I APOLOGISE ON BEHALF OF THE WHOLE OF THE REGIMENT, ROGAN. AND I'M WELCOMING YOU HERE AND NOW BACK TO THE MESS.
THANKS — BUT I DON'T THINK SO. I'VE BEEN A SERGEANT FOR THE PAST FEW MONTHS AND I'VE A MIND TO STAY THAT WAY. I BELONG WITH THE LADS — NOT IN THE OFFICERS' MESS. I RECKON I CAN DO FAR MORE GOOD WITH THREE STRIPES ON MY ARM THAN WITH A PIP ON MY SHOULDER.
BERT WASN'T JOKING.

SO IT WAS THAT BERT KEPT HIS STRIPES. HE BECAME AN INVALUABLE GUIDE AND TRAINER OF RAW YOUNG OFFICERS AS THEY JOINED THE REGIMENT. UNDER BERT'S TOUGH BUT TACTFUL GUIDANCE, THEY DEVELOPED INTO GOOD OFFICERS. BUT THEY HAD TO BE REALLY GOOD EVEN TO TAKE THE EMPTY PLACE LEFT IN THE MESS BY BERT ROGAN!

JUST FOLLOW ME, SIR, AND YOU'LL BE OK!
Commando
THE END

HOTSPUR GLIDER

Here is the Hotspur Glider that carried sergeant-pilot Jamie Locke and his fighting cargo into enemy territory in "GLIDER ACE."

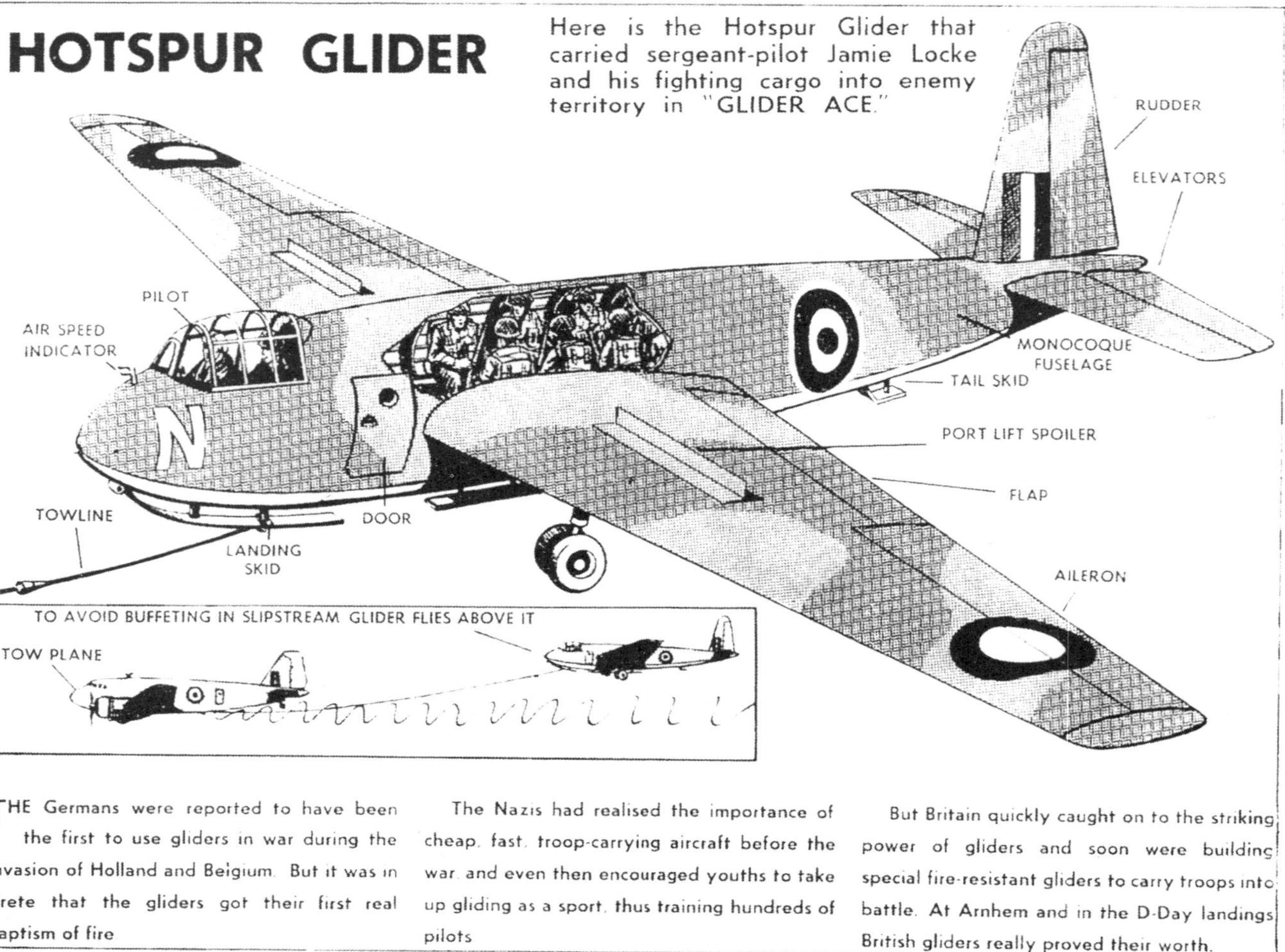
RUDDER
ELEVATORS
PILOT
AIR SPEED INDICATOR
MONOCOQUE FUSELAGE
TAIL SKID
PORT LIFT SPOILER
FLAP
TOWLINE
DOOR
LANDING SKID
AILERON
TO AVOID BUFFETING IN SLIPSTREAM GLIDER FLIES ABOVE IT
TOW PLANE

THE Germans were reported to have been the first to use gliders in war during the invasion of Holland and Belgium. But it was in Crete that the gliders got their first real baptism of fire

The Nazis had realised the importance of cheap, fast, troop-carrying aircraft before the war, and even then encouraged youths to take up gliding as a sport, thus training hundreds of pilots

But Britain quickly caught on to the striking power of gliders and soon were building special fire-resistant gliders to carry troops into battle. At Arnhem and in the D-Day landings British gliders really proved their worth.

GLIDER ACE
FIGHTER PILOTS WERE THE HEROES OF THE BATTLE OF BRITAIN. BOMBER PILOTS HIT THE HEADLINES WITH EVERY THOUSAND BOMBER RAID. BUT WHO EVER HEARD OF THE GLIDER PILOTS? VERY FEW. AND YET EVERY ONE DESERVED A MEDAL.
JAMIE LOCKE WAS ONE OF THESE. NO SMOOTH CONCRETE RUNWAY FOR HIM TO LAND ON, BUT JUST A FEW ROUGH YARDS OF BULLET-SWEPT ENEMY TERRITORY WITH DEATH OR GLORY ONLY SECONDS AWAY.
RAF
FLYING TRAINING SCHOOL
5 M.P.H
REPORT HERE
GOSH! LOOK AT THEM GO! AND NOW'S MY CHANCE TO GET MY WINGS AT LAST.
J.L

BUT BARELY WAS THE LUCKLESS JAMIE SETTLED AT HIS FLYING TRAINING SCHOOL WHEN THERE BEGAN THE LONG TRAIL OF DISAPPOINTMENTS WHICH WERE TO BLIGHT HIS FIGHTING CAREER. THERE ON THE BULLETIN BOARD APPEARED THE BLACK NEWS...

IT'S FROM THE AIR MINISTRY.

21 FLYING

NO MORE AIR - CREW NEEDED

THEY'RE SENDING US BACK TO OUR UNITS!

THEY'RE NOT DOING THIS TO ME!

IF ALL JAMIE'S MATES WERE TAKING THE BAD NEWS LYING DOWN, HE JUST WASN'T. HE MIGHT BE SMALL BUT HE HAD PLENTY OF FIGHTING SPIRIT.
THEY'RE NOT MUCKING ME ABOUT LIKE THIS. I'M GOING TO SEE THE ADJUTANT!

THE STATION ADJUTANT LISTENED SYMPATHETICALLY TO JAMIE LOCKE'S INDIGNANT TIRADE, BUT HE HAD NO CHOICE BUT TO SHAKE HIS HEAD.
SORRY, LOCKE, THERE'S NOTHING I CAN DO ABOUT IT.
BUT I'VE BEEN WAITING MONTHS FOR THIS CHANCE, SIR. THEY CAN'T SEND ME BACK NOW!

THE ADJUTANT GAVE A PATIENT SIGH AND EXPLAINED.
IT HAPPENS NOW AND AGAIN, LOCKE. THE CASUALTY RATE AMONGST OUR AIRCREWS HAS BEEN MUCH REDUCED OF LATE, SO TRAINING EASES OFF.
IT WOULD HAPPEN JUST AS MY TURN CAME UP!

THEN AS THE DISAPPOINTED JAMIE PERSISTED, THE OLDER MAN OFFERED SOME FRANK ADVICE...
HOW LONG BEFORE I'LL BE CALLED AGAIN, SIR?
MAYBE MONTHS, I'M AFRAID. LISTEN, IF I WERE YOU I'D TRY FOR THE AIR-BORNE FORCES. HOW ABOUT BECOMING A GLIDER PILOT? THAT'S TOUGH ENOUGH FOR ANYBODY.
A NEW LIGHT DAWNED IN JAMIE'S EYES. THIS HADN'T OCCURRED TO HIM BEFORE. THE VERY NEXT DAY HE SET ABOUT GETTING HIMSELF TRANSFERRED.

THE AIRBORNE FORCES WAS A WHOLE NEW WORLD — AND A TOUGH ONE TO SURVIVE IN — FOR JAMIE. A GLIDER PILOT HAD FIRST TO BECOME AN INFANTRYMAN OF COMMANDO STANDARD, THEN LEARN TO FLY LIGHT POWERED PLANES, BEFORE HE WAS EVEN SELECTED FOR GLIDER TRAINING. BUT JAMIE'S GUTS AND DETERMINATION SAW HIM THROUGH, AND SOON —

THAT'S FINE, LOCKE ...A LITTLE MORE LEFT AILERON.
OK, SIR.
14

AS THE TRAINING WENT ON, JAMIE BEGAN TO BE HIS OLD CHEERFUL SELF AGAIN.

BY THE TIME HE WAS A TRAINED GLIDER PILOT, AND PROMOTED TO SERGEANT-PILOT, JAMIE FELT THAT THE WAR HAD GONE ON QUITE LONG ENOUGH WITHOUT HIS HELP. HIS FIRST SIGHT OF NORTH AFRICA SENT HIS BLOOD RACING.

LOOK, DAKOTAS AND GLIDERS! THAT'S FOR US, MATE.
ALL SET FOR THE INVASION OF SICILY, EH?

THE NEXT MORNING, JAMIE STOOD ON THAT SAME TUNISIAN AIRFIELD WITH THE HUBBUB OF THE AIRBORNE ATTACK TO COME SOUNDING LIKE SWEET MUSIC TO HIS EARS.

GOSH, AFTER ALL THIS WAITING I'M IN THE WAR AT LAST!
LITTLE DID THE SMALL JAMIE GUESS THAT THE DEMON OF DISAPPOINTMENT WAS TO STRIKE AT HIM AGAIN.

FOR ALL HIS LACK OF INCHES, JAMIE HAD AN AIR OF SHARP AUTHORITY, AND HIS EYE WAS JUST AS SHARP AS HE WATCHED SOME SKYLARKING AMERICAN PILOTS WHO WERE TO FLY THE TUG PLANES.

WHAM HIM, STEVE!
ATTABOY, GUS!
I JUST HOPE MY OWN TUG PILOT ISN'T AMONG THAT BUNCH OF CLOWNS!

JAMIE'S FEARS WERE TO BE REALISED. THE SKYLARKERS BROKE UP AND ONE OF THEM CAME SAUNTERING OVER, HIS MANNER FAR TOO CASUAL TO SUIT THE BRITISHER.

HIYA, BUD! THE NAME'S SKEEFER – YOU ALL SET?

NOT QUITE. JUST A LITTLE MATTER TO DISCUSS OF HOW AND WHERE WE'RE GOING TO FLY, THAT'S ALL.

DETECTING THE SARCASM, THE AMERICAN BECAME EVEN MORE OFF-HAND...

HECK, WHAT'S EATING YA? THERE'S NUTHIN' TO WORRY ABOUT.
LISTEN, YANK, UP THERE I'VE TWENTY GOOD MEN BEHIND ME TO WORRY ABOUT. SO LET'S ACT GROWN UP, EH?

WITH A FLUSH OF ANNOYANCE, SKEEFER WENT SOURLY OVER THE DETAILS. BY THE TIME THE GREAT AIRLIFT BEGAN THERE WAS PRECIOUS LITTLE LOVE LOST BETWEEN THE AMERICAN PILOT AND THE SHARP-MINDED JAMIE LOCKE.

SLAP-HAPPY LOT, THESE YANKS!
THESE DURNED BRITISHERS THINK THEY OWN THIS WAR. HECK, IF IT WASN'T FOR US THEY'D BE GOIN' AROUND BAREFOOT!

BUT FOR JAMIE THESE DIFFERENCES WERE SOON FORGOTTEN IN THE THRILL OF THAT GREAT AIRBORNE ADVENTURE. HIS THOUGHTS FLEW BEHIND HIM TO THE SILENT COMPANY OF MEN ENTRUSTED TO HIS SKILL...

THIS IS THE REAL THING NOW, JAMIE, LAD. YOU'VE GOT TO DO IT RIGHT!

THE SEA CROSSING WAS CALM ENOUGH, BUT WHEN THEY SIGHTED THE ENEMY'S STRONGHOLD OF SICILY, EVEN THE STRONGEST AMONG THEM MUTTERED DARKLY...
LOOK AT THAT FLAK!
A GNAT COULDN'T GET THROUGH IT!

BRAVE HEARTS WENT COLD AT THE SIGHT OF COMRADES PLUNGING TO A FEARFUL DEATH...
GOLLY, BUT THIS IS ROUGH!

WITH HEART HAMMERING, JAMIE KEPT AN ANXIOUS EYE ON HIS SUDDENLY WHIPPING TOW-LINE.

IF SKEEFER DOESN'T KEEP STRAIGHT AND STEADY HE'LL SNAP THE BLASTED THING!

THE NEXT SECOND, LIEUTENANT SKEEFER GAVE JAMIE THE SHOCK OF HIS LIFE.
HECK, THIS IS NEAR ENOUGH TO SICILY FOR ME!
HEY, THAT FLAMING AMERICAN IS CASTING US OFF MILES TOO SOON, SO HE CAN CLEAR OFF!
INSTEAD OF WAITING FOR JAMIE TO CAST OFF THE CABLE FIRST, SKEEFER JUST JETTISONED THE TOW GEAR AT HIS END AND LEFT THE GLIDER TO ITS FATE.

WITH A STAGGERING DISREGARD FOR THE FATE OF JAMIE AND HIS MEN, SKEEFER WAS ALREADY TURNING FOR HOME, LEAVING JAMIE RAGING WITH HELPLESS FURY AND DESPAIR.

LET'S GET OUTA HERE WHILE THE GETTING'S GOOD!

WHY, YOU LILY-LIVERED, FLAK DODGING COWARD!

JAMIE JETTISONED HIS NOW USELESS CABLE, WHICH WAS JUST EXTRA WEIGHT.

DEPRIVED OF ITS TUG, THE HORSA'S SPEED DROPPED UNTIL IT HOVERED WITH SICKENING SLOWNESS OVER THE MERCILESS SEA BELOW. DESPERATELY JAMIE FOUGHT TO MAINTAIN HEIGHT AND COURSE.
WE'LL BE DARN LUCKY IF WE MAKE LAND ANYWHERE!

DESPITE ALL HIS EFFORTS, THE DISMAYED JAMIE SAW THE SULLEN WAVES GET NEARER AND NEARER. FOR ONE BLESSED MOMENT HE THOUGHT THEY WERE LUCKY, WHEN HE REACHED THE ROLLING SHALLOWS.

EVERYBODY, OUT, QUICK!

BUT THERE, ON THAT INNOCENT-LOOKING SICILIAN BEACH, THEIR LUCK RAN OUT WITH FEARFUL SUDDENNESS.
AAGH!
FEUER!... FEUER!
OH, NO! JERRY MACHINE GUNS WAITING FOR US!

WITH HORROR-FILLED EYES JAMIE WATCHED THE BRAVE YOUNG COMRADES HE'D FOUGHT TO SAVE RUTHLESSLY SHOT DOWN AS THEY STRUGGLED ASHORE. THIS WAS TOTAL WAR, SAVAGE AND BRUTAL.

THEY HAVEN'T GOT A CHANCE!

THREATENED BY A FURTHER BURST OF ENEMY FIRE, JAMIE AND THE FEW SURVIVORS HAD NO CHOICE BUT TO SURRENDER.
YOU ARE PRISONERS!
I RECKON IT'S THIS OR BEING MURDERED. AT LEAST THIS WAY THERE'S A HOPE OF REVENGE...

TO JAMIE'S DESPAIR, HE WAS CARRIED OFF WITH OTHERS TO A PRISON CAMP DEEP IN ITALY. ONCE AGAIN HIS HIGH HOPES OF GETTING INTO THE WAR SEEMED CRUELLY DASHED.

...AND IT WAS MY FIRST GO. I'D HARDLY GOT STARTED IN THIS WAR.
NO TALKING!

THE GERMANS WASTED NO TIME IN PUTTING THEIR PRISONERS TO WORK ON DEFENCES AGAINST THE ALLIES NOW STORMING ON TO THE BEACHES OF ITALY.

JAMIE RAGED AT HIS BAD LUCK.

INVASION... THE MOST EXCITING BIT OF THE WAR, AND I'M MISSING IT ALL.

AS THE TEDIOUS MONTHS PASSED, JAMIE'S EARLY ANGER GAVE PLACE TO A COLD, IRON-HARD RESOLVE.

IF I EVER GET BACK INTO THE FIGHT, BY HECK, I'LL MAKE UP FOR LOST TIME!

BUT JAMIE'S SOLEMN VOW, COUPLED WITH HIS HEADSTRONG NATURE, WAS TO LEAD HIM INTO TROUBLE LATER ON.

IT WAS WITH A TERRIFIC JOY THAT JAMIE SHARED THE WILD WELCOME GIVEN A FEW WEEKS LATER TO THE LIBERATING ALLIED FORCES.

THANKS A MILLION, SIR!

A PLEASURE, SERGEANT!

WE'RE FREE! BLIGHTY, HERE I COME!

THAT WAS CHRISTMAS DAY, 1943, AND THE BEST CHRISTMAS PRESENT JAMIE HAD EVER HAD.

EVEN SO, AS HE RESTLESSLY PACED THE SHIP THAT TOOK HIM HOME TO BRITAIN, JAMIE THOUGHT IMPATIENTLY OF THE MONTHS HE'D LOST BEHIND BARBED WIRE.

IT WOULD BE JUST MY KIND OF LUCK IF THE WAR IN EUROPE FINISHES BEFORE I CAN GET INTO IT!

JAMIE'S PATIENCE WAS TAXED TO THE UTMOST BEFORE HE COULD AT LAST REPORT TO HIS OLD AIRBORNE REGIMENT NOW BASED IN SOUTHERN ENGLAND. COLONEL HURST GAVE HIM A WARM WELCOME.

DUNKIRK
CALAIS
LISLE
BOULOGNE
CHANNEL
ABBEVILLE
R. SOME
AMIENS
GOOD TO SEE YOU BACK, SERGEANT LOCKE. BETTER LUCK THIS NEXT TIME!
NEXT TIME, SIR? FINE! WHEN WILL THAT BE?

THE COLONEL'S EYES TWINKLED AT THE EAGER QUESTION. AND WHEN HE REPLIED IT WAS WITH A LOW, TENSE VOICE.

THE INVASION OF EUROPE, LOCKE! THE BIGGEST DARN SHOW OF ALL TIME...AND YOU'LL BE IN IT, RIGHT UP FRONT. I KNOW THAT'S WHAT YOU WANT.

DIEPPE

CHERBOURG

LE HAVRE

CAEN

BUT EVEN NOW THE DEMON OF DISAPPOINTMENT HADN'T YET FINISHED WITH THE LUCKLESS JAMIE.

WHILE UP ON A REFRESHER GLIDER FLIGHT, HE WAS SPOTTED BY A MARAUDING ENEMY PLANE.

WATCH THIS, OTTO!
HECK, A JUNKERS 88!
WITH BOTH EYES, MEIN KONRAD!

FRANTICALLY JAMIE TRIED ALL THE TRICKS HE KNEW WITH THE MOTORLESS GLIDER, BUT NOTHING COULD SAVE HIM FROM THAT DELIBERATE CAT-AND-MOUSE ATTACK.

THE BUZZARD'S PLAYING WITH ME!

THIS TIME WE TICKLE HIS TAIL, JA?

WITH CRUEL TEUTONIC GLEE, THE GERMAN GUNNERS SLOWLY SHOT JAMIE'S FRAIL CRAFT TO PIECES. A CRASH WAS CERTAIN.

...AND I HAVEN'T EVEN GOT A CHUTE! THE RATS!

SOMEHOW JAMIE HELD THE RIDDLED FRAMEWORK TOGETHER AND WITH A LAST DESPERATE YANK OF THE CONTROL STICK MADE A TURF-TEARING LANDING. BUT THERE WAS NO MISSING A CLUMP OF TREES, AND –
AAAAGH!

JAMIE WAS LUCKY ENOUGH TO GET AWAY WITH A BROKEN ARM, BUT WAS RAGING BECAUSE IT KEPT HIM OUT OF THE GREAT INVASION OF NORMANDY.
WHEN CAN I GO, DOC? LOOKS LIKE I'M BEING DELIBERATELY KEPT OUT OF THIS DARN WAR TILL IT'S ALL OVER!
I CAN UNDERSTAND YOUR DISAPPOINTMENT, LOCKE, BUT THAT'S NO EXCUSE FOR TELLING MATRON SHE'S A TUB OF LARD WITH THE MANNERS OF A SERGEANT-MAJOR!

REPORTING FIT ONCE MORE TO HIS REGIMENT'S BASE, THE ANXIOUS JAMIE ONCE MORE HEARD GREAT NEWS FROM THE C.O., COLONEL HURST...
ARNHEM, SERGEANT LOCKE...WE'RE GOING TO LAY ON THE BIGGEST AIRBORNE INVASION IN HISTORY. ANOTHER CHANCE FOR YOU, EH?
STERDAM.
ARNHEM
JUST TRY AND KEEP ME OUT OF IT, SIR!

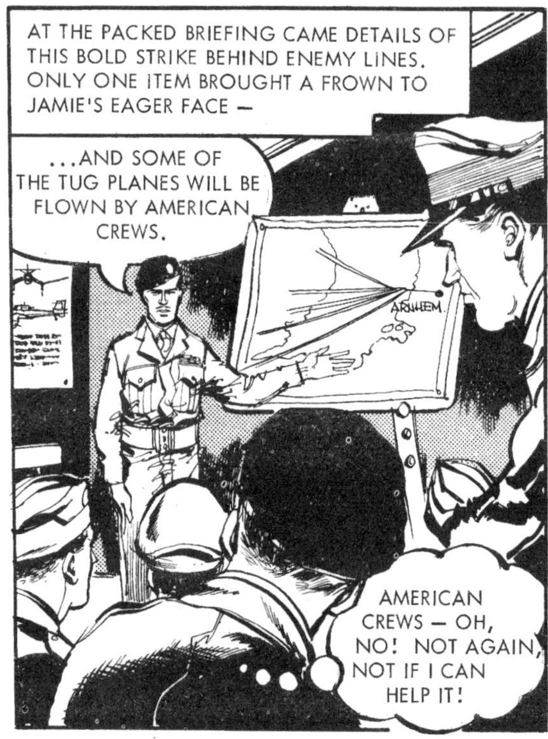
AT THE PACKED BRIEFING CAME DETAILS OF THIS BOLD STRIKE BEHIND ENEMY LINES. ONLY ONE ITEM BROUGHT A FROWN TO JAMIE'S EAGER FACE –
...AND SOME OF THE TUG PLANES WILL BE FLOWN BY AMERICAN CREWS.
ARNHEM.
AMERICAN CREWS – OH, NO! NOT AGAIN, NOT IF I CAN HELP IT!

BUT IT LOOKED AS IF JAMIE'S IMP OF FATE WAS WORKING OVERTIME, FOR NEXT DAY AS THE WARMING-UP THUNDER OF ENGINES SWEPT ACROSS THE AIRFIELD, A LANKY FIGURE STRODE UP WITH A BEAMING SMILE.
GLAD TO KNOW YOU, LIEUTENANT LOCKE! ME AND THE BOYS HAVE THE HONOUR OF BEING YOUR TUG TEAM.
A YANK! HEAVEN HELP US! I MIGHT HAVE KNOWN. AND IT'S SERGEANT-PILOT TO YOU, MISTER.
AND JAMIE POINTEDLY IGNORED THE AMERICAN'S FRIENDLY HAND.

BUT THE AMERICAN'S GRIN REMAINED AS WIDE AND FRIENDLY AS HIS WHOLE FRAME, TALL AND LOOSE-LIMBED AS ANY TEXAN COWBOY. HIS NEXT WORDS AMAZED JAMIE.
OK, SARGE, "LOOTENANT" OFFENBAUM OF TEXAS, AT YOUR SERVICE.
OFFENBAUM!
STONE ME, IT'S BAD ENOUGH BEING A YANK, WITHOUT SOUNDING LIKE A HITLER STORM-TROOPER!

VISIONS OF THE COWARDLY LIEUTENANT SKEEFER STILL HAUNTED JAMIE'S MIND, AND NOW ALL THE LONG SMOULDERING RESENT-MENT AT THAT LAST TERRIBLE FLIGHT AROSE AGAIN.
I DON'T TRUST YOU SLAP-HAPPY YANKS! THE LAST ONE I HAD WAS A WHITE-LIVERED FLAK-DODGER WHO TURNED TAIL AND DROPPED ME IN THE DRINK!
WELL, JUST KEEP YOUR SHIRT ON ABOUT ME, PAL. I DON'T HAPPEN TO BE THAT KIND OF GUY.

WITH A SHRUG, PETE OFFENBAUM TURNED FOR HIS AIRCRAFT.
DON'T WORRY, BUSTER, I'LL TUG YOUR KITE RIGHT TO THE TARGET IF I HAVE TO PULL IT THERE WITH MY FRONT TEETH!
ER, LIEUTENANT...
JAMIE WAS ALREADY BEGINNING TO HAVE SECOND THOUGHTS ABOUT THIS BIG TEXAN — BUT THE DAMAGE HAD BEEN DONE.

NEXT MOMENT JAMIE HEARD THE CHEERY VOICE OF SERGEANT COX, N.C.O. IN CHARGE OF THE AIRBORNE TROOPS HE WAS FERRYING.

WE'RE BOARDING THE GLIDER NOW, JAMIE.

RIGHTO, SERGEANT. I'LL TRY TO GIVE YOU A SMOOTH TRIP.

SECRETLY JAMIE WISHED THESE MEN BETTER LUCK THAN HIS LAST ILL-STARRED PASSENGERS.

PRESENTLY, TUCKED BEHIND THE GLIDER'S CONTROL STICK, JAMIE THRILLED TO THE MAXIMUM TAKE-OFF ROAR OF THE LANCASTER'S MOTORS. THE TOW-LINE JERKED TAUT AND THEY BEGAN TO ROLL...
WE'RE OFF!

AS THEY SWEPT OUT OVER THE NORTH SEA, THE SIGHT OF THAT VAST ARMADA OF TUGS AND GLIDERS FILLED JAMIE WITH THE FIERCE JOY OF BATTLE.

WHEW! SOME ATTACK, THIS ONE. AND THIS TIME I'M REALLY IN IT!

BUT EVEN THIS TIME THE IMPETUOUS JAMIE SPOKE TOO SOON.

WITH AN EFFORT HE TORE HIS GAZE FROM THAT TREMENDOUS SIGHT AND WORRIEDLY EYED THE LOOPING TOW-LINE THAT LED TO THE MAN HE SO MUCH DEPENDED UPON — PETE OFFENBAUM.
THAT OFFENBAUM BLOKE BETTER DO HIS STUFF — NOT LIKE THAT FLAK-DODGER SKEEFER! MUST SAY HE SEEMS ALL RIGHT...

THE ENEMY FLAK WAS EVEN WORSE THAN THE SPITTING FURY OF SICILY. AGAIN CAME THE TERRIBLE SIGHT OF BURNING PLANES, OF CAST-OFF GLIDERS LEFT TO THE MERCY OF HAMMERING ENEMY GUNS.

THIS WAS ALL PART OF THE TRAGIC COSTS WHICH THE HIGH PLANNERS KNEW WOULD HAVE TO BE PAID FOR EVENTUAL VICTORY. BUT THAT MADE NO DIFFERENCE TO THE GRIM-FACED MEN BEHIND THE CONTROLS OF EACH PLANE...

THEN CAME THE TURN OF LIEUTENANT OFFENBAUM AND HIS CO-PILOT TO CROSS THE DUTCH COAST WITH ITS DREAD CURTAIN OF FIRE. HE KEPT A STEADY ENOUGH COURSE, UNTIL...

SUFFERING CATS, LOOK AT THAT FLAK, PETE!
IT'S SUICIDE ALLEY, SMITHY. I RECKON WE'D BETTER FLY AROUND THIS LITTLE LOT.

BUT PETE OFFENBAUM'S GOOD INTENTION MISFIRED. HE ALTERED COURSE TOO SHARPLY AND MADE THE CURSING JAMIE SWING DANGEROUSLY WIDE.

LOOK OUT, YOU IDIOT!

BLAST HIM! WE'RE GOING TO COLLIDE!

DESPITE ALL JAMIE COULD DO, NEXT MOMENT HE FELT THE JARRING CRUNCH OF COLLISION.

WE'VE HIT!

AT ONCE JAMIE WAS IN A FRENZIED FIGHT FOR CONTROL. WILDLY HIS GLIDER ROCKED AND LURCHED, THREATENING TO SPIN IN. THEN THE WORST HAPPENED...

TOW-LINE'S SNAPPED! CRAZY FOOL OF AN AMERICAN!

SUDDENLY ADRIFT AND HELPLESS AMIDST THAT NIGHTMARE BARRAGE, JAMIE RAGED HELPLESSLY AT HIS TUG PILOT.

THAT CRAZY OFFENBAUM!... I'LL SKIN HIM FOR THIS!

I THINK HE DID HIS BEST, SERGEANT.

JAMIE HURRIEDLY JETTISONED WHAT WAS LEFT OF HIS TOW-CABLE.

BUT NEXT SECOND BOTH MEN GASPED IN HORROR TO SEE PETE OFFENBAUM'S LANCASTER BURST INTO FLAMES.

HE'S HAD IT!
DIRECT HIT!
BALE OUT, AND FAST!

BUT THERE WAS NOTHING JAMIE COULD DO, AND HE HAD HIS OWN CRISIS TO FACE. MIRACULOUSLY THEY PASSED OVER THE FLAK BELT, BUT A FORCED LANDING WAS INEVITABLE.

BIT OF CLEAR GROUND THERE, LOOK!

CONTROLS ARE ALL HAYWIRE, SERGEANT COX, SO IT DOESN'T HELP US MUCH.

BUT WITH GENTLE SKILL JAMIE COAXED HIS FALTERING CRAFT TO A SAFE, IF BONE-JARRING LANDING. MOMENTS LATER...
WELL DONE! A FEW BANGS AND BRUISES, BUT OTHERWISE WE'RE OK.
THAT'S FINE, SERGEANT, BUT THIS IS THE CUSSEDEST LUCK!

JAMIE'S DISAPPOINTED EYE SWEPT ALOFT WHERE THE OTHER TUG-PLANES AND GLIDERS STILL STREAMED ON TO THE TARGET ZONE AT ARNHEM.

DARN IT, WHY MUST I ALWAYS BE LEFT OUT OF THE WAR!

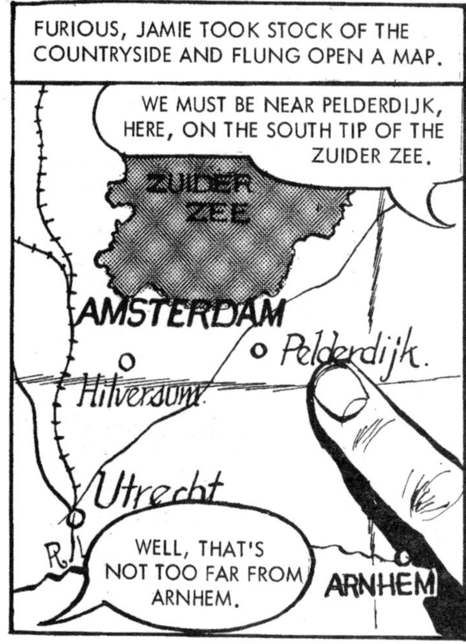
FURIOUS, JAMIE TOOK STOCK OF THE COUNTRYSIDE AND FLUNG OPEN A MAP.
WE MUST BE NEAR PELDERDIJK, HERE, ON THE SOUTH TIP OF THE ZUIDER ZEE.
ZUIDER ZEE
AMSTERDAM
Pelderdijk.
Hilversum
Utrecht
R.
ARNHEM
WELL, THAT'S NOT TOO FAR FROM ARNHEM.

JAMIE GAVE THE OPTIMISTIC SERGEANT A BLEAK LOOK.
ARNHEM'S MORE THAN SIXTY MILES AWAY. BY THE TIME WE'VE WALKED THERE THE BATTLE WILL BE OVER.
ER — YES.

JAMIE'S EYES SWEPT THE LANDSCAPE AROUND THEM WITH A MEASURING, HOSTILE LOOK. HE WAS FIGHTING MAD.

I'VE COME TO FIGHT THIS FLAMING WAR, AND BY HECK I'M GOING TO FIGHT IT! THERE MUST BE SOME ENEMY AROUND HERE WE CAN HAVE A BASH AT.

WELL, WE'RE GAME, SKIPPER.

YEAH! LEAD US TO IT!

FIRST THING WAS TO GET AWAY FROM THE TELL-TALE WRECKAGE OF THE GLIDER. ADVANCING CAUTIOUSLY IN THE LEAD, JAMIE'S EYE WAS PRESENTLY CAUGHT BY A FAMILIAR DUTCH FEATURE.

A WINDMILL — MAYBE THEY'LL GIVE US SOME LOCAL GEN.

THEN A TWIG CRACKED LIKE A PISTOL SHOT AND SWUNG JAMIE ROUND TO STARE IN ASTONISHMENT. IT WAS LIEUTENANT PETE OFFENBAUM, LARGE AS LIFE...

SORRY TO SCARE YA, BUT AM I GLAD TO CATCH UP WITH YOU GUYS!

OUR TUG PILOT!

WE THOUGHT YOU'D BOUGHT IT FOR SURE!

PETE OFFENBAUM SHRUGGED HIS WIDE SHOULDERS...
ME AND THE BOYS BALED OUT OK, BUT DANGED IF I COULD SEE A SIGN OF 'EM AFTER THAT.

BUT THE AMERICAN'S EASY MANNER DIDN'T GO DOWN WELL WITH JAMIE AT ALL.
I SEE NOTHING TO GRIN ABOUT, MISTER! THANKS TO YOUR PANIC FLYING WE HAD TO FORCE-LAND MILES FROM THE BLESSED TARGET.
PANIC FLYING? I WAS TRYING TO TAKE YOU BOYS ROUND THAT FLAK!

JAMIE SNORTED.

YES, I BET YOU MEANT TO AVOID THE FLAK — AND DITCH AND AVOID US, TOO, LIKE THE LAST YANK I HAD!

I TELL YA, I WAS THINKIN' OF YOU GEEZERS!

THEY MIGHT HAVE SWOPPED PUNCHES THERE AND THEN, HAD A DUTCH CIVILIAN NOT APPEARED SUDDENLY BEHIND THEM.

NOT SO LOUD! YOU NEED HELP? I AM JAN WESSEL, I WORK AT THE WINDMILL.

SWIFTLY JAMIE EXPLAINED THE POSITION, AND WAS AMAZED THAT THE DUTCHMAN WASN'T JOYFULLY EXCITED ABOUT THE RAID ON ARNHEM.

ARNHEM! BUT DO NOT YOU BRITISH KNOW THAT STRONG GERMAN FORCES HAVE RECENTLY CONCENTRATED NEAR ARNHEM?

WHAT! NO, I'M BLOOMING SURE NOBODY KNOWS THAT.

HOLY MACKEREL, NOW THERE'LL BE A SHINDY ALL RIGHT!

SUDDENLY THERE WAS A ROAR OF APPROACHING VEHICLES. AS THEY DUCKED, JAMIE CAUGHT SIGHT OF NO LESS THAN A GERMAN GENERAL FLASHING PAST IN A STAFF CAR AT THE HEAD OF HIS COLUMN.

A GENERAL — AND TRUCKLOADS OF INFANTRY!

DOUBTLESS MAKING ALL HASTE TO ARNHEM, MY FRIEND.

IN THEIR HIDING PLACE IN THE RUSHES, JAN WESSEL EXPLAINED.

GENERAL ERNST BOHLEN. HE COMMANDS ALL GERMAN FORCES IN THIS COUNTRY. THE MOST HATED MAN IN HOLLAND.
I CAN BELIEVE IT, MATE. HE LOOKS AS HARD AS NAILS.

AT THE DUTCHMAN'S NEXT WORDS, JAMIE PRICKED UP HIS EARS.

BOHLEN'S HEADQUARTERS ARE JUST DOWN THE ROAD, TWO MILES OUT OF PELDERDIJK.

THE TOP NAZI IN HOLLAND'S HEAD-QUARTERS! WELL, NOW – WHAT A CHANCE FOR A SURPRISE RAID!

BUT ARE WE STRONG ENOUGH?

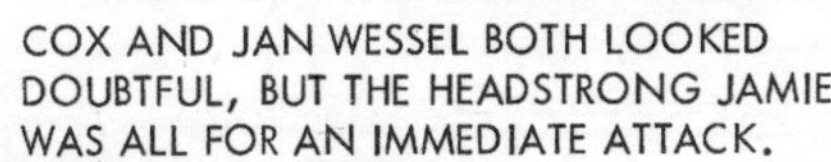
COX AND JAN WESSEL BOTH LOOKED DOUBTFUL, BUT THE HEADSTRONG JAMIE WAS ALL FOR AN IMMEDIATE ATTACK.

OF COURSE! A GENERAL'S HEADQUARTERS – THINK WHAT A SNIP THAT WOULD BE!
AND THINK OF ALL THOSE GERMAN TROOPS JUST ARRIVED NEAR ARNHEM!

JAMIE LOOKED IMPATIENTLY AT THE DUTCHMAN.
WHAT ABOUT THE GERMAN TROOPS?
WELL, THEY ARE VERY STRONG. SUPPOSE YOUR ATTACK ON ARNHEM FAILS...
YEAH, AND BACK COMES BOHLEN TO FIND HIS H.Q. SMASHED. SO HE EXECUTES HALF THE DUTCHMEN IN THE AREA!

STUBBORNLY BENT ON GETTING INTO THE FIGHTING, NO MATTER HOW OR WHERE, JAMIE LOCKE SWEPT THESE DOUBTS ROUGHLY ASIDE. HE SWUNG ROUND ON THE WAITING MEN...
THE ATTACK ON ARNHEM WILL NOT FAIL. IN A FEW DAYS HOLLAND WILL BE IN ALLIED HANDS. COME ON, MEN, LET'S SMASH THIS GERMAN HEADQUARTERS!
VERY WELL, I WILL SHOW YOU THE WAY.
OK, DON'T SAY YOU AIN'T BEEN WARNED!

THE GERMAN H.Q. PROVED TO BE A BIG COUNTRY HOUSE JUST OUTSIDE PELDERDIJK. ALL EAGER FOR ACTION, JAMIE LED THE RUSH.
ACHTUNG! ENEMY ATTACK!
COME ON — LET'S TAKE 'EM!

IF JAMIE THIRSTED FOR ACTION HE NOW GOT IT, WITH INTEREST. THE GERMAN GUARDS THAT HAD STAYED BEHIND WERE FEW, BUT THEY WERE TOUGH, AND THEY COULD FIGHT...

BEAT THE DAYLIGHTS OUT OF 'EM!
UUH!
KNOCK 'EM COLD!

TO GIVE JAMIE CREDIT, HE PROVED AS FIERCE A SCRAPPER AS HE HAD ALWAYS HOPED TO BE — IF EVER GIVEN THE CHANCE.
SHARE THAT AMONG YOU!

NOW THAT THE FIGHT WAS TRULY ON, PETE FORGOT HIS EARLY CAUTION AND THREW HIMSELF INTO THE MELEE WITH GUSTO.

UURRK!
CHIN UP, HERMANN!

WITH THE BRITISH FIGHTING LIKE TERRIERS, THE WHOLE BUILDING WAS SOON IN THEIR HANDS. FLUSHED WITH VICTORY, JAMIE BURST FROM ROOM TO ROOM, MAKING A SHREWD GUESS AT A RICHLY-FURNISHED ONE.
GENERAL BOHLEN'S OWN ROOM, FOR A CERT!

JAMIE TOOK IN THE LITTERED DESK, AND IN A FLASH HE'D SNATCHED UP A LEATHER CASE AND WAS HELPING HIMSELF.
FOUND SOMETHING GOOD?
TOP SECRET PAPERS, SERGEANT. SHOULD BE USEFUL!

HAVING RANSACKED THE H.Q. OF THE HATED BOHLEN, JAMIE AND HIS MEN MARCHED INTO THE TOWN OF PELDERDIJK LIKE CONQUERING HEROES.

OUR LIBERATORS!

THEY BRING US FREEDOM!

FIRED BY THIS WARM GREETING, JAMIE ADDRESSED THE CROWD TRIUMPHANTLY.

THE ALLIES HAVE COME TO FREE YOU AT LAST! YOUR SUFFERINGS ARE OVER!
I WISH I COULD BE SO SURE.
HE'S CERTAINLY GOING THE WHOLE HOG THIS TIME!

JAMIE'S RINGING WORDS EXCITED HIMSELF AS MUCH AS THEY DID THE GOOD PEOPLE OF PELDERDIJK. WORKING HIMSELF UP TO FEVER PITCH, HE FLUNG A SCORNFUL ARM AT THE TOWN HALL.

THE NAZIS ARE FINISHED! TEAR DOWN THEIR HATED FLAG! BURN THE PICTURES OF HITLER AND HIS GANG OF THUGS.

AND THE DUTCH BELIEVED JAMIE'S EVERY WORD. IN CROWDS THEY BROUGHT AND BURNT EVERYTHING THAT WAS NAZI.

ANOTHER PICTURE OF HITLER, CURSE HIM!
INTO THE FIRE WITH IT!

BUT AS THE DAYS PASSED, AND THE FAR DISTANT CLAMOUR OF BATTLE AND THE ROAR OF PLANES AND THE THUNDER OF GUNS WENT ON AND ON, EVERYBODY GREW UNEASY. JAN WESSEL SPOKE HIS FEARS TO JAMIE, WHO WAS TRYING TO HIDE HIS OWN ANXIETY.

MARTINI
I AM SURE THINGS WENT BADLY FOR THE BRITISH AT ARNHEM. I WARNED YOU THAT THE GERMANS ARE STRONG THERE.
NO MATTER. THE ALLIES WILL SOON WIN AND ALL HOLLAND WILL BE LIBERATED, AS I PROMISED.

DESPITE JAMIE'S EMPTY ASSURANCES THE UNEASINESS SPREAD, AND THE NEXT DAY THE TOWNSFOLK HEARD THEIR WORST FEARS CONFIRMED BY A PANTING MESSENGER...

THE BRITISH ARE BEATEN AT ARNHEM AND MANY PRISONERS TAKEN! GENERAL BOHLEN AND HIS TROOPS ARE RETURNING.

GOOD GRIEF!

AW, HECK! NOW WHAT?

AWARE OF THE FEAR-FILLED EYES NOW FASTENED UPON JAMIE AND HIS MEN, PETE OFFENBAUM BEGAN TO GROW ANGRY...
SEEMS YOU'VE BEEN STUFFING THESE FOLKS WITH DANGEROUS IDEAS, JAMIE.
OH, GET OFF MY BACK, WILL YOU? I'VE GOT TO THINK! IF IT WASN'T FOR YOU WE WOULDN'T BE IN THIS SPOT NOW.
FOR JAMIE IT JUST NEEDED THIS PROD TO REKINDLE HIS BITTER FEUD WITH ALL AMERICANS, ESPECIALLY PILOTS.

EVEN THE STOLID JAN WESSEL LOOKED SHAKEN. BUT HE RESPONDED BRAVELY TO JAMIE'S URGENT COUNCIL OF WAR.
WE'RE GOING TO DEFEND THIS TOWN AGAINST ALL COMERS. I CAN'T LET THESE PEOPLE DOWN NOW.
GOT ANY FRIENDS WHO CAN SHOOT, JAN?
BUT OF COURSE!...I'LL TELL THEM.
AS JAN WESSEL HURRIED OFF, JAMIE TURNED AN ANXIOUS EYE UPON HIS FEW MEN AND THEIR ROUGH BARRICADE.
MAYBE WE CAN HOLD OUT UNTIL THE MAIN ARMY ARRIVES ...THAT SHOULDN'T BE LONG NOW.
IT'D BETTER NOT BE, BUDDY! OTHERWISE I HATE TO THINK WHAT BOHLEN WILL DO TO THIS TOWN — AND US!
JAMIE WINCED AT THE ACCUSATION IN THE AMERICAN'S WORDS — THAT IT WAS ALL HIS OWN STUPID FAULT.

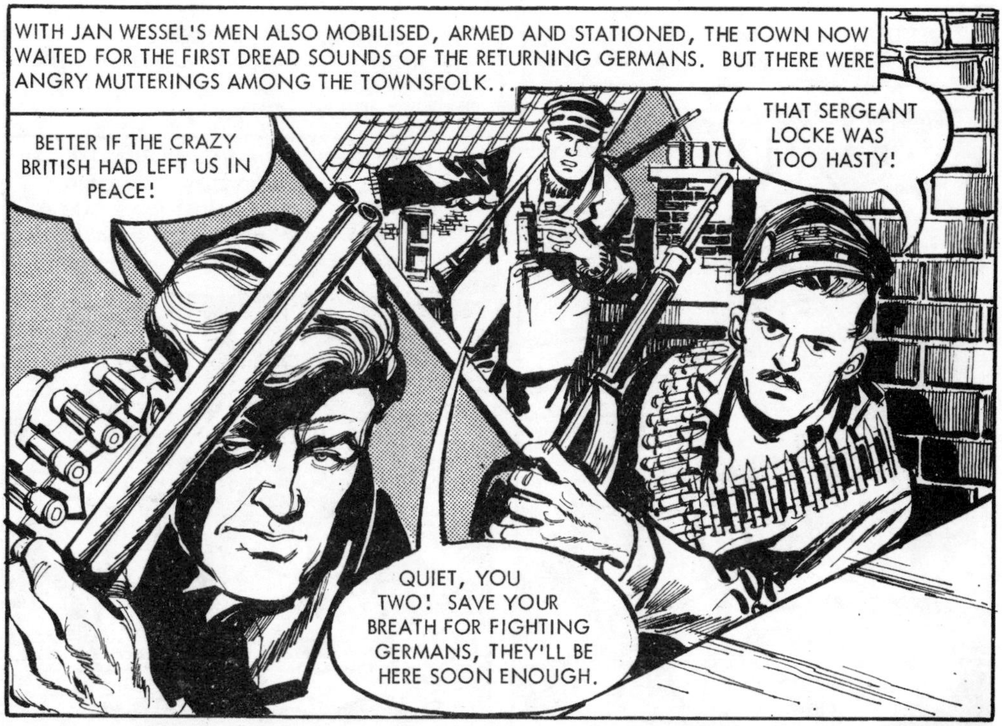

WITH JAN WESSEL'S MEN ALSO MOBILISED, ARMED AND STATIONED, THE TOWN NOW WAITED FOR THE FIRST DREAD SOUNDS OF THE RETURNING GERMANS. BUT THERE WERE ANGRY MUTTERINGS AMONG THE TOWNSFOLK...

BETTER IF THE CRAZY BRITISH HAD LEFT US IN PEACE!

THAT SERGEANT LOCKE WAS TOO HASTY!

QUIET, YOU TWO! SAVE YOUR BREATH FOR FIGHTING GERMANS, THEY'LL BE HERE SOON ENOUGH.

RETURNING VICTORIOUS FROM THE UTTER DEFEAT OF THE BRITISH AT ARNHEM, GENERAL ERNST BOHLEN COULD WELL AFFORD A SMUG, SELF-SATISFIED SMILE.
STRAIGHT TO HEADQUARTERS, DRIVER. AND THEN YOU CAN TAKE A WEEKEND PASS.
JAWOHL, MEIN GENERAL!

BUT MET OUTSIDE BY A QUAKING ORDERLY, GENERAL BOHLEN'S SMILE SWIFTLY CHANGED TO THUNDEROUS ANGER.
EXCELLENCY — A — A BRITISH PARTY ATTACKED AND... AND...
WHAAAAT! WHERE IS THE FLAG OF THE GLORIOUS REICH?

THE FURTHER GENERAL BOHLEN STRODE THROUGH HIS RAVAGED HEADQUARTERS THE BLACKER GREW HIS RAGE. AND WHEN HE GOT TO HIS OWN OFFICE...
SENTRIES DEAD OR VANISHED! HIGHLY IMPORTANT PLANS AND PAPERS — GONE! THOSE DOGS OF BRITISH MUST HAVE TAKEN THEM. HOW CAN THIS HAPPEN IN MY OWN HEADQUARTERS!

AND SO IT WAS IN THE BLACKEST MOOD POSSIBLE THAT GENERAL BOHLEN HEARD OF THE RAID AND THE REVOLT OF THE TOWNSPEOPLE OF PELDERDIJK.
SO! THEN GET READY TWO HUNDRED MEN. I MYSELF WILL DEAL WITH THOSE THIEVING BRITISH VANDALS — AND WITH PELDERDIJK, TOO. TOMORROW NOT A STONE WILL STAND OF THEIR HOUSES, AND THE SCHWEIN SHALL LIE DEAD IN THEIR OWN RUINS!

FILLED WITH A SAVAGE VENGEANCE, THE GERMAN GENERAL LED HIS MEN AT FULL SPEED TO THE OUTSKIRTS OF PELDERDIJK. BUT THERE FURTHER ADVANCE WAS DENIED HIM, AND SO...

USE THE TRUCKS AS COVER! WIPE OUT THOSE SNIPERS ON THE ROOFS!

BUT RETREATING FROM ROOF TO ROOF, JAN WESSEL'S SHARP-SHOOTERS TOOK HEAVY TOLL OF THEIR PURSUERS.
NEVER MIND IF SOME RATS GET PAST US. THEY WILL SOON MEET THE GUNS OF THE BRITISH.

JAN WESSEL WAS RIGHT — THOUGH NUMBERS OF GERMANS WON PAST THE SNIPERS, THEY RAN FULL-TILT INTO A CRASHING BARRAGE OF GRENADES AND BULLETS FROM THE BARRICADED BRITISH.

CHOOSE YOUR TARGETS! DON'T WASTE A SHOT.
AAAAH!

AND NO MATTER BY WHAT STREET THE FURIOUS BOHLEN ATTEMPTED TO STORM INTO THE LITTLE TOWN, HE WAS MET BY A HAIL OF DEFENSIVE FIRE AS THE AIRBORNE MEN ANTICIPATED HIS MOVES.

THERE'S NO COVER FOR THEM IN THESE OPEN STREETS.
IT'S LIKE SHOOTING RATS DOWN A DRAIN PIPE!

BAULKED AT EVERY TURN AND ENRAGED BY THE CASUALTIES AMONGST HIS FINEST TROOPS, THE VENGEANCE-MINDED ERNST BOHLEN CAST ABOUT FOR SOME OTHER WAY — AND PRESENTLY HIT ON IT. HURRIEDLY A TRUCK WAS LOADED.
WELL NOW, SERGEANT, I THINK YOU HAVE ENOUGH — ER — PERSUASION IN YOUR TRUCK FOR THE JOB. TAKE THE ROAD BY THE ZUIDER ZEE.
JAWOHL, HERR GENERAL! WE SHALL NOT FAIL.

AS THE DIN OF BATTLE DIED AWAY TO AN OMINOUS SILENCE, JAMIE SLIPPED ALONG TO WHERE JAN WESSEL CROUCHED.
I DON'T LIKE THIS QUIET, JAN.
NOR I, MY FRIEND. SOMETHING EVIL IS AFOOT, DEPEND ON HERR BOHLEN...

JUST HOW EVIL AND DESPICABLE BOHLEN'S TRICK WAS, THEY DIDN'T LEARN FOR ANOTHER HOUR, WHEN A GIANT EXPLOSION IN THE DISTANCE SWUNG EVERYBODY ROUND.
WHAT THE BLAZES!
HIGH EXPLOSIVES — OR I'M A DUTCHMAN TOO!

JAN WESSEL, HIS FACE BLANCHING WHITE, WAS THE FIRST TO GUESS THE AWFUL TRUTH...

THE DYKE!... THE DEVILS HAVE BLOWN THE DYKE!

JAN WESSEL'S PANIC-STRICKEN SHOUT WAS ALL TOO TRUE. SERGEANT SCHMIDT AND HIS ENGINEERS, AT THEIR MASTER'S ORDERS, HAD BLOWN THE GREAT SEA DYKE.

HURRY, DOLT, UNLESS YOU WANT US TO DROWN TOO!

WITH A THUNDER THAT STRUCK TERROR INTO ALL THE TOWNSFOLK OF PELDERDIJK, THE CRUEL SEA CAME SURGING INTO STREETS AND HOUSES, DRIVING ALL BEFORE IT.

RUN!

HELP!

IF JAMIE'S BARRICADES HAD STAUNCHLY RESISTED THE ENEMY, THEY NOW CRUMBLED BEFORE THAT MERCILESS WALL OF WATER.
COME ON – MOVE!

DRIVEN INTO THE OPEN, JAMIE AND HIS MEN WERE CAUGHT BETWEEN THE HUNGRY WATERS BEHIND THEM AND THE EXULTANT ENEMY IN FRONT.

THEY RUN LIKE DROWNING RATS!...SHOOT!... SHOOT!

AAGH!

JAMIE HIMSELF FELL WITH A SHARP CRY, AND BUT FOR PETE OFFENBAUM AND THE QUICK-WITTED JAN, WOULD HAVE DIED RIGHT THERE.

HE'S HIT IN THE LEG!
QUICK. UP THIS ALLEY! I KNOW A WAY OUT.

BETWEEN THEM THEY GOT THE SUFFERING JAMIE THROUGH THE GERMAN LINES, OUT OF THE TOWN AND BACK TO JAN'S WINDMILL.

I HAVE A SECRET ROOM AT THE TOP. YOU TWO WILL BE SAFE THERE...
YOU'RE A REAL PAL, JAN!

LYING HELPLESS IN HIS LOFTY HIDING PLACE, JAMIE LOCKE HAD PLENTY OF TIME TO REFLECT BITTERLY ON HIS HASTY ACTIONS.
I WAS TOO EAGER TO GET INTO THIS DARN WAR, PETE. NOW LOOK WHAT I'VE DONE!
DUTCH TOWNS HAVE BEEN FLOODED BEFORE, JAMIE. THEY'LL RECLAIM IT IN NO TIME.

TENDED BY THE BIG-HEARTED PETE AND JAN WESSEL, JAMIE FRETTED AWAY THE SLOW DAYS. THEN ONE MORNING THE OTHER TWO BURST IN WITH A HALF-FORGOTTEN LEATHER CASE.
IT'S THE CASE I PINCHED FROM BOHLEN'S ROOM!
JA — ONE OF OUR MEN FOUND IT.
WITH THE TOP SECRET PAPERS STILL INSIDE!

AT ONCE JAMIE SIFTED THROUGH THE GERMAN PAPERS, AND PRESENTLY HE GAVE A LOW WHISTLE...
HEY, THIS IS AN OFFICIAL ORDER TELLING BOHLEN WHAT TO DO IF HE HAS TO CLEAR OUT OF HOLLAND.
AH, THEY FEAR THE COMING OF THE ALLIES, THEN!

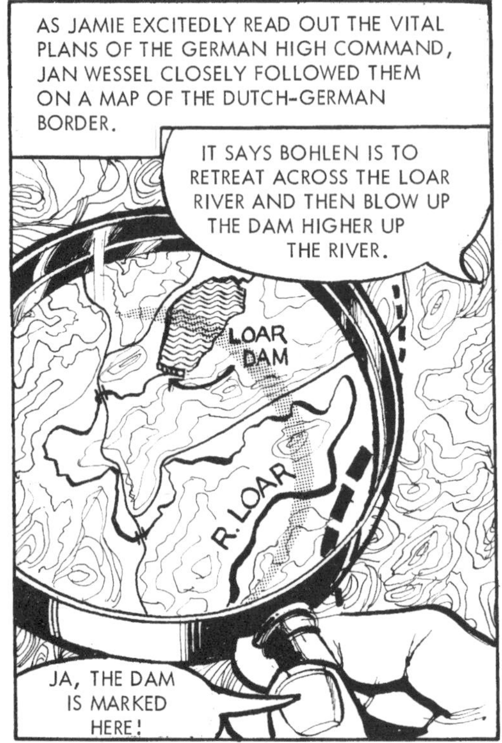
AS JAMIE EXCITEDLY READ OUT THE VITAL PLANS OF THE GERMAN HIGH COMMAND, JAN WESSEL CLOSELY FOLLOWED THEM ON A MAP OF THE DUTCH-GERMAN BORDER.
IT SAYS BOHLEN IS TO RETREAT ACROSS THE LOAR RIVER AND THEN BLOW UP THE DAM HIGHER UP THE RIVER.
LOAR DAM
R. LOAR
JA, THE DAM IS MARKED HERE!

ALREADY JAMIE COULD PICTURE THE TORRENT OF WATER HURTLING DOWN FROM THE BLOWN DAM. HE READ ON...

IT SAYS, "THIS ACTION SHOULD BLOCK PURSUIT BY THE ENEMY, THUS GIVING THE GERMAN HIGH COMMAND TIME TO RE-GROUP ITS FORCES.

WOW!

AT ONCE JAMIE LOCKE WAS IN A FEVER TO GET GOING...
WE'VE GOT TO GET THIS INFORMATION TO BRITISH INTELLIGENCE AT ONCE!
ALL IN GOOD TIME, JAMIE. BOHLEN ISN'T CLEARING OUT YET, AND YOU'VE GOT A BAD LEG TO HEAL.
HE IS RIGHT. WE WILL LET YOU KNOW AT THE FIRST SIGNS OF GERMAN MOVEMENT.

SO, AS THE LONG DAYS SLOWLY PASSED, JAMIE LEARNT TO CONTROL HIS IMPATIENCE. EVEN SO, ONE BURNING AMBITION STAYED WITH HIM, AS HE CONFIDED TO PETE...

I FEEL I'VE GOT TO MAKE IT UP SOMEHOW TO THOSE POOR PEOPLE OF PELDERDIJK. IT WAS ALL MY STUPID FAULT.
YOU'LL GET YOUR CHANCE, JAMIE. JUST YOU WAIT, BUDDY...

AS IF IN INSTANT ANSWER TO JAMIE'S HEARTFELT WISH, JAN WESSEL CAME RUNNING HARD, SO EXCITED HE COULD HARDLY TALK...

THE GERMANS ARE PREPARING TO MOVE OUT! THEY WILL BE GONE FROM HERE WITHIN FORTY-EIGHT HOURS!
YIPPEE!
THIS IS IT!

THE THREE TOOK URGENT COUNCIL. ONCE AGAIN JAMIE CONSULTED THE ORDERS OF THE GERMAN HIGH COMMAND.

BOHLEN WILL RETREAT OVER THE LOAR RIVER AND THEN TRY TO BLOW THE DAM.

NOT IF WE WARN OUR FORCES IN TIME.

YOU TWO MUST START AT ONCE. I AM NEEDED HERE.

TAKING LEAVE OF THE BRAVE DUTCHMAN, JAMIE AND PETE OFFENBAUM SET OUT TO FIND THE ALLIED LINES. AFTER TWO DAYS MARCHING SOUTH THEY HEARD THE RUMBLE OF DIESEL ENGINES.
BARGES FULL OF GERMANS — GETTING OUT OF HOLLAND FAST!
WE OUGHT TO STRIKE OUR OWN FORCES ANY TIME NOW.

IN ANOTHER TWO DAYS, THE FOOT-WEARY PAIR FOUND THE ALLIED LINES. IN TIME THEY STOOD BEFORE JAMIE'S C.O., LIEUTENANT COLONEL HURST, WHO HEARD THEIR STORY WITH CLOSE ATTENTION. FINALLY —
SO BOHLEN IS GOING TO BLOW THE LOAR DAM, EH? WELL, TWO CAN PLAY AT THAT GAME. JUST A MINUTE WHILE I PHONE THE CHIEF PLANNING STAFF.
YES, OF COURSE, SIR.

TEN MINUTES LATER, COLONEL HURST REPLACED THE RECEIVER, HIS EYES SPARKLING MISCHIEVOUSLY.
A GOOD IDEA OF YOURS, LOCKE, TO STOP BOHLEN BLOWING THE DAM. BUT WE'LL GO ONE BETTER — WE'LL BLOW THE DAM INSTEAD!
HOLY COW!
ENJOYING THE MARVELLING LOOKS ON THE YOUNGER MEN'S FACES, COLONEL HURST EXPLAINED.

IF WE CAN BLOW THE LOAR DAM FAST ENOUGH, THE ESCAPING WATERS WILL RENDER THE RIVER IMPASSABLE. THEN BOHLEN AND HIS FORCES WILL BE TRAPPED THIS SIDE OF IT. YOU FOLLOW?
BY GEORGE, YES, SIR!
YEAH, I GET IT NOW.

BUT MORE SURPRISE WAS IN STORE. SUDDENLY HURST SWUNG ROUND —
AND YOU, LOCKE, WILL TAKE A GLIDER AIRBORNE PARTY AND MAKE SURE THAT THAT DAM GETS BLOWN!
ME, SIR? WELL, YES, ER — FINE, SIR!

THEN PETE OFFENBAUM'S DRAWL BROKE IN.
MIND IF I MAKE ANOTHER SUGGESTION, SIR — THAT I GET A PLANE FROM SOME-WHERE AND TOW LOCKE'S GLIDER TO THE TARGET?
I RATHER HOPED YOU WOULD ASK THAT, OFFENBAUM!
GREAT STUFF!

AND SO, FORGETTING ALL HIS OLD ENMITY AGAINST AMERICAN PILOTS, JAMIE WATCHED ONCE MORE AS AIRBORNE MEN CLIMBED INTO HIS GLIDER AND HE LISTENED TO PETE OFFENBAUM'S LAST MINUTE WORDS.

BEST OF LUCK, JAMIE. I JUST WISH I WAS GOING TO LAND WITH YOU GLIDER BOYS!

WATCH IT, PETE! I MAY FLAG YOU DOWN YET IF I GET IN A JAM.

WITH PETE'S MOTORS STRAINING THEIR MAXIMUM, JAMIE EASED THE GLIDER INTO THE DUTCH SKY. MANY ANXIOUS QUESTIONS FLOODED HIS BUSY MIND.
AM I REALLY IN THIS WAR AT LAST — AM I GOING TO MAKE THE TARGET? OR IS MY FLAMING BAD LUCK COMING ALONG WITH ME AGAIN?

PETE SET A COURSE NORTH-EAST, HIS EYE ROVING THE LANDSCAPE BELOW. NEARING THE TARGET, HE SAW MOVEMENT. EXCITEDLY HE SNAPPED ON HIS INTERCOM...

HEY, JAMIE, LOOK DOWN THERE! IT'S BOHLEN'S MOB.

YES, AND THEY'RE NOT FAR FROM THE RIVER. WE'VE GOT TO HURRY!

PETE PILED ON THE SPEED AND PRESENTLY TO JAMIE'S RELIEF THE RIVER LOAR SHOWED AHEAD...AND THEN THE TARGET ITSELF, PERCHED HIGH IN THE HILLS, THE BIG CONCRETE DAM.
RIGHT, THIS IS WHERE I CAST OFF!

JAMIE SLIPPED HIS TOW-LINE AND PETE CIRCLED TO WATCH THE GLIDER'S CIRCLING DESCENT. HE GRUNTED IN ENVY...

I'D GIVE MY FRONT TEETH TO BE WITH JAMIE RIGHT NOW!

JAMIE MADE A TRICKY LANDING ON THE SLOPES ABOVE THE DAM AND WAS AT ONCE UNDER ENEMY FIRE. SPEED WAS ESSENTIAL.
COME ON – HURRY IT!

BY CLEVER USE OF THE SCANT COVER, JAMIE WORKED HIS MEN EVER NEARER TO THE KEY BUILDING, THE CONTROL STATION.

IF WE CAN ONLY CAPTURE THAT AND GET OUR HANDS ON THE SWITCHES THE NAZIS HAVE WIRED TO BLOW THE DAM AT A MINUTE'S NOTICE...

BUT THE MINUTES WERE SLIPPING BY, AND TO JAMIE'S IMPATIENT TEMPER SOMETHING MORE THAN EXCHANGING POT-SHOTS WAS NEEDED.
NO USE SNIPING AT 'EM, BOYS! LET'S GET IN THERE!
RIGHT!

SCORNING THE ENEMY'S REDOUBLED FIRE, THE BRITISHERS STORMED IN TO THE ATTACK. VICIOUS CLOSE QUARTERS FIGHTING BEGAN.

BUT THE ENEMY FOUGHT BACK FIERCELY, AND THE OUTCOME HUNG DANGEROUSLY IN THE BALANCE.

CIRCLING ANXIOUSLY ABOVE, PETE OFFENBAUM SAW JAMIE'S DIFFICULTY. IN ANOTHER MOMENT HIS MIND WAS MADE UP.
HEY, SAM, SIT DOWN HERE AND TAKE CONTROL. THOSE BOYS ARE KIND OF PINNED DOWN. I'M GOING DOWN THERE TO SEE IF I CAN HELP MY PAL.
MYERS
YOU'RE CRAZY, PETE! OK, OK...

ONLY SECONDS LATER, THE BIG TEXAN LAUNCHED HIMSELF INTO SPACE.
GUESS THIS IS WHERE THE GOOD OLD U.S.A. TAKES A HAND!

ABOUT TO LAND CLOSE TO THE DESPERATE FIGHTING, PETE LET FLY WHILE HE WAS STILL IN MID-AIR, IN THE NICK OF TIME FOR JAMIE.

HOLD STILL, JAMIE!

AAGH!

PHEW!

PETE'S TIMELY APPEARANCE SEEMED TO SWING THE BALANCE OF THE FIGHTING. ENEMY RESISTANCE, AS IF EXPECTING MORE PARACHUTE REINFORCEMENTS, SUDDENLY COLLAPSED. JAMIE AND PETE RACED OUT ALONG THE DAM.
SHOULD BE ABLE TO SEE DOWN RIVER FROM OUT HERE!
RECKON BOHLEN'S MOB'S BOUND TO BE ABOUT READY TO CROSS.

FROM THIS DIZZY VANTAGE POINT, JAMIE WHIPPED UP FIELD GLASSES AND INSTANTLY CAUGHT HIS BREATH...
IT'S BOHLEN ALL RIGHT!
WE'RE NONE TOO SOON!

MADLY THEY DASHED FOR THE CONTROL HOUSE. EVERY SECOND COUNTED.
LOOKS LIKE THOSE MIGHT BE THE MAIN SWITCHES — WIRED TO DETONATE, THE GERMAN PLANS SAID...
WELL, LET'S THROW 'EM, JAMIE, AND FIND OUT!
JAMIE GRABBED THE SWITCH AND BEGAN TO PULL...
SILENCE, AT FIRST — THEN SUDDENLY AN EAR-SHATTERING BLAST, FOLLOWED BY A SECOND.
LOOK!

LIKE A GIANT BEAST UNCHAINED, THE PENT-UP WATERS LEAPT INTO THE RIVER BELOW.
IT'S GOING OVER!

THE RUNAWAY WATERS QUICKLY GATHERED INTO A HUGE, DEVOURING FLOOD, SWALLOWING UP THE RIVER AND CRUSHING ALL BEFORE IT.

THE SIGHT OF THAT TERRIBLE WALL OF WATER THREW THE RETREATING GERMANS INTO STUPEFIED CONFUSION. EVEN THE HARDENED GENERAL BOHLEN PALED AND TREMBLED...
HIMMEL, SOMEONE HAS BLOWN THE DAM!
WE ARE FINISHED! THERE IS NO ESCAPE!

THE BRIDGE WAS SMASHED AS IF BY A GIGANTIC FIST. NOTHING COULD SURVIVE IN THAT MAELSTROM OF DEATH.

BACK, FOR YOUR LIVES!

AAAAARGH!

THUS DID GENERAL ERNST BOHLEN MEET DESTRUCTION AT THE HANDS OF THE SAME TERROR HE HAD UNLEASHED UPON THE BRAVE PEOPLE OF PELDERDIJK — WATER.

AS HURST HAD HOPED, THE MAIN GERMAN FORCE WAS NOW CAUGHT WITH THE IMPASSABLE WATERS BEFORE THEM AND THE TRIUMPHANT ALLIED ARMOUR COMING UP FAST.
LOT OF DUST AHEAD — COULD BE OLD JERRY!
IT IS, TOO! STUCK AT THE RIVER, JUST LIKE THE DOCTOR ORDERED. LET'S GET 'EM!

WATCHING THE LAST FUTILE EFFORTS OF BOHLEN'S DEMORALISED ARMY AGAINST THE SWEEPING MIGHT OF THE BRITISH ARMOUR, PETE OFFENBAUM TURNED TO A TIRED BUT HAPPY JAMIE WITH A GRIN...
WELL, JAMIE, YOU FINALLY GOT INTO THE WAR...AND HOLY MACKEREL, WHEN YOU DID, YOU KINDA MADE THINGS MOVE A BIT!
AYE, MAYBE SO. BUT I WANT YOU ALONG, PETE, EVERY TIME I GET IN THE WAR — TO KIND OF HAUL ME OUT AGAIN IN ONE PIECE!
Commando
THE END

Commando
FOR ACTION AND ADVENTURE

THE COVERS

No. 994
7p
AUS. N.Z. 25c
Commando
WAR STORIES IN PICTURES
RILEY'S RIFLE

No. 882
6p
Commando
WAR STORIES IN PICTURES
INLAND NAVY

No. 489
Commando
WAR STORIES IN PICTURES
1/-
AUS. 15c N.Z.
5p
ACES WILD

No. 327
Commando
WAR STORIES IN PICTURES
1/-
TROUBLE SPOT
Suddenly they realised they were in a trap.

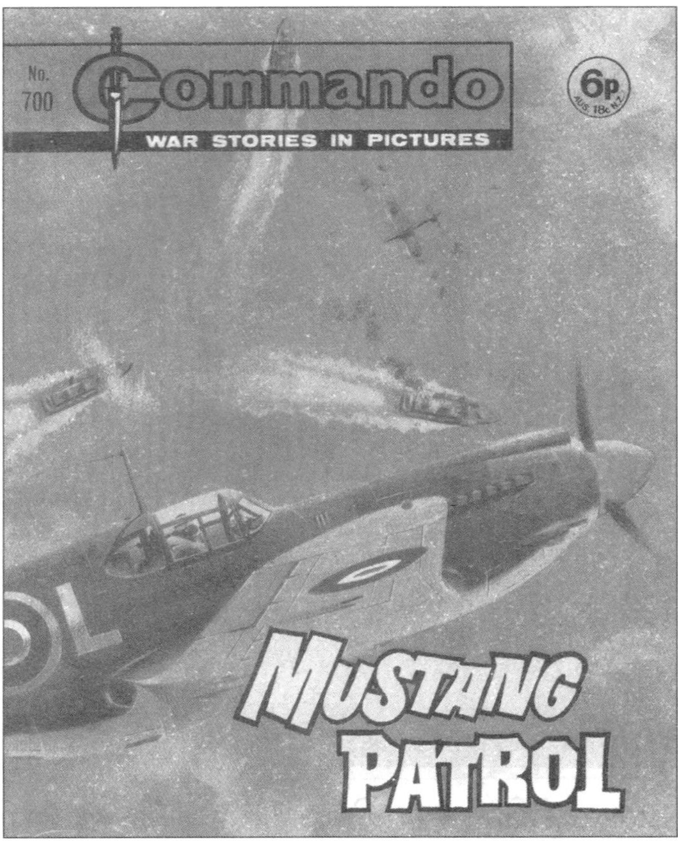
No. 700
Commando
WAR STORIES IN PICTURES
6p
AUS 18c N.Z.
MUSTANG PATROL

No. 404
Commando
WAR STORIES IN PICTURES
1/-
DEATH PATROL

No. 657
Commando
WAR STORIES IN PICTURES
6p
AUS. 18c N.Z.
THE
SHIP-BUSTERS

No. 422
Commando
WAR STORIES IN PICTURES
1/-
BATTLE-
WAGON

No 974
7p
AUS. N.Z. 25c
Commando
WAR STORIES IN PICTURES
THREE...TWO...ONE...ZERO!

No 885
6p
AUS. N.Z. 18c
Commando
WAR STORIES IN PICTURES
MARCH OF THE
MONSTERS

No. 358
Commando
WAR STORIES IN PICTURES
1/-
MAN OF IRON

No. 691
Commando
WAR STORIES IN PICTURES
6p
GLIDER ACE

YOU LOUSY SQUAREHEADS — YOU'VE KILLED THE BRAVEST GUY IN THE BRITISH ARMY.